Becoming One

by Don Meredith

THOMAS NELSON PUBLISHERS
Nashville • Camden • Kansas City

Published in Nashville, Tennessee, by Thomas Nelson, Inc. and distributed in Canada by Lawson Falle, Ltd., Cambridge, Ontario.

Printed in the United States of America.

Library of Congress Cataloging in Publication Data

Meredith, Don.
  Becoming one.

  1. Marriage—United States. 2. Family—Religious
life. I. Title.
HQ734.M473   301.42   79-12691
ISBN 0-8407-5688-7

12 13 14 15 - 90 89 88 87

Acknowledgments

*T*here are many who have contributed directly or indirectly to this book. Greatly influential has been Howard Hendricks. During my years of study under him, I learned valuable lessons and received great encouragement. I cannot remember the countless ways he has positively influenced me and this book.

Five other men I owe significant thanks and credit to are my original partners in Christian Family Life: Jody Dillow, Barry Leventhal, Tim Timmons, Waylon Ward, and Bill Wellons. I have a great love for them, and I deeply appreciate their contribution to my life and their direct responsibility for parts of this book.

In the last three years tremendous support and wisdom has been provided by several dear friends from Campus Crusade for Christ: Ney Bailey, Dennis Rainey, Dave Sunde, Enoch Williams, and Mick Yoder. A special thanks goes to Bill Bright and Swede Anderson for their commitment to marriage in general and to me in particular.

My former secretary, Carol Weirman, has my gratitude

for typing and retyping this material for two years while it was in the beginning stages.

During the last few months of the preparation of the final manuscript, when things really got tough, some faithful friends provided the impetus to get me across the finish line. Next to my lovely wife, Sally, Steve and Shay Freeman were absolutely indispensible. Others who faithfully typed and edited were Skip and Michelle Coffman, Jo Atkins, Nancy Deas, Jim and Micky Grigsby, Gordon and Linda Beth McNulty, Joanne Pryor, John and Merre Putnam, Shelby and Kay Woodall, and Lawrence and Betty Primm.

Last, but far from least, I want to thank Peter Gillquist, whose patience, wise guidance, and literary ability helped cause this book to finally happen.

Dedicated to a special group of people whom God has used to complete and bless me—

My Eve: Sally
My Children: Todd, Carmen, Kathryn, Tiffany
My Mother: Ruth Meredith
My Covenant relationships: Those few singles and couples who have played an equal and supportive part in my life and activities.

Contents

Foreword

*I*n a book like *Becoming One*, I look for four essential ingredients.

First, is it *realistic?* If it isn't, forget it. Something as bottom line as marriage cannot be handled like a fantasy. Authentic realism is a must.

Second, is it *scriptural?* A great deal of nice thoughts and even clever ideas won't cut it when it comes to pulling off a relationship as exacting as marriage. Since this whole concept was God's original invention, it's foolish to think we can accurately address the subject apart from adherence to His Word. A biblical basis is essential.

Third, is it *balanced?* Axes are being ground in pulpits and seminars all across the country, emphasizing various extremes . . . but healthy marriages call for a broad perspective. They require attention and care at every level. To limit the scope of instruction to a few pet (and often obvious) areas of interest creates an unfortunate twisting of the truth or, at best, an over-simplification of some rather deep and involved principles. Balance is basic.

Fourth, is it *believable?* Life's too short to waste our time on unreachable, untouchable directives. People who are married—and often struggling for handles to grab—don't need a long list of high-powered "shoulds" and "musts" that clothe them in guilt and steal their hope. Most folks I know, Christian or not, are searching for helpful, attainable ideas clearly stated and punctuated with practicality. It's got to be believable.

Becoming One by Don Meredith combines all four of these ingredients. Having forged out his thoughts on the anvil of many years of experience both as a husband and a counselor plus a serious, lengthy study of Scripture, Don offers realistic and believable suggestions. They are also balanced and reliable. Being a new author he has a style that is fresh, free from cliches, and relevant—making the book interesting and insightful. He is also honest, honest enough to admit he has not arrived. I look for that in an author of a book that is practical in its content.

This book will be around for some time. We'll be hearing more from Don Meredith in the years to come. He has a lot to say . . . and he says it well.

Chuck Swindoll

1
Bitterness or Blessing

*T*he sensitive young lady in my office was crying uncontrollably. Her face was flushed, her eyes blurred and red. She reached for another Kleenex and struggled as she said, "I didn't know it was possible to hurt so much."

Her husband was telling me of their desperately crushing personal experiences. The details were intimate and humiliating, causing his voice to break repeatedly. When his wife started to cry, the pressure became so stifling that he began to hyperventilate. He had to struggle for breath to speak.

Their circumstances were painfully real and typical in our American culture today. I found myself emotionally involved before I knew it. The emotions of the moment demanded a break, and as the couple left the room my heart quickly responded. "How did these outstanding people allow themselves to inflict such pain on one another?" My mind began to review our first three appointments to search for the answer.

We are not speaking here of a couple with inherent weaknesses in their background. In fact, they were so prominent in their community that they were driving more than a hundred miles weekly to see me to keep local attention at a minimum.

Both had successful family and community histories. They had met during their second year in college. After three and a half years of dating, they were married. He attended one year of law school after college, while she taught school. Both families firmly endorsed their marriage.

What a contrast this session was to our visit a few years back during their engagement period. I had been genuinely impressed with her adoration of him. She viewed him as extremely talkative. In fact, the thing about him that perhaps attracted her most was his ability to communicate easily. They would talk for hours—on any subject. He was so understanding. She had such confidence in his intellect and ability to make decisions. He had held several class offices in school, and she had been proud to be identified with him.

As Jim thought back over their dating period his eyes were alive with pleasant memories. He talked a great deal about how proud he had been and how good he had felt being with her. He had great respect and admiration for her opinions—so much, in fact, that he wouldn't think of attempting anything without seeking her counsel. He loved her sense of humor and they laughed a lot. He was proud of her feminine appearance.

In countless ways I had sensed a wise and practical approach in the timing and planning of their marriage. In addition to this positive beginning, both enjoyed active Christian lives. Each had a personal relationship with Jesus Christ. He had considered attending seminary at one time; she loved her church.

Instead of a fairy-tale finish to this picture-perfect beginning, conflict and hurt resulted. As the months and years passed, life grew very complex. In-laws, children, sexual stress, job changes, disappointments, personality differences, and broken communication seemed to overwhelm the positiveness of their beginning.

Betty no longer found Jim to be sensitive and talkative. Instead, he had grown disappointingly distant. No matter how she tried, attempts at communication almost always ended in conflict.

"I find myself feeling such resentment and anger toward Jim now," she cried. "Last week after feeling guilty all day, I decided to fix his favorite dinner. Every effort to be creative seemed so labored and impossible. I shouted at the kids and blew up at every interruption while fixing the meal. I felt such inner conflict. On the one hand I knew I desperately needed to be creative; yet on the other, I seemed to deeply resent every effort. After my two-hour drama in preparing the meal, I tried to compose myself for Jim's arrival. Just as I lit the candles, expecting Jim to appear at any moment, the phone rang. It was Jim, explaining that he would be home late. What hate and anger I felt! I screamed my deepest resentment!"

After Betty released her anger and hurt, Jim responded, "I never thought I would experience the day when working late in a lonely office would be more inviting than being with you!"

Betty was paralyzed with a frustration so deep that tears wouldn't even flow. The conflict had become so complex that hope was lost and only frustration remained.

Even more tragic, in many ways, was the change

that had come over Jim. I had observed a spirit of sacrifice in his early commitment to Betty—a natural devotion. Betty's every need was an opportunity for Jim's genuine desire to serve her. This romantic drive on his part had resulted in security for Betty in the early days of their courtship and marriage.

How could a man's heart and attitude change so dramatically in just four or five years? A seemingly unlimited capacity for love had turned to the deepest form of resentment, almost to the point of repulsion. Where Jim had earlier sought Betty's opinion, now her opinion included fits of anger and rejection. The soft gentle touch that released Jim to satisfaction had turned to a methodical cold politeness that left both wanting.

My mind was searching for answers as Betty and Jim returned from our break. The tears had stopped, but the evidence of shock and deep uncertainty remained on their faces. Betty spoke first.

"How did this happen to us? What did we do wrong?"

Jim followed with, "Look, the thing that amazes me is that when I stop to evaluate things, I realize I still really love Betty. I am certain I couldn't find anyone better, but when I try to live with her nothing but frustration results. I don't know why."

The question that was born out of Jim and Betty's frustration is being asked by literally millions of couples all over the world. *How could this have happened to us?*

The purpose of this book is to help eliminate the possibility of couples ever reaching that unfortunate and unnecessary point in marriage.

Tragically, most couples naively feel this sort of

situation will never happen to them. "We are different; we love each other so much!" they say.

During the last ten years of counseling and speaking to hundreds of couples, I have observed that the one common factor in all marriages is this: Not one couple has ever married for destructive purposes. The real question that shouts at us is: *How do so many people who mean so well end up so frustrated?*

2

It's Third and Eight, Sally!

*A*ll things considered, marriage today is not a good proposition. In our major U.S. cities during these last several years, applications for marriage licenses and proceedings toward divorce number about the same. *Of all couples marrying in America today, forty percent will be divorced within the next twenty years.*

As alarming as that figure is, an additional shock comes when one adds to it the number of marriages that are tragically lacking yet hanging together. How many couples do you know whose marriages are of such quality that you would trade your marriage for theirs? Certainly not many. Most counselors I have known or read about agree that probably eighty-five percent of marriages today are hurting badly or are somewhere in the process of breaking up.

Is the situation hopeless? No. Not only is marriage as an institution not hopeless, but it can be exceedingly successful above and beyond one's expectations. But couples planning to marry must beware: Happy marriages are made, not found. Do not be deceived by romantic feelings and good intentions. We need to know not only why marriages are failing today, but more importantly, how to succeed in marriage. The blessing of experiencing a great marriage is almost beyond words.

A PERSONAL NOTE

The love and satisfaction I have for my wife, Sally, are almost incomprehensible. Even though she is just another human being like me, with strengths and weaknesses, the complete excitement and gratitude I feel for her could not be higher if she *were* perfect! I am amazed, because all my life I have tended to concentrate on the weaknesses of others. I see Sally's weaknesses in a realistic way, yet I still experience an exhilarating and complete love for her.

One of our first dates was at Disneyland. I can still remember standing close to her in the lines, waiting for the rides. She had on a pretty silk blouse that was very soft to my touch. Emotional charges shot all over me!

In the weeks that followed, I realized that here was a girl I loved to talk to, look at, and be with. In addition, the longer I knew her the more impressed I was with her commitment to Christ and His will for her. Further, she was successful in her vocation; I was proud of her.

I can still remember our first intimate moments together. We were walking in the mountains overlooking San Bernardino on the night I first kissed her. A few weeks later I asked her to marry me.

After three months of seeing each other daily, the wedding day arrived. Sally and I were married just after we both turned twenty-seven. Since we were older and had both been committed Christians for many years, we expected that marriage would automatically be better than average for us. We were certain *our* marriage would be different from most.

We were only partially right. Our years of maturing were a real help, but we were both shocked at the subtle struggles in our relationship right from the beginning.

It was on our wedding day that differences in our backgrounds began to surface. We were to be married at 4:00 on a Saturday afternoon. At 3:00 I turned on the television to catch the opening kickoff of the first football game of the season. I hadn't seen a football game in six months, and I became so involved in the action that before I realized it, it was 3:45 and I wasn't ready. Honestly frustrated at having to leave the game, I rushed off to the wedding.

After the ceremony in Boulder, Colorado, we drove toward Vail, where we had lovely hotel accommodations reserved and waiting. We got away later than planned, and I turned on the radio just as soon as we drove out of the church parking lot, trying to catch the last series of plays of the first Texas game. I *had* to have the score.

Radio reception was limited by the mountains and I could not get a network station. I decided to stop short of Vail and find another motel so I wouldn't miss the 10:00 news and the Texas score.

Mind you, I didn't *intend* to hurt Sally with my obsession. I was behaving exactly as twenty-seven years of living in the family home in Texas had conditioned me to behave.

We stopped forty miles east of Vail, checked into a motel, and went to dinner. We got back to the room about 10:15, just about sports time. As my bride disappeared into the bathroom to prepare for our wedding night, I hurried over to turn on the television. On came the news: Texas had been defeated.

I was shattered. I can still remember trying to clear my mind of disappointment as Sally came into the room. She had no idea how much a part of my life football was, and how affected I was by this loss!

The next day some new conflicts of interest developed. That morning, our first full day of married life, we drove on to Vail. Sally had envisioned us spending time together hiking in the mountains. She was dreaming of a romantic outdoors-type honeymoon in the countryside. I, on the other hand, was not too crazy about walking around gazing at the scenery. Besides, after three or four hours of mountains and trees, I found my mind being drawn to the NFL and the Sunday afternoon activity on the football fields of our wonderful nation. Wouldn't you know, the Dallas Cowboys were to play the Green Bay Packers.

Thinking myself perfectly justified, I began to maneuver Sally toward Denver so we could find a Holiday Inn in time to see the game. I knew if we stopped for lunch we'd miss the start of the game. So we bought some cheese and crackers at a country store and headed west.

When we arrived in Denver, I suggested we get some Kentucky Fried Chicken and take it to the room. She bought a magazine to read while I watched the game! From Sally's viewpoint, the honeymoon (perhaps even the marriage?) was a total disaster. The discussion we had that night was mild compared to the ones to come throughout the rest of football season! Every Saturday and Sunday I was to be found sitting in front of the tube—watching football games.

Sally actually had nothing against football; she had

just never thought much about it. Her idea of a pleasant autumn Saturday was walking or riding through the woods, enjoying the changing colors of trees and smelling the brisk autumn air. Here, already, were seeds of conflict beginning to germinate in our marriage. *We both meant well.* Neither of us was necessarily right or wrong. But our differing backgrounds were beginning to collide and hurt our relationship.

Several things stood out. I was amazed at how my feelings of love for her could change so quickly when I was hurt. A jolted marriage relationship can be intensely painful. Rejection, insults, judgments, insecurity, and lost devotion can ravage one's emotions. I found that after being wounded emotionally, tremendous bitterness in my heart easily replaced the strongest emotional commitments I had made.

Another discouraging force I felt overtake me was the performance struggle. We began to notice every failure and weakness—*in each other.* It became absurd! For example, Sally was a good housekeeper, but because she didn't do one particular thing as my mother had always done, I became obsessed to the point that she might as well have been a poor housekeeper. I was mature enough to know better, but I couldn't seem to help the way I felt.

While meaning so well, we were beginning to find it hard to live together. I can remember thinking to myself that I just couldn't let things continue in the direction they were going. But they did. In just two years, the very best intentions for a model Christian marriage had been diminished to being, at best, a memory of the past. Things were just mediocre.

In our third year of marriage I was involved in student Christian work at the University of Arkansas.

During that year, I noticed that a number of students were getting involved in foolish dating relationships. There was a need to teach these students some guidelines for dating. So I began to page through the Scriptures for some practical thoughts that would apply to dating.

It was during this study of marriage, undertaken to help others, that I discovered the things that eventually changed our marriage—and countless other marriages with which I have had contact. Perhaps those students I undertook my study for don't remember much of what I said, but for the Merediths, marriage has never been the same.

The rest of this book is an attempt to share with you the truths that have been so helpful here in the Meredith household. Believe me, our improvement has not been based on personal strengths. These discoveries stand on the certainty of the Scriptures. For openers, God plainly states that He intends for married couples to inherit from Him a blessing!

> To sum up, let all be harmonious, sympathetic, brotherly, kindhearted, and humble in spirit; not returning evil for evil, or insult for insult, but giving a blessing instead; for you were called for the very purpose that you might inherit a blessing (1 Pet. 3:8,9).

To insure that promise for any couple, certain issues need to be considered.

To begin, I will address the question, "Why are so many marriages failing?" In the last one hundred years, the divorce rate has moved from one in thirty-three marriages to more than one in three. The first step in solving problems is to be able to recognize what the problems are: Part I of this book develops the answer to this question as I expose the five major reasons marriages fail.

All five of these problems will be examined, along with insights into what happens if they are not corrected. A couple who is aware of these matters will be far better prepared for marriage than a couple who marry without a basic understanding of potential problems.

The second and third parts of the book are directed toward a positive solution. Part II describes the spiritual insight necessary to make lasting commitments and changes in marriage. Part III gives directions on how to apply these biblical patterns to everyday married life.

God's purpose for creating marriage will be readily seen as partners understand their roles and thereby open new doors to permanent and growing love. What is love and how does one experience it? How do love and submission work without conflict? These questions and others are discussed in Part II of the book.

Part III integrates the spiritual and practical sides of marriage. What about in-law problems? What is the role of a woman and how is it different from that of a man? How can sexual expression grow? How does one know God's will in marriage? Financial problems, personality differences, life's difficulties, and many more issues are discussed.

A couple who understands why marriages fail, how God intends marriage to work, and who can integrate practicality and spirituality is well on the road to a growing and thriving marriage.

PART I

3

Five Reasons Contemporary Marriages Fail

What will keep you and your spouse from joining the ranks of couples who are discouraged because they cannot live happily together and decide to "call it quits"?

You may say, "We love each other more," or "We are wiser," or "We are better educated," or "We have been Christians longer." Although all of these things are vitally important, they are not sufficient to insure marital success. In considering the five reasons marriages today are failing, I will give the most lengthy treatment to Reason 1, since it is the most complex.

REASON 1: Structural and Cultural Changes Within Our Society

A number of years ago I had the privilege of studying under the outstanding direction of Howard Hendricks. During the course, "The Christian Home," Hendricks displayed a simple chart comparing a home of the 1870s with a home of the 1970s. The comparison provided keen insights into how deeply cultural changes affect marriage.

Thinking back for a moment over our history, it is amazing that so much of what we know and experience today has been developed within the last hundred years. Part of this development is rooted in population growth. It took from the beginning of time until the 1800s for the population to reach one billion. Yet in the last hundred years, that figure has jumped to nearly four billion. Social scientists project that by the year 2000, only about two decades from now, as many as eight billion people will inhabit this planet. The social impact of such growth is staggering!

As greater numbers of people crowd the earth, so greater amounts of information crowd men's minds. With the advent of the computer, the quantity of stored information now doubles and redoubles within months. Cultural changes brought about in this century by this enormous growth have made today's society vastly different from that of any other time in history.

All of this has resulted in some discouraging changes in the home. In 1870, one marriage in thirty-three ended in divorce. As we noted earlier, that figure today is close to one in two and one-half! *More than one child in three is from a broken home.*

To begin to appreciate the impact this century has had on marriage and the home, we need to examine a few of the major cultural and structural changes that have occurred.

RURAL–URBAN CHANGES

In 1870, American society was seventy percent agricultural and rural. One hundred years later, seventy percent of society was industrial and urban. This one significant change in the structure and outlook of society has affected marriage immeasurably.

A hundred years ago I would probably have lived west of Little Rock and farmed about ten acres of land. My wife and I would have been extremely dependent on one another. Daily I would have seen her faithful and hard work. She would have prepared for the family the food I had grown. She would have cared for the children before my eyes. This structure allowed for high self-worth and for development of authoritative people.

In contrast, men today, for the most part, own very little and have real authority in few areas of their lives. They are frustrated by their jobs on the one hand and their democratic families on the other. Comparison with unreal models and low or unseen productivity have cultivated insecure, frustrated, and struggling men.

A hundred years ago women experienced a higher level of being needed. They knew they were vital to family life. Their work was time-consuming and difficult, but they needed and generally developed great versatility and skill. The education of the family and the development of creativity in each member rested on the shoulders of the mother. A significant amount of devotion was given to women because the home was the center of almost all daily activity.

In contrast, today our commerce-centered living makes the home almost an out-of-the-way place. Ingenuity and creativity in the home have often been lost; therefore, women feel those things can only be found outside the home. Today many women feel home is a "prison." This tragic perversion of the true purpose and potential of the home has become a media event, helping to breed women who are angry and resentful.

A NEW MOBILITY

A second significant change in the last hundred years has been the shift from an immobile to a mobile society. In 1870, a thirty-mile trip was an important event. Today we travel that far to shop!

One hundred years ago people tended to live in ethnic groupings—a group of Irish people might settle in one place; twenty-five miles away would be a group of German descent. This resulted in "cultural islands" being formed all over America. If my wife and I had met in 1870, it would probably have been because we had the same ethnic, religious, vocational, and cultural backgrounds. We would probably have grown up less than ten miles apart and our parents would have known each other. Our lives would have been very *similar.*

Certainly I am not saying that the marriage of people from different backgrounds is in itself bad. But I am saying that the mobility unique to the last several decades has opened the possibility of a cultural shock to which some marriages may never adjust.

HOME-CENTERED VS.
COMMERCE-CENTERED LIVING

In 1870, the home was the center of almost all activity. Recreation, education, religious study, vocational preparation, and emotional development were all focused in the home. Creativity was a priority. If there was work to do, everyone was required to help. When it was time to play, everyone took part, including the mother.

There was no place for the odd personality or the unwanted child. Each child was an asset. Girls would help in the home. Boys would help in the fields. Spectator activities were not available; television and movies did not exist. Each person had to be creative.

Today we find a completely different situation. Outside-the-home activities are the way of life. Each child goes a different direction. No longer are we required to be creative and involved in the home; instead, we are spectators. Television, spectator sports, or movies require very little creative imagination. Many fathers, if not at work, are either out playing golf or home watching television. Communication between family members has, in many cases, almost been destroyed by television.

Children today are no longer an asset; they have become a liability. No longer do they help produce food for the family, but instead they are another mouth to feed, another body to clothe, and another educational expense.

The spiritual and psychological implications of these cultural changes on children and marriages are immense. It takes great discernment to recognize and creatively offset the effects of today's cultural system.

PRACTICAL VS. SOCIAL MARRIAGE

Until recent times, marriage was primarily a practical issue. A man generally looked for a woman with physical strength and character. Bearing children and running a farm took real stamina. Certainly appearance and personality were important, but they were tempered with practical balance.

In the past, a woman would have thought a long time before marrying an unstable man. Survival for an abandoned woman with children was extremely difficult. A strong back and courage were important if a man was going to bear up to the rigors of farming and protecting the family. Certainly sexual attraction and romance were important, but the realities of life tended to overshadow these less practical considerations.

Another fact that made people view marriages more practically was that divorce was not a satisfactory alternative and was not socially acceptable. It was not at all attractive. For the woman on the farm, divorce meant fear for survival. For the woman in the city, it meant social rejection. Divorce for the man, too, meant social rejection and the likelihood of spending the rest of his life alone. Certainly these realities caused couples to consider marriage more practically and seriously and to work through problems rather than to glibly end relationships.

Today, however, the decision to get married is almost entirely a social decision. There is usually very little practical consideration given to the commitment people are making in marriage. I have seen this again and again in counseling when I ask a couple long married to recall their original reasons for marrying. So often they say they cannot remember.

Social status and prestige are two keys to marital decisions today. Very few couples must marry for the sake of survival. Women today can support themselves. In May, 1978, forty-one percent of the U.S. working force was female. Divorce is an accepted way of life now, and there are very few factors in our society that encourage couples to consider the *realities* of life before they enter into marriage.

These cultural changes that have affected society so significantly have largely been responsible for three changes in couples' approaches to marriage. Today couples are getting married with differing backgrounds, differing motivations, and with less God-consciousness than they did a century ago.

Let me illustrate with some detail the adjustments we have had to face in our own marriage as a result of the financial, social, and intellectual differences in our backgrounds.

I grew up in Texas, and my parents were outgoing people of modest means. Because Dad was in sales, we were often involved in social encounters. We did not have a great deal of money, but I was fairly free financially. Living in the mountains of Colorado, Sally's family loved people, but they naturally took a much less social approach to life. While she lived comfortably, she had a tighter and more carefully planned approach to finances. I was considerably more free about letting go of money.

When my family took vacations, we usually got up early in the morning and drove all day. We would stop at newer motels that we could be sure were clean and comfortable. We were the "no-surprises" people. We seldom stopped to eat at good restaurants; drive-ins and motel restaurants satisfied our needs. We were very goal-oriented, and for us the vacation started *after* arriving at our destination.

By contrast, the Hills considered the drive part of the vacation. They enjoyed eating out, so they splurged on good meals in good restaurants. To afford that, they economized in other areas, mainly in their choice of motels. They *shopped* motels to find the best deal. (I've learned since that many people do that, but at the time it was a real jolt to my "country-club" pride.) Sally always seemed to head for those old, beige-colored stucco motels—the kind with the creaky furniture, the

1926 chenile bedspreads, and the "everyday low prices."

The first two days of our honeymoon we stayed in what I considered nice motels. On the third day we headed for Tulsa. I had decided to cut the honeymoon short, something which deeply disappointed Sally, but about which there had been no serious dialogue. Being a Holiday Inn man, I kept driving trying to find one. I didn't realize that in that sparsely populated area of the country there might not be motels that suited my standards. I wasn't about to lower those standards, but because we were ignorant of each other's prejudices, Sally couldn't understand why I wouldn't stop. She fell asleep in the car, and after driving through town after town with no Holiday Inns we finally ran out of gas at two in the morning close to a small Oklahoma town, one hundred miles from nowhere.

There were only three motels in town. To me, they were all the pink, unpredictable kind that offended my sensibilities. To Sally there was nothing unacceptable about them. Much to my discomfort, we had to stay in one since no gas stations were open at that time of the morning.

Throughout our travels later that fall, there were many opportunities to stay in motels. Sally, wanting to be a "good steward of God's money," just didn't feel right about paying Holiday Inn prices. Here again, it was not so much an issue of right or wrong, but of two people with different perspectives. We experienced some real hurt and conflict over such differences.

Another contrast that caused almost immediate struggle was the intellectual pursuits of our pasts. All my life I had been an outgoing person who was interested in people and activities more than in reading. Although I had been a decent student, I almost never read a book. I am not sure I had read ten books in my entire life up to that point.

My bride, on the other hand, is the intellectual in our family. She was an excellent student and loves to read. She came from a family who read almost constantly and almost everything. Sally had worked closely for four years under an understanding Christian man who was a dedicated student of the Scripture. She had learned to appreciate his studious example.

In the first months of our marriage, Sally was terribly disappointed with me because I didn't read anything except the newspaper, specifically the sports page. We have since learned the difference between intellect and discipline, but in those early days our divergent intellectual pursuits were a real problem. We simply placed different values on different things.

BASIC MOTIVATIONAL FACTORS

Generally, I see five motivations for marriage in couples today. The most basic involves our *feelings*. "I can't live without you." "I'll die if you leave me." If feelings were not so changeable, marriages might be more solid. But nothing is more deceptive than feelings. Although it is true that feelings are normal and even necessary, they are not a healthy *basis* for a relationship.

Social prestige is another motivating factor in marriage. People concerned about their images and their social standings will choose to marry because their would-be partners are successful or "cool" or socially prominent.

Another dominating factor is *sexual attraction.* Our culture has encouraged the abuse of one of God's greatest gifts by encouraging people to develop sexual identity and to become sexually involved prematurely. There is hardly a greater deceiver than sexual arousal. Emotions, encouraged by physical intimacy, will flare instantly beyond normal proportions. Couples easily mistake lust for love. A relationship based solely on sex is bound for disaster. Today, eighty percent of married couples experience some kind of sexual problem.

A fourth factor that motivates couples is based on a dangerously *false world view.* Young people still believe that being married is a $70,000 brick home, two new cars, and a continual sexual holiday. Instead they find that life is work, debt, problems, illness, and children. Many never recover from the shock when they discover the real road to living "happily ever after."

Too often people are motivated subconsciously to get married to *escape being single.* I can still remember the weekends and holidays when I was single. At the end of a carefree day I would lounge around and dream of my perfect mate. The older one gets, the stronger that dream becomes. Too many of us use marriage as an escape from school, parents, work, or loneliness. Sometimes our emotional needs can rise to the point at which a casual dating relationship can be mistaken for more than it really is.

The motivations for marriage mentioned here are certainly not inherently evil, but if they are not supported by a more practical, mature, and realistic basis for a relationship, they may leave a well-intentioned couple deeply hurt and confused for months or years after the wedding.

LACK OF GOD-CONSCIOUSNESS

The last result of the vast cultural and structural change in society is that Christ and His church are no longer vital factors in marriage today. There is very little real God-consciousness in the midst of marriage. Even many so-called "Christian" marriages have been so affected by our changing culture that God is really not practical to the marriage. Couples consider finances, social acceptance, vocational potential, and many other practical life goals, yet few actually evaluate their marriages from God's perspective.

REASON 2: The Deceptive "Fifty-Fifty" Relationship

There is a saying abroad today that marriage is a fifty-fifty relationship. It sounds good and makes sense.

There's just one problem—it doesn't work! I firmly believe that this proposition is the second major reason for marriage failure. The fifty-fifty relationship doesn't work in marriage because it is counter-biblical. It is the source of a performance or "cause-and-effect" situation that ends in destruction.

"I'll do my part and you do yours." Consciously and subconsciously we have been taught this maxim since birth. Brother-sister relationships, sports, teamwork on the job, roommate situations, and almost every venture of life suggests that it will work in marriage. Certainly in some ways marriage does compare to teamwork. But Scripture presents a basis for relationships that is totally different from the fifty-fifty plan.

The couple who discerns God's order is set free from the bonds of this system.

Why, when it seems to make so much sense, is the meet-me-halfway concept dangerous? It draws the couple's eyes to each other's *performance*, and no one is perfect, or performs correctly all the time. Further, it actually promotes *independence:* You do your job; I'll do mine.

Once we start focusing on one another's performance, we begin to feel rejection and hurt. Sometimes we react with anger—sometimes with silence. The explosions that occur reveal the fallacy of this plan. *It is impossible to believe that the other person has actually met you halfway.* And the minute you believe the other person is not meeting you halfway, you can usually hide your good intentions quickly under the bushel. There's something inside of you that turns you against your mate and resentment begins. That "something" called sin becomes an unbelievable power in your life for potential destruction of the relationship.

David and Ruth, a newly married couple, began to have some of these initial problems. They became so tense and uptight that they would regularly overstate things and then make critical remarks about each other. "Well, maybe we shouldn't have gotten married" or "Maybe I'm not what you thought I was!"

As they argued, Ruth would uncork a cutting remark and David would cut her right back. She would start crying and go back in the bedroom and slam the door. He would get in the car and drive around town, madder than a hornet. His fist would be tight, his stomach in a knot, and he would grit his teeth while driving nowhere. After an hour or so, David would return home, and he and Ruth would have a good time making up, while thinking, "Well, we're working through these problems."

But after those same problems occurred the fourth or fifth time, they began to really struggle in their marriage. While David didn't see it then, he later understood the impossibility for either of them to understand the other's pain. If Ruth couldn't feel his pain, nor David hers, then there was no way they could believe each had met the other in the middle. David could never believe that it was as painful for Ruth as it was for him.

So it wasn't long before David was sure Ruth was not meeting him halfway. The minute such suspicion begins, the journey toward disaster has begun. In each little issue of performance David became very conscious of how Ruth responded. He began to watch her every move. If she didn't respond just right (according to David's standard of performance), he would be bothered by it.

Maybe you are thinking, "Christians don't have those kinds of problems." Evangelical marriages in this country are in a sorry state. Frankly, I find very little difference between the bitterness level in Christian and non-Christian couples. What a tragic commentary on our understanding of God's plan in marriage!

Entering marriage naively, planning to meet your mate halfway, will certainly guarantee the same results as David and Ruth experienced. Christians and non-Christians alike will end up in bitter frustration if they expect another human being to meet them at the proverbial pass. The fifty-fifty relationship is an impossibility if you are looking for happiness and creative love.

REASON 3: Self-Centered Human Nature

People are amazed at how they can feel love for their spouse one minute and hatred the next. Add to this that you remember the negative much more than the positive, and you will begin to realize why almost every couple experiences incredible emotional swings from one end of the spectrum to the other.

Why is this true? How can you so quickly change from having pleasant romantic fantasies to harboring deep anger and resentment? The problem is rooted in self-centered human nature.

We experience rejection, mistrust, physical rejection, intellectual disrespect, or social embarrassment, and quickly love changes to hurt and hate. A friend explained it this way: "I can remember days when I was greatly attracted to my wife. But then she made a cutting remark, and my feelings of attraction quickly turned to resentment. At other times, I was hurt or afraid of some apparent weakness in her—maybe physical or emotional or whatever—and I didn't experience any 'feelings' for her at all."

Hurt and disappointment over a long period of time rob a couple of romantic love. Almost every engaged couple thinks they will not experience deep hurt, but they have no way of anticipating the potentiality or severity of hurt. For that reason, they are shocked at the deep pain that can be inflicted by their loved one.

What's the cause? Why can't this hurt be controlled? Scripture tells us that each person has a capacity for selfishness that is capable of strong destructive actions. Failure to anticipate this tendency, understand it, and know God's solution to it is the third major cause of marriage failure today.

This fallenness of human nature is described best in Paul's letter to the Romans.

> As it is written, There is *none righteous*, not even one; There is *none who understands*, There is *none who seeks for God;* All have turned aside, together they have become useless; There is *none who does good*, There is not even one. Their throat is an open grave, With their tongues they keep *deceiving*, The poison of asps is under their lips; Whose mouth is full of *cursing and bitterness;* Their feet are swift to shed blood, *Destruction* and *misery* are in their paths, And the path of peace have they not known. There is *no fear of God* before their eyes (Rom. 3:10–18, italics mine).

Couples who get married today without knowing how to control this capacity to sin very likely will devastate one another before much time passes.

In fact, this passage is often a good description of the discussions I hear in the counseling room: "He doesn't understand me anymore." "I thought she loved God, but if so how could she say and do what she does?" "He is useless as a husband." "The language and things she says to me are unrepeatable." "He hit me last night and threatened to kill me."

Most of the couples I see are Christians! They get married—certainly with great feelings and good intentions—and then discover that the other person is capable of inflicting great hurt, and feelings for one another are gradually destroyed. Those persons lose the desire to be creative and do what is right. When feelings stop, creative actions usually stop. When creative actions stop, a negative, critical, defensive, unromantic environment is created. This type of environment allows this "Romans 3 syndrome" to function even more intensely.

Criticism breeds criticism. In Genesis 4 we see that because of Cain's disobedience, his countenance fell and he killed his own brother. In other words, because Cain failed to respond properly and confess his disobedience to God, he actually became depressed and continued to live an even more aggressively evil life. He passed these attitudes down to his children and grandchildren (see Gen. 4:23) and they behaved in the same way.

Each of us has a tremendous capacity to be critical. This causes discouragement and defensiveness on the part of our mates. Redirecting a couple who are desperately tied into this type of critical environment can be most difficult. So much resentment and hurt has built up that it is often almost impossible to get creative action going again.

You might be saying to yourself, "My mate doesn't have that extreme capacity for evil." If that is your thinking, my heart shudders with great fear for you. Some of the most outwardly serene people I know are so deeply caught in a pattern of hurt that they have virtually lost hope.

We either are a mirror that reflects approval, appreciation, and encouragement or we are a mirror that reflects failure and disappointment. If your mirror is negative, there will be great struggle and fear in your relationships. Your feelings will become frozen and critical; you will put people under your performance standards, and you will sell yourself into the capacity to sin more.

REASON 4: Inability to Cope With Trials

If couples fail to anticipate and recognize suffering when it comes (and it will come!), later on in marriage they likely will blame suffering as the cause of struggles and trials with their mates.

The apostle Peter says we have been called for the very purpose that we might suffer (see 1 Pet. 2:21). Certainly suffering is not very popular, yet God says we will suffer. The Christ who sweat drops like blood the night before He went to die on the cross is the same Christ who went down the road to Jerusalem carrying the cross and wearing a painful crown of thorns. This was the Man people spit on and cursed and insulted. This was the Man who, when things were tough, had no friends left around Him.

Why is it then that we who have come into union with Him think we are not going to have some of these same sufferings in our lifetimes? Jesus said that if we want to be like Him, we must go through times of suffering.

Time and time again couples come in for counseling, and one or both of them are going through a period of suffering that originally had no connection with their relationship. But because of their failure to recognize and understand God's perspective, they attribute their stress to their mate or marriage. This, of course, results in loss of romantic love and a tendency to judge the other instead of to support the one suffering.

I believe it is because we have "streamlined" our contemporary gospel, leaving out the passages on pain, perseverance, and suffering, that our current crop of Christians cannot handle trials when they come. Theologically, we have tended to teach them that in Christ there are no trials. A couple must know how to recognize suffering and how to give thanks in the midst of it before they can succeed in marriage. Let me illustrate what I mean.

When Renee got married, she had been in Christian

work for three years and was a very effective counselor. Since she had developed an outreach with some girls on a major university campus, girls came regularly to her house for ministry. Before two years of marriage had passed, she had her first child. Twelve months later her second child was born. Girls continued to come by for counsel; often they would babysit, freeing Reneé from the home.

Within a couple months after the second child was born, however, Roy and Reneé moved to another city. With both children in diapers and demanding significant time and care, life totally changed for Reneé. They were geographically isolated from their close friends and were in an older established neighborhood where it was difficult to get to know people. Roy was gone almost every day, supervising his staff in a large five-city area. Reneé was experiencing the first full blast of a twenty-four-hour day raising children without the challenge of counseling with college girls.

Reneé went through nine months of tremendous stress—which Roy didn't understand. Often when he came home she would be so upset and frustrated that they frequently had blow-ups. They experienced very little "feeling" for each other during this period. What did they conclude during that time? They generalized that all of the frustration was because they were married!

Roy thought Reneé didn't really love him anymore. Here he was, growing in the Christian life, having a strong witness, and having mounting marital problems! He was blind to her suffering; in fact, he actually developed a spiritual pride and would say such things as, "Reneé, you've been acting like this for months! When are you going to snap out of it? What's the matter with you—you used to be such a stable Christian."

Reneé was a godly woman, and Roy was destroying her! The confidence she had in her relationship with Christ began to fade away. Fortunately, she came out of it, but it was without any help whatsoever from Roy.

This is suffering!

Roy and Reneé were not out of God's will in moving to another city, or in having two children so close together, or by having different tasks to do. In fact, God greatly deepened Reneé's spiritual life during this time. But they missed some blessings together because they did not recognize suffering and they did not uplift one another. They concluded that it was a spiritual problem.

Many, many people come into my office thinking that their mate has faltered instead of realizing their mate's need to be supported. Raising children carries with it a tremendous burden at times, as does moving to a new location or changing jobs. Yet, with proper perspective, the pain of these things can open the door for compassion and great blessings. Without that godly perspective, we are likely to pick up subconscious or psychological hangovers that can last a lifetime.

Trials and suffering are a regular part of married life. Is this not confessed in our marriage vows themselves? Every couple must anticipate and prepare for these times. How a couple handles these periods of trial determines to a great extent how happy they will be. Having studied successful marriages for years, I have observed that trials actually bless a marriage over the long haul. Yet in less successful marriages, trials become a source of bitterness and division.

Expect your husband to experience many severe ups and downs in his vocation. Expect your wife to experience burdens of the home and the children at times. Support each other instead of criticizing and judging one another, thereby causing needless stress and hurt. (Later, Part III will deal specifically with some of the major trials in marriage.)

REASON 5: A Fantasy View of Love

"After sixteen years of marriage, how could she fall in love with another man?" the man in my office stammered in a troubled voice. "She hasn't spent more than ten hours alone with him and I've already lost her!"

Minutes later his wife was speaking. "It's his fault," she said. "For two years he said he didn't care. I thought I would go crazy. Finally in desperation I turned to Jim and he was so understanding. Without meaning to, we fell in love almost immediately."

The fifth major cause of marriage failure today is what I have come to call *fantasy love*. Fantasy love is more of a "feeling" than anything. "If I cannot have you, I'll die!" It is the kind of love we read about or see in movies and on television. It is the deeply emotional experience that causes us to daydream and fantasize, that sends chills up our spines.

Let me say that I believe God created emotions and I feel they are an important part of human love. However, feelings are a *result* of godly love, not its basis. The tragedy of fantasy love is that it is based on feelings.

If a person doesn't *feel* anymore, he concludes that love has escaped. Like the couple I just mentioned, the majority of people today define love in terms of how they feel. There can be no weaker foundation for a relationship.

Feelings of love become almost a mystical experience for some. Many times I have heard a mate say, "I am sorry, but I just don't love you anymore" or "She has lost her love for me." How tragic it is to think that millions of people actually base a marriage and family life on a love that is capable of disappearing. I find that people today are so confused and frustrated about what love is and how to find it that they are living out their emotional love through books, TV, movies, and fantasy relationships.

Some time ago a single girl came to ask my advice about a man with whom she was "terribly in love." I talked with her for about thirty minutes and knew she believed the relationship was really serious. I finally suggested that she continue to communicate on several points with her friend. Much to my surprise, she answered back with "Oh, I haven't actually talked to him yet." She had created a complete love relationship in her mind without ever talking to the man. She was deeply in love with a myth!

I wonder how much such a myth is involved in American marriages. Recently I read in the newspaper that soap operas are such an important part of American women's lives that when the televised Watergate hearings pre-empted the soap opera programs, the networks were deluged with complaints. The article went on to say that women were so caught up in these stories that when a marriage or death occurred on the screen, TV stations across the nation actually received flowers or condolence cards.

Instead of risking the disappointment of rejection by a real person, some people create fantasies to bring them emotional pleasure. And the end result is often personal mysticism and deep depression.

A type of fantasy love is found in the Old Testament in the story of David and Bathsheba. David had decided to stay home from his military responsibility.

While strolling on the palace roof one day, he noticed a woman bathing. He found out who she was, who her husband was, and when he would be gone. He then began having an affair with her while her husband was away at war.

Doesn't this sound like today? In his book *Prime Time*, Herbert Barks says, "The affair with Bathsheba transformed the knight of God into a liar, a betrayer, a thief (and a murderer) who took what did not belong to him. . . . Perhaps it sounds overdramatic to say affairs can lead to murder. But they can and do. It is certainly not overdramatic to say an affair leads to lies and denials of all that is best and true and honorable—in David or in anyone else."*

All fantasy love relationships, whether real or imagined, are simply counterfeit ways of trying to meet our needs. God's love, on the other hand, releases the only real possibilities for consistent feelings. Thus, relationships are possible with real people who have real faults and real weaknesses—like your mate!

---

*Herbert Barks, *Prime Time* (Nashville: Thomas Nelson, 1978), p. 51.

4
Slip-Slidin' Away: An Avoidable Progression

As a counselor I am constantly faced with couples whose dreams of a solid marriage relationship are being destroyed by one or more of the five enemies discussed in the previous chapter. Many times I have heard a husband or wife say, after I have explained their predicament, "If I had only known these things before we got married . . ."

Yet a person may understand all the pitfalls and still become ensnared in a problem marriage. It is important to recognize the subtle destructive *process* of decay that destroys millions of marriages. Things don't go to pieces overnight; dreams die gradually and subtly. As I have worked closely both with couples and with individuals these last ten years, I have observed a *progression* toward bitterness and isolation in marriage.

This progression of decay seems to develop through four stages:

1) Days of Romanticism
2) Days of Reality

3) Days of Resentment
4) Days of Rebellion

While these stages are not necessarily absolute, they are amazingly observable in almost all problem marriages.

STAGE 1—The Days of Romanticism

Today, as never before in history, our society is being bombarded with tremendous psychological and emotional "public relations" programming. Our five senses are being deluged with the ultimate fantasy: the call to the intellect to experience life through physical freedom without responsibility. A great emphasis is placed on being "in" and upon having all your needs met through experiences or things.

Years of this programming has resulted in a society that is looking for *the* experience or *the* romance. Even the wise person has to fight for real happiness apart from needing a greater or deeper experience. Further, the experiences portrayed and offered in this programming are false. Marriage, raising children, sex, work, and love are so distorted that reality comes as a shock.

All of this results in people from different backgrounds and programming coming together through "experiences." They naively plan their lives and futures as if it were a theatrical production. The secular "citizen of the world" would violently disagree with these statements; programming is so complete that romanticism *has become* reality.

STAGE 2—The Days of Reality

The second stage usually occurs in the first three to five years of marriage, although it is not unusual to see this stage begin in less than a year. Before the honeymoon is over, many myths about sex and romance are usually exposed. But certainly before the first year is past, reality begins to hit.

Today, most young wives work. She is up at six, getting dressed, cooking, and hurrying off to work. She gets home after five, fixes dinner, eats, and finishes the dishes by seven. Washing clothes or house details may keep her busy until nine. By that time she is already thinking about getting up early the next morning, but she has had no real time for herself. Her husband, who has been watching television, is now ready for her personal attention. Emotionally, she is unable to respond.

Perhaps she is "waiting for the day she can have children" so she can stay home. But when that day comes she will enter into a responsibility level previously unthinkable. Instead of viewing marriage as a sexy honeymoon, she is fighting for enough strength and personal time just to hold herself together.

Her husband, likewise, was idealistic when they got married. He thought his job was great. Before long, however, he became frustrated and unsure about his future. He can't change jobs because he is not sure he can afford to go back to a starting salary. His wife becomes frustrated financially because she seems to be trapped by their circumstances. He doesn't want to upset her even more.

In short, it is not long after marriage that the romance ends and the realities begin. Jobs, money, children, observation of weaknesses, and time pressures all bring a very sobering view of life.

During this sobering period, feelings begin to oscillate. Extended painful adjustments and depression appear, and one partner may not have great feelings of love for the other for days at a time. If not checked,

unromantic periods get even longer. This is cata-
strophic, because good feelings were the primary basis
for the decision to marry in the first place. With most
of the motivation for being sacrificial gone, the kind
and sacrificial acts begin to wane. This opens the door
to the next stage.

STAGE 3—The Days of Resentment

When feelings begin to change and creative, sacrificial actions begin to wane, marriage partners begin to
deeply resent each other or blame their mates for the
circumstances: "You're not meeting me halfway" or
"You are so weak" or "You're just not normal sexually."

As a counselor, I can always tell when one or both
individuals reach the conscious point at which they
feel they got "stuck" with one of "those." The one who
feels stuck *resents* the other's inadequacies, and *resents*
God for "allowing this to happen." The other mate
feels judged and misunderstood, and resents it.

When that day of resentment arrives and *if the
couple does not find a solution*, they move in one of two
directions. First, toward *divorce.* Today many are feeling the social freedom to give up and get out. Frankly,
from human perspective and apart from God's perspective, this direction is probably the more realistic
of the two.

The second direction is the *compromised marriage.*
The majority of marriages today fit into this category.
A compromised marriage is one in which people do not
really deal with their mistakes, attitudes, weaknesses,
and differences, but instead each goes his own way,
purposely staying away from the volatile areas. Such
couples will, for the most part, pretend that problems

don't exist even though inside they have deep resentment. Every few months the pressure may build until they explode in anger. Several days of frustration will end with this kind of statement: "Well, I wish things were different. But I am not going to end the relationship because of what it would do to the children. So I'll just put up with the problems."

A compromised marriage often results in sexual dysfunction. The wife has been so hurt that she just has no sexual appetite. The husband tries to ignore her passivity at first, but one night after a social event he observes his wife undressing and his attraction cannot be restrained. Tired, and resentful of his lack of attention earlier in the evening, she refuses him. He explodes. She is angry and guilty at the same time. They go to sleep on opposite sides of the bed and awaken the next morning to "no comment."

Another example is the wife who is raising the children with a husband who is never home. The wife daily sees personality problems or discipline problems developing, and she cannot bear these burdens alone. She knows her husband resents her saying anything about it, so she tries to ignore the problems. One night her husband, who has not had a creative day with their son in weeks, gets angry at the kids and yells at the son and spanks him. Unable to stand it, she explodes, and the gap in their relationship widens.

Many supposedly successful marriages are really just two successful people going their own independent ways, being careful not to step on each other's toes. The husband overemphasizes his job to compensate for the lost intimacy. The wife overemphasizes her relationship with the children to compensate for the lack of a fully developed marriage relationship.

One never knows about such relationships until the

partners reach their late forties or fifties, the children leave home, and all they have is each other. Their *real* relationship can only be measured then.

I counsel more couples in their fifties than in any other age bracket. They always say, "Don, we *thought* we had a good marriage."

Certainly there are many adjustment periods in life. But if resentment continues unabated, it is like a cancer spreading throughout the whole relationship. If it is not dealt with, it will lead to—

STAGE 4—The Days of Rebellion

Every counselor despairs when a man or woman who has been caught in this spiral of resentment for several years enters his office. The results of such years damage lives in many areas. Women often become fearful; men tend to become hardened toward having the relationship healed.

Think for a minute: a wife enters marriage with romantic feelings. She views her mate with trust and sees in him only perfection, and she dreams of a model home and children. Her body is young and her self-image is at its peak.

Several years pass and she finds herself in an absolutely contrasting state. Her feelings for him have long since waned, and she not only lacks trust in her husband, but she now finds herself extremely critical of him. The struggle and disappointment of these few years and her bearing of the children have taken a toll on her youthfulness and her physical appearance. Her days are burdensome, long, and introspective. She is constantly rethinking her situation. Her lost feelings for her husband and her bitter struggle have caused her to fear her future.

Here is a woman at thirty with two children ages seven and four. She knows the tremendous personal responsibility they demand, and it occurs to her that the responsibility will not end for at least fifteen more years. By then she will be forty-five and her youthful years will be long gone. All that will be left is a husband for whom she has lost her enthusiasm.

These realities result in the woman becoming subconsciously fearful and uncertain of herself. Wives come to me saying, "I'm just not as sharp as I used to be. I can't seem to remember things like I used to. I don't enjoy people like I used to." All of these things are a direct result of her lost hope for the future.

Men, on the other hand, handle these painful realities differently. Rather than becoming fearful, they tend to harden and become calloused toward others. They become more insensitive and self-centered in their relationships. Here is a guy who, at one time, would have literally died for his wife. But as his wife becomes more aware of his weaknesses, she becomes more critical. Every failure or uncertainty is closely observed and communicated. After a while, he is covered with guilt and feelings of failure. Because she continually observes his weaknesses more than his strengths, he retreats. His respect for her is replaced by disgust.

Some years ago, this was vividly illustrated by a man who came to see me. He and his wife had been married for nearly twenty years. As I listened to their history, I was amazed at how romantic the initial years of the marriage were. The wife, though, had a strong personality, and after several years of marriage she began to voice her critical opinions of her husband. Over the next ten years, she had dominated him with her thoughts and observations.

Not long after our first few appointments, she called me from the hospital and told me she was going to need emergency surgery for what looked like cancer. She was terribly frightened, and asked if I would call her estranged husband and see if he would visit her.

When I called him, he was preparing to go deep-sea fishing. After I told him the purpose of my call, he said, "That _____ woman has been controlling my life for twenty years. I don't care if she dies and goes to hell, but she isn't going to ruin this fishing trip." And he hung up. Here was a man who had worshiped his wife twenty years earlier and now was so hardened against her that he broke her heart and spirit.

But remember, this erosion of relationship is a *process;* it does not happen overnight. These patterns of fearfulness and hardness, if not corrected, continue until both begin to feel that the best of life was missed because of the mate. The cancer of bitterness becomes overwhelming. Before long this rebellion affects other relationships. Soon each begins to criticize and doubt the children or the boss or friends. It is shocking how few old people really have bitterness-free relationships with anyone.

The culture Americans are born into breeds the destruction of relationships. Even though people mean well, apart from God's pattern they will certainly find themselves alone and wondering where it all went wrong.

A man in his seventies came into my office one day in total frustration. He told me he had not been able to live with his wife successfully since his retirement a few years before. They had been married for fifty years! Both of them were extremely attractive and alert. In fact, this man was so sharp—and set in his ways—that I couldn't tell him anything.

He had traveled to another part of the world and had observed a culture where the women were subservient. He had tried to demand these actions from his wife. The result was separation.

In our first few sessions I tried to talk with him about submission. He was headstrong, and I could not break through. He was saying to me, in effect, "Here I am a millionaire, a man twice your age. How do you think you can tell me anything?"

The next time I met with him I said, "Mr. Beck, you and I are not getting anywhere. Let me ask you a question. How long do you think you have to live?"

He thought for a moment and answered, "Well, probably five or ten years."

"Mr. Beck, I know you have a lot more experience at living than I, but let me ask you another question. If you died tomorrow morning, who would miss you by, say, noontime?"

I could see an immediate change in his tough exterior. I continued, "I don't mean miss you at the funeral, because I know you have done some good things in your life. But I mean who is going to have a vacuum in the middle of the day because you're gone?"

Tears filled his eyes and he said, "I see what you mean. Here I am with all of my experience and wealth, but I don't have a relationship with anyone in the world."

How tragic—a man with every human success but no relationships. I cannot tell that story without being frightened that this could even happen to me! Relationships are what life is all about.

As we prepare to turn the corner—from the discussion of why marriages fail to God's plan for successful marriage—one last point comes to mind.

THE ULTIMATE COMMITMENT

A man recently said to me, "Don, is it necessary for you to bring God in as the answer to my marriage problems?" We had just spent seven hours discussing and agreeing on the destructive process of the five reasons marriages fail.

I answered his question with a question of my own. "Mike, as we have talked about you and Patty—your struggles, conflicts, and rejection of each other—you said you could not seem to control your actions. Why?"

He replied, "I don't know."

"Any counselor will tell you why," I said. "Two people who are egocentric and self-centered have no natural basis for a common relationship."

I told Mike that I was encouraged because of Jesus Christ's ability to help him. "Mike, your struggle is not with Jesus Christ, but perhaps with a caricature of Christ that men have presented. Don't reject Christ's love and power because of some hypocrisy you might have seen in others. God keeps on loving us even while we are still trying to reject Him! Christ died for your sins to reunite you with God the Father.

"Mike," I continued, "have the humility to turn to Christ. If you will, He will start you out all over again as a child of God."

And so it is for all of us. Receiving Christ requires each of us to put away our self-centeredness and come under His reign. If you have never done so, let me encourage you to commit your life to Him. Tell Him you are sick of your self-centeredness. Thank Him for forgiving your sins. Ask Him to enter your life and your home as Lord, teaching you how to live and experience His power in your marriage.

For in Christ, you will have dominion over self-centeredness and sin. You and your mate can find a common basis for marriage and a new beginning in life through Christ, and in His church.

PART II

5

*Oneness: God's Plan,
Man's Hope*

A non-Christian recently said to me, "Why should I become a Christian? It sure didn't stop Bill and Joyce from getting a divorce." Has God stopped working or have we Christians stopped listening to God?

These last ten years of counseling have made one thing clear to me: *There is usually very little difference between a Christian marriage and a non-Christian marriage.*

Here's what I mean by that. As Christians, we tend to have higher standards for our prospective partners. But once those criteria are met, we tend to go right back to the same system for marriage that the world uses.

I met a young man the other day who said he would not *date* anyone who did not adhere to the following criteria: She had to be a Christian; she had to be regularly involved in a church; she had to be learning the Scriptures through Bible study; and she had to be having some kind of outreach ministry.

I appreciated the desire of this gentleman to consider his future mate's spiritual interest. However, too many people have a false sense of security about such criteria. Once they judge that someone has met their qualifications, they drop their guard and before they know it, their marriage is no different from anyone else's.

Obviously, selecting a mate with a track record of spiritual faithfulness is a first step. But the second step is to realize God has given us some very specific guidelines that must be applied daily before one can experience a blessing in marriage. In other words, a successful marriage is not guaranteed by a good beginning; it must be lived out by two people who daily apply God's Word in marriage. It takes two people who individually are monitoring their human existence by a supernatural mindset from God. As these two people obey the Lord, they are directed in a mutually satisfying and successful direction.

The basics of a solid marriage are found in two areas. Internal beliefs and decisions must be developed, and then external actions must be followed. Part II of this book develops these internal beliefs and decisions, while Part III deals with practical action steps.

In this chapter we want to establish some concepts of why God made man in the first place. In light of these thoughts, willful decisions to do what God says will positively affect your marriage. If God created humanity and marriage, it certainly makes sense to consult God's instructions on how to make marriage work.

God's purpose for man and for marriage is stated in the first two chapters of the Bible, Genesis 1 and 2.

First of all, these two chapters (along with Revelation 21 and 22) are written from a totally different point of view from every other chapter of Scripture.

These two chapters refer to a time when sin was not. Both Adam and Eve were perfect—without sin—when God spoke these words. Therefore, we know that God's purpose for man as stated in Genesis 1 and 2 was His perfect intent for man and marriage.

Second, remember that God's authority had already been challenged before He created Adam and Eve. This challenge came from an angel, Lucifer, who had planned to make himself like God (see Isa. 14:12–17). In other words, he was saying he did not need God to have life. This is important because we will see that part of God's purpose in creating Adam and Eve and marriage was to demonstrate to Lucifer and to all of creation that only God can give true life.

Third, realize that marriage was God's first institution. It came long before Israel or the church. Adam and Eve were given a great responsibility in their union to carry out God's great purpose in eternity.

I remember that when I first became a Christian I was amazed that Christ placed so much responsibility on His twelve disciples. Now I realize that the commissioning of the Twelve was the second time in history that God placed His plan in the hands of a few people. Adam and Eve (and therefore you and I) have been given an awesome responsibility before God.

In conclusion, it is clear that God's creation of the earth and of Adam and Eve was not just an "afterthought" of God, but a response to the challenge of Satan. Adam and Eve, and every couple that would follow, would have a tremendous stake in God's plan of the ages. John Barnhouse summarizes the drama that was unfolding best in his book, *The Invisible War:*

We shall give this rebellion a thorough trial. We shall permit it to run full course. The universe shall see what a creature, even the greatest, can do apart from God. We shall set up an experiment, and permit the universe of creatures to watch it, during this brief interlude between eternity past and eternity future, called time. In it, the spirit of independence shall be allowed to expand to the utmost. And the wreck and ruin which shall result will demonstrate to the universe, and forever, that there is no life, no joy, no peace apart from a complete dependence upon the MOST HIGH GOD, possessor of heaven and earth.*

Adam and Eve's dependence on God was vital! As we consider God's plan, we must recognize the important part our marriages play in that plan. Let's see what our responsibility is.

WHY GOD MADE US

With this background, let's look specifically at why God created man. Genesis 1 describes all of creation. Verses 1–25 describe the creation of the heavens, the earth, vegetation, and beasts. Our focus will fall on verses 26–31, which describe the creation of Adam and Eve.

Within these few verses we are able to determine three distinct purposes God had in creating human life and in creating marriage.

1. Reflect His image

Then God said, "Let Us make man in Our image, according to Our likeness; and let them rule over the fish of the sea and over the birds of the sky and over all the earth, and over every creeping thing that creeps on the earth." And God created man in His own image, in the image of God He created him; male and female He created them (Gen. 1:26, 27).

*John Barnhouse, *The Invisible War*

The central thought of these two verses is in the phrases "in Our image" and "according to Our likeness." God is clearly stating that He made Adam and Eve initially (and man in general) to be a reflection of Himself. God desired that He be reflected on earth.

In Matthew 5, believers are exhorted to be the salt and light of the earth. That passage makes it clear that it is the Christlikeness of a person that causes his light to shine brightly. That same thought is initiated in Genesis 1 as the first purpose of man. What a privilege it is to be restored in Christ to being a reflection of God. From the plural pronoun used in verse 26 it is clear that God intended man to reflect the wholeness of the Trinity—the Father, Son, and Holy Spirit—different in person and function but one in nature and purpose.

A very important delineation is made in verse 27. God makes very clear that His reflection cannot be accomplished by a man alone or a woman alone. Even the single Christian is called into relationships and commitments with both men and women within the body of Christ. "In the image of God He created him; male and female He created them."

A powerful statement: God is saying that He is reflected in *both* male and female—a unit. God created Adam and Eve as the parents of a humanity designed to reflect God's image. He further made clear that He wanted "them" to rule.

When a couple displays a real spirit of *oneness*, God is truly glorified. What a waste it is, on the other hand, when a spiritually gifted man or woman does not operate out of oneness with his or her mate. No amount of Christian "giftedness" makes up for that incomplete picture of God's character. Likewise, it is greatly discouraging to see men desiring to be more like women and women desiring to be more like men, as our society tries to dissolve the uniqueness of the sexes. In a very real sense, the fullness of God's image is being diluted at the same time. Instead, God is pleased when one fully man and another fully woman come together to show forth His likeness.

Men and women, God is teaching you in this passage that a right relationship with your mate is *not optional*. If God willed you to marriage as opposed to singleness, then you are bound to your mate in order to experience God's eternal purpose.

Today many people are in a gray zone, either trying to decide whether to marry or, if married, whether to divorce. But if we understand God's perspective and if we are married, we do not have the option of divorce. I would be incomplete without my wife. To lose her without His taking her in death would literally cut part of myself away from God's reflection. I cannot reflect God's image fully without her. Since I have understood the significance of how important she is from God's perspective, I now have a whole different perspective on her importance to me, and to God on my behalf.

2. *Reproduce after our kind*

The second purpose of marriage is discovered in the first half of verse 28: "God blessed them [Adam and Eve]; and God said to them, 'Be fruitful and multiply, and fill the earth. . . .'"

This purpose for man is very clear—to have children. It is important to note that God considered this a blessing—something you are to remember next time your kids are about to drive you wild! This refutes any notion that God created sexual relations in any kind of negative light. He blessed Adam's family and He blessed their sexual union.

Looking at the four billion people alive today, it seems that this is the one purpose of God that man has completed. But if you put this verse in the context of all of Scripture and its drama, it is clear that simply having children is not the full purpose God intended.

This could be better stated, "Reproduce a godly heritage which will also reflect God's image." God created His expeditionary force, Adam and Eve, to reflect God's image. Now God tells us to maintain and to increase that reflection by having children. Remember that the key to being a light or reflection of God is Christlikeness. So when we consider all of Scripture, it is clear that God intended that man, through having children, should increase God's reflection on earth.

3. Reign over the creation

The third purpose God states for man in Genesis 1 is found in the second half of verse 28, to "subdue it [the earth] and rule over [it]." Through *oneness* in marriage two people are equipped to control and rule God's creation.

God intended that Adam and Eve and all couples to follow were to succeed in oneness with each other and, together with Him, to defeat Satan in spiritual warfare. What glory and praise it is to God when a couple, though weaker in creation than Satan, can by dependence on God experience true life and rule over the earth.

God presents three purposes for marriage in Genesis 1. He intended that every couple from Adam and Eve on would: (1) *Reflect God's image;* (2) *Reproduce a godly heritage;* and (3) *Reign in spiritual warfare.*

How many couples do you know who are reflecting the image of God together? How many are raising children who, as a godly heritage, are reflecting the image of God? How many are reigning together in the spiritual warfare going on all about us?

What a challenge to us to develop our marriages in accordance with God's design and purpose.

APPLYING GOD'S PURPOSES

In summary, we see that God, after Satan's challenge of independence, set about a plan that was initially dependent on Adam and Eve's coming together through faith in God to reflect God's image, reproduce a godly heritage, and reign in dominion over the earth. Such a union would demonstrate for all eternity that only a dependence on God would allow man to find life.

It is utterly *impossible* to accomplish these goals for our lives without a husband and wife being *one* with each other. It is one thing for God to desire oneness with us. But it becomes a new matter when we realize we are kidding ourselves by thinking we can raise children or be successful at life without being of one mind and one spirit with each other in the bond of marriage.

Because I have come to believe *God created me to be incomplete without my wife,* I have felt a daily need for her that I did not have before. Only as I am one with her will I be able to accomplish my goals for myself, my children, Sally, and God. I am not able to persist in rebelling against God's will. Because I believe my marriage is vital to God's plan for the ages, I am very sensitive not to discourage His will.

The Spirit of God is not failing to serve marriages today. But because we do not know God's Word and His perspective, He is limited by our unbelief.

God is unchanging: Our Lord Jesus Christ is the same yesterday, today, and forever. Therefore, His plan for marriage is unaltered. We are either going to believe it or we are not. We are either going to follow His plan and experience life, or we are not. It is as simple as that.

6

How Oneness Happens

*A*fter working through God's view of oneness, most couples ask one resounding question: *"How* does a couple find oneness?" The whole point of Genesis 1 is that married people cannot experience fulfillment of God's purpose in creating them without being *one* with their mate. Genesis 2 *defines* oneness and tells you *how* to experience it.

As we approach the passage, let's recall God's perspective. God, after having His very character challenged by Satan's pride and rebellion, creates an expeditionary force on earth to demonstrate that a lesser being who trusts God instead of himself for life can not only be victorious, but one day will be seated at the right hand of God Himself. Right at the focal point of God's created plan were Adam and Eve. As one entity, they were equipped to *reflect* God's image on the earth, *reproduce* God's image through a godly heritage, and to *reign* over the earth, including the evils thereof. All of this was dependent upon marriage oneness.

Genesis 2:18 makes a profound statement: "Then the Lord God said, 'It is not good for the man to be alone; I will make him a helper suitable for him.'"

At the time of creation, Adam was different from you and me. First, Adam had no sin. He was created perfect! Next, his physical environment was perfect.

Finally, and most importantly, Adam had the greatest relationship possible with the living God. Adam could actually experience God with two of his five senses. He could see the Shekinah glory of God, as Moses would, and he could actually hear God speak. Scripture says he walked and talked with God.

God told Adam it was not good for him to be alone. Now put yourself in Adam's feet (he had no shoes) for a moment. You are perfect, with a perfect environment and a perfect and satisfying relationship with the very One who created you. When God told him he was alone, Adam didn't have a clue what God was talking about. What did "alone" mean? Didn't he have God? And the whole earth? Wasn't that enough?

All my life I have heard a subtle thought projected throughout evangelical Christendom. "Me plus God is all I need." I can remember making that statement shortly after Sally and I were married when a student asked what I would do if something happened to Sally. I said something to the effect that I would go on, because, after all, "all I need is God." God put that concept to rest forever in Genesis 2:18!

Every step was according to His perfect plan and timetable. Adam did not give God the thought of being alone; God gave it to Adam! It should be noted that this is the only time God used the words "not good" during His creation of the world. Everything He had created before Adam "was good." God emphasized very clearly that man was not yet complete. He was not created to stand alone—then or now! God was saying, "Adam, in the way in which I have chosen to make you, I need a tool to meet your total needs." God chose to create a need in man for human relationships in addition to Himself. Relationships are not optional; they are vital!

This does not lessen our dependence upon God in the least. *All* that God creates is designed to increase our dependence upon Him. God could have created Eve simultaneously with Adam. But to insure dependence upon Himself, God clearly showed Adam his need so he would trust God for the *fulfillment* of that need. Thereby Adam began a life of total trust in the perfect plan of the Most High.

The words "suitable to" mean "to complete or to correspond to." In other words, God was saying that Adam was incomplete. In Genesis 1, God continually referred to humanity as "they" and "them": "Let Us make man in Our image . . . and let them. . . ." It is clear that God saw Adam and Eve as a single unit of two.

Genesis 2:19,20 further elaborates on this need that God set up in Adam.

> And out of the ground the Lord God formed every beast of the field and every bird of the sky, and brought them to the man to see what he would call them; and whatever the man called a living creature, that was its name. And the man gave names to all the cattle, and to the birds of the sky, and to every beast of the field, but for Adam there was not found a helper suitable for him.

What a shock! Instead of Eve, God brought all the animals to Adam. Why? The answer is given in the last part of verse 20. God rarely gives man anything without first showing him his need. Adam had not yet understood what God meant by "aloneness," so he could not have fully appreciated Eve at this point. How did Adam discover his need through the animals?

To begin with, animals say nothing! He named the first and went on to the next. Same response! Silence. Was he beginning to see a need? Animal after animal was named, presumably without any of them talking back in a language he understood. And he must have observed that even though there were two lions, they were made differently. They were paired off—animal families, if you will. Most important, Adam learned there was nobody suitable for him—no one to talk to, no one to complete him as a companion. The point is, one must see his need before he can appreciate the provision for that need.

I remember when my son Todd was born. I was so excited, I bought him a football right away. Todd didn't appreciate it! Why? He had no need.

On Todd's fourth Christmas I decided it was time for him to be a big boy and ride a bicycle. I had always pictured Todd on a bike. Christmas day found Todd excited, but it only lasted about two hours. In the months that followed the bike sat unused in the garage. He had no need for a bike.

When he was six we moved to Little Rock and Todd observed a neighbor boy with a very special bike—a black one without training wheels and with a rugged look. Todd asked for a bike like Brent's. I am a slow learner, but I was beginning to catch on. "Todd," I said, "Daddy would love for you to have a bike like Brent's, but if you remember you have not ridden the other one much and bikes cost a lot of money."

So Todd rode his bike for four months, all the while praying *daily* to the Lord for a big bike. Not one night passed in four months that Todd didn't ask for that bike.

As we neared Christmas, we were short of money. Sally told Todd he would need to pray for our finances, even to make our house payment. Well, he prayed earnestly for money for our house *and* the bike.

About a week before Christmas a large, unexpected check arrived. Todd was not at all surprised. He expected God to answer. On Christmas morning, under the tree, there was his big, black, rugged bike! How real God was becoming to him through this little trial. The excitement did not stop in two hours or two months or even two years. It's been three and a half years now and Todd still puts that same bike up every night. It is still very special to him because it was God's provision for a need (or at least a *want!*) that he had.

Do you see your *need* for your mate? If Christ returned today and asked how He could help me in working with couples, I would ask Him for a project similar to the naming of the animals. It is so tragic when couples marry before God has prepared them. After experiencing only ten percent of what God intended for marriage, they think they have experienced it all. Couples are getting divorced today without ever realizing what they missed. God showed Adam his need before giving him Eve so that he could fully appreciate God's gift.

God, having first created in Adam a need for marriage, and then having shown him his need, now creates Eve as the satisfaction to the need. We read in Genesis 2:21, 22:

> So the Lord God caused a deep sleep to fall upon the man, and he slept; then He took one of his ribs, and closed up the flesh at that place. And the Lord God

fashioned into a woman the rib which He had taken from the man, and brought her to the man.

God caused Adam to sleep while He created Eve—a picture of God's part, meeting our needs and man's part, resting in God's promises. I've heard it said that God's choosing a rib, as opposed to a piece of the foot or head, signifies the perfect picture of the relationship of woman to man. She is under the protection of man's arm but protects the man's most vital part, his heart. She is not from his head to rule over him nor from his feet to be beneath him, but is alongside to complete him—and he her.

The most strategic statement in the passage is one that at first seems odd. "God brought Eve to Adam." It seems God would have created Eve right next to Adam. Why did God *bring* her to Adam? God wanted Adam to know that just as it was He who had *created* her, it was also He alone who would *present* her to her husband. I believe God asks us today, "Will you trust Me to bring your mate to you?" God desires complete dependence on Him for all our needs!

Adam responded with belief in verse 23: "And the man said, 'This is now bone of my bones, And flesh of my flesh; She shall be called Woman, Because she was taken out of Man.' "

The English text does not fully communicate what the Hebrew words say. Adam was excited! A better translation would be, "Great! Fantastic, Lord! This woman you made for me is my complete joy. I am one hundred percent committed to her." Adam totally received Eve!

Was it Adam's ability to inspect Eve that caused him to totally receive Eve? Certainly not! Don't misunderstand me: I am sure Eve was very attractive to

Adam. But Adam had never seen a woman before; he had no one else to compare her with!

What, then, was Adam's basis for receiving Eve? On what basis was he confident that she was "right" for him? *God* was Adam's hope! Adam was obedient; his confidence was in the Lord. God was the One who had created Adam, created his need, showed Adam his need, and met his need. When Adam fully received Eve, it was based on *who God was to Adam, not Adam's ability to inspect Eve.* Because Adam believed God, he thus received Eve from Him.

What is God saying? That He alone can meet your needs. He has created a need in you for relationships, which He meets primarily through a mate, but also through the church and friends. He put this need in you to teach you dependence upon Him and to equip you to reflect His image to an imperfect world. You can then reproduce a godly heritage and reign on earth. He will meet the need of your loneliness through other people like you who are alone and imperfect. Beware of inspecting with your eyes, because Satan's task is to deceive you as he did Adam and Eve in Genesis 3.

We are at a key point in God's plan. God sought to protect man from Satan's sin of self-dependence by insuring that he would have to trust God to meet his "aloneness" needs. Therefore, God requires that man receive his mate from God. God went out of His way to demonstrate that He clearly created an Eve for an Adam. God's sovereignty in Scripture clearly states that His will for individuals can't be permanently affected by man. God says in Ephesians 6:12 that our struggle is not against men but against evil powers. These powers deceive us into believing that people or God are our problem. Adam *chose* to believe God, which was demonstrated by his response in receiving

Eve as a gift from God, totally perfect to meet his "aloneness" needs.

You are probably saying, "If God will not allow my mate's weaknesses to limit Him in meeting my aloneness needs, how then should I view his or her weaknesses?"

Years ago, when I first understood what God was saying, I was fearful of having to live with Sally's weaknesses, which, I thought, might never change. Viewing these weaknesses as having no limitation on God's ability to meet my relationship needs through Sally seemed almost impossible. Yet, I took a step of faith, believed God, and received her from Him. I asked God to allow me to realize that even her weaknesses were perfect for me in every way. I began to experience a new freedom and hope in my marriage. I began to share this truth with others, and as the first faltering months passed I realized how great our marriage had become.

What began as a tough step of faith ten years ago has since become one of the most blessed realities in my life. Sally might as well be perfect, because God graciously allows me to be totally satisfied. This step of faith opened my eyes to four ways of viewing weaknesses in our mates.

1) Genesis 2 has assured us that we can look beyond our mate's weaknesses to God's perfect provision for our "aloneness" needs.

2) Realize that God's only agent for changing a mate with promised results is *agape* (unconditional) love.

3) God actually uses our mate's weaknesses as a tool to perfect our character (as Bill Gothard teaches).

4) Our mate's weaknesses are an opportunity for us

to be needed. (If our mate were perfect, he or she wouldn't need us).

These truths have released me to experience hope and enjoyment in my marriage. God is reinforcing my belief in them by continually showing me the many reasons He specifically created Sally for me. The very things I would have changed in her in the beginning of marriage have turned out to be the very things I needed to complete me. More and more, I am discovering her value to me. God is so gracious, if we will dare to believe Him.

Can you believe God for your mate now, or if you don't have a mate yet, can you believe Him for your future? *If you don't have the faith to believe God for your mate, don't get married.* If you are married and are inspecting instead of believing, repent of your sin, ask God to forgive you, receive your mate, and give thanks to God for his provision for your need!

We are to accept our mates from God and trust God to meet our needs in spite of our mate's weaknesses. To reject your mate in any way after marriage is to doubt God and His ability to provide. It is to fail to reflect, reproduce, and reign, and it impugns God's motives. We must trust that God still creates Eves for Adams, and that He knew your needs when He created both you and your mate. Adam believed God, not his own eyes; he generated excitement because of God's faithfulness, not because of Eve's performance.

I believe as certainly as God gave Eve to Adam that God gave my wife to me—not because she is perfect, but because God is. Can you believe God for your mate?

If you can, God gives you the promised result in verses 24, 25:

For this cause a man shall leave his father and his mother, and shall cleave to his wife; and they shall become one flesh. And the man and his wife were both naked and were not ashamed.

God gives us, in verse 24, a statement of principle which is repeated twice in the New Testament. He states, "For this cause. . . ." What cause? For the cause that man would have to depend upon God for everything.

For this cause a man shall leave his parents. Obviously, since Adam was the first man he had no parents, so Genesis 2 must have definite application to future ages. Before a new life or family can begin, the old attachment must cease. Again, this is a faith-decision, based on who God is.

Also, for this cause, the man is to trust God for a heart determination to cleave to his wife. The word "cleave" means to "stick together like glue." It has the idea of two alloys melting together to become one metal that is stronger than they were separately. The cleaving is a product of God, effected in us.

The man and woman who truly leave and cleave will become one flesh, and know it! Most counseling situations I encounter come as a result of one or both partners lacking the ability or the will either to leave an old situation or to cleave to the mate.

In verse 25, God finally says His creation of man is now "good." Because they are now one, God says the man and his wife are free to be naked and unashamed. Certainly God is referring directly to the physical nakedness, but in the context of all of Scripture one can say that Adam and Eve were free to be totally exposed before each other and before God without fear. Emotionally, physically, intellectually, spiritu-

ally, and in every way they were exposed and unashamed. Total openness, total transparency. No
walls.

What a promise! Wouldn't you like to have someone
love you to the point that you could be totally exposed,
yet fear no rejection? God has given us the answer to
loving unlovable people. We are to thankfully receive
relationships that are clearly from God, trusting Him
for the outcome, not the other person's performance.

7

Loving When It Hurts

*N*ot long ago I met a man who challenged the concept of viewing his mate's weaknesses as being used by God in his life. "If I don't help her change, she'll never change."

Nowhere in Scripture are we encouraged to change people. Only God changes people. We are told to make disciples of Christ by letting people follow our example as we follow Christ's example. God has ordained only two forces for change in marriage: the *active force of love* (see Eph. 5) and the *reactive force of blessing* (see 1 Pet. 3:8,9).

Most counseling sessions with married couples uncover a struggle for the *rights* of each mate. They want their right to say what they want, do what they want, think what they want, and be what they want. In marriage, God says the only right one has is to love and bless the other. Demanding rights has no place in marriage.

When people marry they get the good with the not-so-good. Do not be deceived into thinking you will subtly be able to control, discipline, or change your mate through your own superiority. Of course, we all *feel* particularly gifted as judge, jury, and executioner, but what we don't understand is that we are totally ineffective to demand change in our mates.

God created humanity. He knows what works. Every other plan fails miserably! Don't think your plans will work if they are not God's plan. Love and blessing, not human ingenuity, produce blessed results in marriage. Let's look at both concepts.

LOVE: THE ACTIVE FORCE

Most people are fighting to cope with the realities of life . . . aging, prejudice, broken relationships, physical problems, rejection, competition, fatigue, impersonalization, isolation, boredom, and all the rest. The one potential blessed isle in the midst of those troubled waters is a love relationship. But when couples come into my office with problems, they are usually there because that once blessed isle has become an erupting volcano. How did it happen?

Much of the problem stems from America's definition of the word "love." In the world, combinations of circumstances almost totally determine "love." Feelings, the need for emotional and sexual attention, social status, escape from home, school, financial, or social pressure, aging, and desire for children are some of the reasons people get married. With the right combination or lineup of influences, couples say, "I think I'm in love. Let's get married." All of these circumstances exist, certainly, but they cannot produce love. Couples considering marriage must settle in their minds what real love is before getting married.

It is sad that some of the greatest love relationships you know of could be destroyed by a change in circumstances. If one changes from rich to poor, sexy to unsexy, young to old, social to unsocial, athletic to unathletic, healthy to unhealthy, skinny to fat, faithful to unfaithful, spiritual to unspiritual, most people would lose what they define as love. With counterfeit love, circumstances and performance are very important.

We need to pursue *commitment-love*, not feelings and circumstances. The Greek language specifically enumerates and defines three levels of love.* The first level is *eros*. This kind of love is totally emotional and physical, with emphasis on meeting the desires of the one who loves: *lust-love*. Sexual attraction and involvement are primary. *Eros* love is ultimately a self-centered or selfish love. Many couples today get married with an *eros* love as the focal point—and most do not even know it! Why are so many of these marriages ending in divorce? Because eros love is selfish.

The second level is *phileo*. It describes mutual, tender affection between two people. It has the connotation of "brotherly love." In contrast with eros love, *mutual love* would be the key phrase here. It has the idea of appreciation of the total person. "I love you because you love me" describes *phileo* love. The overwhelming majority of marriages in America are a *combination* of *eros* and *phileo* love.

The third level of love is far superior to either of the other two. This is *agape* and it is described in Scripture

---

*These definitions are found in W. E. Vine's *Expository Dictionary of New Testament Words*.

primarily as the kind of love that God gave to His Son and then to man. This kind of love is the opposite of *eros* in that it is totally sacrificial. This love can only be measured by the sacrificial action of the giver. It is not primarily emotional or sexual because it is drawn out not by the attractiveness of the object loved but by the commitment of the giver. The lover is acting in obedience to God's commandment; therefore the love is God-directed. It is first an issue between God and man, not between two people, and it does not always run with the natural inclinations of feelings. This love is responsible and does not change as feelings change. It is *commitment-love*.

If you are a Christian considering marriage and you tell your future mate you love him or her, you had better count the cost and discern which level of love you mean. *God never called anyone to marriage without agape love.* Marriage oneness is impossible without it. God teaches dependence on Him in marriage; therefore it is absolutely necessary to trust Him and not your mate.

Biblical *agape* love is best described in 1 Corinthians 13. I would like to define a few of the dimensions of this love and to expand on its meaning for marriage.

Love suffers long: This is the quality of enduring offense from your mate even though there is a tide of emotion welling up within you demanding that you retaliate. Application: 1) Have the kind of patience that waits and prays for the reformation of your mate rather than flying out in resentment. 2) This love suffers many slights and neglects from the person it loves, but waits to see the kindly effects of such patience on them.

Love is not easily provoked: Love does not become

bitter or resentful as a result of continuous irritation or offenses, and love will not respond to these offenses with touchiness or anger. Application: A weakness or offense in your mate should not cause bitterness or anger.

Love bears all things: Love endures offenses from your mate and throws a cloak of silence over your suffering, so that the offenses of your mate are not divulged to the world. Application: If you have a non-Christian or non-spiritual spouse, while this may be known to godly leaders in the church, this should not be exposed in casual prayer groups. Your mate needs to be able to trust you.

Love believes all things: Love chooses to believe the best about your mate and always assumes his or her motives and intentions are right. Application: 1) We make people what we believe them to be. If we indicate that we suspect them, they will be untrustworthy. 2) To trust in your mate gives him or her a feeling of self-worth and acceptance, a key to effecting change in your mate.

Love endures all things: Love has the power to enable one to endure any trial with a confident and joyful heart. Trials produce perseverance and blessings from God. Application: Divorce is not a manifestation of the love that endures all things; the essence of love is permanent commitment.

A study of all of 1 Corinthians 13 is an encouraging pre-marital or marital project. All the verbs in this passage are in the present tense, indicating that these characteristics of love are to be *habitual.* Because a person does not manifest one of these qualities in every instance, however, does not necessarily signal non-commitment, for we are not perfect. Paul is referring to a life-style of love.

God's love leaves no place for the statement, "I don't love you anymore." God's love does, however, hold some absolute promises for us. *Agape* love potentially can solve the most corrosive problem in life today—*fear*.

In Ephesians 5:25–33, a classic biblical section on marriage, the husband is given the same role in the home as Christ Himself has in the church. We find several helpful promises, which are given only in association with God's love.

First, if we love our mates as Paul is exhorting us to love them, we will "sanctify" them or set them apart by our special commitment to them. In other words, a woman who is loved apart from her actions, unconditionally, is set apart from other women who are not loved in this way. A woman who is loved unconditionally is free from marital anxiety and better able to live righteously.

Paul gives another promise that may be applied to changing a mate. Paul says the person who loves in this way will have a spouse who is more "holy and blameless." This describes internal as well as external beauty.

In all my years of counseling, I have never seen any other active approach gain these results. It is not unusual to hear long complaints about having to love God's way. Yet nothing else works. Neither manipulation, verbal assault, bribes, nor subtle lying will work like *agape* love. Don't experience a poor counterfeit of God's love. Experience giving love to your mate and believing God for the outcome. The fearlessness, transparency, and peace of such a relationship is what married life was meant to be.

BLESSING: THE REACTIVE FORCE OF LOVE

With the anger of flashing eyes a woman recently told me this story. "For three years, since my husband started his new business, the children and I have not had a vacation. We have all done without a lot of things so Bob could try to succeed. Then two weeks ago his real appreciation for us came through loud and clear. First of all, I got the Master Charge bill and discovered that Bob had bought an $800 motor boat. When I called him at the office, he exploded and told me that he and some of his buddies were going fishing for ten days in Mexico and needed a boat!

"I was so furious I hardly spoke to him for the next two weeks. The day he left, I took the BankAmericard and all the children and flew home to Mom's for ten days to the tune of $750!"

This couple came to see me nearly three months later, and the hurt, bitterness, and ruin were still flaming! Vickie had done the human thing, and retaliated. She had "gotten Bob back." But how did it help her? Did two wrongs make a right? Was Bob more in love with her than before? Did he appreciate her more? Did it serve *any* useful purpose to have two people hurting instead of one?

Couples today are not prepared for the tremendous shock of the insult potential in marriage. The only means of preventive and corrective action is God's reactive force of love: returning a blessing for an insult. This is an issue that couples almost always resist, but it must be dealt with directly. God's plan of giving a blessing is not only important; it is the *only* thing that works.

INSULT AND BLESSING DEFINED

Scripture gives many exhortations concerning insults. Five are particularly relevant to marriage:

Name-calling: God admonishes us not to revile. Name-calling in marriage is always a threat to any kind of blessing. Any consistent reference to someone that categorizes their negatives is demoralizing. (See Matt. 5:22.)

Sarcasm and ridicule: Implication of ineptness intellectually, socially, or physically certainly hampers marriage oneness. (See Prov. 18:6; Eph. 5:4.)

A nagging wife: Scripture is bold in its condemnation of a woman who doesn't trust or respect her husband enough to keep her mouth closed. (See Prov. 21:9; 27:15,16.)

A contentious man: Scripture speaks just as forcefully of a quarrelsome man and how it leads him into overwhelming traps. (See Prov. 26:21.)

Insult and abuse in general: Immorality, adultery, homosexuality, and unrighteousness of all types are grouped in this last category. (See Gal. 5:19–21.)

In this context the opposite of an insult would be a "blessing." God says to bless a person instead of insulting him. An insult is usually the natural human response, while blessing a person requires a decision of the will. Let us consider four uses of the word "blessing" from Scripture, and apply it to marriage:

1) *Praise* to God. What positive qualities about my mate can I praise him or her for verbally?

2) *Benefits* bestowed—gifts. What benefits—presents—could I bestow upon my mate? In what way can I be of blessing to him or her?

3) *Giving thanks* to God for His gifts and favor. What qualities about my mate am I thankful for and how can I communicate this to him or her?

4) To call *God's favor* down upon. What specific areas of my mate's life should I pray that the Lord will bless?

With these definitions in mind, let's think for a moment about why marriages turn into an insult contest instead of a blessing as God intended. Ever since Adam sinned, men have been born naturally self-centered, not sensitive to other people. We develop ideas and passions that conflict with God's Word and plan for our lives. The following comparisons point out some of the conflicts between the human viewpoint and God's perspective.

MAN'S (THE WORLD SYSTEM'S) VIEW	GOD'S WORD AND PERSPECTIVE
1) People are my problem.	For our struggle is not against flesh and blood, but ... against the powers ... against the spiritual forces of wickedness in the heavenly places (Eph. 6:12).
2) Material security is the first priority.	Seek first His kingdom and His righteousness; and all these things shall be added to you (Matt. 6:33).
3) Hold on to what you've got at all costs or you will lose everything.	Give, and it will be given to you; good measure, pressed down, shaken together, running over, they will pour into your lap . . . (Luke 6:38).

4) Food, clothes, and shelter are the keys to life.

Blessed are those who hunger and thirst for righteousness, for they shall be satisfied (Matt. 5:6).

5) Most of my problems are caused by the one in authority.

Let every person be in subjection to the governing authorities. For there is no authority except from God, and those which exist are established by God. For rulers are not a cause of fear for good behavior, but for evil. Do you want to have no fear of authority? Do what is good, and you will have praise from the same (Rom. 13:1,3).

6) Love your friends, but get your enemies before they get you.

But I say to you, love your enemies, and pray for those who persecute you (Matt. 5:44).

7) If only I had married someone more gifted, I would be happier.

But one and the same Spirit works all these things, distributing to each one individually just as He wills (1 Cor. 12:11).

8) In this life, you've got to take care of Old Number One.

. . . If anyone wants to be first, he shall be last of all, and servant of all (Mark 9:35).

9) My mate can't do anything. If only I had mar-

I planted, Apollos watered, but God was causing the

ried someone God could use.

growth. So then neither the one who plants nor the one who waters is anything, but God who causes the growth (1 Cor. 3:6,7).

10) I'll teach him or her not to cross me.

Never take your own revenge, beloved, but leave room for the wrath of God, for it is written, "Vengence is Mine, I will repay," says the Lord (Rom. 12:19).

11) I'm going to the top and I don't care who I have to step on to get there.

Humble yourselves, therefore, under the mighty hand of God, that He may exalt you at the proper time (1 Pet. 5:6).

The natural bent of man causes hurt and selfishness. God says that only through rebirth and through wisdom and knowledge of God's Word can man override this natural bent. And look at the emphasis the New Testament places on the responsibilities of returning a blessing instead of an insult when hurt by someone.

See that no one repays another with evil for evil, but always seek after that which is good for one another and for all men (1 Thess. 5:15).

Bless those who curse you, pray for those who mistreat you (Luke 6:28).

How does returning a blessing benefit the giver of the blessing? Read 1 Peter 3:8–12:

To sum up, let all be harmonious, sympathetic, brotherly, kindhearted, and humble in spirit; not returning evil for evil, or insult for insult, but giving a blessing instead; for you were called for the very purpose that you might inherit a blessing. For, "Let him who means to love life and see good days *refrain his tongue* from evil and his lips from speaking guile. And let him turn away from evil and *do good;* let him *seek peace* and pursue it. For the eyes of the LORD are upon the righteous, and His ears attend to their prayer, but the face of the LORD is against those who do evil" (italics mine).

Peter tells us that we are called of God to give a blessing, but in doing so we in turn shall inherit a blessing. In other words, just as an insult will beget an insult, so will a blessing beget a blessing! Peter also implies that if you desire a good life, do not insult but bless. God is saying that in order to be successful with life you must bless others, and He favors the man who does good by blessing others. He attends to the prayers of the one giving the blessing.

Why return a blessing? Because it is God's will—as well as the door to blessing, life, good days, and God's favor. It works! The next question is, how do we render a blessing? Four steps in responding to insults can be taken from Christ's example as described in the following passage.

For you have been called for this purpose, since Christ also suffered for you, leaving you an example for you to follow in His steps, who committed no sin, nor was any deceit found in His mouth; and while being reviled, He did not revile in return; while suffering, He uttered no threats, but kept entrusting Himself to Him who judges righteously; and He Himself bore our sins in His body

on the cross, that we might die to sin and live to righteousness; for by His wounds you were healed. For you
were continually straying like sheep, but now you have
returned to the Shepherd and Guardian of your souls
(1 Pet. 2:21–25).

The first step in Christ's response to an insult was
that He committed no sin! Therefore, your first step is
to be sure you have committed no sin when you are
insulted. If you are aware of any wrong you have committed, confess that wrong to God and to your mate.

The second step is to return a blessing when insulted. Christ died to heal the very people that had
killed Him. The implication is clear: Christ not only
refused to insult them, but also blessed them. Each
mate must make a willful decision to return a blessing
for the hurt just experienced. Your will must submit to
God's way. Look for ways to bless your mate, and look
beneath the insult to a *reason* for the behavior or
words. Then look for ways to give praise and communicate that you are thankful for your spouse. Do
something specific to build up their spirits. Tell them
you love them and are committed to them. Do they
need your soothing voice and touch? Do they need time
with you? Do they need peace and quiet after a busy
day?

Most people insult others because they are hurting
inside and have tremendous emotional needs. Insulting someone else is a release mechanism. You inter-
rupt that insult-cycle with kindness so that no other
insults can occur. Jesus uttered no threats when insults were thrown at Him. He had every "right" to
threaten the people who were sending Him to the
cross. But Jesus knew that insults and threats do not

work but only bring out more hatred. By not hurling threats we humble ourselves to where we can be taught by the Lord.

The third step is just as important. Jesus Christ drew His strength and perspective by entrusting Himself to God the Father. Commit yourself and the situation to the Lord. Humanly, Christ did not want to suffer, but as He kept the mind of the Father He knew that even though it was momentarily tough, in the long run the Father's will was the best way. We too must yield to God's wisdom.

We begin to say, "God gave me this person, and my struggle is not against flesh and blood but Satan's deceit." As we catch God's perspective, we thank Him for the situation, which can be used to make us more like Christ. Commit yourself to the Lord's keeping and vow to withdraw your selfish will from the battle so that the Lord can begin to deal with your mate's offense.

The last step implied by Christ's death is that you should be prepared and willing to suffer so that God might heal your offender. In 1 Peter 2:24,25, we see that Jesus purposed to die on a cross so man might be healed. God never says the momentary cost of returning a blessing will be small. In fact, God implies that at times it will be very tough. But even more strongly, God guarantees a blessing for your efforts. It may not be just what you expect, but God will bless you in ways you never dreamed. The wayward one (insulter) will be drawn to the one who is not insulting.

If you cannot believe that God's commands of love and blessing are true, do not get married. If you are married, stop the insult cycle now and start loving and returning blessings instead.

8

Love and Submission: Friend or Foe?

*N*ot long ago a deeply frustrated woman revealed to me her agonizing uncertainty in understanding the woman's role in today's Christian community. She had always thought she knew what God intended for women, but lately she had been confused by discussions over the Equal Rights Amendment. She concluded with, "I have struggled with guilt feelings lately because I've begun to question the issue of submission for a woman. I am confused about what I should and shouldn't do."

Often I find that men are equally confused in their roles. Couples with marital problems rarely fail to mention confusion over biblical headship and submission. In fact, the most heavily talked-about marriage subject today is the roles of men and women. Many marriage seminars taught today deal with this subject exclusively.

When one begins to analyze the frustration in today's preoccupation with headship and submission, two questions seem to be at the crux of the debate.

First, "Did God intend for men and women to be different in function?" And, "Does the man have any advantage over the woman from God's point of view?" These issues have reached great magnitude because of our cultural emphasis today on the "downtrodden" wife.

To answer these questions we will begin with the scriptural "job descriptions" for men and women in marriage. The man's role is stated in Ephesians 5:25–33, and the woman's is found in 1 Peter 3:1–6.

When we approach these Scriptures most of us think to ourselves, "Oh, not that again—if I hear these things one more time I'll scream!" We have all heard them before because most marriage seminars and books place their major emphasis here. Admittedly, these issues are important, yet they must be placed in the larger context of God's holistic plan for marriage or they can become legalistic. From God's perspective, headship and submission are not a source of struggle, but a *hope* of blessed relationship.

IS GOD PREJUDICED?

Let's review these two passages for one main purpose: to demonstrate that there is no favoritism on God's part toward either the man or the woman. In fact, the two passages are parallel in several important ways in their context and structure. This table demonstrates their parallel breakdown.

HEADSHIP (Eph. 5:25–33)		SUBMISSION (1 Pet. 3:1–6)
LOVE without conditions	ABSOLUTE COMMAND	SUBMIT without a word
1. Sanctify her 2. Present her	PROMISE	1. Silence foolishness 2. Husband won to Christ 3. No fear 4. Precious to God

HEADSHIP (Eph. 5:25–33)		SUBMISSION (1 Pet. 2:13–3:9)
1. Love her as your own body	PICTURE	1. Gentle and quiet spirit
2. Nourish her		2. Women of God hope in God
3. Cherish her		3. Example of Sarah
4. Exemplify Christ		4. Exemplify Christ

Each passage begins with an absolute command that is very strong in the original language. It leaves little doubt about the responsibilities of both the husband and wife. Each passage lists a number of exciting promises that result from following the commands. These promises motivate, soften, and become the hope of the commands. The writers of these passages include illustrations to help seal our understanding of each role and give a hint as to how one can apply them successfully.

We also need to consider the similar contexts in which these two passages are written. Ephesians 1–3 says that in light of what Christ has done for us, we are to walk in a manner worthy of His calling. In Ephesians 5:15–20 Paul says to walk in the Spirit of God and four things will result:

1) You will speak to one another with psalms and hymns (understanding God's motivation).

2) You will sing and make melody with your heart to the Lord (praise Him for that motivation).

3) You will be able to give thanks for all things in His name (because you understand His will).

4) You will make yourselves subject to one another in the fear of the Lord (you will understand God's provisions for relationships).

If a man will seek the mind of Christ he will understand the command. Without that perspective, a man will never fulfill his role. In like manner, Peter talks about Christ's perspective just prior to instructing married women. The whole of 1 Peter deals with responding to suffering. It's an interesting fact that Peter first draws their minds back to how Christ suffered before getting into the importance of submission from a woman's standpoint. Peter says that Jesus Christ submitted himself to suffering unjustly and "kept entrusting Himself to Him [God the Father] who judges righteously" (1 Pet. 2:23). Peter is saying, "Women, before you can properly understand your responsibility to your husband, you too must have the perspective of Christ." So, the contexts of both passages are parallel in that they both ask us to keep the perspective of our Lord.

THE ABSOLUTE COMMANDS

As we compare the two passages, the first comparison is the absolute command of each. First we read the command to the man: "Husbands, love your wives, just as Christ also loved the church and gave Himself up for her." The word for "love" used in this command is the word *agape*, which you will recall is a God-given and God-directed love that does not exist humanly. We called it *commitment-love*. That is why it is illustrated by Christ's love for the church, the body of believers.

What was the church doing when Christ came and died for her? She was non-existent! The people were moving in direct opposition to Christ, and they even crucified Him. By this we learn that God's love is totally initiated by the Giver; it does not take into account the actions of the one given to. The same must be true as husbands love their wives. This is a totally sacrificial love, without rights.

Now men, read that command again! Talk about one hundred percent responsibility! There are no exception clauses here. There are no excuses. Should God ask you one day, "How did you love your wife?" you might be tempted to say, "Well, Lord, you know I loved her in certain areas. But it was hard to love her completely because she wouldn't always submit to me. And remember, Lord, she did have an affair and she was untrustworthy. I just couldn't love her unconditionally." You might try to prove she didn't deserve your love. But the Lord would say, "I didn't ask you about your mate's weaknesses; I asked you, How did *you* respond to my command to love her as I loved you?"

There are no exceptions! God knows your mate's weaknesses because He created her. He even knows her sins because Christ died for her. He wants you to love her no matter what she does or does not do. That is your one-hundred-percent responsibility! Hard? Impossible on your own! But by His Spirit you *can* love your wife as Jesus Christ loved us and gave Himself up for us. Otherwise, God is a liar!

The wife, on the other hand, has an equally strong command in 1 Peter 3:1,2: "In the same way [as Christ was], you wives, be submissive to your own husbands so that even if any of them are disobedient to the word [and they will be], they may be won without a word by the behavior of their wives, as they observe your chaste and respectful behavior."

Just as Christ was submissive to the cross, you wives should be submissive to your own husbands. The key word, *submission*, is a very strong word in the Greek language. It has a military usage, meaning literally, "fall in line" or "place oneself under another's authority." Notice, it means that *you* place yourself under; it is one hundred percent your responsibility. Christ placed Himself under the Father to the point that He had to face death on a cross. This kind of submission is not based on emotion but upon the very character of God.

Women are to absolutely submit themselves to their husbands without excuses as they entrust themselves to God. Again, the wife, like the husband, will have to answer the Lord when He asks, "How did you submit yourself to your husband?" No matter how strong the proof of her husband's weaknesses, there are no exception clauses in God's command to her. Peter goes out of his way to make this clear by stating "even if any of them are disobedient to the word."

Then Peter seals the strength of the command by saying the woman must submit herself with a respectful spirit. How many times have you seen women gritting their teeth as they submit? Peter eliminates that as an example of what he means. Certainly it would take a tremendous spiritual perspective to submit as Christ did, but this is His calling for the godly woman. I see no favoritism in these parallel commands to the husband or wife—both are overwhelming commands that are to be willingly followed under a loving and mighty God! So, as the sloganeers of the sixties told us, "Do it!"

PROMISES TO HUSBANDS ABOUT WIVES

The Lord is gracious to quickly draw our eyes from these strong commands to the associated promises. First, the man draws encouragement from the results of Christ's love.

That He might sanctify her, having cleansed her by the washing of water with the word, that He might present to Himself the church in all her glory, having no spot or wrinkle or any such thing; but that she should be holy and blameless (Eph. 5:26,27).

The promise is twofold: (1) that he might sanctify his wife and (2) that he might present his wife spotless. A husband cannot accomplish these things in the eternal sense as God does, but this kind of love on the man's part will effect similar results as Christ's love. And though I have commented already on this passage, let me mention a few additional truths.

To sanctify means to "set apart from the rest." We are set apart in Christ in that we are free from death because of His death on the cross. A wife is set apart by her husband because his love is not conditional on her performance; she is free to be *more* than ordinary.

Just as the Spirit reminds us daily of our forgiveness by washing us with the water of the Word, so a wife must be experientially able to trust her husband's commitment to love her. And men—this seemingly impossible command to love is not so hard when you realize the results will be a receptive and appreciative wife!

Next God promised the husband that if he loves his wife sacrificially, she will be perfected by this love. When I first heard this promise I did not understand how it would happen. Now I envision it this way: When Paul speaks of having "no spot or wrinkle," the word "spot" means "moral stain" and the word "wrinkle" means to be "filled with inner struggles." The use of the words implies the external and internal results of Christ's work. Christ's work results in eternal perfection, but Paul implies a similar temporal result by the husband's sacrificial love.

Christ's love is so freeing and creative in our lives that we are able to experience both external joy and inward peace. The face and presence of a Christian should not show the signs of inward stress and pressure that an unbeliever may have.

God demonstrated the "no spot or wrinkle" promise

so clearly to me last year. While attending a conference with several mutual friends of ours, an old film that was made thirteen years ago was shown. Sally was in the film. All of us were shocked at how her appearance had changed. People have actually said to me that Sally has become prettier over the years.

Husbands, I am not saying here that God will make your wife a "beauty" right before your eyes, but God did clearly show all of us a positive change in Sally. Sally does not spend even minutes a day being distressed over our relationship. My commitment-love has freed her to become characterized by an outward glow and an inner joy that makes her very attractive. I am convinced that one day God will show me that my faith was used by Him to make her more internally and externally beautiful. Added to that is a change that she has expressed to me and others. Sally has actually loved God more and understood the unconditional love of God better because God's love has had "arms" through me.

God promises husbands that if they can keep Christ's perspective in loving their wives, then He will actually use them as instruments of redemption in the lives of their mates. Her peace and joy will be noticeable. People will say, "What a joy it is to know your wife. Her life really motivates me." Even physically she will become more radiant.

PROMISES TO WIVES ABOUT HUSBANDS

Likewise, the woman also has been given promises of results from her submission to her husband.

For such is the will of God that by doing right you may silence the ignorance of foolish men.... And let not your adornment be merely external—braiding the hair, and wearing gold jewelry, or putting on dresses; but let it be the hidden person of the heart, with the imperishable quality of a gentle and quiet spirit, which is precious in the sight of God. For in this way in former times the holy women also, who hoped in God, used to adorn themselves, being submissive to their own husbands. Thus Sarah obeyed Abraham, calling him lord, and you have become her children if you do what is right without being frightened by any fear (1 Pet. 2:15; 3:3–6).

God continually instructs women to submit to their husbands, not because of the husband's perfection, but because of God's faithfulness. Submission is never to be seen as unto the husband only, but also as unto the Lord. God's faithfulness is your hope just as it was the hope of Christ as He went to the cross.

The first promise occurs in 1 Peter 2:15. While not speaking directly of marriage, it deals generally with submitting to any authority. By submitting where God directs, the one submitted will "silence" the ignorance of foolish men. Fighting with your husband only causes prideful, hardheaded ignorance; submission silences ignorance and clears the deck for progress!

This is followed closely by a second promise in 1 Peter 3:1—that wives who submit themselves may win their husbands without words but by their behavior. Again, God is promising the woman that she can be an instrument of the Lord, causing her husband to be won to the Lord when he is obviously wrong. Notice, there is no other way to effect change in a husband. The mouth is neither a way of making peace nor of making a husband do what is right. The woman who struggles with submission has never really believed God that submission is the key to results. Her resistance only leads to frustration.

I have grown to so respect my wife that when I am wrong and she graciously submits to me, I feel overwhelmed to confess my mistakes. As a man, I can bear witness to the power God releases in her life through a gracious attitude of submission. When she does that, I *want* to do right!

Finally, God promises that the woman who keeps His perspective and trusts Him more than human devices (trickery, flattery, physical powers) will be very precious to God. What a promise! God places a very high value on a submissive woman. He says her obedience will cause her to have a "gentle and quiet spirit." *Gentle* means not causing her husband to be frustrated or ruffled. *Quiet* means causing her husband to be soothed when he is upset or frustrated.

To the woman who desires God's way, it means a great deal to be "precious" in the sight of God. Peter says submissive wives will be like Sarah, who had no fear. Most women are paralyzed with fears . . . fears of growing old, losing love, appreciation, wealth, facing death, and more. Most would love to be fearless. God chose Sarah to illustrate His promise. Abraham, her husband, was far from perfect. Yet Sarah submitted herself and was not afraid.

A very wealthy man, Abraham was called by God to leave his home in search of a new place. God promised to lead him. He went by faith, taking Sarah and all their servants. During the trip, Abraham came upon a very violent and prosperous kingdom. Rather than trusting God that he wouldn't be killed, he told Sarah to pretend to be his sister so she would find favor with the king and he would be spared. And Sarah obeyed!

Let me ask you: Has your husband ever told you to do anything quite so ridiculous? Probably not! Abraham pulled his trick not once but twice! Sarah's hope was not in Abraham at this point, but in God who judges righteously. God spared her both times from having to have sexual relations with these two kings. And God will protect you from *your* husband's mistakes.

Considering both the commands and promises to the husband and wife, there is no advantage to either role. The commands call for total responsibility, and His gracious and motivating promises that accompany the commands provide the support we need to obey.

HIS IS TO CHERISH, HERS TO TRUST

Peter and Paul give us two practical pictures of how these concepts are implemented. First, to the husband, the picture of loving his wife.

So husbands ought also to love their own wives as their own bodies. He who loves his own wife loves himself; for no one ever hated his own flesh, but nourishes and cherishes it, just as Christ also does the church, because we are members of His body (Eph. 5:28–30).

We are to love our wives as our own bodies. I am so instinctively aware of the value of my own body that I do not have to consciously think about loving it. If anyone or anything hurts or threatens it, I respond with corrective action. God is telling us that this is how important our wives are to be to us. I am to be so sensitive to her that if anything hurts or threatens her, I should take immediate corrective action to protect her.

I am to *nourish* and *cherish* her. These two words are beautiful ways of describing the love God is talking about. Both Greek words are used only twice in the New Testament. The word "nourish" literally means to keep warm enough to melt. It was used to describe a mother bird's keeping her babies under her wing at perfect body temperature. I am to be so involved in my wife's care that I know from moment to moment what her needs are so I can meet them.

Even better is the word "cherish." This is used one other place in Scripture—in 1 Thessalonians 2:7: "But we proved to be gentle among you, as a nursing mother tenderly cares for her own children." From experience and counseling, this word-picture triggered the key for me. Have you men noticed how women are almost perfect in responding to the needs of their newborn? Even some of the women who come for counsel because they cannot control their anger and resentment toward people have, nonetheless, an uncanny ability to give joyfully, without resentment, to their children. And an infant makes selfish demands with no capacity to appreciate or be sensitive to the mother's needs. But a good mother will reshape her life for her baby with very little struggle. She does it because she senses her absolute responsibility and she has an innate desire to do the task.

This helped turn the light on for me. As I understood that God knew my needs and that I received my wife *from Him,* I began to accept my responsibility from the Lord to nourish and cherish her. I also realized it was an inner desire created by God.

Men, our culture does not teach us to live this way. Such care and concern for wives is not found in the average American home. This is God's pattern. Let me ask, do you love your wife as much as you do your own body? Do you know her needs; are you sensitive to her? Have you altered your lifestyle in order that she might be set apart and glorified? Do you take this responsibility from the Lord as completely as Christ took His responsibility for you? Regardless of performance? Are you totally committed to her?

The wife's responsibility begins with submitting without a word while her husband observes her respectful and pure behavior. Honestly, most women put more hope in their mouths than in their sacrificial behavior. We are all taught from birth to speak rather than to think. But God says, "Love him into right behavior." When your husband is wrong, your first response is usually to tell him so! God says there is a better way—a way that will win him by your behaving in a manner pleasing to the Lord. In the chapter on "Love and Blessing" we have already talked specifically about how to respond in these tough circumstances.

Women who put their hope in God instead of in external values have gentle and quiet spirits toward their husbands. Again, the picture of her outer and inner beauty is contrasted. Peter says not to ignore your physical appearance, but to concentrate on the inner qualities. Wives, you do need to look good for your husbands. But your primary efforts are to be on developing your spiritual walk with the Lord so that "Christlike" qualities will come through to your husband. Jesus loves your husband and died for him. Your life should exemplify that. A gentle and quiet spirit will soothe the soul of your husband like nothing else in the world.

The woman who has her hope in God will be able to call her husband "lord." This means she recognizes God's placement of the husband over her. Without godly headship and submission, a couple cannot reflect, reproduce, and reign properly.

LEVELING OUT

In working with Christians, I have discovered three basic levels of understanding of the husband's and wife's roles and responsibilities. These levels are as different as night and day. Evaluate them and decide where you are—and where you need to be!

The Legalistic Level—I am fearful that most Christians are at this level of understanding. This person only understands that God commands us to be a head or a submitter. Most Christians know these two commands but feel they are impossible to obey. After a talk on headship and submission, these people always try to find an out. The woman may say, "Please pray for me as I try to submit to this monster I'm married to." The husband may say, "I'm supposed to be the head, but she won't do anything I tell her to do."

Down through the centuries men have used this headship issue as a "club" over their wives. Completely missing their responsibility to love, they hear only the command for the wife to submit.

An equally unfortunate response can be seen by some "Christian women's libbers" who have evidently been so shocked and offended by God's command to the woman to submit that in their struggle they deny the very command of God. Letha Scanzoni and Nancy Hardesty, in their book *All We're Meant To Be*, misinterpret Genesis 3, Ephesians 5, and 1 Peter 3. They are clouded by their fear, a lack of trust in God and His commands for women to submit to their husbands. All through their book, one feels a continual fight for their rights. The need to defend one's rights reveals a basic legalistic fear that God is going to deny them something if they do what He commands, or that they will not be fulfilled as a person.

These women have missed the bigger picture of Christ's commands. Beyond the legalism of the commands one finds a new freedom and a new perspective. *We must look beyond the command to the reason why the command was given.* Headship and submission were not given to take anything away from us. They were given to open the door to blessed relationships. Without authority we have no relationships! Unfortunately, Satan has deceived us as we will see in the next chapter.

There is very little hope for the legalistic head or submitter. Either defensive or defeated, they run from one Christian book or Bible study to the next, trying to find the key. This week they might try a new plan. For several weeks their hopes are high. Soon, however, the newness of the project wears off. Things have happened to make them discouraged again, and they begin to search for the next book or marriage seminar. Books and seminars are fine, but the word of God, mixed with faith, is what endures!

The Promise Level—The next level is a gigantic improvement. The promise level of understanding is one in which a person places his hope on God's promises for love or submission, beyond simply a grimacing obedience to the command. Most *successful* Christians are at this level of understanding of godly headship and submission in marriage. They live with a joyful expectancy of God working in their marriages. They *believe* and *act* upon God's Word, which produces results in their lives and reinforces their efforts. They characterize their marriages with hope, which motivates them even further.

The exciting potential results of a life focused on God's promises is clearly stated in 2 Peter 1:3,4.

> . . . seeing that His divine power has granted to us everything pertaining to life and godliness, through the true knowledge of Him who called us by His own glory and excellence. For by these He has granted to us His precious and magnificent promises, in order that by them you might become partakers of the divine nature. . . .

In and through God's precious and magnificent promises, we are assured of everything we need to make a success of life.

The Wisdom Level—As wonderful as the promise level is in enabling us to have a successful relationship, there is yet a higher level of understanding that should be our goal. This is the wisdom level. Wisdom is often defined as seeing life's experiences from God's perspective. It is based upon the expectations of joy in doing God's will.

The legalistic level results from our self-centered wills knocking heads with God's absolute commands. The promise level attracts our wills to new hope in the commands because of the attached promises. The wisdom level dissolves the battle of the wills altogether. This level frees us from the struggle forever by showing us that we struggle only because we have been deceived by Satan. The wisdom level allows us to see headship and submission totally from God's perspective, which results in no fear for either the one who is "head" or the one who "submits." Jesus Christ was at this level when He went to the cross and considered it the door to "joy." Let me illustrate.

Jesus fully understood the awesome responsibility

of the cross, but He asked that if possible the cup be taken from Him. But as He became aware that the cross was an inevitable part of God's plan, He demonstrated not only the promise level of understanding, but the wisdom level of joy.

> . . . fixing our eyes on Jesus, the author and perfecter of faith, who for the joy set before Him endured the cross, despising the shame, and has sat down at the right hand of the throne of God (Heb. 12:2).

Christ's motivation was the "joy set before Him," which was the anticipation of obeying God and seeing the future fulfillment of His promises. This stands in stark contrast to bleak, legalistic obedience, and even goes beyond the promise level of anticipated blessing.

I am sure that as Jesus headed for Calvary, and passed Peter, who had just denied Him, He knew that if He was obedient to the Father to the point of dying on the cross, Peter would be with Him in eternity. The same thought must have been there toward the thief hanging next to him. It must have been there for those who stood at the foot of the cross and watched Him die. It must have been there for you and me. That joy sustained Christ at this terrible time. He had God's perspective, and therefore He simply obeyed.

9

Wisdom or Deceit (Use and Misuse of Headship and Submission)

When a man is sitting in my counseling room moaning over the command to love a woman who has disappointed him and hurt him a thousand times, he may recoil at me with, "I don't *have* to put up with this."

Or when a wife has just reviewed her responsibility in Scripture to submit herself to an almost totally insensitive and irresponsible man, it's not unusual for me to hear, "It's not fair! I cannot submit to a man like him."

How can we handle these situations wisely? Love and submission sound great when we keep them at the fantasy stage. But, regrettably, when they become real and functional in marriage, they become difficult. Let's see if we can discover why we all struggle with these responsibilities.

A REVIEW OF RELATIONSHIPS

Thus far, we have established that God is the author of relationships. It was God who created the need in us for relationships, and God who chose to make Adam and Eve His expeditionary force on the earth.

Since God is ultimately responsible to meet our needs, we know that He will not allow anything to prevent Him from meeting those needs. Therefore, God guarantees the outcome of relationships that are directed by him. In Ephesians 6:12, Paul says, "For our struggle is not against flesh and blood, but . . . against the world forces of this darkness."

Now that's a strong statement. But if we are not limited by people, what about these marriages that are continual battles? Well, Paul says the problem is not people but evil. I am convinced that Satan is in the business of deceit today in whatever form he can devise. And for that reason I am devoting this chapter to addressing the problem of deception in relationships.

As we learned in the previous chapter, God does not consider that either headship or submission is "better." This is not an issue of performance, importance, success, or even superiority. It is a matter, instead, of *order in relationships. Both* are keys to open doors to blessing. When God tells us to love and submit (and we all do both daily in one relationship or another), it is not intended as a source of strife but as a source of joy in the divine plan for successful relationships. There are no successful relationships without loving leadership and loving submission. God is still trying to unite the body of Christ in oneness with His Spirit. There is no oneness in the body without love and submission. 1 Corinthians 11:3 says, "But I want you to understand that Christ is the head of every man, and the man is the head of a woman, and God is the head of Christ."

Here we see order in the Trinity. The Father is the head over the Son in the same way that the husband is the head over the wife. Is it a struggle for God the Son to have God the Father as head over Him? Is Christ any less God than the Father? Any less glorified? Certainly not!

When God tells us to love and submit, there is no struggle intended, only order, blessing, and security. So our struggle is actually not with one another, but *our struggle is in being deceived by the enemy.* Satan wants us to see people as the problem rather than as the blessing. The problem, then, is not that God made a mistake in the job descriptions of husbands and wives, but rather that we have been deceived and have believed the devil's lie.

Our problems start in Genesis 3. Shortly after Adam and Eve had sinned, we read of their response as God inquired into what they had done.

> And the man said, "The woman whom Thou gavest to be with me, she gave me from the tree, and I ate." Then the Lord God said to the woman, "What is this you have done?" And the woman said, "The serpent deceived me, and I ate" (Gen. 3:12,13).

What happened to their oneness? Adam immediately blamed Eve. He failed to take responsibility. But as we look more closely, Adam was really blaming God as he reminded God that He was responsible for giving Eve to Adam. Adam follows the path of Satan, and he now sees both Eve and God as problems.

Who had changed? Not God! Adam had disobeyed and Eve was deceived. The result was the birth of fallen human nature, and a breed of man who loves to sin. From this point on, God's perfect plan has been questioned by men. The self-centered pride of man has become a major deterrent to belief, and to oneness in marriage.

God responds with several actions designed to rescue man and defeat Satan at his own game. First, God creates a redemptive curse for Adam and Eve. It was a curse in the sense that they were given burdens in this life; it was redemptive in the sense that these burdens would occupy their time, limiting their struggle with the flesh and Satan.

The woman was given the burden of bearing children and rearing them in the home. "I will greatly multiply your pain in childbirth, in pain you shall bring forth children; yet your desire shall be for your husband, and he shall rule over you" (Gen. 3:16). The man was given the mandate to toil for life and food by hard work. "Cursed is the ground because of you; in toil you shall eat of it all the days of your life. Both thorns and thistles it shall grow for you; and you shall eat the plants of the field (Gen. 3:17,18).

All through the ages, when men have had abundant free time, their society has tended to degenerate because of sin. Study of historical cultures verifies this fact. Even in America, as the work week shortens and prosperity increases, morality slides. If my own mind is free from responsibilities for very long, I begin to struggle with vain imaginations and lust. So God, in His grace, burdened Adam and Eve to protect them from themselves and from Satan.

In verse 23, God demonstrates His grace even further by removing Adam and Eve from the garden so their struggles with sin and death would not be eternal but temporary. The stage is thereby set for us to receive new bodies for all eternity. These acts were a curse compared to the perfect state of Genesis 1 and 2. At the same time, though, these were gracious and redemptive solutions.

In Genesis 3:16 is a statement that I believe has

become the source of the current debate on love and submission. God said, "The man shall rule over the woman." I am amazed at how teachers today try to deny or misconstrue this absolute statement. Again, however, this was a redemptive act on God's part.

Prior to the fall, Adam and Eve's oneness with God and each other functioned perfectly. Adam and Eve's submission to God was not questioned nor found difficult to accept because of the oneness, the total intimacy and acceptance, among God, Adam, and Eve. God did not even have to mention Eve's submission to Adam prior to their sin, because as they were one with God they were automatically one with each other. When sin entered Adam and Eve, the perfect oneness was lost, and God had to make clear the order of responsibility and authority that had not been an issue before. The line of authority was established at creation: Adam first, then Eve. This order is necessary for oneness in marriage.

RESENTMENT: TRUSTING SATAN'S LIES

A person who is looking at life from God's perspective and who understands God's command to be a head over another knows the one who rules has no advantage over the one ruled. Because of the weakness of the flesh, Satan deceives us to resent any difference; he points to submission, misconstruing the purposes of God.

Take the example of Satan's deceit in the Garden of Eden in Genesis 3. God had created a perfect environment; every need had been met. Adam and Eve had no desire for other things, no longings, no dreams of things being better. God desired this perfect relationship to last for eternity; therefore, he placed within the garden the Tree of Life.

The only threat to this eternal perfection was the Tree of Good and Evil. God told Adam and Eve not to eat of that tree. Since they had no sinful nature, and since they were perfectly dependent on the Lord, they did not even consider the tree an issue of struggle. Adam and Eve trusted God. They knew that not eating from that tree was totally for their good!

In Genesis 3:1–7, Satan distorted the purpose of the tree. He disputed God's purpose by calling His Word into question. He said they would not die if they ate of the tree, and implied that the *real* reason God did not want them to eat of the tree was because they would be like God. "God is really trying to limit you. He is trying to keep you from being like Him." *Satan subtly changed God's purpose from one of protection to one of limitation.* Satan appealed to their eyes, stomachs, and pride in tempting them. They believed a lie and they sinned.

Satan is still in the business of deceiving! He uses the same tactics today. When God originally instructed us to love and submit, what was His purpose? To allow us relationships; to accomplish His plan of the ages; to meet man's needs; to equip man to reflect, reproduce, and reign. God knew that without headship and submission there would be no satisfying relationships.

Satan has distorted God's purpose by suggesting that structure is a limitation, by telling husbands to resist being heads, and wives to resent submitting. "Why should I love her? She doesn't deserve it." Or "Why should I submit to him? He's no better than I am. I'm smarter, more mature, more talented, and more successful."

I believe Satan's second great lie, after the one in the

garden, is in the area of headship and submission. When God said love and submit, there was *only good* intended! Without love and submission, God cannot meet our "aloneness" needs. Without love and submission, Christians are divided and the cause of Christ is seemingly thwarted. If I do not submit myself to you in humility, then I am a threat, a discouragement, a source of rejection and judgment in your life. Unless I love you unconditionally, it will be hard for you to submit to me. There are no *agape* relationships without *both* love and submission.

Satan has again deceived us by appealing to our pride and self-centered nature. Let's evaluate Christ's life to see the ultimate example of the wisdom level of understanding. Observe how Christ did not look at the struggle of these issues, but kept on viewing them from God's perspective.

WISDOM: HAVING GOD'S VIEWPOINT

Christ's trust of God the Father allowed Him to view love and submission not as limitations but as the greatest blessings in all eternity.

If therefore there is any encouragement in Christ, if there is any consolation of love, if there is any fellowship of the spirit, if any affection and compassion, make my joy complete by being of the same, maintaining the same love, united in spirit, intent on one purpose. Do nothing from selfishness or empty conceit, but with humility of mind let each of you regard one another as more important than himself; do not merely look out for your own personal interests, but also for the interests of others. Have this attitude in yourselves which was also in Christ Jesus, who, although He existed in the form of God, did not regard equality with God a thing to be grasped. . . . He humbled Himself by becoming obedient to the point of death, even death on a cross. Therefore also God highly exalted Him, and bestowed on Him the name which is above every name, that at the name of Jesus every knee should bow, of those who are in heaven, and on earth, and under the earth, and that every tongue should confess that Jesus Christ is Lord, to the glory of God the Father (Phil. 2:1-11).

Paul says if anyone desires to experience encouragement in Christ, love, fellowship of the Spirit, compassion or affection in this life, they must be *one* with others and with God. He describes oneness as being of the *same* mind, maintaining the *same* love, *united* in spirit, and being intent on *one* purpose. The goals that Paul mentions describes all of our desires. Oneness is God's goal for all relationships, be they in the church or in marriage.

Paul gives us the key to finding oneness when he tells us to be intent on the purpose of having humility of mind toward others. Obviously selfishness has no place here. Another way of saying "humility of mind" is "have Christ's perspective of love and submission."

Many people fear that to be humble is to be spineless. However, humility is not an emotional cowering but a mark of one with a strong consciousness of God's viewpoint in any given situation. This perspective allows this person to esteem others better than himself. Without humility of mind there is no encouragement, love, fellowship, affection, or compassion.

God's perspective allows us to submit freely or to willingly "place ourselves under" someone else without being resentful or feeling limited. Remember, God created us to be incomplete without relationships. He created us to be unable to accomplish our creation purposes of reflecting His image, reproducing a godly heritage, or reigning on earth without relationships. We are limiting God and His purpose in meeting our aloneness without relationships. As we keep God's perspective of relationships ever before us, the commands to love or submit become, not limits, but the very door to potential relationships and blessings. It allows us to realize that our struggle is not against God or people, but against Satan who is out to deceive us. Therefore, through humility of mind we can actually esteem others higher than ourself even in tough situations. That is how Jesus Christ Himself lived!

In fact, that is Paul's next point! He exhorts us to have the same attitude as Christ when things get tough—in marriage, for example. The Greek word used here for *attitude* is again an appeal, not for an emotional response but for an attitude of the mind. Christ had an attitude of submission such that He did not question or struggle with His Father. Instead, He trusted Him. How many times has someone said to me, "How dare you ask me to lower myself and do that"? In other words, "Do you know who I am?" The eternal Son of God did not question His Father, or grasp for equal *authority* with the Father, even though He shared a co-equal *divinity* with the Father.

So Jesus, in His full humanity, humbled Himself to the point of death on a cross. He was totally submissive to the Father. Did Jesus question the headship and submission "system" that God had instituted? Did He attempt to redefine it through "careful exegesis"? Or did He simply obey? Look, every person will face tough issues in marriage concerning headship and submission. Some will knuckle under to Satan's deceit and question God Himself about His plan. The blessed ones will have the same attitude of wisdom that Christ had.

Finally, Paul shows the result of Christ's obedience. God the Father exalted His Son above every name; every knee will bow to Him and every tongue will confess that Jesus Christ is Lord! Was Jesus Christ "limited" by submission? While momentarily it seemed so as He moved toward the cross, that trial turned to victory. In spite of terrible human suffering Jesus Christ was glorified! Can you trust God in those tough times so He can exalt you and so that others may follow the example of Christ as they see it in you? Will you allow God to show you how to have love, affection, compassion, and encouragement with another human?

Paul then exhorts us to do just that: to pursue these things in the fear of the Lord. To have this kind of response we must have the mind of Christ. Will you accept God's plan, which guarantees successful relationships and glorification of Christ?

Every great marriage has two people who are free from the struggle of questioning headship and submission. Such couples are also mature enough to accept pain and disappointment without reverting to listening to Satan's questions. They know that hurt will sometimes come before blessing. They expect that Satan will attempt to deceive them, to rob them of their joy in following Christ, so they purpose in their hearts beforehand to rebuff him. These same people will also, by God's grace, continue to see that their struggle is not against people. They will be free to submit and receive a blessing.

CONCLUSION

In Part II, four decisions have been introduced as the necessary foundation to a successful marriage.

First, two people need to commit themselves to God's plan for marriage. *Second*, both partners must receive one another from God as His provision for their needs. *Third*, each partner must submit to the only active and reactive force for changing a mate: love and blessing. *Fourth*, each partner must seek God's wisdom to understand the responsibility to lead and submit with joy.

All four of these decisions of the will are absolutely vital in order for the husband and wife to find a common denominator in marriage. Without these commitments, mutual agreement is at best "hit and miss."

If you are typical, at this point you are beginning to say to yourself, "These spiritual thoughts are good, but let's get on with Part III and the practical areas of marriage." Let me say that these four major conditions are the most practical contributions to my marriage. These issues just covered are not things you deal with once and then forget. They are absolutely practical on a daily basis! They are the hope of my marriage. Many times my human experience would seem to be contradictory to these beliefs. At those points Sally's most practical hope is that I would not act humanly but spiritually. These faith issues are the moment by moment practical savior of our marriage. In Hebrews 11, faith is defined as follows:

> Now faith is the assurance of things hoped for, the conviction of things not seen. For by it [faith] the men of old gained approval (Heb. 11:1,2).

Many times in marriage, your human instinct will go against God's perspective. At those times, ideally, faith will take over. Your marriage will then be characterized as one that acts supernaturally, based on the fact of God's Word as opposed to the typical human response that leads to hurt and resentment.

> By faith, he [Moses] left Egypt, not fearing the wrath of the king, for he endured, as seeing Him who is unseen (Heb. 11:27).

Moses stood strong in a seemingly impossible human circumstance, because he kept God's perspective. We need to fight to keep these four issues in Part II a constant reminder before us. There are no greater "practical" issues in marriage. As we keep God's perspective, the daily areas developed in Part III will then fall into place.

PART III

10

A Man of Commitment

Let your fountain be blessed, and rejoice in the wife of your youth. As a loving hind and a graceful doe, let her breasts satisfy you at all times; be exhilarated always with her love (Prov. 5:18,19).

A man asked me not long ago, "What is the mark of a great husband? Is it financial responsibility, social prominence, sexual attractiveness, or being a successful father?" I quickly thought about each of these important areas, only to discard them all for a much greater issue. I responded, "The mark of a great husband is an absolute, unfailing commitment to his wife—based on his agreement to do so before God. As men, we often fail to recognize marriage as a covenant with Him."*

THE MARRIAGE AGREEMENT

This commitment, this covenant a man makes before God to his wife includes (1) overseeing his family

_____
*I want to acknowledge John Putnam for helping me express these thoughts.

in order that they might reflect the image of God properly, (2) raising his children to love and follow the Lord, and (3) leading the way in reigning over what is his. To be God's man, the husband should set a goal of being totally responsible to God for his wife and family.

Our Lord Jesus talked plainly about a man's marriage covenant. "Consequently they are no longer two, but one flesh. What therefore God has joined together, let no man separate" (Matt. 19:6). I feel deep fear in my heart when I think of men—Christian men—who break this covenant. Divorce is not God's will. It's always a second-class solution. A vivid description of how God feels about a husband's commitment to his wife is found in Malachi 2:14–16:

> Yet you say, "For what reason?" Because the Lord has been a witness between you and the wife of your youth, against whom you have dealt treacherously, though she is your companion and your wife *by covenant.* But not one has done so who has a remnant of the Spirit. And what did that one do while he was seeking a godly offspring? Take heed then, to your spirit, and let no one deal treacherously against the wife of your youth. "For I hate divorce," says the Lord, the God of Israel, "and him who covers his garment with wrong," says the Lord of hosts. "So take heed to your spirit, that you do not deal treacherously" (italics mine).

God Himself is a witness and a participant in the covenant a husband makes with his wife. No man can break that covenant and be led by the Spirit of God. God not only hates divorce, but He will judge the one who does the wrong in the divorce. God considers a man's responsibility toward his wife as a covenant with Him, also. He gave man marriage as a blessing;

therefore, the man is responsible to be faithful to that covenant no matter what the cost.

God takes His covenants seriously, and marriage is a covenant! If you want to be characterized as a great husband, expectantly take up your covenant and live it out in Christ. *Put away once and for all any thoughts about quitting or changing mates.* Place your faith in God's promises and commit yourself to sacrificial love that will melt even the hardest heart.

IF YOU HAVE TO "TOUGH IT OUT"

At least eight instructions come from James as he talks about responding to tough trials. This list is helpful to remember during trying times in marriage.

This you know, my beloved brethren. But let everyone be quick to hear, slow to speak and slow to anger; for anger of man does not achieve the righteousness of God. Therefore putting aside all filthiness and all that remains of wickedness, in humility receive the word implanted, which is able to save your souls. But prove yourselves doers of the word, and not merely hearers who delude themselves (James 1:19–22).

If there is a battle, in this case in your marriage, take note of the following:

1. *Don't react,* but listen to your wife and the Lord.
2. *Don't speak* too quickly; wait for your emotions to subside.
3. *Don't be angry;* nothing good ever comes from anger.
4. *Stop your immoral involvement:* lying, cheating, or whatever, in relationship to your wife.

5. *Study God's Word* with a mind of humility for the answers to your problems, seeking counsel if necessary. Then act.
6. *Act on your faith,* not on your feelings. Boldly believe God regardless of your wife's human response. Remake your covenant to your mate by faith.

James 5:16–18 sets forth our final two points of instruction:

> Therefore, confess your sins to one another, and pray for one another, so that you may be healed. The effective prayer of a righteous man can accomplish much. Elijah was a man with a nature like ours, and he prayed earnestly that it might not rain; and it did not rain on the earth for three years and six months. And he prayed again, and the sky poured rain, and earth produced its fruit.

7. *Confess your sins to your wife* so both of you can be emotionally healed.
8. *Pray earnestly.* If God can make and stop rain for Elijah, God can motivate your wife and remove your fears.

FULFILLMENT OF THE COVENANT

The sovereignty of God really motivates me as a man. The thought that God is a partner with me in my marriage gives me a real motivation to serve and please Him. It gives me an awareness that my marriage is part of God's eternal plan. As we go through the Scriptures to determine the husband's role in guiding a marriage according to God's will, here are what I have found to be two of the salient points.

Rule and serve

In the New Testament, God compares a husband's responsibility to that of Christ's to the church (Eph. 5:25). In the Old Testament (see Gen. 3) God says, "The man shall rule over the woman." These truths indicate two major thrusts in the practice of the husband's covenant to his wife. First, he is to *rule.* This word conveys the thought of authority and administration. Second, he is to be a *priest* to his wife. The word priest means minister, emphasizing the role of servant and counselor.

There must be careful balance in both of these responsibilities. If the husband overemphasizes his authority, his wife will lose identity and trust. If the husband is only a servant, she will be insecure and lack direction. Take charge of your wife's needs. Serve her, be her loving administrator, and take authority for her life and needs. Do this in a way that instructs, supports, and encourages her.

Know, sacrifice, and comfort

In searching both Scripture and common sense for what it means to rule and be a servant in marriage, I have discovered several specific areas of responsibility for a man.

- Protect
- Provide
- Initiate love

- Pray
- Take authority in conflict
- Meet physical needs
- Support relationship development
- Share time struggles
- Help with children—discipline, instruction
- Emphasize future hope

There are three major commands given in the New Testament telling us how to *fulfill* those responsibilities.

1. Understand your wife.

You husbands likewise, live with your wives in an understanding way, as with a weaker vessel, since she is a woman; and grant her honor as a fellow-heir of the grace of life, so that your prayers may not be hindered (1 Pet. 3:7).

Peter says that husbands ought to understand, or *know*, their wives. Sometimes after two counseling sessions I get the feeling that I know a man's wife better than he does—after ten years of marriage. Peter is commanding us to be experts about our wives.

Most successful husbands I know make it a point to *ask* their wives about their emotional, spiritual, physical, and intellectual needs. Seek your wife's opinion regularly. Knowing her is not an automatic thing. If you don't work at hearing from her, you won't know when she is under stress or when she just needs some physical exercise, or when she needs a day off or a night out with you.

Do you know what a perfect day is for your wife? A perfect date? What she *really* likes to do on vacations? If not, you'd better find out! Peter commands us to know our wives and to allow them access to us, or he warns that sin and struggle will reign and our prayers will not be answered. How can we be out of fellowship with our wives and expect God to answer when we call?

2. Be responsible for your wife.

We must know our wives so we can uniquely apply our responsibilities to fit their specific needs. Next Paul gives husbands a command from Ephesians 5:25: "Husbands, love your wives, just as Christ also loved the church and gave Himself up for her."

God's command to love includes the idea of giving up your life for her, in the same way Christ gave Himself up for the church. While I do not expect God will require me to literally die, I am willing. God expects me to assume from her all fearful or deadly issues which cause her fear, physically or emotionally. Physical protection, financial protection, protection from being hurt by others, fear of failure, a death of a child, fear of aging, would all be examples. By God's grace you must be a buffer for your wife. This does not mean that the wife does not encounter these things, but only that the husband shields her from the fear of having ultimate responsibility in them.

So husbands, as you prepare to meet your wife's needs, first *know* her and sacrificially *take responsibility* for her fears.

3. Love your wife as you love yourself.

So husbands ought also to love their own wives as their own bodies. He who loves his own wife loves himself; for no one ever hated his own flesh, but nourishes and cherishes it, just as Christ also does the church (Eph. 5:28,29).

Paul commands us husbands to love our wives as we do our own bodies—to nourish and cherish them. These words connote comfort. Paul is saying to sensitively and selflessly attend to your wife's needs, as a mother would a nursing child. Keep her warm by your momentary monitoring of her intimate emotional and physical needs, just as you care daily for your own needs. Practically speaking, God is commanding you in your covenant with Him to give up your own selfishness by putting her first in priority. Put everything except the Lord into a distant second position so that these things are a possibility. The rewards will be unbelievable.

PRACTICAL APPLICATION OF THE COVENANT

Husbands, develop a strategy for your wife and family. Determine the areas of importance in light of your wife's needs, then establish several objectives in each area. Develop a plan for each objective, set priorities, and then schedule their application. A little planning will improve your success significantly. The following are some ideas from counseling; use what might be valuable to you.

Leadership

God's man thrives on being a shock absorber for his wife. He anticipates his wife's needs and fears.

Self-worth: All of us realize the things that affect feelings of self-worth: intellect, appearance, productivity, success in relationships, and financial freedom, among others. Discover a mutual area of interest with your wife and work at communication in that area.

Seek out her intellectual interests and find one where she can teach you. Show interest in her appearance and allow her a sufficient wardrobe to feel good at social events. Become an expert on her abilities. If she has a hobby, encourage her. If she does something well in private, sensitively make her friends aware of these skills or qualities. Look for ways of involving her talents publicly. Help her develop a part-time in-home income if she desires one. Monitor her relationships and assist her in developing friends. Help her organize her schedule.

Spiritual maturity: Your hope for mutual faith in your marriage is related to your wife's maturity as well as yours. Do everything possible to assist her spiritual interest. Encourage her efforts to minister to others or attend church functions. Babysit if necessary.

Hurt: Never allow your wife to experience pain without sharing it with her. A death in the family, a disappointment in relationships—whatever; get involved and take responsibility for finding a solution.

Finances: Work at giving your wife financial hope. A personal savings account for her is important, if at all possible. Special needs like lingerie, hairstyling, exercise classes, and hobbies are not all that costly. And they mean a lot to her.

Children: In the area of protecting your wife, take your share of the pressure of dealing with and caring for the children. Their learning, emotions, and physical and spiritual development can bring her real conflicts. Aggressively seek to understand these pressures as they occur and share them with her. Take responsibility for the development, discipline, and instruction of the children.

Financial provision

> But if anyone does not provide for his own, and especially for those of his household, he has denied the faith, and is worse than an unbeliever (1 Tim. 5:8).

Take finances seriously. Study chapter 13, apply it to your own situation, and make a personal commitment to adjust according to God's will.

Romanticism

The romance of marriage is a man's shared responsibility; romantic moments are extremely important to women. Be a romantic lover of your mate. Get two or three male friends together and start a "Marriage Commitment Club," meeting for lunch once a month. If each is responsible for just one idea, you can schedule a weekly surprise. Women love small, inexpensive surprises. Uniqueness is great, too. Exchange your ideas but not your "war stories." An occasional love letter catches her off guard. Quantity is not as important as quality and consistency. Husbands, never give your wives the silent treatment. Love requires regular communication. Do not withhold yourself but open your life to her.

Prayer

Pray for your wife daily. Ask God to give you love for her, and ask Him to help you be so sensitive to her needs that she will become an even more beautiful person to you.

Authority in conflict

Decisions and conflicts are constantly developing in the home. Men, do not be passive in these issues. Take responsibility and get involved. If a decision is not obvious between the parties involved, take responsibility to make and enforce it.

Time struggle

A major problem for a wife is time. Only her husband with his outside perspective can successfully assist his wife in working out her schedule and priorities. Work out a priority list with your wife. These are the general categories that need to be considered: personal time with the Lord, marriage relationship, relationship with children, relationships and ministry within the body of Christ, work, and recreation.

Set a brief planning meeting, perhaps fifteen minutes each Sunday night, to agree on a week's schedule. Help her eliminate activities that may overcommit her. After understanding her schedule, take responsibility for creativity and diversity of activities. Arrange for her to be out of the home regularly. I have encouraged "Mother's day out" to insure Sally the freedom to get out periodically. When possible, I commit myself to staying home to give her that freedom. We also like to have a "date" once a week. Take charge Friday night and let her sleep in on Saturday morning. If she has preschoolers, relieve her from the five-o'clock "Horror Show" at dinner and the bedtime scene. Putting the kids to bed or washing dishes is like an early Christmas for a mother.

Physical activity

Take an active interest in your wife's health. Exercise with her and make sure she has physical checkups. Convince her that her body is attractive. Do not let her set unrealistic weight goals. Realistic weight goals and

a husband who sensitively cares will result in successful weight control. Allow her to share her concerns
about your physical situation, also.

Children

> Fathers, do not provoke your children to anger; but
> bring them up in the discipline and instruction of the
> Lord (Eph. 6:4).

Husbands, take "first responsibility" for the children in two areas: discipline and instruction.

Discipline: Discipline affects a child's character development. Be very involved in discipline and do not
put it primarily on your wife. Watch for power struggles between your wife and the children. Monitor your
wife's emotional tiredness. When it rises, check her
struggle with the children. Take responsibility for any
special problems like tantrums or hyperactivity. Personally take care of any discipline problems at school.
Do not provoke your child to anger because of your
lack of discipline; establish a relationship.

Instruction: Husbands, you are ultimately responsible for the spiritual development of your children.
Spending an hour a week putting your children to bed
would be a good start. Communicate with your child
to find out where he is spiritually. Work with your
wife, but keep the responsibility on your shoulders.

Future hope

Always oversee your wife's future outlook. Nothing
affects a woman more than low expectations for the
future.

Communication: A woman must communicate to maintain her confidence and emotional stability. She cannot respond adequately without a total relationship. Romance will die without communication. If your wife often says that you do not communicate with her, seek counsel to help define and correct the problem.

Mutual Interests: Too many couples lose their desire to be together because they have lost their mutual interests. If you try, you can develop some mutual interests. Travel is a good possibility. Fun, hobbies, and intellectual stimulation are all vital.

Aging: Without spiritual interest, productivity, relationships, and responsibilities, people really suffer as they age. Protect your wife from this slow depression. Develop spiritual interests and activities that can continue until death.

Allow your grandchildren to become a part of your lives. Even if they scramble your schedule and make you tired, they will keep you involved and make you feel important. Continue to work as long as possible before retiring. Then use your talents part time. Your earlier sacrifices to make time for ministry will really pay off now. As your work-related activities decrease, your activity for the Lord and His people can continually increase. Most of all, maintain your commitment to your wife sexually, intellectually, emotionally, and spiritually.

A MAN'S COVENANT WITH HIMSELF

An old proverb says that where people have no vision, they perish. Most men today, unfortunately, do not have much vision for their lives. But a man who plans his life will experience so much fullness and joy that both he and his wife will be uplifted. Consider these areas of planning in your future.

Spiritual responsibility and leadership

Paul wrote to Timothy, "It is a trustworthy statement: if any man aspires to the office of overseer, it is a fine work he desires to do" (1 Tim. 3:1). In working and counseling with men, I have seen a tremendous need in their lives for authority and respect. In addition, it is very important to their growth in Christ that a large part of their responsibility be associated with spiritual issues. There is tremendous joy for a man in church leadership, especially in a church that views elders' or other lay leaders' roles as a real ministry. If your church does not encourage personal ministry, volunteer to begin a lay program to develop spiritual responsibility. God desires that you would find His perspective on life, and spiritual leadership is vital to doing so. No matter what your gifts or abilities, seek counsel on a plan that helps you develop spiritual responsibilities.

Accountability

As much as men like to be self-confident and independent, they have deep needs in the area of counsel. I have observed a strong need in men's lives for protection from wrong decisions, for wisdom in their marriage and in child-rearing, for encouragement in their jobs, and other important issues.

Not long ago I had to make a significant ministry-oriented decision that was difficult for me and somewhat threatening for my family. Finding myself suddenly under considerable emotional and professional pressure, and feeling intensely the responsibility to provide firm, directional family leadership, I knew I would be unusually vulnerable to Satan's inevitable attack.

To protect myself and my family, I asked five close friends to form an advisory board. I described my situation to them and gave an historical evaluation of Sally and myself. These men stood with me and gave me honest feedback. More importantly, they rallied to my support in developing an aggressive plan for the future, in light of God's leading through these circumstances. Just six weeks later I was totally remotivated, my wife trusted and respected my openness even more, and I had deepened my relationship with these men. The body of Christ demands my accountability to mature brothers. In Proverbs God says there is much safety in the midst of many wise and godly counselors (Prov. 15:22).

Work

In Genesis 3, God instructs Adam to toil and sweat. Many men never face God's statement. Instead, they devise all kinds of ways to get out of work—changing jobs, get-rich-quick schemes, and always looking for "greener grass." The times when I was unsure of my vocation were among the most frustrating and depressing periods of my life.

I have found that about ten percent of the male population has certain gifts and abilities that allow those in this group to easily find job opportunities. Their problem is sticking to one job. The other ninety percent really have to work at getting a good job. Yet most research demonstrates that the men who usually win in the long run are the men who demonstrate perseverance in their chosen field. If you notice inconsistencies in your working experience, seek counsel immediately. Make yourself accountable in your work. Pursue what you enjoy so you can let go and be productive. You and your family will admire your joy.

11

A Woman of Wisdom

The wise woman builds her house, but the foolish tears it down with her own hands (Prov. 14:1).

He who finds a wife finds a good thing, and obtains favor from the Lord (Prov. 18:22).

An excellent wife is the crown of her husband (Prov. 12:4).

Every woman, deep in her heart, would like to be characterized as wise and considered a gift from the Lord. To hear a husband say, "You excell them all" would bring joy to most wives. Do you consider yourself a specific gift from the Lord to your husband? Would you be identified as a wise woman who is skillful at living? I hope this chapter will help solidify some foundational issues and allow you to increase in wisdom.

Over the years I have counseled and worked with many wives. I've experienced joy as I've seen their faith mature, but I've also cried as some have shared the crosses they have had to bear. Out of respect for those women and a deep sense of responsibility to our Lord, I want to share some of my conclusions.

There are four foundational questions every woman must answer before she can be released to enjoy life in the home.

1. Am I limited by my role as a wife?
2. Is the home the key to my success as a wife?
3. Are there limits to submission?
4. How can a wife understand and help her husband?

If you can get a clear direction on these four issues I know you'll be able to have vision and wisdom in your marriage. Ask God, even as you read, to give you understanding of His perspective of a fulfilled woman in marriage.

AM I LIMITED BY MY ROLE AS A WIFE?

Earlier I tried to open your minds to God's perspective concerning the man's role to love and the woman's role to submit. I have tried to demonstrate that there is no special advantage to either role, by comparing Ephesians 5 and 1 Peter 3.

Chapter 8 attempted to reveal God's perspective on love and submission by showing us God's purpose for giving men and women different responsibilities. Love and submission establish *oneness* in relationships, and this accomplishes God's and man's goals of reflecting God's image, reproducing a godly heritage, and reigning in life. Jesus experienced this same love and submission with God the Father and God the Holy Spirit in the Trinity.

God's perfect plan for love and submission was distorted by Satan when Adam and Eve sinned, giving birth to the self-centered nature of man. Lately he has had special success through the media, causing women to question and even doubt their need for submission in what they would call an "equal" marriage.

However, the most difficult part of God's solution is trying to keep His perspective in our daily lives. Women, especially, fight an unbelievable war to maintain God's point of view in face of Satan's deceit. This war must be taken seriously and approached aggressively. Every time submission gets tough we must get back to God's Word. These truths are vital to experiencing real joy in the Christian life.

Wives, God did not load life against you. In counseling, I have suffered with woman after woman about this issue of submission. It can be desperately tough, but God will not fail you. Your struggle is not against flesh and blood (your husband), but it is against Satan and his powers of deceit. To question submission, since it is clearly from God and not from men, is to question God Himself.

After suffering, as "submitters" sometimes do, Job questioned God about why He made him and why He allowed the hardships. God responded with several illustrations from His creation, and asked Job (and us) to answer some hard questions. God refers to the vicious, ugly, untameable crocodile and simply says, "Job, do you question Me on how and why I created such an animal?" Then He explains how the ostrich is cruel to its young, and says again, "Job, do you condemn Me because I made a creature who is cruel to its babies?" Job honestly doesn't understand these things, and he admits he is questioning God about them.

I believe that today many women are echoing these same types of questions along with Job. "Why did You make me a woman? Why must I be under a man's leadership? I deserve to be equal with a man. I am not less qualified, motivated, or capable. Yes, God, I do question your role for me."

God responded to Job and to us, "Will the faultfinder contend with the Almighty?"

Suddenly Job was convicted that the creature was questioning the Almighty God, the Creator. He responded, "Behold, I am insignificant. What can I reply to Thee? I lay my hand on my mouth."

God then says, "Will you condemn me that you may be justified?"

Isn't that what we do with God? God tells us to stop judging Him or condemning Him because of the way He made us. It should be obvious that in our narrow, limited, and finite ways we cannot devise a better way than the God of the universe.

Awestruck at his audacity, Job first recognized God as a God of power, perfect knowledge, and great provisions. In Job 42:2,3 we read:

"I know that Thou canst do all things, and that no purpose of Thine can be thwarted.... Therefore I have declared that which I did not understand, things too wonderful for me, which I did not know."

Next, Job confesses his pride and asks forgiveness (vv. 5,6):

"I have heard of Thee by the hearing of the ear; but now my eye sees thee. Therefore I retract, and I repent in dust and ashes."

Women, can the wisdom of Job be yours? Can you trust God, knowing fully who He is and that His plan for your life is best, regardless of any momentary suffering? (Job lost *all* he had—his children, home, liveli-hood, material possessions, and health.)

Now to the nitty-gritty of maintaining submission on a daily basis! To maintain Job's attitude you must share these faith concepts with others and put on God's full faith armor for protection. Submission is so contrary to our natural human experience that it is impossible to endure tough situations without a defi-nite plan. You cannot stand still in your understanding of submission. You are either gaining or losing ground constantly.

In 1 Peter 1:12–21 Peter exhorts us to holiness and growth. He basically says, "Won't you realize that you are not serving yourselves, but God?" These precious biblical promises are given to you by God's Holy Spirit. They are so great that they intrigue even angels! Submission is not just a trial or something you suffer. As you grow in your understanding of it through God's Word, it becomes a real blessing. You will never be more loved, appreciated, and cherished. Your needs will never be more fulfilled. You see, these are the precious promises of God Himself. Women desire to be loved the way God says a husband should love.

Peter goes on to say, "Therefore, gird your minds for action, keep sober in spirit, fix your hope completely on God's grace." Peter says your struggle is one of the mind. Do not allow Satan to deceive your mind. De-cide that God can sufficiently carry you through those tough situations. Put away your sinful lusts and self-centered rights. Expect the tough situations, but *de-cide to believe.*

Peter continues in verse 18, saying in effect, "Don't trade your hope in God for a hope in temporary or perishable things, like silver and gold. These come from your futile way of life inherited from your forefathers. Place your real hope in life in the precious blood of Jesus Christ."

You will occasionally suffer in your role as an obedient wife, but Jesus called us to follow Him and He was perfectly submitted to His Father. Was Jesus limited in the long run by His submission? Certainly not! And neither will He limit you if you submit.

IS THE HOME THE KEY TO MY SUCCESS AS A WIFE?

With all the negative publicity the housewife has been getting in recent years, along with the glamour attributed to the working woman, it's no surprise that wives question their vocation in the home. I am constantly running into young wives who do not plan to have children. They say they cannot fully express themselves in the home. More and more wives are attributing their struggles in life to being captive to the house and the children. Again, the question must be asked, "Did God make a mistake by placing wives and mothers in the home?"

A wife who does not deal squarely with these questions will experience confusion and frustration in her marriage. Because of the importance and diligence necessary in a homemaker's responsibilities, she cannot afford to be without direction and vision or she will certainly struggle, and perhaps fail. The problem again is one of deceit. Close on the heels of Satan's deceit of submission is his deceit concerning the value of the home.

With the help of our culture, Satan has convinced women that their existence in the home is a barrier to fulfillment. Once a woman's eyes focus on herself instead of on God and His perspective, she begins a lonely uphill battle. With weak vision and lack of determination, the many struggles of the home quickly wear her down and defeat her spirit of hope. She sees her situation as offering no hope in and of itself, and where there is no hope there is only fear. Fear is the enemy of faith.

Note the consistent pattern of Satan. He first catches a woman in a struggle (and a homemaker has plenty of them). At that point of conflict, the woman's consciousness of God's presence is low. The deceit does not directly attack God; instead, it places the blame on a person or situation. The moment a woman sees a person or responsibility of the home as the problem, her commitment is broken. Then she begins passively or subconsciously to resent and rebel against her husband, the one she blames. Once she has begun to resent or rebel, her whole relationship with God is affected.

I believe a woman is equal to a man in every respect with the single exception of physical strength. While a woman's function is different in some ways, she needs equal expression of her intellect, emotions, and physical attributes, and she should have equal opportunities publicly as well as privately. I do not believe God created a woman to be lacking in expression in any way. The problem is not one of equality. The problem is determining how God intended a woman to find expression.

The feminist movement has risen to power by exhibiting "proof" of the plight of the average woman. My disagreement with the movement comes on two major issues: the *cause* of the housewife's problems and the *solutions* offered. These women are in essence saying that God made a mistake in creating love and submission. They imply that God made a mistake in putting the woman in the home.

God's plan has never been for men and women to become more alike, responding to their natural self-centeredness, nor to become more competitive and "rights-oriented." Our hope lies in confessing our rebellion and then, by faith, stepping out aggressively to find fulfillment where God places us.

The biblical woman, the woman of wisdom, finds God's perspective and thus His door to expression through her husband, home, and children. Let's take a closer look.

Godly perspective

In Proverbs 31, the woman's mind is set on a different perspective than we see the world teaching us today. Her mental freedom allowed her creativity to flow. Her perspective of life is mentioned in the last two verses of the passage:

> Charm is deceitful and beauty is vain, but a woman who fears the Lord, she shall be praised. Give her the product of her hands, and let her works praise her in the gates (vv. 30,31).

The word "charm" means superficial graciousness, and the word used for "beauty" means vaporous. God is saying that the woman who places her hope in her superficiality or temporary youthful attractiveness is headed for disaster. But the woman who fears the Lord shall find total expression and praise.

The term "fear" connotes reverential awe. In other words, she doesn't question God's plan for her as a woman. She doesn't place her hope in the ideologies of the world but instead commits her hope to the Lord and His view of life.

This woman is promised praise and God gives it to her! The "product" of her hands is her home and all that it contains. The "gates" are the public places. She will be known by what her home turns out to be.

Can this example of a fulfilled wife be trusted? God may call some women out of the home, but I believe that the home is potentially the greatest place for women to be fulfilled.

Characterized by hope

This woman of Proverbs 31 is characterized by an attitude of hope (vv. 25–27).

> Strength and dignity are her clothing, and she smiles at the future. She opens her mouth in wisdom, and the teaching of kindness is on her tongue. She looks well to the ways of her household, and does not eat the bread of idleness.

Here is a woman of stature! She is not a "trampled-down" woman with a "woe-is-me" attitude. "Strength and dignity" are best translated "a woman of majesty and dignity whose compassion and love free her of future worry." Her faith brings her success, and hope fills her heart.

This woman is able to smile at the future. She is not afraid of the future because she has prepared her household for it physically, emotionally, and spiritually. She is able to meet her husband's and children's needs, and in the process hers are met. She teaches wisdom and skill in the art of living. Here is a woman who can truly lead others to an understanding of God's principles. She views her work in the home very positively. Her role is so fulfilling and far-reaching that she thanks the Lord for it.

Characterized by work

The Proverbs 31 woman is able emotionally and physically to work hard and sacrificially. Work is not popular in our culture, but God commands us to work to spare us from our self-centeredness. Idleness is destructive to our self-image and our spiritual walk. This woman not only gets up early, but she is available to meet the needs of her household at night.

It is important to note that this woman has a great deal of diversity in her work. It takes her in and out of the home. Women who suffer anxiety over their role in the home suffer not so much from overwork as from lack of diversity. Women need authority-oriented, people-oriented, and intellectually oriented tasks. Work is vital to life.

Creative with her abilities

If this woman had heard the feminist appeal to work outside the home, she would have laughed and said, "What foolishness!" Just look at the creativity of this woman. Neither fighting nor questioning God, she believes and becomes creative. Men are motivated by this type of woman and her attitude toward her role. Look at part of her job description:

Looks for wool and flax (v. 13)
Shops in far places for the needs of her home (v. 14)
Cooks (v. 15)
Buys and sells property (v. 16)
Plants a vineyard (v. 16)
Exercises physically (v. 17)

Sews (v. 19)
Works in community affairs with the poor and
   needy (v. 20)
Makes and sells clothes (v. 24)
Teaches in the community (v. 26)

Any way you look at her she was not limited privately or publicly. Few *men* have the freedom to be as
far-reaching and diversified as this woman. Ladies,
you have been deceived into thinking God has limited
you in the home. This woman was wise enough to
believe God and trust Him for creativity. As always,
God was faithful.

Characterized by energy

It is not a small thing that God includes verse 17:
"she girds herself with strength and makes her arms
strong." A lot of women say they want opportunities to
do more things. Obviously, if you are going to be active, you need physical stamina. This woman was definitely active, so she stayed physically fit.

In counseling, I have been amazed at the number of
women who are always physically tired. If a woman
says she is tired it is hard to ask her to do more. Many
women believe the way to restore lost energy is to rest
more. That may be true in momentary cases of over-
exhaustion, but with any long-term problem the opposite is probably true. You need exercise to increase
your normal level of energy reserve. Our friend in
Proverbs 31 kept herself strong and her energy level
high. Exercise is important to mental attitude. If you
are overly exhausted, see a doctor. Otherwise, begin
today getting physically fit.

Husband and children glorify her

Due to Satan's deceit, husbands, children, and home responsibilities are considered to be limitations to wives. But if you assume God's perspective, you see that God has blessed the wife and mother most of all God structured the emotions of children and the desires of husbands to naturally seek her. Because self-worth and self-expression can only be measured by relating to people and to God, this was a gracious act of God. In our case, five people naturally run to my wife daily: me and the four kids!

In Proverbs 31:10, the value of a wise woman is stated: "A wife is worth far more than jewels." Verse 11 indicates that her husband trusts her so explicitly that money loses its importance in comparison. Verses 28 and 29 tell how her family responds to her. Her children will grow up and bless her. They will give her the highest expression a woman could desire, and her husband will say she is the very best woman in the world!

Let's look at these promises of esteem and honor. Do you know of any other role in life that guarantees this result? Does the woman who succeeds in business or public life have these promises? Not at all. In fact, like men, the better she does in business, the more competition and jealousy she will experience from men and women alike. In fact, if a woman chooses the independent life she will probably follow the path of men—a quicker death by heart attacks and ulcers.

What is the key to success for a married woman? First, it is constantly seeking God's perspective on life. Second, it is modeling a personal plan for utilizing herself and serving her husband, children, and home. And last, it is allowing God to meet her needs through her husband, children, and opportunities found through the home.

ARE THERE LIMITS TO SUBMISSION?

I think the question of limits is a valid one. I also believe that God may ask wives to go to unbelievable ends to be submissive to their husbands, even to the point of risking personal sin as Sarah did. But, if possible, they must not allow suffering or personal feelings to determine how far they go in submission (see 1 Peter 3:8,9; and Num. 30:6–16). Scripture clearly communicates that submission by both men and women will be tested in suffering.

While I believe that God's Word absolutely assures the greatest blessing to the one who submits, God will not absolve you from responsibility for sin just because someone with authority told you to do it. In other words, submission cannot be used as an excuse for sin.

On the other hand, a wise woman will use this as an opportunity to be creative in understanding her husband's real need. You must ask yourself. "What is the need in my husband's life behind the request he is making?" Next, try to meet that need without contradicting Scripture. Trust God as Sarah did. God may want to intervene and demonstrate His power as He did with Sarah.

An example of submitting to the point of sin is the story of Ananias and Sapphira in Acts 5. Sapphira agreed to sin with her husband and as a result God took both of their lives. I encourage you to seek counsel if your husband has asked you to do something you think is sin. For most, it will never go that far. As your husband sees your submissive attitude toward him, he will more than likely love you more and be more concerned with how you feel and think.

Before leaving this question, perhaps a word about what submission is *not* is in order. Submission is not simply keeping your mouth shut and doing whatever your husband says. This may be complying with the *letter* of God's admonition, but certainly not its *spirit*. Some women seem to grit their teeth while they act submissive. Throughout Scripture God tells us He is more interested in our heart than our actions. If a man lusts in his heart for another woman, Scripture says he is guilty of adultery. Likewise, if we rebel inwardly while submitting outwardly, we are as guilty as if we had refused to submit.

Communication

In an effort to help our understanding of this important area, let's begin by looking at the example God set for our communication with Him.

> Be anxious for nothing, but in everything by prayer and supplication with thanksgiving let your requests be made known to God. And the peace of God, which surpasses all comprehension, shall guard your hearts and your minds in Christ Jesus (Phil. 4:6,7).

God desires that we express to Him not only our needs, but our very wants. He doesn't promise to give us our wants, although many times in His grace He does that; but He does promise peace beyond our understanding. The key thought is that He wants us to *tell* Him. What is prayer but simply talking to God? Now if God wants us to do that with Him, would He ask that wives not even talk to their husbands? I do not believe He is requiring that.

God is simply saying, "Women, if your husband has an attitude of being disobedient to God's Word, then do not provoke him further by nagging or hitting him with Bible verses again and again." Instead, inwardly make a faith decision to trust in God at that moment, so you can outwardly win your husband with your positive actions. The submissive woman hopes in God and, by grace, does not resist her husband. You must allow your husband to be wrong, even fail, so that the Lord can convict him. You simply love him and encourage him by how you treat him. Colossians 4:6 says, "Let your speech always be with grace, seasoned, as it were, with salt, so that you may know how you should respond to each person."

Women, once you have told your husband you think he is wrong in some way, do not continue to nag on that issue. Turn it over to God and let Him deal with it. I feel that the submissive woman can express her opinions freely; in fact, her husband will want her to do so. However, your hope should never be in your husband's ability or willingness to change but in the Lord, who does the changing. You must at this time assure him that you love him and that no matter what, you are behind him.

The balance to this freedom to communicate feelings is the strong warning God gives us about the poison of our mouths. Paul, in Romans 3, tells us that the mouth is an open grave, capable of unbelievable destruction. James tells us that we should be slow to anger and slow to speak or we will lose God's blessing in trials. A good thermometer of a submissive wife is how she uses her mouth. Proverbs 15:1 says, "A gentle answer turns away wrath," and "How delightful is a timely word!" (15:23). If a woman has God's perspective she will:

(1) Wait for the proper time to tell her husband her negative thoughts.
(2) Talk to the Lord about it in the meantime.
(3) Speak peaceably when the time comes, without anger, bitterness, resentment, or belittling.
(4) Trust the Lord for the outcome, even when no change is seen.

HOW CAN A WIFE UNDERSTAND AND HELP HER HUSBAND?

At a time in our history when women are shouting, "I am not going to take this oppression anymore!" men are suffering unbearably themselves. What a paradox—the women are shouting about oppression but the men are closer to defeat. Consider for a moment the following statistics:

• There are over six million more women than men in America today.
• Men move toward death faster than women after age forty.
• After age twenty-four seventy percent more men commit suicide than women. After age sixty-five eighty percent more men than women commit suicide.
• Far more drug addicts and home deserters are men.
• Men alcoholics outnumber women alcoholics five to one.

• Estimation of male homosexuality in America is as high as ten percent.*

Probably the single greatest problem in America, as well as in Christendom, is the lack of male leadership. Women may feel put upon in our society, but men, according to medical records, show the greatest emotional stress resulting in ulcers and heart attacks.

What is happening to our men? It is not a simple question. Our culture seems to strike hardest at the role of men. Try to understand some of their struggles. Few men own a home free and clear, and fewer own land. Almost all men work for someone else. Because their lives are monitored by loan institutions or bosses, men do not feel control or dominion over their lives. They feel that "Big Brother" is constantly watching them, and "Big Brother" can be a lot of things to different men.

Furthermore, men are frustrated because they no longer experience natural authority over those in their care. The authoritarian influence of the past has turned into the democratic home of the seventies. The father is often just another vote in the family. Men experience anxiety and loss of personal dignity in their families. All of this has resulted in an identity crisis for many, which tends to promote hostility or withdrawal.

Another thing I have observed in counseling with men is a lack of effective male models. With over one third of our children coming from broken homes and with the community-oriented society of today, young men move through their developmental years without

---

*Statistics taken from *Statistical Abstract*, U.S. Department of Commerce, Bureau of the Census, 1978; and The World Almanac and Book of Facts, 1979 by Newspaper Enterprise Association for Doubleday.

identifying with assertive, confident, aggressive, and sensitive men of direction.

Just like women, men are affected deeply by the tremendous pressure of comparison with other fantasy supermen images. Mass media and electronic marvels daily program us with the president, the senator, the executive, the stylish athlete, or the many-faceted TV detectives. Christian women even compare their husbands to well-publicized Christian male celebrities. There seems to be less emphasis placed on the inner qualities of a man, such as faithfulness and consistency, and more emphasis placed on outer qualities like athletic ability, wealth, appearance, and personality. A slight self-image problem in a man can quickly become a serious issue under this barrage of comparison and competition.

The godly woman must create a vision in her heart and mind for her husband. Without a plan or direction from God, the natural tendency would be to ignore these things. But a woman who desires to be God's wife to her husband will look beyond his weaknesses, releasing him to total fulfillment. The question is not any longer, "Do you desire it?" but, "Is it God's will and plan for you?" What a privilege it is to understand, love, and help your husband to be a fulfilled, motivated, and responsible man. To do this, a wife must make two commitments.

Compassion (aggressive belief)

As much as Christ must hate my failure and sinfulness, by God's grace He always maintains a compassion for me that is stronger than His hatred of my sin. He knows what I am missing and desires that I experience the best. In the same way, a wife should not allow her dissatisfaction with her husband to ever overshadow her compassion for him. Compassion is deep, unselfish concern for another that demands action.

Historically, women have had problems losing perspective concerning their husband's weaknesses. A wife can become so discouraged and distrustful of her mate that she can no longer believe God for him. Proverbs 27:15,16 speaks of such a woman:

> A constant dripping on a day of steady rain and a contentious woman are alike; he who would restrain her restrains the wind, and grasps oil with his right hand.

A woman who pursues a course of nagging her husband daily in a quarrelsome and strife-ridden way will eventually be unwilling to follow his leadership at all. The writer then says that to reverse that process would be more difficult than stopping the wind or grasping oil in your hand. A wife must pursue insight that will protect her from Satan's deceit concerning her husband.

Knowing his needs

Your husband has certain God-given needs that must be fulfilled. Needs to protect, to own, to have authority, to be productive, to love, and to reproduce his image—these are some of the major needs implied in Scripture. Consider the areas where you can specifically help him meet his needs. Some will be mentioned briefly, since they are covered in more detail elsewhere.

Vocational needs—A wife who is sensitive to her husband can do more to motivate her husband vocationally than any other person. Usually a man's work sets the pattern for the other areas of his life. A man who is satisfied in his work is a man of real potential. A wife is in an excellent position to study her husband to see what he enjoys doing. Watch him play as well as work, since many times what he does with his free time is a good indicator of what he really enjoys. Glorify your mate in his work. Many men enjoy what they are doing, but secretly feel others do not adequately respect them for it. To hear that his wife is proud of him can make a tremendous difference to any man.

Be willing to adjust your spending and standard of living to allow your husband to change jobs. Anything you do to stabilize and increase *his* happiness helps you, too. A man has an almost constant need in life to reevaluate his vocation. He needs the freedom of knowing his wife will support him whatever his decision may be.

Spiritual needs—Scripture places a significant importance on spiritual leadership in a man's life. Encourage any inclination your husband shows toward taking spiritual responsibility. Especially after thirty, a man's feeling of importance can be increased if he is involved in church leadership or in a discipling process. This may require you to have a Bible study in your house or to get a babysitter to pursue this end. It might even require you to make friends with one of your husband's friends' wives. Whatever it takes, help all you can. If your husband is not gifted in aggressive ways, ask the Lord for ways to support others more aggressively gifted. However, never feel that you have to push him in this direction. Remember, God does the changing.

Sexual needs—This area is very important to most men. Unless you are naturally motivated sexually, do not get under the pile of trying to keep up with mythical "national averages." Detailed information is contained in the next chapter.

Relationship needs—Many husbands are loners. If you add to those the large number of couples who do not develop mutual friends, the problem becomes staggering. Relationships are very important in a man's life. A wife benefits from her husband's relationships. Communication, diversity of interest, and increased hope in life are just a few of the possible benefits. Observe people your husband naturally likes, and create social settings where he feels comfortable. When possible, pursue his interests in friends. The more you do sacrificially for him, the more he will become responsible and be encouraged to return the blessing.

Intellectual needs—A man people listen to is one who can communicate well. Especially if you are a more assertive or disciplined student, do what you can to recognize your husband's intellectual interests. Everyone is interested in something. If you can start a mutual discussion on any issue, your husband will begin to look forward to sharing his thoughts with you. A husband who feels his wife cares about his intellectual interest feels a special closeness with her. She's a real friend. In addition, if she listens to him in even one area, he can then listen to her without feeling she is preaching.

Authoritative needs—A wife who encourages her husband's authority in her life is a protected woman. This sounds good, but how do you do it? The following ideas illustrate some ways to give your husband authority and revive his natural protectiveness.

Many times a wife will come to me to ask if I could lead her husband to Christ, or convince him of some spiritual truth. She usually has asked several women's prayer groups to pray for him. The place I have to start is with the wife. Her attitude and feelings of superiority or "spirituality" toward him have usually enraged him subconsciously over a period of time. This man is really rejecting his wife's attitude, not Christ. If I can get her to go home and ask her husband's forgiveness and believe God for him as he is, the husband is usually open to talking about a God powerful enough to get his wife to say she was wrong!

Wives also come to me and say, "If you could just get my husband to spend more time with the children, things would be fine." Unfortunately, this wife has usually so covered him with guilt and rejection that every time the children enter the room he subconsciously feels whipped. These feelings retard his natural aggressiveness and make him want to stay away because they are a reminder of failure. Again, if I can help the wife see that she will never motivate him this way, I can help her trust God with her children alone if necessary. She can then ask his forgiveness for judging him and give him the freedom to treat the kids as he feels he should. This man is free to be convinced by the Lord without being sidetracked by feelings of anger and rejection.

I have seen men treat new cars better than their wives. Why? Because a car is their total, unabridged responsibility. A man senses *real* dependence, so he naturally feels more responsible for a wife who's there for better or worse.

In Genesis 4, Cain tried to please God by sacrificing his very best vegetables. It was God's desire for him to sacrifice an animal, so the Lord was displeased with Cain's offering. Cain tried to please God in his way, not in God's way. A wife who is obediently attentive to her husband's desires is a wise woman and knows how to really please him. A man cannot easily change his self-image, but a wife has the ability to be blind to his faults and that will cause her to fall in love. As she visualizes him as near perfect, he will try to be.

IN SUMMARY

The wise wife knows that God provided her mate for her and therefore knows her struggle is never really against him, but against Satan. This woman can honestly love her husband so completely that severe lack of self-confidence would be a contradiction of his importance to his wife.

The mother is a model to the children. If she doesn't respect him, neither will they. If she respects him, so will they. Give your children a blessing—let them respect their father.

Allow the Spirit of God to teach you how to understand your husband. The woman of God is freed through wisdom to defeat Satan's deceit. She can then release her mate to take authority in her life as she hopes in God, seeing him fully expressed and at the same time viewing him as a gift from God with no limitation to her.

Verbal praise is extremely vital to a man. My heart burns with excitement for a man when I hear his wife praise him when he is not present. At the same time, I die a little inside when I hear a woman criticize her husband. A wife who makes a strong commitment to never utter a critical word about her husband does wisely.

12

Naked and Unashamed

What a powerful drive God gave men and women for sexual expression! Anyone considering marriage should plan to pursue God's full gift of sexual expression within marriage. You might say, "What an unnecessary statement! Sure, I plan to do just that." Yet marriage counselors all over America report that up to eighty percent of couples seeking counsel mention the sexual relationship as one of the key struggles in their marriage.

God emphasizes and devotes an amazing amount of space in Scripture to marital love, demonstrating its place and importance to the marriage bond.

Our biblical discussions of the sexual relationship will include six major areas. They are:

1) Why the problems?
2) Biblical absolutes on the sexual relationship
3) Cultural and religious myths concerning sex
4) Sexual differences in men and women

5) Wisdom from counseling
6) Pre-marital sex

The most important thing to realize as one prepares for a successful sexual relationship is that God is the author of the sexual relationship, and that He intended pleasure and blessing in its creation. Israel's king and his wife stated it best in the Song of Solomon 1:15,16:

"How beautiful you are, my darling,
how beautiful you are!"

"How handsome you are, my beloved,
and so pleasant!
Indeed, our couch is luxuriant!"

This is only one of many references in God's Word to the happiness of marital love. Let's ask for discernment in finding what God intended to be a blessing in the physical relationship.

WHY THE PROBLEM?

"I am angry and bitterly disappointed in my sexual experience," a woman told me recently. "I was so expectant and excited when I got married, only to find shock, hangups, and mediocrity. It is not at all what I had thought it would be. What shocks me most is that I realize I am probably more of a problem than my mate."

I never cease to be amazed at the number of men and women who say similar things three or four years into marriage. It is not necessary for this to happen.

There are three basic reasons why couples experience sexual frustration today. The primary cause of sexual frustration is the *cultural programming* they have received. The film industry and television create a false image of the act of sexuality. The implication of the media is that only the socially and physically "attractive" people really succeed sexually. On film, the sexual act never fails! Reality is hidden and replaced with an image that is fantasy. Advertising bombards us daily with "super" bodies in exotic situations, while the fantasy is destroyed in the reality of the bedroom at home. This wholesale merchandising of sex contributes significantly to growth of the American pornography industry. False comparison, false image, guilt, and disappointment reign in our culture as a result of these influences. We all have been brainwashed, to varying degrees, by these factors, which give us a poor idea of God's truth relating to the sexual relationship.

Another major cause of sexual frustration today is the *nature of man himself.* Because of sin, men and women are self-centered beings; problems in the sexual relationship are a prime example. The human will can bring devastation to a marriage. Each partner brings to the bedroom different standards, inhibitions, and hangups about sex. Each carries a certain amount of scar tissue from the past. Pride is also involved; we want to be self-sufficient and therefore we don't want to admit we don't know it all. We have difficulty asking for help.

The third major cause of sexual frustration today is the often *inadequate job being done by Christian teachers.* For the most part, Christian leadership has not responded properly to people's needs in this area, and has not taught positive truths concerning sex from God's Word. When there were attempts in the past, the teaching was often legalistic: a bunch of "no's." Sex was only for having children.

Of the hundreds of women I have worked with through counseling and seminars, ninety-five percent tell me they never received specific instructions on sex from anyone with authority in their lives. Ninety-one percent of today's students state that their parents gave them no instruction prior to dating and forty-three percent said they had *never* received any instruction about sex. Yet God has spoken boldly on sexual matters. Our culture, man's nature, and ineffective teaching have resulted in a sexually frustrated society.

BIBLICAL ABSOLUTES ON THE SEXUAL RELATIONSHIP

In gaining God's perspective on sexual relationships, the starting point is to learn the absolutes of the Scriptures concerning sexual love. The following ten points are of absolute importance to a successful sexual relationship.

1. Sexuality is God's creation.

It is important that every man and woman realize that their sexuality was unquestioningly created by God. Any uncertainty about that fact affects sexual perspective and freedom. Genesis 1:27 says, "And God created man in His own image, in the image of God He created him; male and female He created them."

God clearly states that man and woman were two different entities, but "one flesh" in reflecting His image. Clearly the creation of sexuality was no accident, and the sexuality of a husband and wife is important to

God in His plan for marriage. To accept one's sexuality and to seek positive fulfillment of its purpose before God is not only good but required by God.

2. Physical love is for procreation.

The innate and emotional needs of men and women, and even their vocational productiveness, is very closely tied to reproducing children in their image and God's image. God commanded Adam and Eve to be fruitful and multiply and fill the earth. God further states in Psalm 127:3–5: "Behold, children are a gift of the Lord; the fruit of the womb is a reward. Like arrows in the hand of a warrior, so are the children of one's youth. How blessed is the man whose quiver is full of them."

The second major absolute of God concerning sex is that God's norm for marriage is to have children. Certainly there are exceptions, but the emphasis is clear.

3. Physical love is for pleasure.

From the very first statements in Genesis, God refers to His command to have sexual relations as a blessing. This refers to a very high and positive experience, one that is deeply fulfilling. God devotes a whole book to His vision for sexual love—the Song of Solomon. In Song of Solomon 8:6 it says of love, "Its flashes are flashes of fire, the very flame of the Lord." Without a doubt, God associates pleasure and excitement with the sexual relationship.

4. Physical love demands a time priority.

In 1 Corinthians 7 and in the Song, God places a time priority on the sexual relationship. Solomon created a special bedroom and took his bride away from the activities of life. The preparation and time taken imply that God ordained special emphasis in sexual matters.

In Deuteronomy 24:5, the young men were instructed: "When a man takes a new wife, he shall not go out with the army, nor be charged with any duty; he shall be free at home one year and shall give happiness to his wife whom he has taken."

The words "give happiness" refer to sexual pleasure. These older men of God knew how vital the sexual relationship is to a marriage, so they committed time from other very important matters to allow the successful establishment of the sexual relationship. Any couple who expects to be sexually satisfied must spend time developing their relationship.

5. Physical love requires a transfer of body ownership.

Sexual love is so vital to Christian marriage that God removes the rights of the individual to control his or her own body. We read in 1 Corinthians 7:3,4:

> Let the husband fulfill his duty to his wife, and likewise also the wife to her husband. The wife does not have authority over her own body, but the husband does; and likewise also the husband does not have authority over his own body, but the wife does.

God steps boldly to the point, finishing any fainthearted commitment to the sexual relationship once and for all. My body is not mine, but my mate's. I am here to please her. Hereafter, to demand rights over my body is to disagree with God's instruction. God makes sex a sacrificial act that is redemptive, in that it gets my eyes off my needs and onto the needs of my mate.

6. *Physical love is passionate and creative.*

As you look closely at Scripture, there are many practical issues on which God did not specifically comment. However, He speaks specifically about the sexual relationship. The Song of Solomon describes a beautifully passionate physical love.* No one could read the following passage and not be convinced that God has established passionate sexual love.

How beautiful are your feet in sandals, O prince's daughter! The curves of your hips are like jewels, the work of the hands of an artist. Your navel is like a round goblet which never lacks mixed wine; your belly is like a heap of wheat fenced about with lilies. Your two breasts are like two fawns, twins of a gazelle. Your neck is like a tower of ivory, your eyes like the pools in Heshbon by the gate of Bath-rabbim; your nose is like the tower of Lebanon, which faces toward Damascus. Your head crowns you like Carmel, and the flowing locks of your head are like purple threads; the king is captivated by your tresses. How beautiful and how delightful you are, my love, with all your charms! Your stature is like a palm tree, and your breasts are like its clusters. I said, "I will climb the palm tree, I will take hold of its fruit stalks." Oh, may your breasts be like clusters of the vine, and the fragrance of your breath like apples, and your mouth like the best wine! It goes down smoothly for my beloved, flowing gently through the lips of those who fall asleep (Song of Sol. 6:13–7:9).

Hebrews 13:4 says, "Let the marriage bed be undefiled." Creative and passionate marital love is good in the sight of God.

---

*I encourage you to read *Solomon on Sex* by Joseph Dillow (Nashville: Thomas Nelson, 1976).

7. *Consistent physical love is important.*

Stop depriving one another, except by agreement for a time that you may devote yourselves to prayer, and come together again lest Satan tempt you because of your lack of self-control (1 Cor. 7:5).

God specifically instructs the married couple to have regular sexual relations. He warns that to disobey this command would leave the partners open to lust problems. The issue here is not a certain number of times per week, but physical love sufficient to meet your mate's needs. Notice that there is no age limit mentioned. The Bible gives accounts of sexual love for the elderly. Abraham and Sarah were in their nineties and still gained pleasure, as recorded in her statement to the Lord about her conception of Isaac. Regularity may change, but there are biblical, medical, and psychological reasons why the sexual relationship is as important at sixty as it is at twenty-five.

8. *Scripture illustrates creative sexual communication.*

In the Song, God implies the importance of verbalization to sexual relations. The wife as well as the husband creatively communicate their thoughts sexually. In 4:1–7 Solomon excitedly describes his wife's body, starting at the top and progressing downward. In 5:9–15 Shulamith reponds with an equally verbal description of Solomon's body. In 2:6, Shulamith even gives specific instructions during the act of making love. In chapter 7, Solomon describes a dance Shulamith does to excite him sexually.

God clearly demonstrates how vital verbalization is to sexual love. For most of us, when we first get married, verbalization is difficult. But when you know that God wants you to talk, you start talking!

9. *Physical love is more than physical.*

Anytime one focuses on physical love, there is a tendency to separate the physical from the emotional, spiritual, and intellectual needs of the couple. Scripture never makes this mistake. When God said Adam and Eve were "naked and unashamed," He was obviously speaking of more than physical transparency. When studying the Song, one sees the communication of the total person's needs throughout the book. Shulamith rejects Solomon when she has been hurt by his lack of attention. He responds to her with love and blessing. The importance of the whole person in the physical area of marriage is clear. Several times God compares sexual love with the union of Christ and His church.

I highly recommend chapters 2 and 3 of Tim LaHaye's book *The Act of Marriage.* These chapters communicate the "wholeness" of the individual man and woman.

10. *Sexual attitudes of parents are transferred to children.*

To a large degree, children learn from their parents. Deuteronomy 6 tells us that parents teach more by what they do than what they say. If Dad is not excited about Mom, the children will not likely sense or observe what God intended for them to feel toward their own mates.

Couples may think they can subtly hide their sexual attitudes from their children. Not so. If a father doesn't have a good relationship with the mother, it will affect the daughter's concepts of femininity and her role in life. By the same token, if the father doesn't have a good relationship with his daughter, it will affect her relationship with her future husband. This is also true of the father-son relationship and the son's concepts of manhood and marriage.

In summary, all these absolutes of God's Word teach one thing: sexual relations were created by God and He wants His children to get with the program!

CULTURAL AND RELIGIOUS MYTHS CONCERNING SEX

Over the centuries, the self-centeredness and guilt in man in relation to sex have produced certain background struggles for couples. These patterns from the past need to be identified to allow couples to escape their disillusionment. Usually, just identifying them is all that is needed to begin the process of overriding their effect. Occasionally, it may be necessary to see a counselor to overcome some of the effects.

Male sexual image

Culturally, we have been educated to see the virile male as Johnny-on-the spot and always ready to perform sexually. The man who is not instantaneously ready at all times is subtly suspected of being less of a man. Men as well as women subject themselves to this thinking. The result is that men may try to prove themselves on the one hand, or they may develop an insecurity about their manhood. Either of these can add real pressure to the natural sexual experience.

All things considered, a man's motivation and function sexually are not all that different from a woman's. He, too, experiences times of low interest, and needs sensitivity and motivation.

Early female conditioning

Every couple needs to consider the fact that a woman who has exercised modest restraint for twenty years needs a creative adjustment period to turn into an aggressive lover. The more legalistic and rules-centered her background, the longer the adjustment will probably take. While the woman needs to aggressively seek God's attitude, the husband needs to exhibit tremendous sensitivity, patience, and acceptance. His goal should be to attract her with personalized love that motivates her.

Required romance and feeling

The film industry has created a false image that couples need to recognize immediately. The lie is, "If you really love me, you would be romantic and want to be sexually involved."

Certainly any *agape* marriage will experience romance and sexual desire, but feelings and romance usually are the *result* of a relationship, not its *cause.* Sexual love is "believing and doing," not "waiting and feeling."

Frigidity

"Frigid" is a term used to describe a woman who is not naturally aggressive sexually. She may not need sexual involvement very often. Her husband, after six months of quoting the national weekly average for sexual intercourse, finally concludes his wife is frigid. She, in self-evaluation, agrees that her desire does not keep up with the national average, so her husband must be right. But is he? Never label your mate "frigid" without seeking counsel.

SEXUAL DIFFERENCES IN MEN AND WOMEN

God purposefully made women's sexual needs different from men's. Over a period of time, these differences reveal a great deal about the total relationship of the couple. The couple who is experiencing an *agape* marriage relationship will begin to see these differences as opportunities to serve and broaden the sexual experience.

First, women are motivated greatly by the emotional side of the sexual relationship. Romantic love and the total person cannot be separated. Tender moments all evening that demonstrate admiration and respect for her prepare her for an exciting sexual experience. In fact, in the absence of romantic tenderness and emotional appreciation, she sometimes enters into sexual love with a feeling of "being used."

Many women tend to be cyclical in their sexual desire—their desire tends to rise, then drop after a sexual experience for several days, only to rise again later. Women tend to be excited more slowly and respond to tender touch and caresses. Privacy, no distractions, warmth, and darkness are usually important and help release emotional fears. Sensitive verbal encouragement can soothe and motivate her.

Men are much more physical. A man can be struggling with a problem all evening and still be tremendously attracted by his wife's body. His sex drive is a continual thing. Tim LaHaye mentions several related issues in his book *The Act of Marriage*. A man's sex drive is connected to his ability "to be the aggressor, provider, and leader of his family. The woman who resents her husband's sex drive while enjoying his aggressive leadership had better face the fact that she cannot have one without the other."*

A man usually responds spontaneously to any stimuli, and is as likely to be stimulated through the eye as the touch. He normally likes to caress his wife in the light so he can see her clearly. A man is excited much more quickly than a woman and distractions usually don't bother him.

A man experiences immediate release in the sexual experience at orgasm. He could fall asleep immediately. With a little effort on his part, however, he too can greatly enjoy those moments after intercourse—which are extremely important to his wife. She enjoys tenderness before, during, and after the sexual experience. To hold her afterward is probably the most vital gift a man can give to his wife.

The couple should anticipate these differences, never allowing resentment in their lives over them. A creative plan can turn these differences into a real blessing. The woman who understands a man's natural God-given sexual drive is overwhelmed when he tenderly meets her needs in spite of his own natural desires.

Nothing is more enjoyable to a man than being able to satisfy his wife sexually. There are comparatively few things in life that a man feels he completes or finishes, yet satisfying his wife is like wrapping up a package and tying a ribbon around it. The sexual part

---

*Tim and Beverly LaHaye, *The Act of Marriage* (Grand Rapids, Mich.: Zondervan, 1976), p. 22.

of marriage is exciting. The spiritual and emotional commitments between two people are sometimes best expressed in sexual oneness. You will spend hours over the next thirty or forty years discussing, reading, preparing for, and being involved in God's adventure of sexual love.

Be prepared for the fact that sexual love takes time. Sexual love changes constantly all through marriage. Early marriage experimentation, hormonal and physical changes during pregnancy and nursing, years of small children with little time for privacy, the middle years, and finally the older years all are different phases. Yet, all of these seasons can be extremely satisfying. All the changes that take place can be beautiful tests of your mutual love.

WISDOM FROM COUNSELING

About eighty-five percent of sexual problems fall in seven or eight categories. Most develop because of ignorance in the early years of marriage. Couples will ask advice on buying a house or car, or even about discipline of the children, but only a few will seek help sexually. Again, I encourage each couple to read together at least one book on Christian sexual love each year and to seek counsel when a problem continues over several months.

To husbands

Men, your responsibility is to love your wife sacrificially as your own body. If you relate to her in a godly manner, you will enjoy a rewarding sexual relationship for the rest of your married life—dividends of great blessing. Here are some simple guidelines.

1. *Belief:* In the Scriptures, God tells us men to be excited and satisfied with the bodies of our wives. Regularly communicate your acceptance of your wife's body to God and to her. Fall in love with her so completely that you will not be affected by the inevitable changes produced by aging. Sell your wife on your love of her body. With every change in her body that comes with age or having children, fall in love with that change. What appears to be a flaw in actuality becomes a mark of beauty!

A man who is not excitedly communicating his acceptance of his wife's body will eventually discover that she begins to hide her body from him. The result sexually is devastating. A husband has the power to change his wife's self-image about her body and to see her develop pride in it.

2. *Acceptance and communication:* God says in 1 Peter for husbands to dwell with their wives in an understanding way. A husband must take responsibility for helping his wife understand her sexual frustrations. A woman who develops sexual anxiety usually is not aware of it initially. Insecurities about her appearance, the size of her breasts, her thighs, her middle, or whatever, can cause a woman to lose her desire for sexual intimacy. By your continued assurances, keep your wife from labeling herself negatively.

3. *Sacrificial love:* Since so much of a woman's sexual enjoyment is tied to her emotional preparation, the husband must be prepared to take charge of easing his wife's burdens. A messy house, unattended children, uncertainty of personal attractiveness, and social pressures are the types of problems that keep a woman from releasing herself emotionally. The sexually effective husband gets up Saturday morning and lets his wife sleep in while he dresses and feeds the children and helps clean the house. He might also take the

children for several hours that afternoon so she can bathe or have her hair done, thus releasing his wife to relaxation. These things unburden the wife emotionally, and that allows her to become aware of his needs and desire to meet them.

When we first married, I used to blame my wife when she was not "up" sexually. Now I blame myself. Don't feel rejected, men. Do something creative!

4. *Wisdom:* Men, protect your wife from sexual anxiety. Never take your cleanliness for granted! Brush your teeth and let her help you select your clothes. Do things that take the pressure off the intercourse experience. Hot baths, rubdowns, and walks together just prior to intimate involvement foster communication and association of pleasure with the sexual experience. Candlelight and soft music reduce anxiety and promote uninhibitedness. Holding her and talking for ten or fifteen minutes before sex adds definite pleasurable associations with the act itself. No man can guarantee a woman's sexual response every time, but he can foster a positive experience for both of them.

Never allow your wife to endure pain sexually! Occasional momentary pain on entry is not abnormal but if pain is a consistent problem, seek medical help together. There are a number of medical problems, such as rashes or infections, or more severe things such as endometriosis, that cause pain. If the problem stays around for an extended time in spite of proper medical help, follow alternative sexual involvement that your doctor will suggest.

To wives

I believe when a marriage is functioning correctly, according to God's perspective, women are as sexually active as men could ever desire. Unfortunately, many times pressures cause women to be emotionally restricted sexually, while causing men to be overly active or preoccupied with sexual activity. Try to find how perfectly you can meet one another's needs sexually. Here are some thoughts that will help:

1. *Natural motivation:* There is a natural, somewhat predictable, level of sexual aggressiveness in women. The following line represents the total spectrum of all women's natural sexual desires.

Naturally Aggressive	Not Naturally Aggressive

Most women tend to be to the right of center on the line—they would initiate sexual activity infrequently. These women are not at all anti-sex or even disinterested. They simply do not naturally think aggressively toward sex. If properly motivated and stimulated by their husbands, they would be open to a much more frequent response to sexual advances. They will usually respond when properly approached. Some women are even more aggressive than their husbands. Neither situation is better; both require creative approaches.

This natural aggressiveness is only a problem when the husband and wife do not understand that it has nothing to do with their ultimate fulfillment. The level of her natural aggressiveness should not be a measure of sexual success.

2. *Enjoy sex:* When I first married, I thought if I could just have my sexual needs met I would be happy. It was not long before I realized that the greatest need I had was not my own enjoyment, but my wife's. The greatest gift a woman can give her husband is to enjoy her own sexual experience.

Too many women look at their sexual activities as a responsibility to their husbands. Every woman should know that God wants her to feel good sexually, to enjoy sex. If a woman has the freedom to look at her sexual involvement as an enjoyable emotional and physical experience, her attitude will change tremendously. A woman needs to sense personal freedom in the areas listed below:

- Satisfaction with her mate
- An understanding of the Scriptures concerning sex and marriage
- Security in her sexual setting
- Relaxation of daily responsibilities
- Cleanliness of her mate and herself
- Respect from her husband
- Freedom to discover what feels good
- Security that her body is beautiful to her mate, and to herself
- Freedom to verbalize enjoyment, feelings, instructions

3. *Femininity:* Men have been given by God a tremendous desire to pursue, keep, and serve a woman. In the natural sense, this drive manifests itself through sexual attraction. But a wise woman takes advantage of every God-given drive in her husband.

A man loves to sense his wife's cleanliness and attractiveness. It is not the shape of your body that matters in the long run, but neatness. How you dress is very important. Feminine-looking undergarments are really motivating to a husband.

I personally like to see women wear dresses as much as possible. Many women dress only to please other women as opposed to dressing to please their husbands. Makeup and perfume also play a part in natural attractiveness and can be very pleasing to a man. Wives, seek your husbands' advice on maintaining femininity.

To husbands and wives

1. *Naked and unashamed:* Each couple should place the focus of their sexual relationship on being "naked and unashamed" as opposed to having a climax in intercourse. God intended that a man and wife would be intimate in a way that would be unique to their relationship. Every married person needs this intimacy to experience God's complete love. God's emphasis is on being naked, totally transparent, and unashamed. Many of our physical, emotional, and spiritual needs are met in this intimate experience of total openness.

While sexual intercourse is a very important icing on the cake, it is not the cake. No couple can be assured of a successful intercourse experience every time, but every couple can be assured of a successful intimate experience. Do not limit most of your sexual experiences to just intercourse. Characterize your physical lovemaking by time spent in total transparency— emotional as well as physical.

2. *Body freedom:* Since the sexual relationship is primarily a physical act, it is very important that partners be excited about their mate's body as well as their own. Research indicates that sexual feelings intensify when the couple is open and creative with each other's body. The woman, for instance, who can uninhibitedly open her mind, body, and body movements to her husband's direction will certainly experience increased enjoyment and success sexually.

God clearly states the view of both Solomon and Shulamith toward one another's body in the Song of Solomon. It is common for men to be attracted to their wife's body and to even express that verbally; yet it is not so common for the wife to express her appreciation of her husband's body. It's good to know that it is scriptural for a woman to think sexually. Shulamith comments, "and he is wholly desirable. This is my beloved and this is my friend."

It is generally much easier for a man to develop freedom with his body and with his mate's body. Women are not as free as men sexually. They compare themselves with the youthful, unblemished bodies of models on TV, which results in great insecurity. Christian teaching has not helped women to be free with their husbands. Some women believe that the lower parts of their bodies are extremely unattractive and even unsanitary. This sets them up for sexual anxiety. Yet men, when polled on what part of their wife's body was most attractive, overwhelmingly said the genital area.

Because of these attitude gaps between the sexes, a husband's early sexual aggressiveness in marriage can cause great harm. However, if he is patient and sensitive, within several months the couple can be open and free with one another's body. So many couples give themselves ten minutes in the bedroom with the lights off at bedtime when both are very tired, and then they wonder why sex isn't all it's cracked up to be! No wonder some women are turned off by sex. It has become an animalistic approach with very little romance and sensitivity. Once a woman is motivated by her husband's tenderness and patience, sex will become a most enjoyable experience for her.

3. *Sexual verbalization:* Sexual communication is an

absolute must in any successful marriage. Talking about sexual excitement, instructions, hurts, fears, disappointments, joys, and anticipations are very important. The couple's ability to verbalize these to each other is imperative.

Several problems occur in sexual verbalization. It is not natural for men or women to verbalize during lovemaking. Fear of losing their feelings is prevalent. Any verbalization that is natural is likely to be a negative response. "Don't do that" or "I don't like that" are said all too often instead of positive things like, "That feels good" or, "One thing I love for you to do is . . ."

Because of the personal aspect of the sexual relationship, prides are easily desecrated. A wife who is trying hard to please her husband and gets criticized for her efforts is deeply hurt. And vice versa. A beautiful sexual experience can quickly turn into a bitter exchange of insults.

In approaching the problem of learning to verbalize, there are a number of things a couple can do. Learning a sexual vocabulary is a first step. Sally and I took the example of the Song of Solomon and developed words that we personally felt comfortable with. We laughed a lot and have had a good time developing our sexual vocabulary. After years of marriage, our vocabulary is very free.

A very helpful adventure was reading the Song of Solomon out loud to each other, Sally taking the part of Shulamith and me taking Solomon. You will laugh at some of the terminology but you will begin to feel natural using sexual terms from this book. I would also suggest regularly reading together Christian books on the subject of sex. I definitely recommend four: *Intended for Pleasure*, by Ed Wheat; *The Act of Marriage*, by Tim LaHaye; *Solomon on Sex*, by Joseph Dillow; and *Physical Unity*, by Shirley Rice.

4. *Time priority:* The longer a marriage lives, the greater the sexual blessing. Couples need to moderate any past disappointments with the hope of the future being better. A good sexual relationship is strengthened if a couple applies the following two time commitments.

First, have one two-hour sexual experience weekly for the rest of your marriage. Schedule it if you have to, but make it happen. Plan an evening without the children (or wait till they have gone to bed) with no TV. You will be surprised at how creative you will become with your two-hour encounter.

The second major time commitment is very important as children come along. I suggest to couples that they take a twenty-four-hour time period alone together once a month. You can "switch-off" your children with another couple who is doing the same thing. It's fun to sometimes have breakfast in bed or sleep late or have an early morning "love-in." Be creative!

I all but guarantee that if a couple takes a night each week and a day every month to concentrate on their physical and emotional needs, there really aren't too many problems that will arise that they cannot conquer together as one flesh. All I can say is, "Try it; you'll like it!"

PRE-MARITAL SEX

Today in America, many counselors and well-meaning friends contend that pre-marital sex releases people from their inhibitions, strict morals, and so-called religious hangups. I would agree that certain "hangups" need emotional release. But I do not believe that pre-marital sex is the answer. Pre-marital sex does *not* make a couple free emotionally, but in fact adds emotional pressure and puts them in bondage. It can rob them of the freedom to clearly see God's will for marriage. To God, sexual love is a physical expression of a more important spiritual commitment between two married people. Sexual love apart from this total commitment simply reduces sexual love to a purely physical level.

Some of you have had pre-marital sex. Some of you are now involved in pre-marital sex. First of all, you must recognize that it is sin. God didn't tell us not to be involved in pre-marital sex because he wanted to take away our fun. He told us no because He loves us and has for us a better way.

We must recognize that sin is forgivable, no matter what form it takes. You need to repent and ask Him for forgiveness. If you are presently involved in pre-marital sex, you must now make a decision of your will to stop. This will insure a much better transition into marriage.

Because of the nature of man and the cultural fantasy that is perpetrated on couples today, sexual involvement before marriage causes an unnatural emotional response. An air of false excitement and expectancy alters the normal marital sexual response. Therefore, a couple involved prior to marriage may have problems adjusting when this false expectancy is removed after the wedding. Stopping now will allow God to begin to give you an anticipation of a sexual relationship in marriage that is free from guilt and open to godly expression.

Since we are all victims of the tremendous emphasis on sexual involvement today, let me give you some practical ideas that will help with this struggle. First, make a spiritual and verbal commitment together to stop your pre-marital sexual activities. Men, you take the leadership in this decision. Women are as responsible sexually as men, but it bothers a man much more to be rejected or limited verbally concerning sex.

Let me give you an alternative to sexual involvement that has worked for many couples. I have found that while actual sexual involvement frustrated a relationship, the real need is not sexual contact but sexual recognition and communication.

I suggest to couples that after making their commitment to stop all sexual involvement, they try the following: Each day, just before they part, they should excuse themselves from family or friends and privately kiss affectionately. Then both should express their deepest felt sexual need. The statement should be brief and stated as unto the Lord. Yet it should be a complete expression of what they feel and need in general terms. The woman might say, "Darling, I want you to know that I am excited and expectant of giving myself to you sexually after the wedding. Today especially you are so attractive to me. I am going to pray specifically tonight that God will cause me to be a great lover to you after we marry." I have found that a brief statement communicated sincerely can meet the need of being recognized and appreciated sexually. Creativity by both will aid the development of sexual verbalization.

The key to this project is to be certain to only attempt this communication just as the couple is parting. The sexual battle is usually lost not at the point of contact, but at the point of being together too long. A couple who plans a day at the apartment watching television is in trouble from the start. Try not to resent waiting sexually; instead, be creative in meeting the other's need for physical attention.

If you still struggle with sexual involvement after these suggestions, the next step is to make yourselves accountable to someone else. Go together to a godly person in your church whom you can trust. Communicate your frustrations and make a commitment to do as you are told. Usually, this type of accountability will do the job.

Most importantly, remember that God is fighting for your sexual life together. Trust Him that He wants you to be more fulfilled than you even desire for yourself.

13

Financial Freedom

A few years ago the powerful importance of finances to marriage was permanently imprinted on my life through a dear couple. The wife, a delightful person and a spiritual leader among the women in the city where they lived, came for counsel.

When she first contacted me I had not met her husband. She loved him, but revealed with a certain disappointment in herself that over the years she had accumulated a great deal of resentment toward her husband's financial habits. She had prayed and prayed, but she could not resist being critical of him.

It seemed that her husband was always late paying the bills. She would receive the bills in the mail and give them to him. Months later he would pay them. All of this came to a head one day when, with three friends along at a department store, she attempted to charge a dress and was refused because of a record of late payment of the bills. She was severely embarrassed. The problem had become so bad that she felt the need to seek counsel.

Financial stress is a major problem in most marriages.* Every couple spends restless nights over financial fears, but entirely too many couples actually lose their marriages over financial stress. Few things cause bitterness and resentment more than money.

Paul was certainly correct when he said to Timothy:

For the love of money is a root of all sorts of evil, and some by longing for it have wandered away from the faith, and pierced themselves with many a pang (1 Tim. 6:10).

The key phrase is "some, by longing for it." The first financial problem to be solved in a marriage is attitude. What importance do you as a couple place on money? 1 Samuel 2:7 says, "The Lord makes poor and rich; He brings low, He also exalts."

Is your attitude such that you are willing to believe God even if you have little money? The question points to the fact that any couple considering marriage needs to agree on some financial absolutes to protect them from attitude problems. The solution is a proper combination of attitude and financial discipline. Some couples become trapped in spite of a good attitude because they are not diligent to anticipate, record, and control their finances.

Responsibility in financial matters entails proper attitudes and faithful control or discipline in financial disbursements. The problem occurs when our worldly desires conflict with God's perspective. Our culture subtly says one thing about real joy in life, while God's Word says another. The following chart gives examples of some of these conflicting concepts.

---

*I want to acknowledge James Squires, John Maisel, and Jody Dillow for their help with these thoughts on finances.

OUR CULTURE'S VIEW	GOD'S PERSPECTIVE
1. Fix your attention on money and possessions.	But seek first His kingdom and His righteousness; and all these things shall be added unto you (Matt. 6:33).
2. Wealth and possessions determine happiness in life.	Beware, and be on your guard against every form of greed; for not even when one has an abundance does his life consist of his possessions (Luke 12:15).
3. I'll be satisfied when I have more _____.	He who loves money will not be satisfied with money, nor he who loves abundance with its income. This too is vanity (Eccl. 5:10).
4. A man's wealth is his security.	God is our refuge and strength, a very present help in trouble. Therefore we will not fear, though the earth should change, and though the mountains slip into the heart of the sea; though its waters roar and foam, though the mountains quake at its swelling pride (Ps. 46:1–3).
5. Financial success is the first priority.	Matthew 6:33 (quoted above) ... not addicted to wine or pugnacious, but gentle, uncontentious, free from the love of money (1 Tim. 3:3).

You might have a tendency to read quickly over these conflicting statements without a lot of personal application, but don't! Any person who has grown up in America cannot help but be influenced by our culture's thought patterns. The resultant pressures and conflicts are painful. The more a couple adheres to God's thought pattern, the more freedom and blessing will result. As you try to develop God's perspective on finances, look first at the example of Christ Himself. Jesus mentions that the basic issue of financial faithfulness is a thermometer of our relationship with God.

> He who is faithful in a very little thing is faithful also in much; and he who is unrighteous in a very little thing is unrighteous also in much. If therefore you have not been faithful in the use of unrighteous mammon, who will entrust the true riches to you? And if you have not been faithful in the use of that which is another's, who will give you that which is your own? No servant can serve two masters; for either he will hate the one, and love the other, or else he will hold to one, and despise the other. You cannot serve God and mammon (Luke 16:10–13).

The first thing Jesus does here is compare money to a "little thing." He makes it clear in His analogy that in comparison to the important things in life, money is a small item. But this "little thing" is a big indicator of a man's faithfulness in serving God. The way a man handles his finances is a strong indication of his trustworthiness as a person. In verse 11, Jesus says that if you cannot be trusted financially, how can He give you "true riches"? This refers to the "grace, hope, and peace" that God gives to a person or couple who adheres to God's perspective. Today men acquire money to find peace, but God says money does not bring peace.

The issue for a couple is whether they choose to serve God or serve money in married life. Jesus says that every person is either serving God or trusting in the security of money. What is your choice as a person or couple? Couples who apply faith in finances experience a blessing that results in real praise of God. Couples who put their hope in money, however slightly, struggle greatly in this life. Often the struggle results in cursing God or feeling depressed. There is seldom any middle ground. *I am convinced that God uses finances as few other things to teach dependence upon Him.*

I believe that in finding God's perspective financially, you should consider the following issues.

FOUR PILLARS OF FINANCIAL MATURITY

Ownership

The minute I bought my first car, I began to feel a compulsion to own things. This compulsion forced me to compare myself with others who owned more. Then came resentment and discontentment. Over the years, God has given me a control over my appetites. My new attitude developed around 1 Chronicles 29:11–16:

Thine, O Lord, is the greatness and the power and the glory and the victory and the majesty, indeed everything that is in the heavens and the earth; Thine is the dominion, O Lord, and Thou dost exalt Thyself as head over all. Both *riches and honor come from Thee*, and Thou dost rule over all, and in Thy hand is power and might; and it *lies in Thy hand* to make great, and to strengthen everyone.

Now therefore, our God, we thank Thee, and praise Thy glorious name. But who am I and who are my people that we should be able to offer as generously as this? For *all things come from Thee*, and *from Thy hand we have given Thee*.

For we are sojourners before Thee, and *tenants*, as all our fathers were; our days on the earth are like a shadow, and there is no hope. O Lord our God, *all this abundance* that we have provided to build Thee a house for Thy holy name, it *is from Thy hand*, and *all is Thine* (italics mine).

God says He is the dominion and head over all; that *all* things come from Him. We are simply tenants of God's possessions for a short time. We are to worship and glorify God with what He has given us. When others have need of what we are *tenants* over, we should be free to give. Sally and I talk about how God plans to use the possessions He gives us.

Eight years ago we bought our first washing machine. At the time we were close friends with a couple in seminary who didn't have any money, and we told them they could wash their clothes in our machine. Every Saturday they came over to do laundry. Sally began to feel uneasy about this, thinking that the machine might break because of overuse, and then we would be stuck with the bill. We reminded ourselves that the machine was not ours but the Lord's, and that we had given all our possessions to Him to be used by Him in any way He chose. Once again our attitude changed from one of possessiveness to gratefulness that the Lord had so blessed us with a machine that could be used by others.

We don't struggle very long on possessiveness, because it seems the Lord always reminds us *who* gave it, *who* is going to use it, *who* is going to pay the bills, and *who* may even take it away! Today that machine is still going strong, without ever having been repaired.

Learn to be a tenant.

God's providence

Another constant struggle for Christians is the problem of comparing our financial situation with others. Feeling superior over the one with less or hating and resenting the one with more can destroy God's perspective in our lives. The opposite can also be true. Today there is a great tendency by some to feel proud about their "simple" life-styles. God clearly speaks about differences in financial situations.

> But you, why do you judge your brother? Or you again, why do you regard your brother with contempt? For we shall all stand before the judgment seat of God. For it is written, "As I live, says the Lord, Every knee shall bow to Me, and every tongue shall give praise to God." So then each one of us shall give account of himself to God. Therefore let us not judge one another anymore, but rather determine this—not to put an obstacle or a stumbling block in a brother's way (Rom. 14:10–13).

> The Lord makes poor and rich; He brings low, He also exalts. He raises the poor from the dust, He lifts the needy from the ash heap to make them sit with nobles, and inherit a seat of honor; for the pillars of the earth are the Lord's, and He set the world on them (1 Sam. 2:7).

God leaves us no doubts on this issue: He makes both rich and poor. There are no accidents in business.

Whatever your state, it was not the "breaks" that put you there; it was God. We have all seen "sure deals" fall unrewarded, and totally "hopeless deals" pay tremendous financial dividends. Don't waste your time blaming or watching your friend, because the One to be glorified is Christ Himself. It is not man but God who causes all things to happen. The issue is not what you have or don't have, but what you do with what you have. You are accountable to God for what He has given you. God's ultimate purpose is to conform us to the image of His Son, Jesus Christ. He may use finances to do part of that shaping. Can you thank Him at all times for what you have or don't have? *Everything* we have is a gift from Him to us, and a part of His plan for our lives.

Contentment

So we do not really own anything, and God is the One who makes men rich or poor. Then what should my attitude be?

For we have brought nothing into the world, so we cannot take anything out of it either. And if we have food and covering, with these we shall be *content*. But those who want to get rich fall into temptation and a snare and many foolish and harmful desires which plunge men into ruin and destruction (1 Tim. 6:7–9, italics mine).

Let your character be free from the love of money, being *content* with what you have; for He Himself has said, "I will never desert you, nor will I ever forsake you," so that we confidently say, "the Lord is my helper, *I will not be afraid. What shall man do to me?*" (Heb. 13:5,6, italics mine).

Apart from basic food and clothing, there is no real hope in things; there is only the appearance of hope. So be content with food and clothing, if that's all you have. If you have wealth or desire to seek it, then you need to be very cautious. Remember that God is still responsible for meeting your needs. God Himself said He would not leave us nor forsake us. Trust Him to meet your needs. He has promised to do so and in many cases has given us many of our wants as well. And consider this insight:

> Give me neither poverty nor riches; feed me with the food that is my portion, lest I be full and deny Thee and say, "Who is the Lord?" or lest I be in want and steal, and profane the name of my God (Prov. 30:8,9).

These thoughts need to be reviewed regularly and prayed about because of our humanity, which "wants." As hard as it is to grasp, we must realize the difference between needs and wants, and claim God's promises to meet our needs. The ability to be content in these promises is a major ingredient in God's recipe for financial maturity.

Security

> Instruct those who are rich in this present world not to be conceited or to fix their hope on the certainty of riches, but on God, who richly supplies us with all things to enjoy. Instruct them to do good, to be rich in good works, to be generous and ready to share, storing up for themselves the treasure of a good foundation for the future, so that they may take hold of that which is life indeed (1 Tim. 6:17–19).

The last pillar of God's perspective on finances is security. What is real security? It is not found in the uncertainty of riches. Security is found by fixing your hope on God, who gives us everything. Scripture is full of this concept both in finances and in human relationships. If a person will place his hope or security in God to the point that he can release himself from riches and actually be generous in sharing with others, then God promises "life indeed." Faith is acting on a statement from God even when it goes against human thought. Financial freedom and security are in God, not in earthly possessions.

UNDERSTANDING AND APPLYING GIVING, SAVING, AND SPENDING

The four financial pillars are actually tested and proved in the practical financial activities of giving, saving, and spending. Scripture instructs us in all three of these important activities. Develop a careful strategy for each one.

Giving

The importance of giving financially to the church and to others is a theme throughout Scripture. The Old Testament gives very specific direction on amounts to give and when to give. Paul states New Testament instructions in 1 Corinthians 16:1,2:

> Now concerning the collection for the saints, as I directed the churches of Galatia, so do you also. On the first day of every week let each one of you put aside and save, as he may prosper, that no collections be made when I come.

Paul instructs each believer to give regularly on Sunday and to give according to how much God has given him. In the Old Testament, men gave more than twenty percent; in the New Testament, we are to ask the Spirit of God to direct our giving. For some it will be ten percent, some twenty, and some more. Sometimes the less a couple earns, the more possessive and materialistic they become. A couple should take seriously God's command to give liberally.

Giving is a redemptive act; it forces my eyes off myself and my needs. It allows me to keep the right perspective on who really owns my money and who gives it to me. Believers will receive a blessing from God if they give sacrificially to others. I challenge you to let the Holy Spirit tell you what to give and to whom.

Paul gives additional instruction in Galatians 6:6, "And let the one who is taught the word share all good things with him who teaches." We are taught to give to those who minister to us. The ability of God's full-time servants to be available depends on your faithfulness to support them financially.

Above all, be visionary in your giving. Believe a mighty God who has given so much to you.

> Give, and it will be given to you; good measure, pressed down, shaken together, running over, they will pour into your lap. For by your standard of measure it will be measured to you in return (Luke 6:38).

God wants to use you as a reservoir to meet needs! Allow God to use you greatly so He can enlist you as a supplier for His work. What a joy there is in giving to others. Even when you loan money to brothers, you should consider giving the money to them. Deuteronomy 15:10,11 describes a giving spirit that God can use.

You shall generously give to him, and your heart shall not be grieved when you give to him, because for this thing the Lord your God will bless you in all your work and in all your undertakings. For the poor will never cease to be in the land; therefore I command you, saying "You shall freely open your hand to your brother, to your needy and poor in your land."

There are many other ways to give to people out of our abundance—food, clothing, furniture, cars, and other material blessings. Your part is to give and God's part is to bless.

Saving

Saving is vital to financial peace and joy. I am constantly dealing with the struggles of couples who are in debt or who have no money at the end of the month. A poor person with a little money in savings is much freer financially than a rich man who is overextended. Scripture speaks of the wisdom of saving. Proverbs 21:20 tells us that the man who keeps a little treasure and oil stored up is a wise man in comparison to the foolish man who swallows up his excess. Proverbs 13:22 says that a good man leaves an inheritance to his grandchildren.

No matter how small the amount, even $5 a month, begin immediately to save. If you run out of money at the end of the month, the pressure is much less if you have an additional $65 in savings.

God speaks a great deal about making wise investments. God graciously gives us some guidelines to investments. First, avoid "get-rich-quick" schemes.

A man with an evil eye hastens after wealth, and does not know that want will come upon him (Prov. 28:22).

But those who want to get rich fall into temptation and a snare and many foolish and harmful desires which plunge men into ruin and destruction (1 Tim. 6:9).

Build security slowly. Putting a little aside weekly, following a hard week's work, is your best strategy. "Wealth obtained by fraud dwindles, but the one who gathers by labor increases it" (Prov. 13:11).

The best advice is to always seek counsel from someone who has invested wisely. "Prepare plans by consultation, and make war by wise guidance" (Prov. 20:18). Seek out several men who are not prejudiced and who are experienced in investing. Older, more mature men often have more wisdom. Don't be afraid to ask questions. Find someone who will take the time to listen and help you model a plan.

Be very cautious about borrowing against projected future income to make investments or to cover expenditures in the present.

Come now, you who say, "Today or tomorrow, we shall go to such and such a city, and spend a year there and engage in business and make a profit." Yet you do not know what your life will be like tomorrow. You are just a vapor that appears for a little while and then vanishes away. Instead, you ought to say, "If the Lord wills, we shall live and also do this or that." But as it is, you boast in your arrogance; all such boasting is evil. Therefore, to one who knows the right thing to do, and does not do it, to him it is sin (James 4:13–17).

Debt has literally killed many marriages and may even ruin our country. Debt is "normal" and accepted today. Be different; do it right the first time!

Spending

Most financial problems occur in the spending area. Paul exhorts the Romans to "owe nothing to anyone except to love one another." Although he was not speaking directly of finances, the application is valid. Establish a set of standards to govern your purchases. If you don't do this, you will have struggles in your marriage. Often two people come together in marriage with totally different ways of looking at spending.

The following chart is an example of the type of questions you might ask yourself to determine if your expenditures are in line with God's perspective. You may want to study this together.

Question	Scripture
1. Is my spending motivated by the love of things?	1 Timothy 6:9 1 John 2:15
2. Has God already led me to meet a need with this money?	2 Corinthians 8:14 Proverbs 3:9,10
3. Do I have a doubt about it?	Romans 14:23
4. Have I given God an opportunity to supply it?	Psalms 37:5 Proverbs 10:3
5. Will it be disadvantageous for my spiritual growth?	1 Corinthians 6:12 Hebrews 12:1

6. Is it a good invest-   Proverbs 20:14
   ment?

7. Does it put me in debt?   Proverbs 22:7

8. Will it be meaningful   1 Timothy 5:8
   to my family?   1 Timothy 3:4

Each of these factors should be balanced against all others in making a decision. Wise counsel from another person helps. A couple who keeps tight control over their purchases should have little trouble keeping God's perspective.

BUDGET

Any family that desires to get control of their finances should set up a monthly budget. A budget is simply a projection of future income and expenses. A simple budget really does not take much time, but over a period of five to six months it can help a couple get on top of their finances. It is not important that the budget be absolutely accurate at first, but it should be reviewed and adjusted faithfully each month. The couple can then evaluate together any problem areas, find solutions, and adjust their financial plans. Several good financial management books are usually available in any public library. Consult one of these for more specifics on budgeting.

It is very important to compare your actual expenses each month with your budget. Then you can see exactly what you are spending, and where you tend to spend too much. Budgets are only of real value as you continuously review and update them. Couples who plan usually tend to "make do," and their money goes further.

SPIRITUAL ISSUES

A couple are never more aware of their lack of oneness than when they are dealing with finances. Both will have different ways of handling money.

Attitudes carry over into marriage, so you and your future spouse must discuss how the two of you are going to approach the issues of finances and the problems that are encountered. You must agree on priorities for purchasing and agree on financial values. To apply the faith commitments of Genesis 1 and 2 to finances is absolutely essential. Then you must agree upon the transfer to the Lord of all things owned. Much conflict can result where there is not mutual commitment and action.

INDIVIDUAL RESPONSIBILITIES

Men have primary responsibility financially. God has instructed the man to provide for his family, and He has never changed that mandate. Men are to provide the income, control the expenditures, pay the bills, initiate giving, and save for a rainy day. That does not mean they are smarter, more gifted, or even more successful at these things, but they are primarily responsible.

Women need to recognize their husband's authority to take responsibility for the finances. Authority in this case means he has the freedom to fail. Wives, when your husband fails, don't take over and pick up the pieces. Even if creditors give him a bad credit rating or repossess the car, just keep referring his creditors to him. If you don't get involved, but continue to love him, he *will* ultimately come to such conviction and scorn from other men that he will change. If you come to his rescue and do it for him, he will let you, and you will end up carrying the financial weight and resenting him. Instead of his respecting you for your help, he too will feel guilty and resent you for it.

As long as men take the responsibility financially and emotionally, and feel secure in that, the wife can do the book work. But if the man begins to hedge on his responsibility or if the wife is struggling, she should give the book back to him.

The husband, on the other hand, should take responsibility for the wife's needs as well as her advice. He should always seek her input, and include her in financial decisions. He might also consider setting up an operating account for her so her freedom and responsibilities increase.

Both the husband and wife should maintain a spirit of joy, freedom, and creativity in the household. Some people become extremely creative when they are low on money. They have joy in giving and yet have a tight budget. Refinishing furniture, crafts, garage sales, and do-it-yourself is the name of the game, as well as being keys to making a problem become a blessing.

14

Loving Those In-Laws!

Although all of us have heard the standard jokes concerning in-laws, this is a "joke" a lot of couples must deal with in reality. I'm not sure that couples fully realize the potential stress and anxiety that can come from problems with parents or in-laws. I have known couples that have been hurt a great deal in life because they were unprepared for potential in-law problems. To be forewarned is to be forearmed!

About the time invitations are being sent, wedding showers begin, and planning for details of the ceremony are all underway, the couple begin to realize that opinions are surfacing and feelings are being stepped on. By the time the week of the wedding arrives, simple parent-child relationships have turned into complex anxiety struggles. The bride is crying, "Oh, why can't Mom understand?" and the groom is asking, "What did I do that upset them so much?" Caught off guard, the couple has unintentionally become a party to a conflict that cuts deeply into the emotional needs of both the couple and their parents.

The toughest thing about preparing for a solid in-law relationship is that usually you don't get a practice run! Your initial introduction to them is tremendously personal and power-packed. The future of their son or daughter is at stake. Only after having children of my own have I started to understand this pressure. Even though my oldest daughter is only eight, I can already imagine how suspect and observant I will be that day in the future when some "hot-dog" tells me he deserves my little girl! I believe parents really want to be closely related to their future sons- or daughters-in-law, but the initial introduction can be emotionally hard on them.

Often, these initial introductions take place while planning the wedding. Many couples have known each other a long time and have lived in the same hometown; but in our transient society it is just as common for a person to bring his or her future mate home just months prior to the wedding. To force two different families, often complete strangers to each other, to come together amiably is not the most natural environment for the development of healthy relationships.

I can still remember my initial introduction to Sally's parents. Because we were older and working for the same organization a considerable distance from her home, I didn't meet her family until one week before the wedding. (As I tell this story, remember that Mom and Pop Hill are extremely likeable people. The slight problems encountered were not related to the people but to the awkward situation.)

When I arrived in Boulder, Colorado, it was about two in the afternoon. I had stopped earlier to clean up and put a suit on before going to meet Sally's family. They lived in the mountains above Boulder, so I decided to drop in on Sally's dad at work and have him direct me to their house. Pop was a well-known auto mechanic in Boulder, and I had gotten careful directions to his shop. When I entered, the supervisor told me Pop Hill was working under a car, several cars down the line.

I was spotlessly dressed, overly aggressive, and somewhat nervous. I walked up to the car and said to his feet, which were sticking out beneath, "Mr. Hill, I am Don Meredith." Stunned, Mr. Hill got about halfway out from under the car before I grabbed his greasy hand and said, "Hello!" He was embarrassed about the grease, and we both felt rather awkward. He gave me directions to their house and I left with my clean suit and greasy hand.

That night the pressure mounted quickly. All my life I've been a very modest person. I quickly discovered that the house they lived in at the time had only one bathroom, and you had to go through her parents' bedroom to get there! After going to bed, my worst fears came true. I had to use the bathroom! I waited as long as I could, and then walked on through their bedroom to the john. I turned the water on in the basin and it sounded like Niagara Falls. I was so embarrassed, I almost died!

I felt emotional pressure from that point forward. The first verbal problems surfaced later in the week— over the phone expenses. Sally and I had made some long-distance calls the month before that were necessary to make our wedding plans. However, we didn't communicate to the Hills our intention of paying for the calls. All the calls were long—full of questions, congratulations, and general catch-up—and they were all expensive. Finally, Sally mentioned to me her parents' concern over all the calls we were making. This was perfectly understandable, but in light of the tension of the atmosphere I reacted strongly against Sally. I took pride in my financial responsibility and felt my integrity was being questioned.

These problems sound so foolish as I retell them, but at the time they were very serious. Four people, who under normal circumstances would have hit it off perfectly, started out on a slightly wrong foot. Since then, things have smoothed out remarkably and, by God's grace, our in-law problems have been very minor. Our family greatly enjoys our times at Sally's parents' home, and we all look forward to our visits.

But many couples start off wrong and are then burdened with poor in-law relationships for years. God makes some clear statements about in-laws and I would like to add some practical suggestions for developing successful in-law relationships.

Let me repeat Genesis 2:24. God communicates the vital importance a strong faith commitment plays in a successful marriage. Even though Adam and Eve did not have parents, God makes a statement that reveals the role future parents will play in the lives of their children. "For this cause a man shall leave his father and his mother, and shall cleave to his wife; and they shall become one flesh."

God makes it clear that children are to leave their parents when they marry. The Hebrew word used here for "leave" means to "abandon" or break off completely. God is saying that before a significant new relationship can begin, the old child-parent relationship must cease. By this, God means that in issues of authority the parents no longer have responsibility; He does not mean that the parental relationship should end altogether.

Is God against parents? Absolutely not! But without

the strong command for men and women to put their full trust in their mates, no marriage would ever experience real success. Total mate satisfaction and respect cannot occur if there is any question concerning where allegiance lies.

God knew that after twenty or so years of responding to parental authority, there would be a tendency to continue even after marriage. Therefore, God clearly requires the formal termination of parental authority and the firm commitment to the new marriage.

While the authority of the parents ends with the creation of the new authority, the couple's responsibility to honor their parents continues. Deuteronomy 5:16 tells us that the duty of a child is to honor his parents. This word "honor" speaks primarily of "valuing at a high price; deep respect or reverential awe." In marriage, parental experience and advice is very important, but decisions are made by the couple independent of parental control.

FOUR CRUCIAL CORDS TO CUT

I have discovered in counseling with couples that there are four ways they fail to leave their parents. These examples of failure to leave can be so subtle that the couple may feel frustration without even understanding why.

Parental wealth and social benefits

This is a conscious or subconscious hope of future inheritance or dependence on present financial and social benefits to the point that the couple fails to acknowledge their own financial or social independence. A husband may allow his mother to criticize his wife so that his relationship with his parents will not be endangered. Other couples tend to spend too much time at the home of parents because of social or financial advantages, even to the point that it hinders development of the new relationship, or to the point that they become dissatisfied with the financial situation at their own home.

Parental model

Some couples, again consciously or subconsciously, compare some area of their mate's performance with that of their parents. This comparison can ultimately cause dissatisfaction. I have seen men become completely disillusioned with their wives over not developing a particular housekeeping habit their mothers may have had. On the other hand, I have seen women lose respect for their husbands because they did not project the same financial stability as their fathers. Any continued dependence on parents can destroy marital commitment.

Parental approval

Usually as a result of an extremely strong or domineering parent, some mates are so dependent upon the need to feel approval from their parents that this need discourages the new relationship. Women have told me that they love their husbands, yet I soon learn that they perform to please their mothers because they need that approval. These women are frustrated in the same way if their mothers disapprove of their husbands. They clean house the way Mother would want, discipline the children with Mother in mind, all the while hoping for her recognition or approval.

One woman told me that every time she and her husband had bought a house, her mother's approval would be on her mind. Therefore, she wasn't really free to make a decision with just her husband's and her family's needs in view. A woman's need for approval in this way can jeopardize a man's sense of authority. Men who work for or with their fathers can do the same thing. A man's misdirected dependence can affect a woman's sense of self-worth.

Parental relationship substitute

Nothing deflates a person more than for a mate to continue conscious or subconscious emotional dependence upon parents, especially when their own emotional needs go unmet as a result. I have counseled men and women who will call or go see their parents about most key issues in their lives. They will give affection, receive most of their security, share their criticism, and even express most of their creative personality to their parents. All of this not only excludes their mates, but terribly hurts them.

SUGGESTED SOLUTIONS

To fail to leave your parents hurts *them* in the long run as well as your mate and yourself. Agree together on a mutual plan to communicate, recognize, and deal with any failure to leave the authority of your parents. Consider the following suggestions.

First of all, parents are not the enemy! Parents just do what comes naturally. Never explode or punish your parents for loving you, even if their method is wrong. Both mates have an innate need to be at peace with their parents, so do not be in conflict with them.

Instead, when frustrations occur, analyze the situation with your mate and agree together about the cause. Evaluate *everyone's* real need, what went wrong, and most importantly, look for a creative solution. If either mate has wronged a parent, ask forgiveness. If a decision is needed to protect the integrity of the marriage, make it together. Then look for a creative way to communicate this to the parents.

Second, commit together to never share any intimate needs or decisions with either set of parents without your mate's permission. A husband may be dreaming of a new car, and the wife simply mentions it to her dad. The father then voices his disapproval to her husband, and the husband feels betrayed. A couple must build their lives together, and everything should be intimate unless agreed otherwise.

Third, never be critical or allow critical statements about your mate to be made to or by your parents. The cruelest thing a person can do to their parents, as well as to their mate, is share something critical about their mate. Why? Because parents never forget or never allow that person to change in their minds.

I know of a situation where a wife shared a financial irresponsibility on the part of her mate in the first year of their marriage, and her parents are still bringing it up after twenty years. Parents don't have the opportunity to see your mate change and improve as you do. They only have your comments to go on. Never be critical of your mate to your parents.

Do yourself and your parents another favor. The next time they make a critical statement about your mate, respond with a strong but loving rebuff. I know of one man whose mother was just leading up to a critical remark about his wife. He interrupted with, "Mom, I love you a lot, but please don't be critical of Joan. I want you to know she is God's gift to me, and I don't want to hear those criticisms."

His mother hastily replied, "Don't be silly; I wasn't going to be critical of her."

The wise son responded with, "Forgive me, Mom. I just so want you and Joan to be friends, because I love you both so much." He was strong but kind to his mother.

Obviously, a strong blockage to critical statements must be followed with a sensitive ear. If this man wouldn't allow critical statements from his mother, he certainly owed it to her to get her opinion. This particular mother was about to make an observation about Joan's discipline of the children. So he sent his wife the next day to ask his mother's opinion about discipline. Everyone's opinion was expressed without threat or hurt.

Fourth, before visiting parents, especially in the early years of marriage, be in agreement about the length of time you stay. Don't plan long days of forced communication.

If at all possible, allow your wife to go home to her folks a few days earlier than you so she can give her parents the attention they need before you arrive. Men, occasionally go home to see your parents alone. If you live close to either parent, this will not be a problem. Sometimes parents need special times with their children after the children are married. Most importantly, when visiting as a couple, let the son- or daughter-in-law in the situation have the freedom to just love your parents.

As an example, you might want to go somewhere

with your wife while at her home. She is the one who is naturally accepted in her home, so take her aside and tell her of your need. You are free to go back and visit while she, at the appropriate time, announces the need to go, and she takes total responsibility for the decision. You are free from the possibility of hurting her parents, and they better understand and accept the decision.

Fifth, the husband should work out a definite plan for receiving any money offered by parents, and then communicate the plan to both sets of parents. If a man will communicate with the wife's father the first time he attempts to give them a gift, the father will always respect his son-in-law. Although I discourage parental loans in almost every situation, I do believe parents should have the freedom to give gifts to their children. However, a husband needs to set controls that will insure his authority as well as the parents' respect.

Sixth, be creative toward your parents. Ask your mother-in-law and father-in-law what they would prefer that you call them. Let them know you will be glad to call them Mom and Dad if they prefer.

Another thing that demonstrates care would be dropping your parents-in-law an occasional card thanking them for their role in your mate's life or for allowing you to visit. Courtesy with parents not only brings joy to them and to you, but increases the possibility of an exciting grandparent-child relationship in the future.

A WORD TO PARENTS AND PARENTS-IN-LAW

Regarding her married children, one mother said, "Lord, give me the wisdom to bite my tongue." My hope for you as parents is to be able to so trust the Lord in your children's lives that you *let* them make some "mistakes" (by your standards). Parents tend to want to give advice on how they would run things, how they would spend money, how they would raise kids, and so on. This causes guilt on the part of your children if they don't do what they know you expect them to do.

Realize that *times* have changed, not scriptural values. Your children may live in nicer housing at their age than you did at the same age. Your children may leave their children with a baby-sitter far more often than you did. Don't get into the habit of being critical of things they do or have. Criticism will eat at you like a cancer and destroy any joy you could be having watching your children grow to maturity.

It would be wise to say to your children, "Listen to what I say, and then do as you please." This assures you of always having the freedom to offer advice and suggestions based on your experience, yet it assures your children that they can make their own decisions. This leaves the door of communication open for all of you. Allow them to then do as they please without further unsolicited advice or an "I-told-you-so" attitude.

15

God's Testing Times

*E*arlier I mentioned unexpected trials and sufferings as a major cause of marriage failure. Because many of the trials encountered in marriage are universal, you would do well to prepare for a positive response to those that can be anticipated. Normally, the thought of trials is not a very popular subject.

As a new Christian, I remember when I first began to understand the biblical importance of trials. My immediate assumption was that the successful Christian was the one who missed the most trials, possibly because of his "spiritual maturity." Years of study, counseling, and personal times of testing have changed my perspective.

A biblical key to deeper understanding of trials is in 1 Peter 2:21: "For you have been *called* for this purpose, since Christ also suffered for you, leaving you an example for you to follow in His steps" (italics mine). I had never imagined that it had actually been part of God's plan for me to experience trials. The more I thought about it, the more it made sense. If I had been called to salvation by Jesus Christ and given His inheritance, it only made sense that I would be called to share in His suffering too.

I have begun to see that without trials I probably would not depend on the Lord. My humanity is bent on lustful desires and self-centeredness. God, in His grace, is committed to teaching us dependence. Dependence on God brings humility, with the result of being "other-oriented" as opposed to "self-centered." Trials, while sometimes momentarily tough, are redemptive in my life. Many times the only anchor I have is the reality of Christ and His Word.

The Book of James gives a clear statement of God's purpose for trials.

> Consider it all joy, my brethren, when you encounter various trials, knowing that the testing of your faith produces endurance. And let endurance have its perfect result, that you may be perfect and complete, lacking in nothing (James 1:2-4).

He says *when*, not *if* we encounter trials. Suffering is inevitable. The word "various" means diversified, trials of all kinds. James is telling us that we *will* have trials and that we *should* count them a joy. That's a different perspective than our human nature has. God says trials will produce endurance and perseverance in us.

In a world that is falling apart emotionally and where unfulfilled marriages are robbing people of their best hope in relationships, endurance is no small blessing. God promises that the result of endurance will be that we may be "perfect, complete, lacking in nothing." Trials not only promise endurance but maturity. The phrase "lacking in nothing" means equipped with every resource. Endurance, complete maturity, and being equipped with every resource—that's quite a promise!

To keep a joyful spirit when either you or your mate is experiencing a trial is not a natural human response, but a faith-oriented response. Christ suffered because He knew that if He went to the cross, you and I would someday be with Him in eternity. ". . . for the joy set before Him [He] endured the cross, despising the shame . . ." (Heb. 12:2). Will you join Jesus in experiencing a blessing? James adds in verse 12 the following:

> Blessed is a man who perseveres under trial: for once he has been approved, he will receive the crown of life, which the Lord has promised to those who love Him.

The word "blessed" means "the very highest experience." The man who perseveres will be approved by God and will receive a blessedness. "Approved" was the word stamped on cookware after it came out of the fire with no cracks. The same is true of us. After being tested, each person is promised a stamp of approval.

With a thought of joy and expectation, let's look at some possible trials most of us suffer in marriage. We must not be caught off guard by trials when they come. When we are shocked by trials we have a tendency to blame others; many couples go through trials and blame their mates for what God is allowing to happen in their lives.

THORN IN THE FLESH

I have found that almost every person has one or two areas in his or her life that are just plain tough. Paul mentions one such problem in 2 Corinthians. In order to limit his pride, God gave him a thorn in the flesh to keep him from exalting himself.

We cannot be sure what Paul's problem was, but he clearly calls it a weakness.

> Concerning this I entreated the Lord three times that it might depart from me. And He has said to me, "My grace is sufficient for you, for power is perfected in weakness." Most gladly, therefore, I will rather boast about my weaknesses, that the power of Christ may dwell in me. Therefore, I am well content with weaknesses, with insults, with distresses, with persecutions, with difficulties, for Christ's sake; for when I am weak, then I am strong (2 Cor. 12:8–10).

I am convinced from working with people that many of us, if not all of us—and our mates—have a similar burden to bear. Unfortunately, our acceptance of our thorns or our mate's thorns is probably not as positive as Paul's. You can prepare yourself for the possibility that your mate will have at least one area that will probably never change and you will have to view it as Paul did his thorn.

For some people it might be stubbornness or a weight problem, or temper, or sloppiness. I have seen some great men with pride problems and some with insecurities. I know in my own life that my insecurity about public speaking is definitely a thorn in my flesh. I am convinced that it is there for my good and that it will become a source of strength in my life. This is an area I have fought with God about; it has caused my family some trauma, and me some heartache, yet it is still there.

In working through *my thorn*, I have been able to

recognize *other people's thorns.* I know there are millions of marriages where mates are paralyzed because of some unchangeable weakness in themselves or their mates that has robbed them of all hope and joy in their marriages.

If you or your mate has a problem that seems impossible to work with, approach it as Paul did. If it never changes, then thank God for it and ask Him to use it in your life to develop endurance, patience, and maturity.

JOBS

We each have a need to work hard and feel productive and appreciated. As career men and women move through life, they go through many cycles in their working relationships. There are a number of factors that affect a person's happiness in work, such as knowing he or she is in the right job and in the right place, being excited about going to work, enjoying the work, and being proud of the job done.

Men and women (including wives and mothers) need to prepare for some real trials in their work. You can be happy one day and dissatisfied the next. Wives need to trust and support their husbands during periods of dissatisfaction, which can last for extended lengths of time. Husbands, likewise, need to understand and encourage their wives who work either in the home or in an outside job. Job frustration is a normal and regular problem in life.

It would help a man to become accountable to several older men—preferably in his church—to help him evaluate and keep perspective during trials. Husbands and older, mature Christian women can provide this authority and support for wives.

FINANCES

We have already dealt with financial trials, so we will not cover them again here. But let's not forget that desire for things, financial disappointments, or inability to provide the basics for the children's schooling can bring on real trials and testing. Keeping a faith perspective in these trials is a must for happiness.

CHILDREN

Children, while a major blessing in life, are also a source of major trials along the way. Men, if you stand by your wife in these trials you will make these times much easier and a greater blessing for the family. A woman's major mission field is often her children. She has a tendency to evaluate her worth in life in terms of her children's success. It is not a surprise, then, that God would use children to teach women dependence. If the husband shares this responsibility properly, the wife will feel less stress.

The initial trial concerning children can develop during the first pregnancy. Stress can also come if a woman cannot conceive. If sickness occurs during pregnancy, an understanding and patient husband will help with meals and the housework. As her body begins to change, compliment her on her new beauty and your appreciation of her faithfulness.

There are many momentary trials with babies such as sickness, sleeping problems, and scheduling. The husband must be able to help the wife during these times, and not allow her to take full responsibility. The husband needs to be aware of how to help through sleepless nights and hectic times of the day (usually the supper hour). When your wife's schedule is hectic, give her a part of a day away from the house and children. This will help her mental attitude greatly.

When children reach school age, parents begin to observe potential emotional, intellectual, and spiritual needs. Anticipate these trials and support one another.

The process of disciplining children is a continual trial, especially for mothers. A mother who lives with her children twenty-four hours a day can lose perspective and end up in power struggles with the children. I have found that a husband can literally save his wife's spiritual life by taking responsibility for discipline. If I take a three-day period every two months to run a discipline check and fine-tune my children, I can tremendously support Sally. The children respond beautifully to a father who is in authority. It also relieves the mother's mounting tension.

RELATIONSHIPS

Couples who do not prepare and anticipate pain or trials in relationships are opening themselves to bitterness and wounded spirits. If you anticipate trials in relationships, you will not only reduce the hurt, but you will limit the bitterness, protect yourself from striking back, and allow yourself to return a blessing.

Prepare for trials in working relationships. Realize that people will fail to appreciate you, use you for selfish purposes, blame you for failure, question your abilities, even cut you out of future plans. These typical hurts all cause bitterness. Husbands and wives, gear up for these occasional shocks. Protect one another! Losing a job or missing a promotion is a small thing for the Lord to overcome. Remember—long-term bitterness is faith's enemy. I meet people regularly whose lives are distorted because they see a particular person as their enemy. Draw one another's hope back to the Lord and His Word at these times.

Church relationships, close friends, family, and neighbors are sources of potential trials. Apply aggressively the law of love, but expect occasional hurts. When it happens, I hope a red flag goes up in your mind, and you pull together as a couple. Above all, don't be critical of others.

MOVING

You might be surprised by this one, but it is big! America is such a mobile society that almost everyone moves many times in life—yet few things affect the emotional security of a family more. The selling of your home and the buying of another one, followed by the move, is only the beginning. Many things are changed: relationships, authority, organizational ties, friends, and security. New frontiers must be forged, new relationships built, a new job begun, and a new church home established. Probably the most difficult part of the move is the fact that even as you make new friends, it usually takes a long time to really develop comfortable relationships with them.

Almost everyone moves; you cannot stop that. But you can as a couple agree to support one another in the move. First of all, make the decision together, including the whole family when possible. Then, work out a total plan that gives everyone hope. God doesn't often move people into a spiritual vacuum. Consider a vital church in your new location as primary.

Pray about everything. Before our move from Dallas

to Little Rock, we prayed for specific things: a house, a neighborhood with children, a church, and friends for Sally. God *specifically answered all* of these requests. With our other moves we had not prayed specifically and, for the most part, those moves caused much anguish. I am convinced that if we spend time on our knees, the trials won't seem nearly so insurmountable!

TIME

One of the biggest trials in married life is time availability: time for yourself, for romance, for the children, for ministry, for hobbies, or even just time to read a good book. I am convinced that Christians really desire to do what is right in their marriages, but they usually lose the battle in their schedules. You must *get tough with your priorities.* There is no other way. There are so many responsibilities and "good" things to do that only an unbending commitment in time priority will help.

Men, take responsibility here. A wife cannot do much without her husband's involvement. First, decide on your major priorities. Then list three things you need to accomplish in each area. After that, you will have to eliminate almost everything else.

Because of the importance of time control and schedule in relation to a man's priorities, I occasionally will ask two or three close brothers to sit down and go over my schedule. I like to bring Sally in to share her perspective. I try to schedule a meeting with them six weeks later to evaluate my accomplishments. If Sally and I make ourselves accountable like this and have other men agree with us on our busy schedule, then we know it is momentarily workable and our priorities are in order as the Lord would have them.

The better you are at anticipating trials and the more determined is your faith in facing them, the greater will be your manifested joy and spiritual maturity, for:

Beloved, do not be surprised at the fiery ordeal among you, which comes upon you for your testing, as though some strange thing were happening to you; but to the degree that you share the sufferings of Christ, keep on rejoicing; so that also at the revelation of His glory, you may rejoice with exultation. If you are reviled for the name of Christ, you are blessed, because the Spirit of glory and of God rests upon you. By no means let any of you suffer as a murderer, or thief, or evildoer, or troublesome meddler; but if anyone suffers as a Christian, let him not feel ashamed, but in that name let him glorify God (1 Pet. 4:12–16).

16

Winning, Losing, and Other Strange Games

*I*f you stop to think about it, we in America are naturally geared to think in terms of "winners" and "losers." Almost every issue is evaluated in terms of who won or who lost. It's true in business, in club elections, in sports—and in discussions. "If I am right, then you must be wrong." "I cannot afford for you to be right because emotionally I would feel that if you're right, it would make me a loser."

In this chapter, let me talk about winners and losers, and other practical matters. As silly as it sounds, this winner/loser syndrome really affects our marriages negatively. I work hard in the counseling room trying to convince couples to think in terms of "creative alternatives" instead of winners or losers. If a couple can trust the sovereignty of God in their relationship, then there never needs to be a winner or loser. If God makes a promise available and we take advantage of it by faith, He guarantees only winners in the long run, regardless of human weaknesses. Therefore, when a couple bumps up against a disagreement, a frustration, a weakness, or a problem of any kind, they simply search for a creative alternative rather than looking for someone to blame.

A couple came into my office recently and each mate took thirty minutes to list the areas in which his mate was a loser. The husband was a loser in spending time with her and the children, in being insensitive sexually, and in social involvement. The wife was a loser in keeping house, in responding sexually, and in disciplining the children. Each of them could have presented full-scale proof of their convictions. By the end of the hour, I was a loser, too, because I was depressed! I wanted to shake them and say, "Don't you see what you're doing to each other?"

In the weeks that followed, I was able to show them that they didn't need to fear one another; in fact, they began to see that they were each other's best potential assets. After re-establishing hope, we were able to review their opinions of one another, but this time we listened to understand why each was not performing well. With just a little discernment and creativity, we were able to develop a plan that synchronized their strengths and resulted in both being "winners."

With *creative alternatives* ringing in your minds, I would like to share with you some problem areas in marriage and demonstrate the possible creative alternatives to each. Review these regularly in your marriage. They are: (1) personality differences; (2) intellectual differences; (3) vocational struggles; (4) spiritual differences; (5) physical appearances; and (6) putting fun in your marriage.

PERSONALITY DIFFERENCES

Historically, dating relationships tend to bring out the positive side of people's personalities, while marriage naturally tends to bring out the true, unpolished character of a personality. Couples who are dating tend to put their best feet forward, and are more aggressive in establishing real friendship and trust. Also, each tends to communicate total acceptance and hope to the other, which allows their personalities to risk more openness.

After marriage, men and women sometimes react with intolerance to personality differences. Any form of criticism or rejection stifles acceptance and hope, and results in defensiveness. The natural relaxation in aggressiveness that settles in after marriage, along with the tendency to become critical, starts a slow progression toward problems.

A man in my office a few years ago characterized his wife as extremely introverted and antisocial. From his description of her I would have thought the woman could not think, feel, or even talk at times. The next hour his wife came into the office. I found she was not an outspoken woman, but she was pleasant and attractive. After a few minutes of slightly uncomfortable talk, we found a mutual interest in University of Arkansas football! Any woman that loves football cannot be all bad, and for the next fifteen minutes I had a vibrant conversation with a delightful person who could relate intelligently and sensitively. I thought to myself, "How could this man have gotten that view of this attractive woman?" As I began to ask questions, the answer came quickly.

The couple had met during their senior year in college, which just happened to have been the wife's peak of social involvement. In reality, she had always been a shy person. The husband, on the other hand, was a hyperactive perfectionist. After marriage, she had to adjust simultaneously to a high-pressure teaching job and to running a house for a perfectionist. Two years later, her first pregnancy drained her physically. She became emotionally depressed six months after the baby's birth, when her husband asked her to go back to work. With communication at a standstill because of feelings of rejection and failure, this wife's personality could not muster up the confidence to fight back. Happily, after just two months of counseling, God was able to reveal to them what had happened and they were able to virtually begin again.

You must keep alert for such personality differences in marriage. The key is not that one personality is better than another, but rather that *any* personality can be forced or driven toward problems. With proper understanding, most personalities can be challenging and exciting to live with.

In trying to understand your personality as well as that of your mate, consider the wide range of personality types. The following chart represents some discernible personality ranges.

GENERAL RANGE OF PERSONALITY TYPES

Aggressive	Fun-loving	Calm	Sensitive
Active	Outgoing	Cool	Introspective
Intense	Emotional	Assured	Quiet
Logical	Affectionate	Unemotional	Takes things personally

No matter where your personality fits into this chart, one is no better than another. Every personality, functioning properly, has strengths and weaknesses. For instance, an aggressive person usually has the important strength of being a self-starter but at the same time can have the devastating tendency of being critical. The quiet personality usually is more sensitive, yet may have a problem of being withdrawn.

Whatever personality you or your mate has, re-member it is simply a measure of social involvement, or how you encounter people. Personality is not a valid measure of such important things as intellect, feelings, love, commitment, attitude, ideas, or spiritual per-spective. When people start dating, they draw out the other person's attitude, beliefs, opinions, and intellect, no matter what the personality. After marriage, we often forget the person we married is not really con-trary, but rather a totally equipped human being, with a special personality different from our own.

Your view and reaction to your mate's personality will become a most determinative factor in its de-velopment—whether it is positive or negative. The most important issue, then, is to become creative, not critical, in drawing out the positive aspects of each one's personality.

Begin by believing that God knew your needs when He gave you your mate and that He will meet your total needs with that personality. Faith, again, is the foundation of creative action. Never be critical or apologetic, publicly or privately, about your mate's personality. I shudder when a wife says about her husband, "John is not upset; he's just quiet." The poor guy is standing there not knowing how to respond. He's been labeled by his wife so often that it would be hard for him to come out of his privateness if he wanted to. Instead, she might say, "John could com-ment on that; he's got such neat ideas." He would think, "Who, me? Why sure!"

Freely merge your personality with your mate's so that you can develop a public "couple" personality with both of your strengths. Do not treat your mate as a social outcast. Stick together at social events, arm in arm. Look for a natural opportunity in the conversation to involve your mate. If you know your wife is well-read on child discipline and the conversation moves toward children, you might say, "Joan was telling me an interesting story on discipline. What was that story you were telling me the other day?" Joan may never have entered the conversation by herself, but if you give her a lead she will usually be delighted to enter in and feel accepted.

After social events, talk about your evening and look for ways to help one another feel more at ease socially. Again, look for creative alternatives, not for winners and losers. Develop a strategy for your "couple" personality. Work together, allowing each other strong expression intellectually, socially, emotionally, and spiritually—regardless of personality.

INTELLECTUAL DIFFERENCES

Another area of potential problems is intellectual differences. During pre-marital days, a man was told his IQ was quite a bit higher than his future wife's. That stuck in his mind, and it subconsciously colored his evaluation of her. Years later he was telling me that she didn't read books and he couldn't have an intellectual discussion with her. This man was convinced he was "stuck" with an intellectual weakling! His attitude had affected his respect for her in every area.

He was deceived and didn't understand the difference between being intelligent and being a disciplined student; between knowledge and wisdom; between talking a good life and actually living one; between quickness of mind and faithfulness of mind. Almost every person has adequate intelligence—more than he or she will ever use—but each person has certain strengths and certain weaknesses in intelligence.

I mentioned earlier in the book that Sally and I had to make an adjustment in this area. I was a "Cliffnotes" man in college; she was a good student. On Sunday afternoons she would curl up in a chair and read a good book while I would watch football on TV. We were also different in how we *applied* what we knew. She had more knowledge, but applied it more slowly and sometimes less practically than I. We discovered that one was not better or worse, but we complemented each other.

We have since looked for creative alternatives in this area. God didn't make a mistake after all. In recent years, instead of rejecting each other because of the differences, we help each other. Sally will read a book for me, underline its key points, and explain its overall message to me. I then go back and read her underlinings. The value to me with our hectic schedules is unbelievable. This allows Sally an opportunity to minister to me, makes her a part of what I am doing, and also stimulates her intellect.

Don't be critical. Be grateful for your mate's intellectual pursuits and work your strengths together. Believe God and motivate your mate.

SPIRITUAL DIFFERENCES

A very subtle form of deception comes with how you view your mate's spiritual maturity. Your view of your mate in this area is vital to his or her growth, and a poor view of their spirituality can be the greatest growth retardant.

In all my years of counseling Christian marriages, one of the three or four areas I would classify as most touchy is one mate's dissatisfaction with the other mate's spiritual maturity. *If you make your mate feel like a loser in this area, then for him or her to aggressively pursue spiritual things would mean subconscious agreement with your evaluation!* The mate who judges gives the other reason to reject God.

You may think you're being "loving" in your evaluation, with spiritual-sounding rhetoric like, "I am accepting by faith today that tomorrow you will be better." That *really* sounds spiritual. I'm convinced that is exactly the kind of subtle statement Satan himself would make! It sounds good, but it is still saying to your mate, "You are less than adequate today."

God hates my sin, but He does not retract any commitment to me because of it. I am perfectly acceptable to Him today as Christ covers my sin. I am overwhelmed by God's graciousness in giving so much when I am so undeserving. I am stimulated to worship Him because of His gracious love, which He demonstrates in His acceptance of me through Christ. You don't have to like one another's sin, but God does expect you to trust Him with that sin, as with any other problem.

That kind of belief will allow you to be concerned with *motivating* your mate instead of *judging*, so that your partner will not experience rejection or feelings of dissatisfaction from you. If you are not yet married and are concerned about your future mate's spiritual maturity, *don't get married.* If you are married and are struggling with this problem, ask your mate's forgiveness and look for creative alternatives. Seek counsel if you are overwhelmed and don't know how to resolve this problem. For both husbands and wives it would be good to reread 1 Peter 2 and 3 on what motivates a person toward spiritual maturity.

VOCATIONAL STRUGGLES

A large portion of a person's life is spent working. In the very beginning, God told Adam and Eve to rule, reproduce, and reign. He told Adam to keep and cultivate the land. God added other commands concerning our attitudes toward work later in the New Testament. All such commands imply that God equipped men and women with a need to be productive.

Since the very beginning, happiness in life has been tied to success and productivity. How motivated a person is in his work affects his productivity. His pride in his work, and his mate's respect of it, affects his sense of value. The gifts or abilities of a person also affect his or her sense of value to other Christians. Being certain of being in God's will in your job is very important to self-confidence and happiness.

Men come into my office hurt because their wives are embarrassed at what they do vocationally. Other men leave jobs they like because a wife is not satisfied financially, or because a wife does not like the schedule or her husband's boss. And it's not always the wife— men evaluate themselves in the same ways. It's not unusual to meet a highly successful man who does not respect what he does and therefore is not happy.

And men, don't forget: in one sense, your wife's vocation is homemaking. The husband often does not understand or respect the overwhelming tasks of a housewife, so he is impatient with her. Men who will not help their wives, nor give them the opportunity to establish reinforcing, encouraging relationships outside the home contribute unknowingly to making her feel the home is a "lesser" place to be. Then she feels confined. Men who are critical of the housekeeping and the children's behavior, but won't help her with any of these "womanly" responsibilities, are hypocrites. No wonder women suffer self-image problems and seek outside employment to meet the needs the husband could have met if he had been sensitive. A woman needs the same support in her vocation as a wife and mother that the husband needs in his chosen field. Couples need a strong mutual commitment in two basic areas to support each other vocationally.

First, acknowledge that your mate's gifts or talents are from God. 1 Corinthians 12:11 says, "But one and the same Spirit works all these things, distributing [gifts] to each one individually just as He wills." In other words, the Spirit of God distributes each person's gifts. Whatever gifts you and your mate may have, accept them from the Lord and trust God to bless you through them.

Next, do not make the mistake of throwing the diamond out with the rocks. Over the years I have met people who seemed to be just raw material; they didn't develop or produce quickly. Then after a series of events—perhaps a spiritual reawakening or the faithfulness of a patient spouse—that person blossomed. Give your mate time to develop.

Years ago I had to release a man from my organization after several anguishing years of trying to utilize his talents successfully. I followed him for the next several years, and he continued to flounder. Eventually his wife had to seek counsel. About the third year after leaving me this man got involved in doing some fairly menial tasks with another organization. While doing his new work, he got excited as never before about an idea associated with his job. A new drive and attitude literally changed that man's life. He went back to school and began to write and teach on the subject. Now, he is nationally known in his field. His wife is elated, and grateful to God for giving her some much-needed patience.

To insure that you don't lose the diamond in yourself or in your mate, consider the following suggestions. Always at the top of the list is: Never allow criticism of your mate's abilities. Be creative with what you have. View your mate as your hope and part of yourself, and trust God with both your gifts. Join your gifts together and begin to think of them as "couple" gifts. A husband and wife who synchronize their gifts can accomplish unbelievable things.

Become an expert on what you and your mate do best, and emphasize it. Protect each other from placements that do not emphasize what you enjoy and do well. If your husband is most fulfilled by washing the car, don't reject him. Stick with him and who knows—you may end up managing a chain of car washes! And even if you are poor, you will be married to a happy man.

Men, if your wife does something well, do everything you can to bring her joy by letting her pursue it. Be an expert on what she does well. Encourage her by allowing her time to develop her talents.

PHYSICAL APPEARANCES

In a world that places so much emphasis on physical appearance, it is impossible to ignore its role. Some couples tend to be imbalanced in the direction of spending large sums of money on clothes and cosmetics. Diets and physical fitness are emphasized to the point that all life revolves around these activities.

Other couples can be just as imbalanced in the opposite direction, and allow their physical appearance to become sloppy.

If there is a proper commitment between two people in marriage, one particular body shape should be no more satisfying than another. However, three issues are very important about a person physically: they should be *neat, clean,* and *reasonably trim.* Whatever the shape of your body, remember, your mate chose you like you were. If there is a weight problem, however, set some long-term realistic goals.

Get involved in a positive way in helping each other buy clothes. If your husband wears white socks with dark clothes, get him some dark socks. If your wife wears her underclothes until they have holes in them, buy her some new ones. A husband can really help a wife please him in her dress if he goes with her to buy clothes. I try to shop with Sally so she will know what pleases me. A wife can do the same with her husband.

MARRIAGE FUN

You would think that nothing need be said about having fun in marriage, but unfortunately it does. Many Christian couples are so intense in their sobriety that they miss the enjoyment of having fun.

Let me tell you a story that unfolded several years ago. A couple came for counsel, and before they sat down the wife started crying. She said, "Don, I don't want you to think I don't love David, because I do. But this year of marriage has just been terrible for me."

After her last year in college, where she had a delightful time, this young woman had married. They moved to another city and attended seminary. Her husband had picked out an apartment the previous spring, without her seeing it. It was old, and furnished with even older furniture. The curtains were supposed to be white but were so old they were off-white. In addition, the apartment was filled with insects and was located in a less desirable part of town. This was a far cry from the year before. She landed a teaching job that began before she was able to finish cleaning the apartment. This was her first full-time job and resulted in multiple pressures and time commitments. All of these adjustments overwhelmed her positive expectations of marriage, and brought great frustration.

Let me pass on to you some of the suggestions I gave to this couple. First, become an expert on what your mate enjoys. That sounds easier than it is. I make a habit of asking people what their mates really like to do. It is amazing how few married people really know what their partner honestly thinks is fun. So work to find out.

When you do, don't judge. It may be something like watching TV. I have seen people decide that their mate's fun was not spiritual or intellectual so they refused to participate. The result is that they belittle their mate. Look—don't you try to put the Holy Spirit out of a job! You be concerned instead with having some fun in your marriage.

Also try to have fun doing *necessary* things—don't let them become drudgery. Clean the kitchen together while you let the kids watch an acceptable TV show. Work on the lawn together. Weed the flower beds together. Wash the car, eat by candlelight, walk around the block and discuss the day's activities. Set aside some time for organizing the pictures, slides, a movie . . . and reminisce at the same time.

All this adds up to doing the "have to's" together—

and enjoying one another. If your wife works, especially help her with cleaning and other duties so she can share her world with you.

Develop hobbies. If your wife paints, has musical talent, is a writer, or whatever, encourage her to continue.

Set some family goals that you can both work toward. Sally and I worked on a plan to see the entire country in the first ten years of marriage so we could take the children to see it again in the next ten.

Work on your relationships with others. Even though you might not feel a need initially, relationships with others are vital to having fun. Doing certain activities with others is a lot more fun than doing them alone as a couple, and such involvement also encourages sharing of oneself. Invite people over, have picnics, potlucks, go to the beach, have an evening of parlor games, take a vacation with another family.

Some romantic ideas for the two of you would be to go out to lunch together or to breakfast without the children. The husband can pick up the baby-sitter and occasionally surprise his wife with a pre-planned night out. Wives, return the blessing by planning your own surprises. How about a twenty-four-hour campout or a drive in the woods? Have fun learning once again to be romantic with each other. Never stop dating. Ask the Holy Spirit to give you creative and fresh ideas for fun ways of spending time together.

17

So You Want To Get Married

Some of you reading this book have not yet decided to get married. You probably want to ask, "How can I be sure I should get married?" This is one of the most important decisions of your lifetime.

I have found over the years that each couple is a little different. Premarital counseling is helpful. Yet, there are three basic areas for consideration that I feel are universally important. First, is the couple mature enough to handle marriage? Second, how clearly do they both understand the biblical concepts of marriage? Third, are they willing to work through a strategy for addressing practical areas of life together? Let's look at each of these areas to get a better perspective on their meaning.

SPIRITUAL MATURITY

Recently a couple asked me if I could ever be sure in advance that a marriage would be successful. I told them there is only one reliable way of anticipating the outcome of a future marriage, and that is to look at the individual track records of the two people involved and see how they have responded to tough situations they have encountered in the past.

Obviously, the longer the track record, the more evidence there will be of success or failure. Experience and ability to adjust to major issues in life come only with time and knowledge. Nearly every person performs well at *some* level of pressure, but we all differ as to the levels at which we perform less effectively as pressures rise. Therefore, the performance of a man who has finished school before he marries is more measureable as to how he responds under pressure than the freshman in college. And the man who has graduated from college and worked for three years is even more measurable and predictable in regard to response under pressure. The woman who has been a Christian for five years is much more measurable than the woman who has been a Christian for three months. Even more measurable is the woman who has been a Christian fifteen years, and has gone through some tough testing periods. This woman is much more predictable as a partner.

A single person who has a history of being faithful in tough situations can be expected to continue to apply faith in tough marriage situations. An untested person with an unmeasured track record is almost a total gamble, a shot in the dark as a successful marriage partner. That's a strong statement, but it's true!

Therefore, how can a couple considering marriage evaluate their own maturity and that of their mate before deciding to get married? The famous passage called the Beatitudes contains the best statement of spiritual maturity ever set forth. And it is Christ Himself who describes these marks of maturity in Matthew 5:1–16.*

The passage develops eight specific points of spiritual maturity and success in living life. Jesus describes a person who is "blessed," which means that they experience the very highest in life. The word was used during the time of Christ to refer to a "blessed isle" of joy, and was used to mean "being set apart as an island in a sea of turmoil." Jesus says that the person who has these qualities is one who will be able to experience joy and fulfillment in life despite continued trials. The ultimate in human joy, then, stems from our fulfillment in Jesus Christ.

1. Poor in spirit

Christ says that the successful and mature person is one who is poor in spirit. The literal meaning is, "having no power at all." Here is a person who sees himself as he really is apart from God. He is not hopeless in his weakness because he turns to God. This person knows it is better to seek the Lord than to gain the world. This person is not prideful or inflated in his self-evaluation. Therefore, in marriage, this person will most likely be accepting of another's weaknesses, because he knows his power must come from God.

2. Those who mourn

Christ here is referring to a person who so hates to sin or to hurt someone else that when he does sin his sorrow visibly pierces his heart. This person is so compassionate that he does not hold a grudge. Here is a

*I would like to acknowledge Tim Timmons for initially giving me these thoughts.

person who confesses his mistakes and is broken about his sin and the sin of others. This person will say, "I'm wrong. Please forgive me."

This type of maturity is extremely important in marriage. Be honest about any bitterness, grudges, or inability to forgive. No matter how good the reason, grudges are deathly because they are contagious.

3. *Gentle*

Jesus communicated a strong and aggressive obedience to pursue truth without making a lot of noise about it. A mature person diligently seeks God's truth as it applies to any life situation. Here is a person who does not get depressed or pout when stress is encountered but seeks God's solution to that problem. In marriage, he does not condemn his mate but instead looks for solutions.

Are you or your potential mate a pessimistic or negative person? Do you fight about solutions to problems? Is there evidence of prolonged periods of depression or inactivity? Even small tendencies in these directions prior to marriage can become monumental leanings in marriage.

4. *Hunger and thirst after righteousness*

Jesus Christ is talking here about a person with a starving soul and a passionate desire to seek after God. This person cannot stand to be out of fellowship with God. He will actively correct any problem in a relationship. In marriage, this factor is an indispensable part of a happy relationship.

Do you and your mate-to-be really have a track record of seeking after God? Are you both characterized by wanting to be in fellowship with God and others? After marriage, this may be the difference between insult or blessing.

(It is interesting to note that the last four Beatitudes have a cause and effect relationship with the first four. For example, the person who has a right evaluation of himself (poor in spirit) will tend to be merciful toward others. Evaluate the implication of this cause and effect relationship on marriage.)

5. *Merciful*

A study of this word reveals that it is best characterized by "outgoing kindness." Kindness that acts. A mate in marriage that is merciful will be compassionate. Nothing is more important at times than a compassionate mate. Look for evidence of compassion on the part of your future mate toward others. How does he or she approach the failure or unfortunate situation of others.

6. *Pure in Heart*

This is a person who truly sees God, which results in significant loyalty to both God and man. Here is a person who is free from guilt. This loyalty to God carries over to his or her mate. Again, because of this person's transparency before God, he or she is open about personal failure and more free to love others. Observe your future mate's openness with others, especially with those in authority. Look for signs of honesty and pure motives.

7. *Peacemaker*

The person mentioned here causes peace among others because of his security and peace with himself,

God, and others. This peace again results from having God's perspective. One of the greatest attributes a person can bring to marriage is that of being a peacemaker. Peacemakers solve problems with truth and love. To determine if your future mate has this quality, look for signs that people seek him or her out for counsel and encouragement. Negatively, look for signs of sowing discord in relationships and groups.

8. Persecuted

This is a person who puts the opinion of God above the opinion of others. A strong identity in Christ is involved. Here is a mate who is recognized publicly as being truly Christian. How a person spends free time tells a lot about his or her characteristics. Do they play at Christianity as if it were a Sunday hobby, or is it daily, personal, and a part of every circumstance?

Jesus goes on to say that people who possess these characteristics are the salt and light of the earth. Remember that in marriage we are to reflect God's image. Only a mature person can do that.

Who do you and your prospective mate reflect—the god of this world or the God of creation? There are no shortcuts to these dimensions in your life. If they are not already present, wait! Do not deceive yourself about the presence of these qualities in your life or your future mate's.

No one is perfect. If you demand perfection, certainly no one would qualify except Christ Himself. However, you should have the discernment to evaluate yourself before God and before your future mate. I always ask couples, "What really concerns you about your future mate?" It scares me to death if they say, "Nothing." That is either naiveté, dishonesty, or mental illusion!

I ask couples to get away by themselves and go through the Beatitudes—first alone and then with their future mates. They should consider these things in relationship to behavior around parents, other authority in their lives, fellow workers on projects or jobs, roommates, and relationships at church.

Then after going over the lists privately, they should get together and share them. The openness and thoroughness of each is probably the greatest evidence of maturity. After gaining the Lord's direction, they should ask a wise counselor who is older and more spiritually experienced to double-check the conclusions with them. If this step checks out, they can begin to consider the other issues in determining God's will for marriage.

AGREEMENT ON FOUNDATIONAL FAITH CONCEPTS

Couples considering marriage should understand and commit themselves to the basic biblical concepts of marriage, presented in Part II of this book. A couple who desires marital unity must possess the common bond of oneness that God provides in His Son, Jesus Christ. In Genesis 1, as we have seen, God introduces His purpose for man and for marriage. That plan requires two people who become one unit to reflect God's image, reproduce a godly heritage, and reign spiritually in life together. Both partners must first feel a burden and commitment to God's plan for their marriage.

Each partner must understand that God specifically places people together in order for this plan to be carried out. Therefore, each should be able to receive the other from God as a personal provision for blessing. Each should trust God for the success of the relationship, not the performance of the mate.

A successful marriage foundation requires two people who understand that there are only two avenues of effecting change in their mate: love and blessing. Both must confess the futility of human manipulation.

The husband and wife must understand Satan's deceit in their responsibilities to love and submit to one another, and be on guard against his stratagems.

It is easy to read over these issues quickly. But these concepts, if understood and enacted, will bring the security and joy to your marriage that is provided only by God Himself.

AGREEMENT IN PRACTICAL AREAS

The last imperative to evaluate before deciding to get married are these practical issues we have discussed in Part III. In my opinion, every couple should research and develop mutual agreements on each issue. Write out your plans and discuss them together. It would help to evaluate these plans with a counselor.

Finances, sexual relationships, in-laws, personality differences, vocational goals, children, and spiritual issues will be less of a problem if both partners have contributed to a positive plan of action. Agreement on these issues is one confirmation of the relationship being God's will. There are other issues—such as God's timing to get married—but these mentioned here are the basic issues and should give clear direction as to choice of mate and potential areas of problems that will be encountered. God bless you in your decisions!

Epilogue

As we think back to the beginning of this book, to the story of Jim and Betty, we must conclude that they, like us, meant well when they got married. But meaning well was not enough to elude the pain and shock they experienced. Great marriages do not just happen. They are made through wisdom, work, a little suffering, and faith in a loving God.

If Jim and Betty had understood something of why marriages fail, how to make permanent and faithful commitments, and how to live practically with life's ups and downs , they could have avoided their predicament right from the start.

In this book you have been introduced to God's plan for lasting, joyful marriage. You may have identified with people you met on these pages, learning from their backgrounds and how they helped or hindered their marriages. You saw that natural man runs contrary to the love and blessing made possible through Jesus Christ. You also read about how love and submission open the door to a most satisfying relationship, one where it is possible to *reflect* God's image, *reproduce* a godly heritage, and *reign* on this earth together.

You have also seen that marriage is not a fifty-fifty proposition, but that both partners are to share a one-hundred-percent commitment in order for the relationship to work. Of course, living all this out is impossible without knowing personally the God of Creation, made known through Jesus Christ.

Commit yourself to these faith principles of marriage. Receive your mate from God. Place your focus on God's faithfulness as opposed to your mate's performance. Love your mate and give a blessing if you are wronged. God will surprise you with positive results. Begin to look at the Lord's command to love and submit as opportunities for relationships instead of issues for resentment. While they are difficult to understand through human thought, living these concepts will result in your receiving a blessing.

A secondary benefit of making these faith commitments is a new freedom in the practical areas of life—sex, finances, in-laws, vocation—which will produce not winners or losers but opportunities for creative alternatives. Give God a chance to release the old areas of conflict and hurt.

Christian marriage not only can work, it *must* work if the name of our Lord Jesus Christ is to be honored in this nation. You and I can do more than *survive;* we can live victorious and joyful lives and be fulfilled in our marriages.

Acclaim for *How to Catch a Prince*

"A stirring modern-day fairy tale about the power of true love."

—CINDY KIRK, AUTHOR OF *LOVE AT MISTLETOE INN*

"*How to Catch a Prince* is an enchanting story told with bold flavor and tender insight. Engaging characters come alive as romance blooms between a prince and his one true love. Hauck's own brand of royal-style romance shines in this third installment of the Royal Wedding Series."

—DENISE HUNTER, BESTSELLING AUTHOR OF *THE WISHING SEASON*

"*How to Catch a Prince* contains all the elements I've come to love in Rachel Hauck's Royal Wedding Series: an 'it don't come easy' happily ever after, a contemporary romance woven through with royal history, and a strong spiritual thread with an unexpected touch of the divine. Hauck's smooth writing—and the way she wove life truths throughout the novel—made for a couldn't-put-it-down read."

—BETH K. VOGT, AUTHOR OF *SOMEBODY LIKE YOU*, ONE OF *PUBLISHERS WEEKLY*'S BEST BOOKS OF 2014

Acclaim for Previous Books

"Rachel Hauck's inspiring Royal Wedding Series is one for which you should reserve space on your keeper shelf!"

—*USA TODAY*

"Hauck spins a surprisingly believable royal-meets-commoner love story. This is a modern and engaging tale with well-developed secondary characters that are entertaining and add a quirky touch. Hauck fans will find a gem of a tale."

—*PUBLISHERS WEEKLY* STARRED REVIEW OF
ONCE UPON A PRINCE

"Both books, *Once Upon a Prince* and *Princess Ever After*, are a good blend of uplifting entertainment with a mystery twist—not too heavy, not too light, just right! Five-plus stars awarded to these most excellent books by Rachel Hauck."

—LAURA PALMORE

"A completely satisfying read. I've read *A March Bride* three times!"

—J. GOLDHAHN

"Upon entering the world of Brighton and now Hessenberg (*Princess Ever After*), my mind was awash with the colors, sounds, sights, and even smells of this delightful, fictional city. So much so, I wish it were real so that I could schedule a visit! All in all, this was a world I did *not* want to leave."

—THINKING THOUGHTS BLOG

"I just finished my ARC of *Once Upon a Prince* and I LOVED IT! I don't say that often because I do so many book reviews and it's hard to find a real gem, but this one fit the bill!"

—LORI TWICHELL OF *RADIANT LIT*

"*The Wedding Dress* is a thought-provoking read and one of the best books I have read. Look forward to more . . ."

—MICHELLE JOHNMAN, GOLD COAST, AUSTRALIA

THE WEDDING CHAPEL

Also by Rachel Hauck

The Wedding Dress
The Wedding Chapel
The Wedding Shop

Novellas found in A Year of Weddings

A March Bride (e-book only)
A Brush with Love: A January
Wedding Story (e-book only)

The Royal Wedding Series

Once Upon a Prince
Princess Ever After
How to Catch a Prince
A Royal Christmas Wedding

Lowcountry Romance Novels

Sweet Caroline
Love Starts with Elle
Dining with Joy

Nashville Sweetheart (e-book only)
Nashville Dreams (e-book only)

With Sara Evans

Sweet By and By
Softly and Tenderly
Love Lifted Me

THE WEDDING CHAPEL

CHAPEL

Rachel Hauck

ZONDERVAN

The Wedding Chapel
Copyright © 2015 by Rachel Hayes Hauck

This title is also available as a Zondervan e-book.
Visit www.zondervan.com.

Requests for information should be addressed to:
Zondervan, *Grand Rapids, Michigan 49546*

ISBN: 978-0-7180-7781-5 (Mass Market)

Library of Congress Cataloging-in-Publication Data

Hauck, Rachel, 1960-
   The wedding chapel / Rachel Hauck.
   pages; cm
   ISBN 978-0-310-34152-9 (softcover)
   1. Man-woman relationships—Fiction. I. Title.
   PS3608.A866W425 2015
   813'.6—dc23
   2015023680

Any Internet addresses (websites, blogs, etc.) and telephone numbers in this book are offered as a resource. They are not intended in any way to be or imply an endorsement by Zondervan, nor does Zondervan vouch for the content of these sites and numbers for the life of this book.

Publisher's Note: This novel is a work of fiction. Names, characters, places, and incidents are either products of the author's imagination or used fictitiously. All characters are fictional, and any similarity to people living or dead is purely coincidental.

Interior design: Mallory Perkins

Printed in the United States of America

16 17 18 19 20 21 / QGM / 20 19 18 17 16 15 14 13 12 11 10 9 8 7 6 5 4 3 2 1

For my sister, Rebekah Gunter

CHAPTER ONE

JIMMY

Jimmy's journey began with a photograph. One of two girls standing next to a slender bride gripping a weak cluster of flowers, the shade of a stone chapel falling over their faces.

"My cousins." Clem's heavy exhale pushed him down to the family's brand-new sofa. "From England."

"All of them?" Jimmy remained planted in the same spot he'd been standing when Clem passed over the picture. In a warm swath of afternoon sunlight falling through the square front window.

"Nooo, golly geez, just the two flower girls, or bridesmaids, whatever you call them. *They're* coming to live with us." Clem whistled low and slumped down against the couch cushions, his dark hair buzzed in a close crew cut. "If all three of them came to live with us, I'd have to move out. And you know Mama wouldn't cotton to losing her baby boy."

Jimmy's eyes watered. Dang. He was too old for tears. He cleared his throat, then said, "She'd hunt you down."

"You don't say." Clem made a wry face, but Jimmy knew their joking etched around the truth. Clem was now his mama's *only* boy. Big brother Ted had died on Iwo Jima just a week after his twentieth birthday, and the family had never been the same.

Though more than three years had passed since the telegram arrived, Jimmy's soul still vibrated with the echoes of Mrs. Clemson's wailing as her husband read the news. Everyone in Heart's Bend had loved Ted. No exaggeration. *Everyone.* The whole town shut down for his memorial.

Jimmy jerked around, glancing at the stairs, for a moment imagining he heard the big guy's thunderous footsteps.

"Come on, lazies, let's get up a game. Jims, you staying for dinner? Mams, set an extra place for dinner . . ."

". . . but what's a fella to do?" Clem's question brought Jimmy out from the shadows. "They lost everything in the war. Their folks, their home . . ."

Right. The cousins. Jimmy studied the picture again. "They're orphans?" His heart moved with understanding.

"Yessiree, and they're coming here to live." Clem leaned toward the radio console and upped the volume, the velvet voice of Doris Day giving energy to the sunlight.

"Gonna take a sentimental journey / to renew old memories."

"So why're you showing me this?" Jimmy held up the

photograph. Did Clem want him to decode something between the shades of black and white? "Might be kinda nice, Clem, having kids around. The house won't be so . . ."

Lonely. He wanted to say it, but the tone sat sad in his ears. If Jimmy knew about anything, it was loneliness: the hollow shadows of a dark house, the chill of walking into a cold kitchen, the loudness of silence.

"Lonely?" Clem made a dismissive *phffbt* sound and waved Jimmy off. "What're you talking about? I just got things the way I want around here. Got the whole upstairs to myself." He flipped his hand toward the stairs, feigning more protest than Jimmy believed true. "Now I'm going to have girls hanging their stockings and *unmentionables* in the bathroom—*my* bathroom— and getting their powder and rouge all over the sink."

"Girls get their powder all over the sink?"

Clem sat forward, jamming his thumb over his shoulder toward the neighbors. "Bradley told me everything about living with sisters." Clem shook his head. "Just when we thought the war was over and things were getting back to normal, I got to have *girls* moving in."

"Big deal . . . So what, maybe they'll bake or something. I bet they'll do the dishes and cleaning." At least he'd heard that's what womenfolk did around the house. But in the Westbrook men-only home, Jimmy did most of the "girl" chores.

"I'd gladly do the dishes to have the upstairs to myself." Clem glanced away, a glossy sheen spreading across his eyes.

"I'd not want anyone to take Ted's place either if I

was you," Jimmy said quietly, taking a final glance at the girl cousins before passing the photo back to Clem.

Clem took the picture, running the heel of his hand over his eyes, and with a final gander dropped it onto the coffee table.

"Can't stop missing him."

"Yeah. Me too."

But Jimmy's gut told him Albert "Clem" Clemson, his best friend since Miss Tuttle's second-grade class, was wrong about these girls. They were special. He didn't know how or why, just that they were more than powder-spreading inconveniences.

Besides, they were *pretty*. Especially the one on the right with her sweet, heart-shaped face and head of curls.

Jimmy recognized the look in her eye as she squinted through the shadows. It was the sad glint of losing a parent. And he sure as spitting knew what that felt like.

"If they do the housework, you know what that means? Dad'll have me putting in more hours at the store." His jaw set, Clem was determined not to be consoled. "Did I tell you he's pert-near ready to open a third store in Ashland City?"

"What's her name?" The words came out, *slipped* out, without Jimmy's consent. But there they were, hanging in the air. He dropped to Mr. Clemson's well-used leather easy chair as the image of the girl with the curls and tender gaze made him feel all hot and fluttery inside.

"Of the store?" Clem curled his lip. "You think it's a she?"

"No . . ." Jimmy grimaced, making a face. "Th-the

cousins." It was hard to act casual when his pumping heart made his voice all quivery.

"Which one?" Clem reached for the photo on the coffee table, then regarded Jimmy for a moment.

Jimmy ducked his head, fearing he'd be discovered. He could sense a red heat flushing his cheeks. If Clem ever told the fellas . . .

"Um." He cleared his throat and rose from the chair. "Either, I guess. Man, it's hot in here." Jimmy glanced toward the window and its stream of July sunlight.

"Guess it don't matter 'cause I don't know their names." Clem popped up, reaching for the football wedged between the couch and the end table. "Let's get up a game. We need the practice."

"You don't know your own cousins' names?"

Jimmy had one cousin, April Raney, who was off to college now but the closest thing he'd ever had to a sibling. He liked her a lot, and every year he saved some of his earnings to buy her a birthday and Christmas present.

"Why should I? I never met them. Their mom is . . . *was* . . . my mom's sister, but they only saw each other once in twenty years. When Mama went to England." Clem tossed the football between his hands, then fake pumped to Jimmy. "Mama says they'll be in our class."

"They're twins?" Jimmy leaned to squint at the picture, his interest more in memorizing the face of the girl with the curls. He took up the image and flipped it over. Maybe her name was on the back. But the only imprint was the date: *May '48.*

"Naw, not twins. That I know. Just in the same grade.

Something to do with the war and being shipped to the country to live. Then they got orphaned." Clem tossed the ball toward the ceiling, jumping to catch it while moving toward the door. "Let's go, Westbrook. I'll holler at Bradley. We can pick up Spice on the way."

"Coming." Jimmy dropped the photograph onto the table just as the breeze skipped through the open doorway, skidding the picture across the coffee table's smooth surface into Mrs. Clemson's collection of *Saturday Evening Post*s.

Can't wait to meet you . . .

Outside, Clem jumped from the porch, slapping the rafters, the ball tucked under his arm. "Braaadleeeey Green, we're getting up a game. Need to practice if we're going to make first team. Let's go. I'm working this afternoon so it's now or never."

Jimmy jumped from the porch onto the grass, trying to shed the strange sensations lingering in his chest. *Get over it. It's just a photograph.* But confound it, Clem's goofy girl cousin made him want to hug her, protect her. He'd always promised himself he'd not go moon-eyed over a gal. He'd learned from Dad that women weren't worth the effort.

His ole pop seemed pretty clear on the fact that loving a woman caused a man a whole heap of trouble. And his father was a swell, stand-up fella who told the truth.

Besides, what did Jimmy know of girls? Nothing. Other than Nana and April, he had no experience with women *whatsoever*.

Bradley ran out of his house, still tying his sneakers. "I called Spice," he said.

Sure enough, from across the street and three houses down, Spice Keating hurried out of his house. His old man was a boozer, a bit rough. But Spice was all charm and smiles.

Jimmy didn't know how he managed it.

"Coach said we could practice at school if we promise not to tear up the turf," Clem said, walking backward, tossing the ball to Jimmy.

But Jimmy missed. *Missed!* The ball slipped through his hands and hit the pavement.

"Westbrook, is that how you're going to play this fall?"

"Shut up, Clem." Irritated, Jimmy scooped up the ball, ran down the middle of the street, and spiraled it back to his quarterback. "You get it to me and I'll catch it."

See what girls did? He was already distracted and he hadn't even met her. That was the trouble with girls. They could mess up a guy in all sorts of ways. Humiliate him.

"Hey, fellas," Jimmy said, a teasing melody in his voice. "Clem's having girl cousins move in."

"Girls? What kind of girls?"

"Westbrook, you big mouth." Clem fired the ball at Jimmy.

"Ah, what's the big deal? They were going to find out sooner or later." Jimmy caught the ball and shoved into Spice. "What do you mean, 'What kind of girls?' There's more than one?"

"Yeah, sure, pretty and ugly." Spice laughed, shuffling around Jimmy, reaching for the ball, a saucy grin on his face, his dark hair flopping over his eyes. "So which is it? Pretty or ugly?"

"Yeah, Jimmy," Clem echoed. "Which is it?"

"They're your cousins." Jimmy tossed the ball to Bradley, who dropped it.

"Exactly." Clem scooped up the ball, twisting around, barely missing Mrs. Grove as she turned the corner in her big new Cadillac. "I ain't got no skin in this game."

"Nice car, Mrs. Grove." Young or old, Spice tried to charm them all. "Anyway, we could use some new girls round here. Pretty ones." He glanced back at Mrs. Grove's driveway. "Young ones too."

"Well, if you'd quit loving 'em and leaving 'em, you'd have more choices." Jimmy ran long for Clem's pass, catching it in stride, feeling the lingering grudge he had against Spice. They were friends all right, but last year Spice knew Jimmy was keen on Rebekah Gunter. He moved right in anyway, even though he had no intention of ever going steady. Love was just a game to him.

"Ah, don't be bitter, Westbrook. You know you didn't have the guts to ask Beka out."

"Take that back, Keating." Jimmy shoved him, hard.

"See, girls are nothing but trouble." Clem stepped in between them, waving the ball. "Focus. We've got a season to win. That tailback from Memphis who ran through our D line last year? Heard he bench-pressed three hundred in the spring."

Bradley moaned. He was a defensive lineman.

"Yeah, we got some work to do." Clem sprinted forward, then whipped around, sending the ball in a high arc toward Jimmy. Man, he could throw a shot. Jimmy caught it and ran through Bradley's soft blocking.

If all went as planned, Clem would start as quarterback and Jimmy as halfback. They were juniors but the best ones for the job. So they hoped.

With the ball tucked in his arm and the sun peeking in a patch of blue sky, Jimmy left the street, the football field in view, cutting through Mrs. Whitaker's backyard where Spice chased the old lady's cat up a tree.

Jimmy raced ahead, the end zone in sight. Clem ran a close second, Spice and Bradley lumbering behind.

Jimmy spiked the ball as he crossed the goal line.

Yeah, this was what he needed to clear his head. To be on the field. Looking forward to the season. Fixing on his goals.

Dad was looking forward to his boy starting this season, and Jimmy didn't want to let him down. He liked to brag on his son's football talent to the fellas on his crew.

Jimmy would do his dad proud. He'd not allow a girl to get him off track.

Nevertheless, when he lined up behind Clem for the first practice play, his pulse thudded in his ears. Not from racing with his friends to the field, but from the lingering image of the girl in the photograph.

CHAPTER TWO

TAYLOR

Taylor glanced up with a wash of anticipation as she heard his key in the lock. Jack was home.

Her computer-tired eyes adjusted to the dark shadows filling their fourth-floor apartment, the glow of Brooklyn streetlights muted against the windows.

"Look, Hops, it's a great campaign. Let's just make the presentation and see what they say." Jack moved through the apartment, phone pressed to his ear.

"Hey—" Taylor said, standing, smoothing her hand over her hair. She ached from sitting so long. Now that her husband was home, she longed to nab a bit of his attention.

Husband. Six months and the word still felt so foreign.

But Jack crossed to their bedroom without pausing or even nodding her way, his laptop case swinging from his shoulder, his broad, muscular presence and over-the-top confidence a light of its own, consuming the dim apartment.

Taylor sank back down to her chair, the ache in her muscles creeping toward her heart. If he didn't want her here, then why did he propose?

Even more confounding, why did she say yes?

She sat with her fingers poised at her keyboard, the angle of light from her desk lamp glinting off the silver sheen of her wedding band. A platinum symbol of their trailer park commitment.

She'd preferred things free and loose in the beginning. The whirlwind of their romance had launched her to the moon. An emotional place she never wanted to leave.

But after their Martha's Vineyard elopement, she slowly sank back to earth, leaving the moon and stars behind. The seasons changed—spring to summer, summer now giving way to autumn—and Taylor sensed their love fading and withering.

They fought lately, often over money. She claimed he spent too much. He charged her with being a skinflint. But he had more shoes than she did, and his clothes took up two-thirds of the closet and a whole chest of drawers.

With a sigh, Taylor returned to the image she was editing on her screen. A wedding gown, of all things, she'd photographed for a new designer. The shots were due tomorrow.

The touch-up work had been body-tensing tedious. All the gowns had dirt on the hems from the outdoor location. For the last ten hours she'd been enhancing light and shadow in each photograph, the setting, the models, the dresses, and at last, making brown spots white.

After a few seconds, Taylor lost her concentration. Sitting back, she checked the time. Ten o'clock.

"Jack, you hungry?" she called toward the bedroom, waiting, listening.

She'd worked through the dinner hour, ignoring her rumbling belly, determined to get this job done.

If she wanted to grow her résumé as a commercial photographer, she needed to deliver excellent work on time.

"Jack?"

The closet door clicked shut, but otherwise there was no response. Okay, back to work. Three more dresses and *done*.

Breathing in, Taylor hunkered down, willing herself to press on.

Right after she eloped with Jack, she landed her first commercial client, Melinda House Weddings, a European designer famous for dressing the Grand Duchess of Hessenberg, Princess Regina.

Landing Jack Forester and Melinda House in the same month? Serendipitous. Dreamlike.

"What are you doing?" Jack entered the room and dropped down to the couch, reaching for the remote. He was dressed for exercise in his basketball shorts and oversized Ohio State National Championship T-shirt.

"Working . . ." No kiss. No tender hello. No sultry gaze like in the days of old—six months ago felt like the days of old. "Are you hungry?"

"No, ate at work. Is this the Melinda House job?"

"Yes, the hems are dirty. I told her it would happen, but she insisted on an outdoor shoot." Which had taken Taylor and her assistant, Addison, on an exhausting yet exhilarating ride all over the city.

"By the way, Keri texted me today. She wondered if you had her wedding done yet."

"Why is she texting you? She's got my number . . ." Taylor doubled down on the image on her screen. Why did Keri insist on using Jack as an unnecessary middleman?

"Don't snap, just asking."

"I told her the end of the month." *End of the month . . .* a hundred times.

"Fine, just shoot her a text or an e-mail. She's dying to get her pictures. I can't blame her."

"Guess not. A girl has a right to revel in her wedding."

The only pictures she had of her wedding were snapped with her iPhone by the officiant presiding over their vows. She'd not even thought to take her Canon with her to the ceremony.

That's how head over heels she was for Jack. Giggly. Forgetful. Spontaneous.

She hadn't wanted to shoot Keri's wedding because the job wouldn't build the commercial résumé Taylor wanted. But Keri was a friend of Jack's, a former client, and probably an ex-girlfriend, though Taylor wasn't sure about that last part. Either way, she would do just about anything for Jack.

Even marry him when she didn't believe in marriage.

He was her weakness. Her shoe sale, her milk chocolate, her ice-cream cone on a summer day, her high
school crush come to life.

She didn't know he was in Manhattan until that cold
January afternoon when she literally ran into him coming around the corner of Madison and 67th. She'd just
finished a job and thought a perusal of the Tory Burch
store would be a nice reward.

Not that she had Tory Burch kind of money to spend,
but looking and dreaming never hurt. She'd get a latte
on the way home as another reward.

Instead, she'd rediscovered Jack. So much better than
drooling over clothes she couldn't afford. Yes, that's it.
Drool over a man she couldn't *afford* either, but somehow her emotional bank was willing to risk investing in
one Jack Forester.

At first it was, "Wow, hello!" Two friends from Heart's
Bend, Tennessee, in the Big Apple.

Then dinner, followed by lunch, and dinner again.
Eight weeks later, he whispered two stunning words
on a Martha's Vineyard beach. *"Marry me."* She didn't
hesitate or take one contemplating breath. *"Yes."*

Eyes tired and blurry, Taylor closed her laptop. She'd
finish in the morning and get them to Melinda on time.
"A-are you going out?"

Jack cut a glance her way, then back to the TV where
he'd landed on SportsCenter. "Yeah, Aaron called.
Wanted to play basketball."

"Now?"

"It's been a long day. I need to burn off some energy.
Hops is all in a wad over the FRESH Water account."

Jack was an up-and-comer in the New York advertising world. *Ad Age* called him the "Charmer." His work on a Super Bowl spot had won his agency their first CLIO Award.

"What's going on with FRESH Water?"

She'd wanted Jack to recommend her for a FRESH shoot. But his boss, Hops Williams, deplored nepotism. It didn't matter how good Taylor was, or how cheap—did free count? He'd not entertain the thought of his main man's wife working on one of the accounts.

"Nothing, just working all the angles."

Nothing? It didn't feel like nothing. "Hops is in a wad over nothing?"

"Taylor—" Jack stood, moving to the kitchen. "It's just business." He jerked open the fridge.

She felt all this keenly, a sign their relationship was dying. In the beginning, they'd lain together in bed, legs and arms entangled while they talked about their work, their dreams, the funny bits on Jimmy Fallon. Then they would fall asleep in each other's arms. But now they went to bed at separate times. Jack clammed up about his job, and by Taylor's calculations, it'd been awhile since they'd . . . well . . . *entangled*.

"How's Aaron's new baby?"

Jack twisted the cap from a bottle of water as he returned to the sofa, laughing low. "Why do you think he wants to play midnight basketball? Burn off some tension. I guess the thing is colicky or teething or something."

The *thing*? One of the conversations omitted in the whirlwind was how many babies, if any, they wanted.

Besides his standard response of "not now," Taylor wasn't sure of Jack's feelings on family.

Other than that he loathed his own.

Taylor studied him, the palpitation in her chest tangible. Try as she might to get a realistic grip on her marriage, she was still a bit mesmerized by Jack. The troubled, brooding, *gorgeous* boy from high school who walked among the wounded yet excelled in everything. For some unknown, aggravating reason, she had this desire to get and keep his attention. To make him smile at her, *because* of her, *only* for her. To see in his eyes that she mattered to him. Made his life complete.

"Why do you have to do it?" she asked without pre-amble.

Jack peeked her way. "Do what?"

"Be . . . *perfect.*"

"Perfect?" He made a face and swigged from his water. "You mean besides spending too much money?"

"Jack—"

"I'm determined, purposeful, precise, maybe a *per-fectionist*, but hardly perfect." Another swig of water. "I don't have perfection scheduled until I'm forty-five." His wink and grin flooded Taylor with the warmth of want. "So relax."

Beneath the fortitude and confidence, Taylor caught a glimpse of the boy from Heart's Bend who wrestled with demons only he could see. He'd used all his skill and unique talents to act as his own healer; Taylor had yet to determine if he was becoming whole by his efforts or only more wounded.

Was his impulsive proposal another Band-Aid on

the wound? Another way to forget his pain? Had they been too impetuous? Too full of lust or something? Out of their heads?

Never mind that Jack could have *any* woman he wanted. Underline *any*. Models. Actresses. Beauty queens. She'd scanned his Facebook friends.

So why did he pick her? A throwback-hippie photographer. From their small hometown?

Back at the fridge, Jack checked a carton of leftover Chinese.

"Do we have anything to eat besides three-day-old fried rice?" He arced the small white box toward the trash, basketball style.

"I thought you weren't hungry." Taylor held her tone low and cool, trying not to be defensive.

"Changed my mind. Wow, we have a fifteen-hundred-dollar fridge with nothing but leftovers."

"There's milk," she said as she went to the couch and sat next to where he had been. "And cereal."

"Cereal?" His heavy sigh irritated her.

"What?"

"It's just . . . you're here during the day. At home. I thought you'd handle the food, the kitchen . . . dinner."

"Handle dinner?"

"You know what I mean."

"No, I don't."

"It's just . . . you're home."

"I'm not *just* home, Jack. I'm working." She motioned to her little office set up in the corner of their apartment. The space was small, but she had an amazing view of the East River and the lower end of Manhattan.

"Fine, but can we clean this out once in a while?" He made a show of it by tossing another carton of Chinese into the trash, then slamming the fridge door shut.

"Feel free, Jack." Taylor reached for the remote, changing the channel. Resentment bubbled under her skin. He was gone all day, then walked in without a tender word, changed to go play basketball, and criticized her for having too many leftovers.

What was on TV at ten thirty? Something funny . . .

"What's with you and leftovers anyway?" she asked. "I wanted to throw that stuff out two days ago and you said, 'No, keep it.'" She landed on a rerun of an eighties show. "So eat it, Jack."

He folded his arms and leaned against the counter. "I'm just saying, Taylor, the kitchen is sort of your domain."

"My *domain*? What's yours? Telling me what to do? I already do the cleaning, the laundry, the shopping and errand running."

"Your time is more flexible than mine, Taylor."

"That's so not true, Jack. I'm every bit as busy as you, and I don't have a big-name company to back me up. If I don't have a job, I have to *find* one. Once I get said job, I have to book the studio, rent the equipment, do the scheduling, and organize the shot list. Then I do *research*, without assistants to help me."

"What do you call Addison? She's your assistant. One I agreed we could pay for out of the household budget."

"Said the man with twenty-five pairs of shoes."

"What do my shoes have to do with anything?"

"Your shoes, your spending . . . and you're bust-ing me because I wanted a bit of money to hire an assistant."

"And is she assisting? Why are you doing Melinda House edits instead of Addison?"

"She's not that good at it. Yet."

"Then find someone who is good at it."

"What? No. She's organized and detailed, keeps me on track."

She was too tired for this. And weary of this merry-go-round. *You do, I do.* How did they get *here* within a few words?

Jack opened one drawer, then another, making a racket of shoving the contents around and every few seconds flashing her with his blue eyes. "Don't we have any paper and pens in this place?"

Taylor pointed to the canister by the phone. "What are you doing?"

"Making a list of chores."

"Jack, come on."

"Come on, what? I hear you. Things need to be more equitable. Let's write *Taylor* on one side and *Jack* on the other."

Why was he doing this? Taylor wanted to fly across the room and grab his arm, shake him, say, *"Let's get back to where we were in the beginning or end this."*

With a sarcastic flair, Jack started detailing their respective chores. "You do . . . shopping, cleaning, laundry . . . Is that right? Did I get them all?"

"Finances."

"Right, of course, the budget Gestapo."

Taylor's eyes misted. He'd asked her to do them because she was good with numbers. Good with denying superfluous expenses. But lately he didn't even talk to her about his spending. Just handed her receipts.

"I handle the dry cleaning—" he began.

"Because you insist on that crazy cleaners by your office. He charges too much, you know."

"—garbage, earning the money, supporting the house and your business—"

Taylor bolted off the couch and snatched the paper from under his pen, wadding it up. "Stop, just . . . stop. I said I'll pay you back for Addison's salary."

"Did I ask you to pay me back?" He stooped for the wadded-up list. "I'm just trying to figure out the great divide in our responsibilities."

"Then why did you say, 'I earn all the money around here and support your business'?"

"Because I do. I don't know why you're so upset." He tossed the pen back in the canister. "I was just commenting—"

"You were putting me in my place."

"And you're not putting me in mine? I get it, you don't want to be responsible for dinner. Good to know. I should make another list. 'Things to discuss before eloping.'"

There. Doubts, out in the open. She knew he had them. *Knew it.* So what choice did she have but to reel in her heart?

"I've got to meet Aaron." Jack disappeared in their room, returning after a second with his keys. "Don't wait up." He glanced back to her as he reached for the knob, a flicker of something soft lighting his face. "Taylor, I—"

"Yes?" Her heartbeats thundered in her ears.

"I just want to say—"

The doorbell sounded, startling Jack backward and jarring the intimacy from the moment. Jack frowned, opening the door. "Who's here at this hour?"

Doug Voss stood on the other side. Taylor exhaled, trembling. *Oh no.* Her Big Mistake. The one she escaped.

"What are you doing here?" Taylor moved toward the door, standing between her past and her present, the shadows in the room seeming longer and darker.

He smiled his perfect, oh-so-sly smile. "I was in the neighborhood. Thought I'd visit the newlyweds." He crossed the threshold without invitation, surveying the room as if he owned it.

"J-Jack, this . . . this is Doug Voss."

"I know who he is," Jack said, offering the publishing mogul a stiff handshake. "Publisher of *Gossip*."

"Number one celebrity magazine. Thanks in part to this girl here." Doug motioned to Taylor as he moved through the living room. "Nice place. They're doing a lot with these old refurbed buildings."

Old. Refurbed. A put-down if Taylor ever heard one.

"Again, why are you here?"

Doug's gaze passed over her as he angled to see out the stacked panes. "Nice deck. Great view of the river."

"We like it," Jack answered, tense and suspicious, his tone marking his territory.

"Can I offer you some . . . tea or coffee? Water?" Taylor gave Jack a pointed look. *What? I don't know why he's here.* She felt trapped between Doug's invasion and Jack's stony stance.

"No, nothing for me." Doug gave Jack the once-over. "You play ball?"

"Yeah, a little. Relieves the—"

"Tension. I'd agree. I shoot a bit of hoops myself."

"Doug, I know you didn't come here to talk basketball with Jack." His presence seemed overbearing, nosy, as if inspecting where Taylor landed. Well, it wasn't his business.

"I need you for a job."

"A job? What sort of job?" Working for Doug and *Gossip* had kept her busy when she first came to the city eighteen months ago, kept her name out there and the bills paid. But they were the fame jobs. Not the fortune ones. Commercial jobs, like working for an agency like Jack's, were where the money could be found.

"Don't worry, not another Brandon Colter shoot."

"Thank goodness. He was a real *treat*," she said. The teen rocker showed up late, with glassy eyes, slurred speech, and five beautiful, very skinny girls as his entourage. It took Taylor two days to do what should've taken her one.

"Oh, say, how did the gig from CBS work out?" Doug asked, his eyes steady on her. "I told them you were the best."

"It turned out. I'm shooting the cast of *Always Tomorrow* in the morning." He was marking his territory. Letting Jack know he, the mighty Doug Voss, took *care* of his girl. But she wasn't his girl anymore.

"Excellent. See, babe, I got your back."

"What's this CBS job?" Jack shifted his stance over

the restored hardwood. "Does it pay money? Voss, you seem to send her work that ends up costing her more than she earns."

"Ah, husband and agent, I see."

"'Husband' pretty much covers all the bases, I think."

Doug made a face, turned to Taylor, rolling his eyes. *Get this guy.* "So, you're shooting the cast of *Always Tomorrow*?"

"In the morning, yes."

"The pay is good? I told them not to go cheap on you."

"Better than most." CBS wanted a photo spread of their first and longest-running soap opera cast as they marked the end of the show's sixty-two-year run.

"The last show airs at the end of the month," Taylor explained to Jack. "Doug got an exclusive for *Gossip*."

"They have fans all around the world," Doug said. "*Gossip* will be going into forty languages for that special issue. Taylor's photo will be on the cover."

"Is that why you're here? To check on the job?" Taylor asked.

"No, actually, I have another job for you."

"You seem to be swimming in jobs for my wife, Voss." Said with an edge, a hint of possession rather than affection. Taylor cut Jack a sharp glance.

But Doug chuckled, easing down into a chair, slowing the game, playing at his pace. "What about your aunt? Did you contact her?"

Colette Greer, Granny's sister, was the madam and star of *Always Tomorrow*. She had played Vivica Spenser all sixty-two years—from teen to grandmother, from cheerleader to business tycoon and matriarch. Though a familiar face on daytime television, she was a stranger to Taylor and the family. Since moving to New York, she'd seen Aunt Colette once.

"I called her. Doug, really, what is the job?" The tension wafting off Jack pressed against her, stealing her strength.

"Are you looking forward to seeing her?"

"Voss, she's asked you several times. What's the job?" Jack's phone pinged from his pocket. Probably Aaron. *Where are you?* But he didn't answer.

"Pardon me." Doug remained in control, undaunted by Jack's presence. "Taylor is my friend, despite our . . . past."

"Which is exactly what you are. Her past. Now state your purpose and go." Jack's elevated voice boomed into the space between them.

Taylor felt it beat against her heart. "Jack, please."

"State my purpose?" He glanced about the small but airy, modern apartment. "I wanted to see how you fared." His tone, his gaze bored into her. "To see if you were happy. After all, you left me and next thing I know you're married to this man."

"Stop, right now." Taylor held up her hand and moved to the door, somehow commanding her weak legs. Doug was maneuvering, manipulating. She could feel it, and if she waited another moment, he'd soil her soul with his brand of charm.

"Listen, Tay," Doug said, still seated. Reclining. "LA next week, you and me, the staff, at the Emmys."

"What? You're kidding."

Doug Voss was beyond her Big Mistake. Her time with him had been a desert. A season where she'd stopped hearing the heartbeat of God. She never wanted to go there again. So why spend a week in LA with him? Even for a job.

"Would I kid about business? Never. I need you for the Emmys. You're the best photographer in the business for the red carpet."

"I'm not the best—"

"Jack, tell her, she's the best." Doug baited Jack, but he was in advertising, used to the cloak and mirror of swindlers.

"She's the best."

"Are you and that fancy firm offering her any gigs? You know she wants to go commercial."

"Doug—"

"So, what do you say? You and me in LA for a week? Visiting our old haunts? Seeing the old gang?"

The old gang were his friends. And Taylor saw more than just work in his thinly veiled offer. He didn't like losing things. Especially the women in his life.

"No, Doug, I'm busy."

"If you change your mind . . ." With a cocky grin, Doug left, unfazed by her rejection, as if he had a plan to change her mind. When the door clicked shut, Taylor shivered, peering sideways at her husband.

"What did you ever see in that guy?"

At first, everything. "I'm just glad I saw the light." She smiled at Jack, inhaling. "Go, play ball. Have fun. Tell Aaron hello." She motioned to the door, pushing every ounce of merriment to the surface. *All is well!*

"You okay?" Jack slipped his hand lightly about her waist, kissing her temple.

"I'm fine." Now. Really fine. She rested her cheek against his chest where the soft motor of his heart reached her ears and reminded her why she'd said yes.

CHAPTER THREE

JACK

He looked toward the door, a familiar dark wave crashing over him. Doug Voss had come to his house and mocked him by flirting with Taylor. An unease belted his middle.

Voss would be back.

Jack had known about Voss before they married. Taylor dated him briefly in LA when he flew in for business. Then she moved to New York to be with him, breaking up shortly after.

What she saw in Voss confounded him. He was arrogant and rude. But he was also wealthy, powerful, and some sick version of charming.

Yet she chose you, man. You.

However, in the moment, the private confession carried no weight.

Jack exhaled, holding Taylor a bit closer. She seemed flustered. Bothered. "You okay?" From his pocket, his phone buzzed again. He pulled it out to peek at the screen.

Aaron. He'd have to wait.

"Yeah, I'm fine." She pushed out of his arms, leaving

him instantly cold, aching to reach for her. "Aaron is going to wonder what happened to you."

"I don't have to go . . ."

"Sure you do. Blow off steam and all that . . . Plus, I have work to do." Taylor waved toward her computer.

"Right. Well then." Jack reached for his gym bag. "I won't be long. And, Taylor, you are a great photographer. One of the best."

The best. In every sense of the word. Since he first met her in tenth grade, Taylor Branson captured his imagination. He just never had the courage to do anything about it until they ran into each other on Madison Avenue one cold January day.

He'd come to love the city, the avenue, the job that brought him the life he dreamed of during the dark days of his youth in Heart's Bend, Tennessee. The city, the avenue, the life that brought him Taylor.

"See you," he said without moving toward the door. Should he stay?

"Have fun." Her smile caught the light of her desk lamp and filled Jack. "Really. Have fun."

"Oh, Taylor, I forgot." Jack leaned on the doorknob, watching her, moving from insecure husband to confident ad man. "I have a job for you."

She glanced up from her computer. "You have a job for me? What sort of job? Not another 'old friend's' wedding. Jack, I won't do it—"

"A shoot for *Architecture Quarterly*." His boss, Hops Williams, would kill him for giving a job to his wife, but Jack could endure his pseudo wrath. He earned the man boatloads of money.

Besides, Hops had asked Jack to relocate. Head up a client's foundation. In London. A request he had yet to pass by Taylor. What was a bit of nepotism in light of moving across the ocean?

She gasped. "*AQ*? A commercial shoot? Jack, really?" Her expression softened. Joy sparked in her blue eyes.

"Kind of. It's part of their new brand. With all the DIY shows and HGTV, there's a new interest in architecture. They have a campaign going and there's a building—" Jack had no clue about the details. He'd only overheard pieces of conversation between Hops and *AQ*'s publisher, Cabot Grayson. "Somewhere." Jack smiled, determined to do this for his wife. Let her know, in some way his words could not, that he believed in her. "I'll get the details."

"And they want me?"

"They asked for a photographer. I put you forward." Was it so wrong to shade the truth for love? He wanted to be her hero. He wanted her to not regret taking a leap with him.

He'd have a whale of a tale to tell Hops in the morning. But it was a small job. Surely he could bend a few of his rules for Jack, for his new bride.

"Really? When were you going to tell me?"

"Tonight. Like I said, I meant to when I walked in—" And London. He needed to tell her about London. But he had a presentation this week and he wanted to shut out everything else until it was perfected.

Nevertheless, he felt the weight of his lie. If it boomeranged, he'd be in trouble with his boss *and* his wife.

The dark wave rolled toward him again, crashing

over the rocks of his soul. Nothing good stayed the same for Jack Forester. Ever. This issue with Hops, his job, his new marriage were simply illusions.

"Jack, I'd love to do the job. Thanks for thinking of me." Taylor moved across the room toward him, the long angle of the kitchen light kissing the top of her golden-brown hair. "When is this job?" She kissed him, wrapping her arms around his neck, leaning her body against his.

"I-I th-think next week." Jack buried his face in her long, silky hair. "I'll have Petra e-mail you and Addison."

"Th-thank you."

And his heart sighed.

"As for earlier, the household chores and stuff, we'll figure it out, Taylor. We will—" Again, his phone buzzed. More demanding than the last time, if possible.

Taylor stepped out of his arms, returning to her desk, and for a second time a cold chill rushed his chest. "Go! We can talk later. Aaron is going to be livid."

"Taylor," Jack said, easing the door open. "About Doug—"

"Forget him, Jack. He just likes to get his way."

He nodded. "But he's pretty persuasive."

"What are you saying, Jack?" The glow of her computer screen highlighted the smooth, high planes of her face, and the sight knocked the gumption out of him.

"Nothing. Just an observation."

Just a fear that Jack could lose her. How could he tell Taylor, show her, how much he was all hers? Love was such foreign ground for him.

What he wanted to ask was if she still loved him.

Their whirlwind romance and marriage happened on the edge of Taylor breaking off her relationship with Voss.

But asking would make him look weak and sound pitiful.

"Don't work too hard, okay?"

She nodded, smiling. "Don't play too hard."

"With Aaron? No way. It's all out."

He needed to play hard. Needed to exorcise doubt and the scum of Doug Voss from his soul. Perhaps happily ever after was not in the cards for them—surely they leapt without looking—but Jack held on to hope. Giving Taylor the benefit of the doubt where *that guy* was concerned seemed like a good place to start.

CHAPTER FOUR

Colette

Her day began in the back of a taxicab, riding to a photo shoot, being whisked across the river to a Brooklyn studio where she and her *Always Tomorrow* cast members would pose together one last time.

The end of an era. A very long, glorious era.

Colette twisted her handkerchief around her fingers. She'd not become weepy or sentimental. But the *end of an era*? Well, what was an old soap opera siren supposed to do with her life now?

There had been several endings in her life, the most painful ones occurring before she turned twenty-one. Being sent out of London to live in the country at the start of the Blitz. Though that was seventy-five years ago, there were days, like today, when it felt like yesterday.

Then the death of her parents during the war, and leaving England at sixteen to live with her aunt and uncle in Tennessee.

Running away from Heart's Bend at nineteen. Leaving *him* and her very core behind.

"Zoë said your niece is going to be the photographer on this shoot. I didn't know you had a niece in town."

"What?" Colette turned to Ford, her manager of fifty-one years. Her most constant friend besides her alter ego, Vivica Spenser, whom she embodied on *Always Tomorrow* since the summer of '54.

"Your niece? She's the photographer today?"

Her niece? "Oh yes, Taylor. My sister, Peg's, grand-daughter."

"Peg?" Colette knew that expression, the raised eyebrow and lowered chin, peering at her with expectation. "Don't tell me that's not bringing up some buried feelings," he said.

"Really, Ford, you should've been a psychiatrist instead of a talent manager."

"I didn't know there was a difference."

Colette pressed her hand on his arm. "Seeing Taylor won't bring up buried *feelings*." Thanks to her career on the small screen, she'd perfected the art of pretending. She could sell water to a drowning man. "We're practically strangers. I met her when she was a girl, twenty-plus years ago. The last time I was in Heart's Bend. When you coerced me into being their Christmas parade marshal."

She'd been out of the country when her Aunt Jean had died the summer of 1990, so when the parade marshal offer came, Colette's longing for home, for some part of her roots, won the day. Before the parade, she spent an afternoon with good ole Uncle Fred in the nursing home, grateful he was tender and sleepy with age. That he never asked the hard question, though she read it in his eyes. *"What happened, Lettie?"*

"Coerced? It was great publicity. Especially after the Daytime Emmy debacle between you and Marilee Jones."

"She told the world I was a horrible actress. A fraud. What did you expect me to do?"

"Oh, a number of things besides saying, 'Take that, Marilee. *Pfffbbtt!*' when you won best actress."

"Now *that* was great publicity." Colette laughed. Comedians, sitcoms, talk show hosts turned the moment into a bit. One Colette parodied on *Saturday Night Live* and spoofed on Carson and Letterman.

Ford's low chuckle made Colette smile. She liked the man now as much as ever. He'd been a young, hungry talent scout for a big New York agency when he decided to launch out on his own. He met Colette at a reception for the mayor and wooed her endlessly until she became his first client, the anchor of his agency.

And his lover.

It was an act beyond her sensibilities and moral boundaries. But she was so desperate to move *on*, to bury her wounds and fears. To *feel*. When the affair ended, she fled to England for the summer. Why England, with its rude and rough memories, she could never say. Except the fact that she'd been invited to tea with the Queen . . .

Colette gripped her handbag, a Diamatia-Greer, named after her by the exclusive, in-demand designer Luciano Diamatia, who had been in love with her. But she had not loved him.

There were other men. Spice Keating, an old friend from Heart's Bend and a fellow actor. And Bart Maverick, her *Always Tomorrow* costar.

All romance found its end road. Because her heart belonged to another.

So she had fame, fortune, and celebrity as her companions. Awards, acclaim, honorary degrees, and a Park Avenue penthouse.

The car jostled from side to side, hitting uneven pavement.

Colette stared out her window as New York passed by. Just like life, if she were honest. She'd slid inside the "ride" of her career and watched life pass her by. She had accomplishments the world envied. But inside she was empty. Though for over sixty years she'd filled herself with foolishness. The hype of the show. The grandeur of being one of the most beautiful, then one of the oldest actresses on television. A career that spanned the ages.

But since the taping ended a month ago, she found her days long and silent. Lonely. And it was then that she began to hear the beating of her own heart.

So much so she thought it might drive her mad.

"Did you decide about the book?" Ford pulled her attention back inside the cab, back to the moment. The cab jerked again as the driver wove through traffic, muttering in Arabic, as orange cones narrowed two thick lanes down to one. "The show is over. You've had a month to enjoy your freedom. I declare I don't know why you didn't go down to your Caribbean home. Anyway, now that you've had some time, you can start work on the book. I've been promising your publisher a manuscript for the past three years."

"Yes, the book." She'd agreed to the book but only because she was angry with Peg, who in light of her sickness had suddenly wanted to make amends. To undo the past sixty-plus years as if nothing had ever happened. Colette forgave her, then threatened her with a tell-all if she didn't leave things be.

But she'd never write such a memoir. Not while Peg was alive. Because it wouldn't fix anything, change the past, or bring back those Colette had loved and lost.

"I don't know the first thing about writing a book, Ford."

He sighed, angling forward as the driver surged through traffic and through a yellow light. "You have a cowriter, Justine Longoria. Remember? You tell her your stories and she handles the writing magic."

"I can't imagine anyone wanting to read about me."

"Everyone wants to read about you, Colette," Ford said, exasperation molding his thin features. "You're an award-winning actress, a patron of the arts, a world traveler, a spokeswoman. You acted on the same show for six decades. Yet your personal life is a mystery. You've had many suitors but no husband. No children. You've lived in the same penthouse for fifty years. You don't even own cats or dogs."

"Animals die." She'd had enough death in her life. People. Dreams. Love.

"They also bring joy and comfort."

"And I have children."

Ford laughed low. "As Vivica Spenser? That doesn't count, Colette."

"Don't talk to me like I'm one sentence away from the old folks home, Ford. The actors who played Vivica's children *feel* very much like my own. Caron Seitz and I talk once a month, at least. And Jenn Baits has her children call me Granny."

"Sweet stories, but you can't lie to me. No one really knows you." Ford said this while answering a text to his phone. "I'm not sure I know you all that well."

"You know me as well as anyone."

"Then tell me. How do you feel about the show ending? That the last episode airs this month?"

"I'm . . ." Colette paused. What words fit the swirl in her soul? Sad? Lost? Lonely? Such pitiful words for a woman who had a life others envied.

But really, there were days Colette Greer didn't know where she ended and Vivica Spenser began. The women were one and the same. One's reality was the other's fantasy. She was the blended shade of her real life and TV persona.

"You'll have to read about it in my autobiography."

Ford's laugh filled the cab. "Touché. So you'll do the book?" He flashed his phone. "I'll get Justine scheduled. How's Monday?"

"Fine, but not too early. I like mornings to myself."

"Noon it is. The publisher will be thrilled. I can hear the ka-ching of foreign rights dollars. You're practically a goddess in Latin America."

"They don't love *me*, Ford. They love Vivica Spenser." Was that it? The world loved Vivica, not Colette. So the show's end meant the end of the only love she knew?

"Of course they love Vivica. But who is Vivica without Colette Greer?" Ford's big hand covered hers. "It'll be therapeutic. Writing. You can exorcise your demons."

"You think I have demons?"

On Colette's last word, the taxi eased alongside a curb with nothing in view but brick buildings.

Ford offered the man his credit card while she stepped out of the car without waiting for assistance, raising her face to the thin, crisp morning breeze, to the sights and sounds of New York.

Fall in the city was magical, with a kind of cool-breeze ethereal energy that reminded her of her youth. When she had skipped down the sidewalk, turned cartwheels on the lawn, and collected gold, red, and orange leaves for a treasure box.

"Top floor," Ford said, pointing to the building as he joined her by the curb, tucking away his wallet.

Colette wobbled with her first step, the ground beneath her quaking. So this was it. Her final call with the cast.

The End.

Nothing but the blinding glare of endless blank days ahead.

"I can't—"

"Excuse me?" Ford glanced at his ringing phone, then tucked it away. "You can't what?" He cupped his hand against her elbow and tried to inch her forward.

"I can't go up there, Ford." Her voice warbled and she sounded feeble, old, like she was a hundred and one instead of vibrant and cultured at eighty-two.

Ford shielded his eyes as the morning sun fell between the buildings. "What's going on? Talk to me."

"It's just . . . over." Colette regarded Ford for a moment. Then without so much as a deep breath, she evoked Vivica Spenser. The old broad had twice her strength. "Well, shall we?" She smiled, raising her chin, stepping toward the building. "Bart Maverick will never let me live it down if he arrives before me."

"Colette?"

She glanced back at Ford. "I'm fine."

"Are you sure?"

"More than anything." A famous Vivica Spenser line that served her well.

Ford led the way to a bright, well-lit studio. Music with a light, toe-tapping melody added texture to the atmosphere. A smooth tenor sang about being happy.

Some of the cast had already arrived, including ninety-seven-year-old Wilma Potter, who played Colette's first mother on the show. The two never got along. Wilma greatly resented playing Colette's mother when they were only fifteen years apart.

Greeting the cast, both old and new, current and retired, Colette walked in Vivica's shoes and postured herself as the dame she was and drew the room under her spell.

All the while, however, she avoided the slender blonde working with an equally slender brunette setting up behind the camera. She'd face Taylor soon enough.

She joined in the jubilee when the legendary Bart Maverick arrived, who played the rich and handsome Derek VanMartin, Vivica's first and truest love, and patriarch of the VanMartin fortune.

"Gorgeous Colette." Without missing a beat, Bart swept Colette backward and kissed her, making a show of it for everyone.

Applause rose and floated around her, through her, never landing. Never finding space in her heart. Because she never craved applause. Colette craved the escape of being another character. Of living a life written by others.

When Bart released her, Colette swatted at him. "Such a ham, Bart. Don't you ever change? Act your age."

"This is my age," he said with a wink, turning to greet the rest of the cast.

Still a charmer, that Bart. Colette realized how much she missed him. He'd left the show in the late nineties due to a heart condition, and, well, the show had never been the same. At least for her.

"Are we all here?" Taylor stood in front of them, looking trim in a pair of jeans and a fitted top. She was gorgeous. So like Colette's memories of Mamá. She had the Greer eyes and full lips.

Annoying, telling tears burned in Colette's eyes, threatening to expose her. She batted away the sheen and held her smile in perfection, nodding when Taylor's gaze swept past her and back again.

Oh my, she *was* beautiful. And when she smiled at Colette, the floor crumbled from under her feet, sending her tumbling through time.

> *Standing on the stool next to the London house stove, watching Mamá cook supper, laughing as Papá's deep bass song filled the house. Happy Christmases by the fire before the war. Running home after church, the melody of God's love in her heart.*

Cozy nights listening to Mamá reading bed-time stories, Colette curled up in bed with Peg. Dressed in lace and ribbons for Mimi Blanton's wedding. At that old chapel in Nottingham. Summers at the shore. On the boat with Peg to America, so scared, yet so full of expectation.

Aunt Jean and Uncle Fred, Clem, and the warm welcome of their home.

Jimmy. Every moment with him.

Seeing Heart's Bend disappear on the horizon as Spice's old Ford headed north out of town, tears dripping from her chin, soaking her blouse.

She couldn't stand another moment. Colette reached to pull herself from the memory, grabbing at nothing but air, desperate to steady herself.

"Colette, good to see you." Taylor offered her hand and Colette escaped her reverie.

"It's good to be seen." It was the first answer that came to mind. What else could she say? "Are we sitting here?" Colette motioned to the large, red velvet sofa. To her own ears, she sounded distant and a bit snobby. But that was the voice of ancient walls.

"Yes, if you don't mind. Colette, here, in the middle." Taylor deposited her on the cushions.

"Naturally," Bart said. "Colette is the sun and we are her moons."

"Hush, you, and sit next to me." Colette patted the soft surface, avoiding Taylor's face, avoiding the storm surge of emotions pounding against her.

"Perfect. Bart Maverick?" Taylor said, offering her

hand. "I'm Taylor Branson." She smiled and had old Bart mesmerized right off.

But was she still going by Branson? Colette gave Taylor the once-over. Wasn't she married? To an ad man, if memory served.

"Addison?" Taylor called to the brunette. "Why don't you set up the cast while I test the light?"

Watching Taylor, Colette battled a rising heat of regret. Since arriving in New York the spring of '51, she'd never allowed herself to look back, to dwell on the past. Because the pain threatened to be her breaking.

But for a split second, in this moment, she pinged with a sliver of truth. All of her life's work and accomplishments were rubbish compared to what she could've been, what she *should've* been. And nothing reminded her more than beautiful Taylor Branson.

CHAPTER FIVE

JIMMY

Well now, wasn't that weird? Twice in one week? What turn of events had the Lord brung his way?

Jimmy settled the kitchen receiver on the phone's base and stared out the window over the sink. His chapel. Left dark and alone, silent for sixty-plus years now, suddenly had folks popping out of time for a gander at it.

With the chapel tucked back off River Road, he didn't reckon anyone knew about it except him, his dear departed dad, and the property appraiser.

But some fella from *Architecture Quarterly* had called wanting to send a photographer down. Said they were doing an issue on classic American wedding chapels. But Jimmy didn't have a pie-eyed guess as to how they discovered his place.

When Jimmy inquired, the man said he didn't know.

But if Jimmy indeed had a wedding chapel tucked up in the woods, they'd like to feature it in their magazine.

"We heard it was a beauty."

From who? Property appraiser Arnold Rowland didn't have *Architecture Quarterly* connections. Of that Jimmy was sure.

It was a mystery, to be sure.

And just now a real estate agent called. Keith Niven said he wanted to look at the place and if Jimmy was interested he had a buyer.

"I'm out here on your property, and boy, Coach, what're you doing with this thing?" Keith had whistled loud and shrill, giving Jimmy the impression he was wowed by the place. Or was that strictly salesman hype? "Do you want to sell?"

"No," was Jimmy's gut response. But he held off saying it. Maybe it was time. After the *Architecture Quarterly* photographer showed up next week, he was bound to get all kinds of interest. He might as well give the lead to Keith.

"I'll head on out there. Give me ten minutes."

"Fantastic."

So with this quagmire on his mind, Jimmy fished his truck keys from the fruit bowl by the kitchen door and stepped into the midday sun, summer's grip still hot and strong on the passing September days.

But that's the way it was in Middle Tennessee. He'd spent more than his share of autumn afternoons baking under the sun's rays, running football practice, building boys into men.

Then one day God would flip the switch, drop the

temperatures, color the trees with the beauty of heaven, and cheer up life with full-on football weather.

He missed those days. Missed filling his life with meaning. But nine years ago, when he turned seventy-four, he heard the bong of time in his chest and knew it was time to hand over the reins of Rock Mill High's football program to a younger man.

Tom Meyers was doing a good job of it too. Hadn't won a national title yet, but it was harder today than in Jimmy's day.

As he walked to his truck, his thoughts bounced from football to the chapel, to Keith's proposition. He was a young buck, this real estate agent, and a good man as far as Jimmy knew. His daddy had played on one of Jimmy's championship teams.

Settled behind the wheel, Jimmy fired up the engine, then paused with his hand on the gear shift. His old chapel . . . The memories surfaced . . .

Shoot fire, he had forgotten the chapel key.

Leaving the truck engine idling, he traced his way back to the house, crossed the kitchen to the living room, then made his way up the stairs. In his room, under the dormer eaves, he opened the narrow half door leading to the attic and climbed up.

Stooping down, he reached through the dark, retrieving a small cedar box. When he raised the lid, the scent of the wood enhanced his memory.

What are you going to do with the place?" Dad had followed Jimmy into his room, not willing to leave it be.

"*Lock it up.*"

"*After all your hard work? Jimmy, let it be useful—*"

"*I'm locking it up since you wouldn't let me burn it.*" Jimmy searched his dresser for something, anything, he could use to store the key. He spied a dust-covered cedar box he'd made in Sunday school eons ago. Popping it open, he dropped the key inside.

"*You won't always feel this way,*" Dad said. "*She might come back.*"

"*Yeah? Did Mama?*" It was a low blow, but anger threw mean punches.

"*What have I been telling you? Don't be like me. Move on. Find another gal.*" Dad moved to the door, his wide, large shoulders rounded down with the weight of the conversation. "*Just promise me you won't throw away the key.*"

He wasn't talking about the metal piece in the cedar box. Jimmy knew it. Falling on his bed, stretching out, locking his hands behind his head, he nodded. "*I won't . . . I won't throw away the key.*"

Returning the box to its hideaway, Jimmy shook away the fragrance of the past. But he had thrown away the key. To his heart. While the physical key to the chapel remained, Jimmy kept the letter of the law but not the grace.

He squeezed the key against his palm. "Sorry, Daddy." Even at eighty-three, he missed his father.

But today represented a new chance. To pass the key on, give the old chapel the life it never had. It was too late for his heart but not for the chapel's. Not his dreams for her.

But did he have the courage? Jimmy wouldn't know until he opened the door and stepped inside his past for the first time in a long time.

With that in mind, Jimmy left the house, nurturing a sense of purpose. Perhaps the Divine was intervening, answering an unspoken prayer in his heart.

He drove slowly down the street, the slightest touch of fall painting the edge of the green hills.

He jutted his elbow out the open window and caught a whiff of burning firewood. Change was in the air, and it had him hankering for something he could not see nor touch.

Turning off Dunbar Street onto River Road, Jimmy headed north for three short miles.

Along the sloping hills, another housing development seemed to have popped up overnight. Heart's Bend hardly looked the same in recent years, what with Nashville expanding her borders and stretching northwest, posting new construction all over Jimmy's rolling hills and along the Cumberland River.

He'd lived out this way for so long he felt personal about the land. Back in the day, he'd wanted Daddy to buy the property surrounding their house. He managed to set money down on the first track when ole Rise Forester Sr. came along and gobbled up the rest.

Now his son, the scalawag Rise Jr., was selling to anyone who could buy. Word was he had no choice.

He'd blown through the family fortune in a couple of decades. Not to mention he was a mean cuss. What he did to his kid, Jack . . .

Jimmy shifted in his seat, twisting his hand on the wheel. He'd coached hundreds of kids in his forty-five-year career, but Jack Forester remained a standout in his mind. Jimmy had gotten the chance to coach him right before he retired. The boy worked hard, played hard, studied hard. Did everything that was asked of him all the while being tossed from foster home to foster home. And his durn daddy watching it all go down, doing *nothing*.

The road to the chapel peeked out from underneath overgrown summer shrubs and Jimmy steered onto his property, a gem of a place smack in the middle of Forester's holdings.

Down a short, lean path, the truck broke into a bright, magical clearing, and the chapel rose from the earth and commanded the devotion of everything around her.

Jimmy breathed in. She was a beauty. Like her inspiration.

Majestic with her stone walls and weather-worn beam trim, the chapel drank in the sunlight through the cupola, then reflected it back out through the windows. The canopying beech and cottonwood trees stretched leafy branches over the slanted slate roof, creating a thicket of serenity.

Pulling alongside a thick carpet of late-summer grass, Jimmy stepped out of the truck, easing the door shut. "Hello, old friend," he said, a cord of emotion in his voice.

The breeze shimmied through the trees and coiled on the ground as if in response. *Hello to you too, old friend.*

His boot heels crunched on the gravel as he made his way to the pebbled concrete walkway—the final touch he'd put on the chapel thirty years ago. He used to visit about once a year, making sure she still stood whole and unbroken.

But one year had turned to two, two to three . . . Now Jimmy reckoned he hadn't been out here in six or seven years. And when he did come, it was only for a quick inspection. He hired Andrew Votava to keep the grounds trim and in shape. But otherwise . . .

He regretted his absence now, seeing how beautiful she became with time.

Stepping up on the minuscule portico, he pressed his hand against the sun-warmed gray stone.

She was part of him, this place. He'd deposited his sweat, his tears, and his heart here. And buried them with time.

At one point he saw the chapel only as a monument of sorrow. He'd intended to burn her to the ground until Daddy intervened.

"Finish what you started. Make peace with it, son."

He'd finished the construction but never made peace with it. No, for years he clung to anger and fed bitterness like a hungry bear. Until he woke up one day, looked in the mirror, and realized he'd become the man he never wanted to be, never even *tried* to become the man he dreamed to be.

He'd been content in his crotchety ways, being the tough yet winning coach, the old bachelor.

Then Peg Branson died four months ago, which sparked a new interest in religion for Jimmy. He realized he was an old man hoping to get into heaven but doing little to ensure his entry. He'd been darkening the door of Grace Church ever since. Even managed to read through the New Testament. Jesus had a whole heap to say about the dangers of being bitter.

Peg's funeral stirred something else in Jimmy—a desire to make peace with her sister, Colette. He'd searched the packed sanctuary for signs of her coming to say good-bye to her sister, but to his disappointment she only represented herself with a large bouquet of flowers.

The river of hurt ran deep between the sisters. Though Jimmy never understood all the whys. He had his own river to manage.

"Mr. Westbrook, Coach . . ." Keith Niven approached, waving, with a young African American woman accompanying him. So engrossed was Jimmy in his reverie that he hadn't heard Keith's car pull in.

"This place . . . Wow!" Keith shook Jimmy's hand with a force that needed reckoning. "This is Lisa Marie, my associate. Man, Jimmy, when did you buy this place? I didn't even know it was *here*."

"Nice to meet you." Ignoring Keith, Jimmy shook Lisa Marie's hand. She was pretty, with a sharp eagerness and an intelligent glint in her eye.

"Mr. Westbrook," she said. "This chapel is incredible."

"Thank you."

"Did you build it?" Keith shoved back his jacket to

anchor his hands on his belt. "I'm like, *bam*, blown away."

"Dug up the foundation the summer of 1949, right after I graduated high school."

Keith whistled. If he wanted to win over Jimmy, it was working. He loved anyone who loved his chapel. "What in the world . . . Summer of '49, huh? What inspired you?"

"A photograph, really." And a girl. But Jimmy would leave off with the short, simple answer. "I had a drafting class in school and made the wedding chapel drawings my project."

"So it *is* a wedding chapel?" Lisa Marie said, swatting at Keith. "I told you."

Keith narrowed his gaze at Jimmy. "Why a wedding chapel?"

"Because—"

"What's her name?" Lisa Marie said.

Jimmy cleared his throat. "H-her name?"

"Of the girl who inspired a high school boy to design a wedding chapel." So he wasn't so transparent.

"What's this?" Keith elbowed his way between Jimmy and Lisa Marie. "There was a girl?"

"I told you, I was inspired by a photograph." Now it was Jimmy's turn to prop his hands on his leather belt. The same one he'd slipped through his jeans' loops for the last thirty-six years. The belt was probably older than this whippersnapper, Keith.

"What makes it a wedding chapel, though?" Lisa Marie asked a downright good question. "Why not just 'a chapel'?"

"Because I said she was a wedding chapel." Jimmy

jutted out his chin. End of discussion. Maybe it wasn't such a good idea to meet Keith here.

When he designed this place, he had more than a plan for a building, but a plan for his life, one that included *her*. Because he'd loved Colette Greer more than himself.

And she'd loved him.

"Can we take a look inside?" Keith motioned to the front door.

Jimmy slipped the single key from his pocket, unlocking the door. "Here she blows." He stood aside to let Keith and Lisa Marie go in first. They exhaled their "Wows" in harmony.

Jimmy moved just inside the door, the emotion in his throat thick and rough. It felt like yesterday that he'd brought *her* here, snow falling all around, the world white and quiet. The world turning just for them.

Lisa Marie glanced back at Jimmy, holding up her phone. "Do you mind if I take some pictures?"

He shook his head. If he was going to sell the place, he'd best let go, let them do their job.

"The craftsmanship . . ." Lisa Marie aimed at the vaulted, exposed beam ceiling, stone walls, and slate floor, capturing image after image. "Did you cut the stones yourself?"

Jimmy nodded toward the part of the chapel's stone wall he could see from the tiny foyer. "Every one." And set each one in place too. With joy.

"This is fantastic." Keith stood under the stained glass window depicting the scene of Christ at a wedding. "Where did you get this?"

"An old church in downtown Nashville. It was torn

down during the reconstruction years after World War Two."

Keith whistled low, trying almost too hard to impress Jimmy. Slipping into the back pew on the right side, Jimmy rubbed the ache out of his old bum knee and inhaled a long breath.

The midmorning light cascaded through the cupola to the chapel floor where tiny diamond sunbeams floated and drifted in the wide swath.

"Coach, what did you intend to do with this place?"

Marry my girl. The thought no sooner skidded across his mind than he heard *it*. The resounding *thump-thump* of a heartbeat. So strong, so thorough, Jimmy gripped the pew in front of him and struggled for a deep breath.

"Coach, you all right?"

Jimmy nodded, rising, inching his way out of the pew and toward the door. The drumming . . . the reverberating *thump-thump* . . .

He had to get out of here. Escape. How was it possible? That sound? After so many years.

"Jimmy . . . Mr. Westbrook?" Lisa Marie's call trailed him through the chapel.

The first time he heard the thumping was sixty years ago, when Peg came by that day with her boy. He thought he was trapped inside an episode of the *Haunted Hour*. Or was experiencing a latent bout of shell shock. He'd only been home from Korea a couple of years.

But the sound was . . . real. All too real. Too close. Resounding in his chest. In his ears. And in a way Jimmy couldn't explain, it felt life-giving.

The sound, from wherever it came, gave him hope. But that hope fruited nothing except to make him wonder if he'd darn near lost his mind.

And he'd been to Korea. Faced the enemy's gun. But nothing spooked him like the sound of a living heart beating.

As far as he could remember, he'd not heard the sound since that day with Peg. Now, after sixty years, he heard it again?

Outside, he gulped the air. Dang if he wasn't too old for this sort of shenanigan.

In the yard, Keith and Lisa Marie caught up to him. "Coach?"

"It's yours if you want to buy it." It was time. At eighty-three he needed to be rid of lingering, silly boyhood dreams, rid of that *sound*. He'd be the very definition of a crazy, foolish old man if he didn't let her go.

"Yeah, we want to buy it."

A stony sensation filled his chest. "Wh-what're your plans?"

Lisa Marie glanced back. "I didn't see any electricity—"

"Ain't none. Gotta use candles and lanterns."

"Oh my," she sighed, smiling at Keith, then at Jimmy. "This is the most romantic place I've ever seen. Keith, we can sell this."

"Coach, we can have it listed by next week." Keith leaned toward him, encroaching on his personal space. Jimmy gave him a light shove in the chest.

"Hold up now, let me think about it." Maybe selling didn't appeal as much as he imagined.

"Talk to me. What would it take to make you sell?" Keith folded his arms, angled backward, and waited.

Jimmy tucked his hands in his pockets and walked around the dynamic real estate duo and faced his ole girl, his chapel. It'd been a holy place, full of communion and promise.

Yet here she stood. Silent. Rejected. A wedding chapel that had hosted no wedding. Not a real one anyway. There was that one night, with Colette, before he shipped out when . . .

Jimmy grunted, shoving the memory back down. Weren't this whole thing kind of pathetic when he considered it?

The hours he spent ringing his hammer against the stone. The golden-red dawn of summer days, when he walked onto these very grounds with his thermos full of coffee, his hand swinging a bag of Donut Haven's donuts, his heart full of dreams.

Among the trees, tucked in the shadows were the memories of voices, the deep bass laugh of his father, the lively banter of Clem—one of the best friends a man could hope to find.

Mercy if he didn't have tears from missing that old boy. *Clem Clemson* . . .

But it had all been in vain. *Vanity, vanity* . . .

He swung around to face Keith. "All right, let's put her on the market." There. He'd said it. Out loud. It was a verbal contract as far as he was concerned.

Lisa Marie pumped her fist in the air and Keith's big, cap-tooth grin did all his talking.

"But no promises," Jimmy said, striding toward the

chapel door to lock her up, hearing the comforting tick of his own small heartbeat. Not the one haunting this place. What *was* that? "I hold the right to refuse any buyer. And the price has to be right."

"Of course, of course. We can do that, Jimmy. We'll treat this place as if we built it ourselves."

So it was done. Keith went on about papers and listings as Jimmy headed for his truck and slid behind the wheel.

"I'll be in touch," Keith said.

"Fine, fine, you obviously know how to find me." Jimmy backed down the path, shooting onto the main road, an old pain in his back flaring up.

He tried hard to think of nothing as he arrived home, but the laughter and play of the neighbor children caught his eye, awakened his heart.

He watched them, jiggling his keys against his palm, as he took a slow walk to the kitchen door.

Too late . . . The truth branded his brain. The twist in his back intensified.

Of course it was too late. He was an old man. Too late to do anything about unfulfilled dreams. Too late to win a love that was lost. Too late for everything the chapel represented.

He, a hall-of-fame football coach, had ridden the bench in the game of life, waiting to be called in for a play that never came.

CHAPTER SIX

JIMMY

FRIDAY NIGHT UNDER THE LIGHTS

With each long stride, his hot breath swirling out from under his helmet, he sprinted toward the goal line, the football tucked tight against his ribs, his chest expanding with each deep inhale.

Peeking around the edge of his helmet, Jimmy saw the crowd on their feet, arms raised, their cheers inaudible against the pounding of his own pulse. Another two strides and he risked a backward glance, expecting to see a Bolton defender on his heels.

But he was alone, charging across midfield, not a defender in sight.

Ha-ha. Jimmy settled into the run, lengthened his stride, and . . .

Touchdown!

The roar of the crowd pierced him through—two hundred volts of human electricity. He loved every tingling one of them. Spiking the ball, he jutted his arms in the air and let rip the deepest, truest gut-wrenching holler.

"Go, Rockets!"

A weight hit him from behind, toppling him to the ground. Jimmy barely heard Clem's voice before he was buried under a mound of teammates, hammering his helmet and shoulder pads, shouting and laughing.

He'd done it. Scored the winning touchdown. With ten seconds remaining on the clock. *This*, right here, was the magic of Friday night under the lights. May it never end.

The referee's whistle ended the celebration and Jimmy crawled from under the pile, running back to the bench as the special teams lined up for the extra point. The crowd roared as the ball sailed through the uprights.

Coach Wilmer patted Jimmy on the helmet as he passed. "Good job, son. Defense, let's go. Hold 'em for ten measly seconds. You think you can do that?"

Removing his helmet, Jimmy raised his gaze to the stands, looking for Dad. The other reason he loved football season was bonding with his pop. He was a man of few words, so the fact that he never missed a game spoke volumes.

Jimmy spotted him halfway up in the center seats, standing, hands in his trouser pockets, cigarette smoke twirling out from under the brim of his fedora.

He acknowledged Jimmy with a single nod. That was about the extent of their affection—grunts and nods. Dad claimed the womenfolk were responsible for the mushy stuff, like prodding fathers to hug their sons and say things like, "I'm proud of you, boy." But they didn't have any womenfolk at their house since Mama ran off—save for Nana when she came over to make Sunday dinner—so Dad let love fall between the words, between the nods and handshakes.

Though there was that uncomfortable time when Jimmy was thirteen and Dad sat him down for a talk. Jimmy squirmed, thinking Dad was going to give him the business about the birds and bees again.

Instead, he cleared his throat and . . .

"I'm going to say this to you 'cause your nana's been on me about it. So here goes. I love you, you're my son . . . and I'm proud of you. I mean it now and always. No matter what."

Jimmy downed a cup of water and sat on the far end of the bench. It was crazy, the thoughts a fella came up with after making a touchdown. Must be all the running jarring his brain loose, letting memories leak.

He downed his water and tossed the paper cup in the trash, giving a shout for the defense just as Bradley sacked the quarterback. The Wildcats didn't stand a chance. Not with only five seconds left and the Rocket defense fired up.

"Westbrook, over here." Clem motioned him to join the rest of the O line.

As he moved, Jimmy took another gander at the stands, stopping cold when he saw *her*. She passed by, just on the other side of the chain-link fence, laughing, her hair gleaming in the stadium lights.

Clem's cousin. The girl from the picture. He'd seen her the day she arrived, moving into the Clemsons' house with her sister. But Dad had him working with his crew so Jimmy had no time to stop and welcome her properly to Heart's Bend.

In school he'd learned her name. *Colette*. Prettiest name he'd ever heard. And for the past three weeks he'd passed her in the halls, after lunch, on his way to trigonometry. He said hi but she kept her gaze down, clutching her books close.

According to Clem, they were quiet as mice, Peg and Colette, and twice as sad.

"Poor kids, lost everything in the war. First their mama in the Battle of Britain. Then their dad in the Battle of Berlin. Shot down."

About to climb the bleachers, she glanced back and stared right at him. Like they were lovers on the movie screen. Jimmy's heart thumped even harder than when he'd raced for the touchdown. He wanted to score a touchdown all over again, just for her.

The final whistle blew and the air horn burped into the cool night air. Game over. The Rockets had won!

Jimmy gathered his helmet and ran into the locker room, shoving aside thoughts of her, willing himself to bask in the team victory. *Celebrate!* he told himself. *Stop mooning over a girl.*

Coach stood on a bench and whistled everyone's attention to him. "Game ball," he said, the ball in his outstretched hand. "Jimmy Westbrook. Best run I've seen in a good long while. Keep it up."

The fellas erupted, cheering, their voices bouncing off the block walls. *"Jimmy . . . Jimmy . . . Jimmy."*

Grinning, he ducked away from his friends and

their aggressive back-slaps and accolades. He'd earned the game ball! Dad just might bust his buttons.

Less than thirty minutes later, he was showered and dressed, his dirty uniform stuffed in his duffel. The last of the team had wandered from the locker room. Jimmy's big night was over. In the history books.

The last one out, he cut off the lights and walked toward home, against a breeze that was a blend of late summer and the coming fall. Slices of moonlight haloed the darkest shadows.

Clinging as best as he could to his triumph, the game ball tucked close, he wanted to do something. Go somewhere.

He wasn't ready for his night to end. But moment by moment, the night ticked away. All the fellas were home now, or off with their girlfriends. Nearly all of his friends had moms and dads at home, siblings. By now they'd be getting ready to watch *Break the Bank* with a big bowl of popcorn.

At least that's how they did things at the Clemson household. Where Colette lived.

Colette . . . Colette. He rolled the name around in his head, then let each syllable whisper from his lips. *"Co-lette."* Her name was as pretty as her face.

Maybe he could celebrate with Dad, pop some kernels, catch a radio program. Dad hadn't signed onto the idea of owning a television yet. *"What do we need all that noise in the house for?"*

A mile to home, a mile to relive his touchdown over and over. Jimmy knew he'd have this moment for the rest of his life. And it made him want more.

Cutting across the Bostic and Philpott backyards, he crossed the road and finally skipped up the back steps into the kitchen. The screen door clapped closed behind him.

"Daddy-o, you here?" Jimmy draped his letterman jacket over the back of the kitchen chair and set the football in the empty fruit bowl. The house was dark save for a lone lamp shining from the living room. "Dad? Do we have any popcorn?"

Jimmy opened all the cupboards and scoured the pantry. Empty. When was the last time they'd been to the market? Rats, he kind of had his heart set on popcorn.

He collected the football to show his dad, but when he approached, his old man was fast asleep in his chair, a book open and pressed against his chest.

Jimmy gently tapped his foot. "You'll get a crick in your neck if you sleep like that, Pop."

"Wh-wha?" Orie Westbrook jerked upright with a snort, running his hand over his thick hair. "Hey, son." Jimmy couldn't gauge it really, but he considered his dad to be a handsome man, maybe even good-looking in a John Garfield kind of way. The gals in town seemed to take a second glance when he passed by and said his name all sweet like. *"Heeey, Orie."* "When did you come in?"

"Just now. Coach gave me the game ball." Jimmy spun the ball between his hands, dropping to the sofa.

Dad lowered the footrest, shaking the sleep from his head. "Congratulations."

"What say we do something, Dad? You know, celebrate."

"Like what?" Pop jutted his chin toward the ball. "I can build a shadow box for that if you want."

"S-sure, that'd be great." So his moment of glory could fit into a glass box. Dad's kind gesture deflated Jimmy's enthusiasm.

"Got that old wood from the trees we logged and stacked in the barn. Good solid walnut." Pop eased up from his chair, stretching, yawning. "Any of that strawberry pie left?"

Dad wasn't much of a cook, but he loved pie so he'd mastered the art of crust making. The summer Nana taught him, Jimmy never ate so many dry, doughy, burned, runny cherry, apple, strawberry, peach, pecan, and pumpkin pies.

He swore off pie for the rest of the year. But now? Pop's pies beat the bakery's.

"Dad, let's go to the movies. Or down to the soda fountain."

"We already saw the movie. Weren't one I'd pay a nickel to see again. You know, in my day that's all a picture show cost. A nickel."

"So you've said."

"And what would I do at the soda fountain?" Jimmy heard the refrigerator door open, then close. "Got to be up early in the morning. So do you, boy. We're pulling rock from Crawford's field. I'm going to need your help."

"Pop, I don't want to spend my Saturday digging limestone from Crawford's field. I don't know why you do either. You've got a good surveying job. Why do you have to work on the weekends? Don't know what you're collecting all the stone for anyway."

They had their own ten acres and then some that Pop never did anything with other than to ride a tractor over all summer, cutting the grass. He'd hemmed the property line with Tennessee limestone and that was that. Otherwise, he filled their barn with the stone and lumber he collected for no apparent reason.

"Watch your tone." Pop came through the kitchen door with a slice of pie on his plate. "You never know what good those stones will be one day." He eyed Jimmy across the room. "I'm heading out at six. Be ready."

"Why do I have to break my back, spend my time and sweat on your stones?"

"Because those stones are yours too. Ever think you'll get married one day, have a family? I got six acres I'm planning to give you. The materials I'm collecting will build a nice house for your wife. Save you a boatload of money too. That is, if you can ever smell good enough for some girl to go out with you." Pop arched his brow and wrinkled his nose.

"Hey, I showered after the game."

"You still have to be ready at six tomorrow morning. I'll buy you breakfast from Ella's."

Food was a small motivator, but enough. "I'm getting extra bacon then," Jimmy said, moving to the window, leaving Dad to shovel pie in his mouth.

Pinning back the curtain with the nose of the football, Jimmy stared in the direction of the Clemson home. Three wide streets over there was a girl who made his heart flutter, and she just might be sitting on the sofa with another boy.

A flame of jealousy burned the thin edge of his football hero confidence. Colette was the only girl who ever made him lose concentration in math class. Yet he never found the gumption to speak to her save for "hi" and "good-bye." He needed to get up some courage or else he'd end up an old bachelor like Dad. After his wife left, he never even considered another woman.

Jimmy didn't call her Mama. Because she'd never been one. Just a woman who gave birth, then ran off to seek fame and fortune—

From the window, Jimmy regarded his pop for a moment. The limestone, the lumber . . .

"Dad," he said, low, slow. "She's not coming back, you know." His old man stared at his empty plate. "Don't know why you waste your time, breaking your back and mine, collecting materials to build her a dream house when she's not come round here in a dozen years. And if she did, would we even want her?" Jimmy sure as shooting didn't. Just thinking about it made his gut rot. "What about Miss Jackson, down at the bank? She'd go on a date with you if you'd—"

"I'm a-warning you, James Allen—" Dad wielded his full name, piercing Jimmy's bravado. He *never* used his full name. "You're sixteen, but I can still take you to the woodshed if need be." Pop moved to the kitchen, and from the clatter, it sounded like he'd tossed his plate into the porcelain sink. "Don't ruin your big night by sassing me. Your grandpa would've already decked me across the room by now."

"I don't mean any disrespect." Jimmy collapsed

against the wall, restless. He itched to move, do something. No, what he itched to do was to be around Colette. Not stuck in the dark with Dad. Not tonight.

"What say I go over to Clem's?" If he couldn't talk to Colette on the night he was a hero, then he never would. "The kids gather over there, you know, after the games."

Jimmy went a few times last year, but he hated to leave Dad sitting home alone on a Friday night listening to Frank Sinatra or Bing Crosby croon love songs on the hi-fi. It seemed sort of pitiful. Jimmy shook his head. He didn't get it. Dad loved the ballads but he never made a move toward romance.

"Fred and Jean will be there?" Dad said, starting for the stairs.

"Where else would they be?" Jimmy headed for the kitchen and his jacket, smoothing his free hand over his hair, the ball still under his arm. "Do you think they'd leave Clem home alone? With a bunch of football players hanging around?"

"Guess not." Taking one step up, Dad paused, his hand resting on the banister, his face lost in the shadows. "Don't be angry, Jimmy, about your mama. You didn't know her. She was a fine woman."

"She left us. How fine can she be?"

"She was . . . full of life. A free spirit. Too pretty for her own good. And smart." He whistled, shaking his head. "She'd have gone to college too if she hadn't been expecting."

"That wasn't my fault." He'd heard the stories, about how Mama, the valedictorian, was pregnant the day she walked for her diploma. That summer Mama gave up her college scholarship to marry Dad—who had her father's shotgun pointed at his head.

"No, that one's me. It was my fault." Dad disappeared up the dark stairwell, not even bothering with the hallway light when he got to the top.

Jimmy didn't care whose fault it was. And while he didn't have any experience with baby-making, he was pretty sure it took two to tango. It wasn't right what Vera did, leaving, crushing Dad, and abandoning Jimmy.

But Dad blamed himself. The burden of guilt left him with enough heart to work and come home. Not much else. He was an old man at thirty-five.

Well, Jimmy wasn't going to be an old man at sixteen. He flew out the kitchen door and jogged toward Clem's. Tonight was his night. He was going to celebrate by talking to Colette. Because he'd be hanged if he'd choose a life like Dad's.

Waiting on a woman who weren't never coming home.

CHAPTER SEVEN

JACK

The apartment was silent and dark when Jack entered, not bothering to be quiet. Out of habit, and with skilled movements, he tossed his keys onto the table by the front door. They landed with a clatter against the old, scuffed wood.

Taylor had rescued the thing from a junk heap on the side of a street with the intention of "reclaiming it." She said it had character and once she restored it, the table would be a hallmark of their apartment.

However, it remained battered and scuffed. Not even the afternoon sun could get a shine from the thirsty wood.

Jack dropped down to the club chair facing the fireplace, the muted glow of the city his only light.

He felt sick. No, ill. Morbidly ill. Kicking off his shoes, he stretched his tie away from his neck and dropped it to the floor beside him. He shrugged out of his jacket, wadded it up, and tossed it against the white brick fireplace.

Was he really so naive? How did he *not* see this coming? He never even suspected. Never. How could she?

He shoved up out of the chair and paced to the balcony door. Pushing it open, he stepped onto the wide, tiled space. The mellow midnight air breathed a swallow of life back into his cold bones and stony emotions.

Betrayed. He hated it. There was nothing worse. *Nothing.* This particular betrayal cut to the core.

Jack slapped his palm down on the flat, cold metal railing. The small noise barely made a ripple against the sounds of the streets. From the river, a tugboat horn moaned. And the melody of lights bursting toward Brooklyn from the Manhattan skyline layered long, wavy sabers on the water's surface.

Raising his hand, Jack grabbed at the city—the buildings, the lights, the bridge, the teeming streets, the promise of success. It was supposed to be just that easy. Reach out, take what you want, and hang on.

But no, he was Jack Forester. How could he forget? Life refused to let him all the way in. Everything he wanted got ripped away. Ripped. Away. Eventually. No exaggeration. He could write a freaking *book* about it.

On top of losing a longtime 105 account today, Hops still pressured him about London.

"What are you doing out here?" Taylor's voice broke in, a soft chisel against the rock of his thoughts.

He glanced around as she stepped through the door onto the balcony, the hem of her nightshirt barely brushing the top of her legs. Man, she looked good with her hair mussed up and twisting over her shoulders, the ghostly streetlights touching her profile.

"It's late. You should be asleep."

"It's not late." She came alongside him, propping her arms on the railing, leaning into the air. "It's early. One a.m. early. Where have you been?"

"Working."

He'd been bothered and jammed up that afternoon he ran into her on his way back to his ad agency after arguing with a client. The cold, along with the salting of January flurries, only aided and abetted his irritation.

Hey, watch out." He tried to sidestep the human barricade coming around the corner of 67th, but she moved in the same direction.

"Sorry . . . I wasn't looking . . . Jack? Jack Gillingham?"

When he glanced into her royal blues, the ragged edge of his tension eased. "Taylor Branson?" He hugged her and when her laugh kissed his ear, the growl in his chest silenced. "What are you doing in New York City? And it's Forester. Gillingham was my foster parents' name." He stepped back, letting her go, but not wanting to as the cold claimed the spot on his chest where her warmth had radiated.

"I'm here now." She patted her photo bag. "I moved from LA in June."

"Why? Because all that sunshine was getting on your nerves?"

She laughed again, and his ad man brain said if he could bottle that sound, he'd be a billionaire. "Needed a change of scenery. A friend lined up a couple of jobs and wham, I loaded up and drove across the country."

"How's ole Heart's Bend? Have you been lately?"

"Christmas. And it's fine. My granny's not doing well, but it was . . ." She shrugged, a slight sadness invading her tone. *"You? Been back lately?"*

"Naw, work keeps me busy. I'm an ad exec for 105." The snow thickened and he detected a blue shiver on her lips.

"105? Very nice. I'd love to get some work with them. But I hear Hops Williams is a bear to manage."

"He is, but if you know a few tricks . . ." He winked, loving her responding smile. *"Say, I'm freezing. Can I buy you a cup of coffee? Tea? Something?"*

"Well . . ." She glanced skyward, assessing the snow clouds, then back at Jack. *"My job just canceled on me. But what's behind the door marked 'Something'?"*

She captured him. Right then and there. *"Lunch?"*

"Perfect. I'm starved."

Lunch turned to window shopping, a stop at a café, and then dinner. Then a meet-up for coffee in the morning. Dinner again. Dinner every night, actually, until their spontaneous wedding.

"Jack?" Taylor's touch ended the memory. "You were working?"

"Yeah, sorry, I meant to call. How'd your day go?" Didn't she have a shoot or something? Right, for *Always Tomorrow*. Brought to her by the arrogant Doug Voss.

"Fine." Her answer, in quick movements. "The *Always Tomorrow* shoot went well. Saw Colette."

"Yeah, what'd she say?"

"Nothing really. I mean, we're like strangers. Same blood in our veins, but that's about it. Though Addison thought we looked alike."

"The power of suggestion. It's an ad man's best tool."

"And why we think a pill can make us skinny."

She leaned near him and he exhaled a bit of his anger, but not enough to move him from the edge. He was comfortable there. Lived most of his life there. "Did she say anything about your granny's death?"

"Nope. She introduced me to one of her costars as her niece, but otherwise you'd never know we were family. Oh, Jack, she's gorgeous. Looks like she's still seventy."

"How old is she?"

"A year younger than Granny. So, eighty-two?"

"Hmm. Probably took a pill to keep her young."

Taylor bumped him with her hip. "Very funny."

"What'd you decide about Voss?" The edge was back in his voice. He heard it. He felt it.

She stepped back. "What do you mean, what did I decide?"

"Are you shooting the Emmys?"

"Really, Jack? You'd want me to go to LA with Doug?"

"It's a job." He heard himself. And he sounded stupid. But he wanted to be confident. Let her know he could handle whatever came his way. "I don't have anything to worry about, do I?" If she still had feelings for Voss in some way, then by all means, let them surface.

"You can't be serious." He felt the heat of her sigh. "Jack, why don't you tell me what's wrong?"

"Nothing."

She slid to the right, away from him. "By the way, the *Architecture Quarterly* people called. Thanks for the job. Said they needed me next weekend. Guess where?"

"LA?" Sarcasm was his default.

"Okay, Jack, fine." Taylor turned for the door. "Be out here brooding by yourself. I don't have time for this."

"Taylor, wait." He reached for her, his fingertips brushing the soft underside of her forearm. "Bad day. So, where is this *AQ* shoot?"

"It's okay, Jack. You don't have to care."

"I care. Look, I just . . . Things didn't go well at work."

"What do you mean, 'didn't go well'?" Taylor gasped. "Did Hops get angry with you for giving me the *AQ* job?"

He laughed. Her sincerity moved him. "No, he didn't get angry."

Hops was the opposite of angry. He wanted Jack to move to the London office. And really, Jack should tell Taylor sooner rather than later. But fear of rejection inspired all kinds of procrastination. If Taylor refused to go, then what? Did he go without her?

Just how committed were they in this six-month-old marriage? The one that bloomed from passion and spontaneity on a Martha's Vineyard beach.

When he proposed they hadn't even talked about things like finances or kids. Or how she might feel about moving across an ocean. But for now, in the immediate, Jack must focus on winning back an account.

"We have a kink in the FRESH Water account. So, where's this AQ shoot?"

"What kind of kink?"

"The shoot, Taylor. Where's the shoot—"

"Heart's Bend."

"Heart's Bend?" Jack glanced down at her, surprised. "Good ole HB? What's the job? Photos of decrepit Main Street buildings?"

"A wedding chapel, if you must know."

"A what? There's no wedding chapel in Heart's Bend."

"Apparently there is. Off River Road. Jimmy Westbrook built it."

"Coach Westbrook?"

"I guess . . ."

"He built a wedding chapel? Off River Road?" Jack scanned the back roads of his memory. He used to hunt out in the meadows, stealing away from one foster home or another.

Until Sam and Sarah took him in. Then he picnicked out there with their extended family. All one hundred of them eating fried chicken and collard greens. But he never saw a chapel.

"So, you're going home?"

"Looks like it. Guess it's serendipitous since I've been meaning to get down there, deal with Granny's house."

Taylor had inherited her granny's house, but she'd

only been home once in the past four months to deal with her inheritance. Her sister sent updates on things she'd taken or given away, but Taylor was needed to finish up. But like Jack, she seemed happier avoiding their hometown. Avoiding memories. For Taylor, it was her parents. Mainly her father.

"I thought I'd stay down there for a week, deal with the house. I've been leaving all the work to Emma."

"Sounds good."

"Y-you want to come with?" Her question came softly, tentatively.

"To Heart's Bend?" Jack shook his head. Once he left, he never looked back. "No, I've got work here. We lost the FRESH account."

"Oh, Jack, I'm sorry." She lightly brushed his arm and he accepted her comfort, though he otherwise remained ticked off. "How could you lose an account you've had for so long? Didn't they like your presentation?"

"Oh, they loved it. Very much when Alpine & Schmidt presented it to them."

"Huh? They presented your campaign?"

"They stole it."

Taylor laughed until his sharp glance cut her off. "What? You're serious? Someone *stole* your campaign? Are they in third grade?"

"Apparently Carmen gets chatty when she's had a few drinks. She blabbed the whole thing to her boyfriend over dinner one night." Jack left the rail for the balcony table they'd purchased the first week they'd moved in with visions of dinner under the stars.

But so far they only used it to catch bird droppings.

"Carmen?" Taylor sat next to him. "The top copy-writer at 105?"

"Yes, and her boyfriend is the head copywriter at Alpine & Schmidt."

"Jack, no . . . Surely she knows better."

"One would think. FRESH Water has been my account for three years. Hops won the account ten years ago. Thanks to Carmen, Alpine heard FRESH was coming to town to meet with us about a new brand ad campaign and invited them to a meeting at their office yesterday."

"And gave them your pitch." Her sympathetic tone bothered him. He wasn't used to commiseration. Or solidarity.

"A version of it. Close enough that FRESH laughed in the middle of my presentation. 'What is this, Jack? Some kind of a joke?'" He intoned Lennon McArthur's Ten-nessee accent with each syllable. "'We heard a similar presentation from Rob Schmidt last night. Did you steal it from them?' Har, har, har, har." Just repeating Len-non's mockery fired up Jack all over again. "Hops and I tried to recover. Spent the whole day trying to find out what happened. Then it all came to a head tonight."

"I'm so sorry, Jack." The breeze blew Taylor's hair over her shoulder, exposing the high, God-crafted planes of her face and the long, slender slope of her neck. She was lovely, so very, very lovely. He'd always thought so. But when he crossed her path back at Rock Mill High, he was arrogant, high on himself, and bar-ricaded like a war zone. He asked her out because he knew she'd say yes. Then he ignored her afterward, dissing her like poo on his shoe.

How'd he get so lucky? Lord above, how'd he get so lucky to be with her now?

"What happened?"

"Carmen came into my office around seven. I was packing up to leave. She was all tears, snot-nosed, bawling, confessing the whole thing. That was *after* she had acted appalled and disgusted all day over the Alpine news and pretended to be shocked when she heard they gave our presentation."

"She had to be devastated, Jack."

"She hung herself with her own stupidity. If you can't hold your liquor, don't drink. She's forty years old, Taylor. Been in the business for fifteen years. She's not some innocent freshman, unaware of the pitfalls."

"Maybe she never believed her boyfriend would steal from her."

"Technically, he didn't. She just brainstormed with him and it happened to be our idea." He peered at Taylor.

"So what now?"

"I fired her." His confession boomeranged in his chest and vibrated with the frequency of a car horn blaring in the distance.

"Whoa, that's a bit harsh, Jack. Really? She didn't mean to—"

"If she did it once, she'll do it again. Loyalty and confidentiality are everything in this business. If you're not loyal to me, then be loyal to the firm. If you're not loyal to the firm, be loyal to the client, and if, for some heinous reason, you can't do any of the above, then be loyal to yourself. Otherwise, you can be bought for the highest price."

Taylor sat back, shaking her head. He could feel her closing off. This was where things broke down with them. He was too direct. Harsh. A mode he learned long ago. It was how he survived.

If *he* knew anything about life, it was to cut off traitors. He had no time for the disloyal, for the betrayers. His heart already bore the scars of their work.

So if she was in any way leaning back toward Voss—

"You once told me you couldn't do your job without Carmen. That she was a life saver."

"Until she proved to be a thief."

"Oh, come on, Jack, really? You're so perfect no one needs to forgive you once in a while?"

"I try to never mess up."

"I thought you didn't have perfection scheduled until you were forty-five."

He shot her a hard glance. "She lost a client, Taylor."

"Fine, fine . . ." She turned away, staring toward the water.

Jack felt the power of his tone, as if he'd crushed her. Taylor . . . Unlike him, she was soft, easy on the eyes and the heart. She trusted too much—with Voss being Exhibit A—but held things close. Spoke up for the underdog.

"Don't worry about Carmen. She could go work for Alpine, but she has a two-year noncompete clause. She knew the rules, Taylor. Hey, I forgave her. We hugged it out. Gave her my handkerchief to dry her eyes, blow her nose. Then I fired her. If I hadn't, Hops would've."

Taylor drew her knees to her chin, anchoring her heels on the edge of the chair. "Remind me never to mess up."

"Don't ever work for me." He laughed, trying to remind her of his lighter side, but from the flash of ire in her eye, his answer achieved the opposite.

"Do you want the *AQ* job back?"

"Nope, that's all yours. Consider yourself a contractor." He leaned toward her. "Here's a question for you. Why would Voss walk in here and ask you to go to LA with me standing in the room?"

"I told you. He's that arrogant." Her expression hardened as she regarded him for a long moment. "But would you rather have him ask *without* you in the room?"

"I can't believe he only wants you for a job. I don't trust him. He still loves you."

"What?" She sounded incredulous. "He never said he loved me. You hear what you want to hear. Besides, what does it matter? I'm not into *him*. I'm married to you." She stood up and moved for the apartment. "I'm going to bed." As she passed by, the wind caught the loose edge of her collar, exposing the round sculpture of her breast.

"Taylor . . ." *Apologize and go inside with her.* Yet he couldn't make himself move or surrender to her charms, to his own urge to pull her onto his lap and kiss her enticing skin. *Tell her you appreciate her. Love her.* His early anger faded into an ache. He loved her, but he couldn't paint his feelings with the brush of action.

"Jack, sooner or later, you're going to have to deal with it," she said, pausing at the door.

"Deal with what?"

"That ghost you carry around in your soul."

This again? She insisted his father haunted him. "Rise Forester is alive, Taylor. So there's no ghost."

"There's the ghost of what he did to you. I live with its shadow every day."

She slipped through the door and Jack dropped his head to his hands, his entire body aching to follow her inside.

She was right, his biological dad haunted him. But he had no idea how to chase it away.

Taylor Branson was the best thing that had ever happened to him. Better than the ten million dollars he'd brought into 105 last year and the subsequent bonus.

If he could channel the energy he had for advertising into his marriage, he'd have the happiest wife on earth. But he had no idea how to be a husband, how to be raw and real, how to tell her that if she disappeared from his life he just might not be able to breathe.

. . .

TAYLOR

Taylor lay in bed, listening to the movements of her husband through the house. The red digital glow of the alarm clock on the corner dresser flashed 2:00 a.m.

After she had crawled in bed, she debated about

readdressing his Doug question, but decided to let it go. Bringing it up might seem as if she was defending herself. Or it might make him more suspicious, like she was hiding something.

The truth was that she hated her time with Doug. Regret coated every memory.

Sitting up, Taylor glanced toward the door, tuning in to the sounds of Jack in the kitchen—making a sandwich, pouring a glass of milk, moving to the sofa where the blue glow of the TV edged around the open bedroom door.

She'd shopped today, filled the cupboards and fridge, thinking they could have dinner together. After all, he'd said he wanted her in charge of *food*. But when he didn't come home or answer her call, she'd poured a bowl of cereal and done some work.

The TV hue flickered as Jack changed the channels. He'd pause on SportsCenter, then move to the home improvement shows. She smiled when she heard the muffled sound of a saw.

Should she go out there and watch with him? A salami sandwich sounded kind of nice. But did he want to be alone?

One thing was for sure, he didn't want to be in bed with her.

Six months in, weren't they technically still on their honeymoon? Shouldn't they be rushing home every night to be together, make love, take weekend drives to upstate or across New England?

Flopping back on her pillow, Taylor rolled over on

her side, burrowing under the thin sheet and Jack's Ohio State sports blanket. A road trip was how they got married in the first place.

Six months ago, if someone had told her she'd walk a Martha's Vineyard beach with Jack Gillingham, rather Forester, over-the-moon in love, she'd have . . .

Laughed. Yes, laughed. Loud.

But the feel of his hand in hers as they walked the Edgartown shore, laughing and running from the frigid Atlantic waves, was perfect. Real. True. Strong.

What do you think?" Jack wrapped his arm about her waist, drawing her close. Their footsteps came in unison. "You like the Vineyard?"

"I love it." He'd woken her up at five this morning, banging on the door of her New York apartment, surprising her with a breakfast basket of pastries and coffee. Then he kidnapped her for the five-hour drive across New England to the Massachusetts shore where they caught the ferry.

"I like when you're happy. You get this crystal glow in your eyes."

Taylor turned to walk backward, still holding his hands and peering at him eye to eye. "What do you see?" She held her eyes wide.

"Someone willing to take a chance."

"Yeah? On what?"

"Me."

His tone shifted something in her. They

weren't kidding around anymore. "What if I am?"

"Then marry me."

She stopped her backward motion and he walked into her, gripping her in his embrace. His sigh brushed his sweet breath across her face. "Marry me."

"What? Jack—"

"I know it's only been a few weeks."

"Eight."

"I know, but—" His gaze did not falter. "I want to be with you."

They'd been mad about each other since their first date. Went to movies, watched sports, talked about today and tomorrow. Never yesterday, which she loved about him. He was about the present moment, and the future. Each night when it was time for him to go home and leave her cramped apartment, they made out like teens, crushing the cushions on the oversized couch. Then Jack pushed away and went to the door. He'd never taken it any further. And Taylor was relieved.

That's where things had gone wrong with Doug. So she stayed with him because she'd "been" with him. Wasn't that the right thing to do?

But Jack? He never pushed the boundaries, and Taylor fell for his gallantry. Then he surprised her with this spontaneous Martha's

Vineyard getaway, booking two rooms at the Lighthouse Keepers Inn.

He was a gentleman. And she so needed a gentleman. But marriage?

"I don't know . . . Jack. I mean . . . You can't be serious."

"Stone serious. Right here, right now. Why not? We're good together."

"I adore you. I can't imagine being with anyone but you right now, but I'm just not sure—"

"Aren't you tired of playing it safe? There are plenty of stories of couples who got engaged after one or two dates. Married a week later. Then they went on to be married fifty, sixty, seventy years."

"It's not a contest, Jack—"

"No, it's not." He slipped his hand along the side of her neck and stroked her cheek with his thumb. "Have I told you how beautiful you are, Taylor? And that I've never felt this way about anyone? Ever."

"What about Abby Conrad? You were all over her at our senior prom."

"Not even Abby Conrad."

"How about the way you dumped me in eleventh grade? One date and you never spoke to me again. I'm sorry, but I have to raise the issue. That hurt like crazy, Jack."

"I know. I'm sorry."

"So what's all this, a do-over? You don't have to marry me to prove you've changed."

His kiss laughed against her lips. "Taylor, I was a blockhead. A jerk."

"You were smart and funny, and captain of the football team and a drummer in your own band. All the girls liked you."

"But I only liked you."

"So you dumped me?" She pulled free of him and walked away with a flirty flounce of her hair.

"I know, I know." He slipped his hand around her waist, picked her up, and twirled her around. "So I bolted, but now I have a chance to do what I wanted to do twelve years ago. Be with you." He lowered her feet to the sand. "Taylor, there's only you and me standing in this moment."

She searched his eyes. This was so outside her lines. Saying yes to a spontaneous marriage proposal when she wasn't even sure she believed in marriage and happily ever after. But what she saw radiating behind his blue irises was an eager sincerity. This was love.

"Leap with me." He squeezed her hands, slowly bending to one knee. "Taylor . . . Branson, will you—"

"You don't even know my middle name."

"Alice?"

"No."

"Jean?"

"No."

"Drusilla?"

"No." With a laugh and light swat on the head. "Jo."

"Taylor Jo Branson, will you marry me?"

"Okay, Jack . . . whatever Forester—"

"Spratt."

She grimaced. "Your name is Jack Spratt Forester?"

"Andrew. Jack Andrew Forester. But when I used Gillingham my initials were JAG, thus—"

"Your high school nickname." Pictures became clear. Understanding enlightened.

He rose to his feet and cradled her against him. "What do you say? Marry me?"

"Yes, Jack Andrew Forester, I'll leap. I'll marry you."

His lips against hers were thick and hungry, asking for her heart. And she responded, leaning against him, drifting away from the clouds of doubts stirring in her soul that told her love never lasted.

Popping up, Taylor dragged the blanket from the bed and tiptoed into the living room. "Jack?"

But he was asleep, his head resting on the back of the sofa, his breathing deep and even. The sandwich plate teetered precariously in his loose grip.

Taylor set it on the end table, then stepped over Jack's outstretched legs and settled next to him on the couch, the room crisp and cool from the open balcony window.

When she'd phoned Mama announcing that she'd

eloped with Jack Forester, she was not pleased. Nor was sister Emma.

"What in the world? Are you crazy?"

"Your sister is getting divorced and you eloped?"

Taylor endured an hour-long inquisition in which her long-time divorced mother and newly divorced sister tag-teamed her, passing the phone back and forth, summing up all their sage wisdom with, *"Don't put up with anything from him."*

Jack roused when Taylor fluffed the blanket over them, opening one eye. "Hey, babe—"

Babe. The smooth endearment dropped into her heart like coins in a jukebox and played a romantic melody. "Shh, go back to sleep."

"Taylor?"

"Yeah, Jack?"

"You're hot." He cocked her a saucy, barely awake grin.

"Yeah? You're *hot* too." Jack was named Most Handsome in high school and he'd only improved with age.

But her idyllic views of romance were crushed when she was fifteen by her father and her parents' subsequent divorce. So she didn't dream of fairy tales and white wedding gowns.

Reaching for the remote, Taylor aimed to turn off the TV but paused when a young image of Aunt Colette walked across the screen.

"Did you know you landed on the soap channel? Look, it's Colette in an old episode of *Always Tomorrow.*"

He peeked at the TV. "Looks like you."

"Please, she's so stunning." Taylor had Granny Peg's square face and sturdy features. Like Katharine Hepburn. Colette Greer was a genteel beauty with a girl-next-door face. The next Loretta Young, they'd called her.

Taylor pressed the remote's guide button to see the show's description. *"Vivica Spenser testifies in court about her CFO's embezzling. Aired 1985."*

Colette sat on the witness stand with eighties big hair and lots of makeup, her shoulders back, chin raised, giving life to Vivica. She answered the questions without faltering. Then when she was released from the stand, she walked to the defendant's table, picked up a glass of water, and tossed it in his face.

"Ha-ha, way to go, Vivica." Taylor shimmied Jack's hip, trying to wake him. "Look, Jack, Colette, or rather Vivica, tossed water in a guy's face. She was famous for doing that. Maybe you could get her for the FRESH account. She could start to throw a glass of FRESH water on someone but then stop and say, 'No, wait, this bottle of FRESH is too good for you.' Then she picks up a glass of *not* FRESH water or something and tosses it in their face. See? Brilliant." Taylor settled down in the cushions. "Shoot, this advertising thing ain't so hard."

To which Jack replied with a deep, rolling snort.

She stared at him, sleeping, his bangs sticking up, his full lips pink and sweet. "There's no Doug Voss, Jack. There's only you."

But confessing her heart to his awake-face never seemed to find space in their day. Even when he proposed, and again when they stood on the beach at sunset exchanging vows with matching platinum bands, the words "I love you" were oddly never said. As if they were both afraid to declare it. Or require it. But when they made love for the first time, and the second and third, she knew she was in love.

Then they came home, and gradually the waves of life washed away the shallow shore of their relationship and their expression to each other.

"Lord, if You can hear me, help us."

She believed God cared about people, about her. Otherwise, the whole Jesus-on-the-cross thing made *no* sense. But all she had was her Sunday school faith.

And the heartbeat. The one she heard as a kid when she crawled in bed at night and said her prayers.

It's why she left Doug. With him, she never heard the heartbeat, no matter how hard she tried. She knew the light within her was burning out.

But was leaping and eloping with Jack only more of the same?

Gently Taylor rose to her feet, rotating Jack so his long legs stretched the length of the sofa. "Night, Jack."

"Tay?"

"Yeah?"

"The salami was good."

"I'm glad. Go to sleep."

Back in their room, she took another blanket from the linen cupboard and curled up on the bed. As she drifted to sleep, the clock flashed 2:30 a.m. and a childhood prayer whispered across her dreams.

. . . *I pray the Lord my soul to keep.*

CHAPTER EIGHT

COLETTE

PARK AVENUE WEST, MANHATTAN

Since the taping of the show ended, Colette had taken to staying in her robe until 10:00 a.m. But no later. She pushed the edge of decorum as it was by lounging around, and she couldn't bear it much past midmorning.

Eighty-two or not, she had a life to live. Or so she hoped. Besides, some things were just too ingrained for her to change. Since the age of seven, she'd been waking up at 6:00 a.m. to do morning chores on the Morley farm. A time she did not care to remember or cherish.

A time of war. A time of death. Oh, the ache of missing Mamá and Papá.

Colette peered out the window of her bedroom suite. Central Park spread out below her, reminding her in some mystical way how small she was, how minute her success. In the vast scheme of things, she was nothing more than a speck. A gnat in the span of time.

But for the little girl who'd lost her parents, her

innocence, her one true love, her sister, her . . . everything, not even the great park could contain her heartaches.

But yet I see you.

Colette pressed her hand to her chest, the pace of her pulse rapid. *I suppose You do.*

She'd heard the internal voice of God before. He whispered past her from time to time, but she'd never paused long enough to ask Him what He wanted. Deep down, she knew. Her. He wanted her.

But she could not surrender. What if the Almighty broke her heart the way life had broken it? Then where would she be? In whom could she place her hope?

Stepping away from the window, the divine whisper, and the ridiculous travel down memory lane, Colette retired to her en suite to shower and dress.

By eleven she was in her office waiting for her co-author, Justine Longoria, and feeling restless.

The whole retirement business was a rather nasty lot. She found it disagreeable. Eighty-two or not, she wanted to work. To *do* something, put her hand to a good deed. Empty space just gave her too much time. That's when those old memories popped in for a visit.

No, thank you. Colette never understood the glory of reminiscing. Now with Peg gone, Colette imagined the past would be buried for good. All six feet under.

But she found herself mourning, wishing for someone to talk with about jolly old England, about Mamá and Papá, about the war years. About the joy and pain of Heart's Bend.

Colette sank down to her chair. She supposed

Justine's lot would be to hear her out, hear what she had to say. Whether Colette let her write it or not was another matter.

Seeing Peg's granddaughter had awakened a longing in Colette she'd not encountered in years. Decades, really. And more secrets pushed to the surface.

Peg had ruled Colette with an iron hand. She could not, would not, tell their secret.

They were sisters bound more by pain than by love.

Seventy years later, Colette was right. It wasn't over. Did she have the courage to write about it? Peg was no longer around to protest.

Could Colette tell the truth? The one that sent her away from Heart's Bend? Should she tell the story of how she never planned to stay in New York? How she longed to return to Heart's Bend? How acting was a fluke, her fame a charade?

"Ms. Greer?" Zoë, her girl Friday, appeared in the door. "Would you care for some tea?"

Zoë, an industrious young woman, was educated and athletic. She bustled about her work as if trying to burn more calories. She was Colette's recent replacement for Anna, her assistant for more than twenty years who resigned six months ago.

"At the moment, no. But when the writer arrives, we'll have tea and sandwiches. Nothing fancy. And the library and the living room need a good cleaning. There are still newspapers in the media room."

"I'll take care of them today." And young Zoë was gone, bouncing in such a way her ponytail swung up over her head. Colette must remember to inquire of Ford where in the world he had found the ball of energy called Zoë.

At one o'clock sharp, the writer rang and Zoë brought her to the study.

Justine was short and cute with her hair cropped in a wispy style that framed her features. She wore glasses that, oddly enough, were the single component that gave Colette confidence that the woman had any writing chops at all.

Writers should wear glasses.

"Ms. Greer. It's an honor to work with you. I'm Justine Longoria."

"Of course you are." Colette shook her hand, then motioned to the chair by the coffee table. "Please, have a seat."

Instead, Justine set her laptop down and roamed the room. "This place is incredible." She leaned to see out the window, down to the busy avenue. "Have you been here long?"

"Fifty years," Colette said.

"The park . . . wow. You can see the whole thing." Justine faced the room, hands on her hips. "This feels so big. Like I could move in and you'd never know."

"I suppose I'd find your little mouse droppings here and there." Colette sat in her chair by the end table. This was the same spot where she drank her juice in the morning and tea in the afternoon, watching the clouds move over the city.

"Yes, but not for a *very* long time." Justine settled down finally and reached for her laptop.

"So, how does this go?" Colette's restlessness intensified now that she was on the mark for telling her story. "I ramble on and you record? Or shall we do this interview style?"

Justine opened a thin silver computer with an apple emblem. "I thought I'd record while we talk. You tell stories. I'll ask questions. The publisher provided your basic bio and some older interview material, clips of the *Tonight Show*, *Dinah Shore*, and *Michael Douglas*. Your first soap opera, *Love of Life*, which I believe you got fired from, and your beginning days on *Always Tomorrow*."

"I was replaced. Not fired." In truth, she *had* been fired, but the network told the press Colette had been "replaced." But if she was going to make this book a tell-all . . .

Justine tapped on her keyboard and asked about WiFi—at which time Colette called for Zoë—and after a few moments, Justine declared she was ready to go.

"The publisher would like a first draft by the beginning of the year. Seems doable. Did they tell you it's set to release around the anniversary of the first episode of *Always Tomorrow*? Next summer sometime, so we have to get busy. In the publishing world, we're already behind."

"Well then," Colette said, leaning forward, evoking the courage of Vivica Spenser. "What would you like to know?"

Justine set an iPad on the coffee table for recording, then kicked off her shoes and curled her leg beneath her, balancing her laptop on her knees. "Tell me how you got to New York."

"A truck."

She laughed. "Just a truck? You woke up one morning and said, 'I think I'll get in a truck and drive to New York'?"

"How did you get to New York, Justine?"

She shrugged, thinking. "I came after college. My boyfriend was here and I wanted to work in an art gallery. But there were no art gallery jobs so I ended up blogging about art and city life. Next thing I know I'm writing other people's stories. Found out I was a pretty good cowriter. And seven years later, I'm in your living room."

Justine's transparency challenged Colette. She answered honestly, without sarcasm.

From the end table, she picked up her father's old cigarette lighter, the one treasure she brought from England—everything else was lost—and used it as a prop. She had vague memories of Papá cupping it in his hand as he lit a cigarette. "I came with Spice Keating."

Justine nodded, tapping on her computer. "You came with the big guns."

"He wasn't a big gun in 1951. Just a young man looking for a break in show business. We had no idea he'd produce shows like *Go West* and *Mulberry Street*."

"My mom loved *Mulberry Street*. But she was one of the lucky ones where her family life was exactly like the show. Too bad she couldn't find a husband to do the same for her own kids."

"Same with Spice. *Mulberry Street* was a show about the family he always wanted. Not the one he experienced." Colette's first honest confession felt good. Even if it was about Spice.

"We watch the reruns every Christmas as a family. My mom worked her fingers to the bone to keep us safe and happy, giving us our own version of *Mulberry Street*." Justine ran her fingers through her hair, ruining the style and making it stand on end. "What a loss to entertainment when Spice Keating died."

"Yes, too young. Only fifty-two."

"He lived large, from what I read. Were you in love with him?"

"In love?" Colette fiddled with the lighter, turning it in her hands. "No, no, we were friends. I'm not sure I even knew what love meant in 1951." The words twisted around her heart and dug in. *Lie.* She knew love, and its name was Jimmy Westbrook.

"How did you meet Spice?"

"High school. Then we seemed to be ready to change at the same time. I wanted to go places and Spice was offering a ride."

"How did your first soap opera, *Love of Life,* audition come about?" Justine appeared to pull the question from her notes.

"Spice's cousin worked on the show. She managed to get auditions for both of us."

"Did you always want to be an actress?"

"Mercy, no. I'd never acted in my life, but I had a lot of pent-up emotion to draw upon. I'd lived through a war and a ship ride to America, and moved to small-town Tennessee to live with relatives I'd never met. I was terrified but excited, afraid yet hopeful."

"What were you afraid of? Death? Being alone?"

"Life."

"Just life?"

"War paints life in very frightening colors."

"I imagine so." Justine scanned her notes while typing something on her computer. "You and your sister were sent out of the city during the London bombings."

"In August of 1939. I was barely seven years old. Peg was eight. We were put on a train and sent to live with a family in the country. My father was a pilot in the RAF and my mother worked with the signal corp. I was terrified to leave them. Convinced I'd never see them again."

"And did you?"

"Not my mother, no. Because Peg and I were so young, Papá thought it best we not attend her funeral. He came after the fact to tell us Mamá was safe in heaven and when he flew through the clouds, she'd be with him."

Justine glanced up, regarding Colette, then whispered, "I can't imagine."

"No, it's nothing to imagine."

"So you stayed on with your host family?"

"Papá didn't want to disrupt our life. And there was really nowhere else to go. Our grandparents were not able and Mamá's sister lived here, in America. We did get to see Papá over the years. He came out to the farm whenever possible." Colette smiled. "Oh, those were happy times."

"And when did he die?" Justine tapped on her computer.

"The Battle of Berlin. In '44. Shot down."

Justine shook her head, then stared toward the window. "You hear history, you read history, you watch it in movies or on TV, but you never understand how it impacts people until you encounter someone who was there." She returned her attention to Colette. "How did you find out? I mean, that your father had died? A telegram? And how did you feel? Scared? Alone?"

"Our host family told us. And yes, we, I, felt very much alone. Terrified."

"Who was your host family?"

"The Morleys. Farmers in Carmarthenshire."

"They were childless?"

"They had a son. Nigel." Colette shifted in her chair. She never cared for him.

Justine smiled. "This is good stuff, but we're just scratching the surface, getting into the life of the great Colette Greer."

"The great Colette Greer was nothing more than a silly girl who became a silly actress, playing the same silly woman on TV for sixty years." *Sixty years.* Was she more Vivica than Colette? Or was Vivica simply the light side of Colette?

If Justine was smart—Colette suspected she was—she'd eventually see the truth. Colette hadn't been a girl looking for adventure or for her name to be in white lights. She'd been a girl looking for a place to hide.

"What about boyfriends, lovers? You said nothing happened between you and Spice, but you were, *are*, a beautiful woman. You must've had your share of suitors."

"Are you married, Justine?"

She sighed. "No, I'm not."

"What happened to the boy you moved here for?"

"We broke up."

"Do you have a boyfriend now?"

She rubbed her forehead with the edge of her thumb. "I work too much."

"So you understand, then. Sometimes life takes you on a path that never leads to love."

"That's a morbid thought. I want to get married, maybe move to Long Island and have a couple of kids."

"Sometimes it's not in the cards," Colette said, straightening her stiff back and motioning to her penthouse walls. "This is where my life took me and I'm quite pleased with it."

"But you had lovers, right? Just not husbands."

Colette pressed her finger to her lips. "Shh, darling. A lady never tells."

"Really? 'Cause I got a contract that tells me I'm to get your entire life story." Justine narrowed her gaze at Colette. "What are you not telling me? Being evasive speaks to me of 'the one that got away.'"

Colette squeezed the silver lighter into her palm.

"Colette, was there one that got away?"

"Perhaps. Or maybe I came to my senses and let *him* go."

. . .

September 1948

After Friday Night Under the Lights

Aunt Jean's wide, warm kitchen was full of light and the laughter of red-cheeked boys. Cousin Clem had many handsome chaps as friends, strapping and rugged from playing sports.

Sitting among them, Colette sipped from her iced tea, a new drink she rather adored. In Carmarthenshire they drank hot, bitter tea most of the time, or black coffee, without sugar as it was a scarce luxury during the war.

Each Friday Uncle Fred allowed Clem to host parties after the football match as long as the kids behaved and helped clean up. Although she'd only lived in Heart's Bend for a month, Colette found these parties wonderful for making new friends.

Because of Clem, she and Peg had been easily accepted at school. The lads greeted Colette as she walked the halls. The girls insisted she dine with them at the lunch hour. Everyone especially adored Peg, so classically lovely with her reddish-brown curls, curious brown eyes, and pouty lips. She'd taken to wearing red lipstick and Aunt Jean said not a word.

Peg also charmed the kids with her mimicking skills. Voices. Drawing. Handwriting. She forged Shakespeare's script from a photograph on the wall at school and nearly gave the English teacher a heart attack when Peg claimed the piece was original. *"It's been in our family for generations."*

How the kids had laughed at Mr. Bruner's expense.

Last week Peg wrote a letter for one of the senior boys, Larry, who skipped school to see his girlfriend in another town. He brought his mum's grocery list for Peg to use as a sample. Peg's copy was flawless.

Larry exited the principal's office with a big smile on his face, giving Peg the thumbs-up.

She meant her skill to be a lark. A way to gain favor. But three more kids had asked for her talents in the last week.

Colette had warned her just last night that the habit would be her demise.

>*You'll get caught, mark my words. You think you're doing good, but you're causing harm."*
>
>*"You're such a worrywart. Leave me be, I'm having fun. Wait until I write a letter to myself from Princess Elizabeth."*
>
>*Her laugh gave Colette chills. "Peg, you can't—"*
>
>*"Colette, we've already faced the worst thing possible." Peg pursed her lips, lowering her voice. "After something like that, how in the world can a bit of princess handwriting fakery harm anyone?"*
>
>*"You said we were not to speak of their death."*
>
>*"Did you hear me speak of it? I certainly didn't." Peg switched off the light. "Go to sleep."*
>
>*"Go to sleep? No. I want to speak of it now that you've cracked the door." Colette switched the light back on. "Peg . . ." But her sister had gone silent, rolling away from her, leaving her to simmer in her own grief.*

Music burst into the kitchen from the living room, bringing Colette into the moment. She spun around to see Clem rolling back the rug and grabbing pretty

Sharon Hayes for the jitterbug, twisting her round and round until her skirt billowed and her long blond ponytail bounced about her shoulders.

"Come on, gang, let's get on the floor." One of the chaps ran by, tugging a dark-headed girl with round hips behind him. "Can't let Clem have all the fun."

The lads scooped up the other girls, and Peg, who'd become quite good at the jitterbug since living in Heart's Bend, danced with a bloke called Spice.

Colette loved to dance. She practiced in her room before the mirror. But, oh, she'd be too scared to dance with one of these chaps. When Peg caught her practicing the boogie-woogie, she laughed, telling Colette she looked silly.

Clem jumped in front of her, startling her, bowing with a grand sweep of his arm. "My dear English cousin, might I have this dance?"

"Oh no, I don't know." She'd feel so self-conscious. "I've never really da—"

"Never fear." Clem grabbed her hand, jerking her to her feet. "I'll teach you."

"Go on, sugar, dance." Aunt Jean took Colette's iced tea, pressing her forward from the confines of her chair. Her words of Southern affection carried her English breeding, and her bright eyes were so like Mamá's.

"B-but I'm so awkward. Truly I am." Colette took Clem's hand. She looked silly, according to Peg's assessment. "Clem, you'll be embarrassed to dance with me."

"What're you, crazy?" Shoving aside her protest, Clem twirled Colette onto the dance floor. "Come on, let's see what you can do."

A new song dropped on the hi-fi and on the down-beat, he started juking and jiving. Colette stumbled as he twisted her about, reeling her in and out, moving, turning, never letting his feet stop.

"Clem, you're a hepcat," one of the chaps hollered between the beats. "Go, daddy, go."

"Come on, Colette, get with the swing." Clem spun, tapping his feet, gyrating his hips. "You're too stiff."

She tripped around and caught Peg's disapproving posture. Who was she to be so condemning? Was she not dancing for her very life just two minutes ago? With that darling Spice Keating?

With the song nearly half over, Colette found her determination and fell into the rhythm, tapping, kicking, spinning, twisting from side to side, and following her cousin wherever he led. When he jerked about like a pecking hen, she did the same.

"Thatta girl, Lettie. Come on now. Hit that jive. I'm going to send you out . . . now come back through, do the shoulder twist. Yeah, like that . . ." Clem laughed, exerting an energy that spread a rosy glow across his high cheeks.

Note by note, Colette let go and danced. The song ended in a flurry of music, brass overlaying piano, and Clem spun her round to his father's Barcalounger where she collapsed, laughing and gasping for air as the kids applauded.

"Colette, where have you been hiding all your talent? You're wonderful."

One of Clem's friends danced alongside Colette. "Dance with me next, Lettie, okay?"

"Ice cream is ready out back if anyone's interested." Aunt Jean's announcement elicited a shout, and the whole gang surged through the house to the back porch.

Colette stumbled behind them. She adored dancing. Outside, the cool air felt good on her warm face. Taking a seat at the picnic table, she fanned herself with her hand, waiting for the ice-cream line to thin down.

Now that she knew she did not look silly, she'd listen to no more of Peg's insults. Colette would relish the freedom. Was it really all behind her? The war. The death. The Carmarthenshire farm. The nightmares.

Maybe she could dream about good things. About the possibilities—

That's when *he* appeared in the doorway. A tall, rather somber boy with a mop of dark hair and beautiful eyes. He wore a letter jacket like Clem's and had a football tucked in his arm.

He hesitated, glancing about, his gaze easing past her and then back again. He smiled and offered a short, stiff wave.

Her? Was he looking at her? Colette peeked around. She sat alone at the table. So, in polite and kind reply, she smiled and waved back.

"Jimmy, goodness, welcome." Aunt Jean shuffled over to him, a big ice-cream spoon in her hand.

"Hey, Mrs. Clemson. Is there room for one more?"

"There is always room for you. You needn't ask. Come on out, we're dishing up Fred's homemade ice cream."

Still clinging to that football, Jimmy stepped out on the porch.

"Jim-Jim." Clem jumped up to greet his friend. "The man of the night."

Jimmy was an instant hit. The other kids clamored around him, patting him on the back. Poor chap, he seemed rather overwhelmed by it all.

But he was the one who'd scored the winning try, or rather *touchdown*, as they called it in America.

"How'd it feel crossing the line?"

"Are you ever going to put that ball down?"

"Going to do it again next week, Jimmy?"

Peg emerged from among the throng, brandishing her pretty smile, and tiptoed up to kiss Jimmy on the cheek—when had her sister become so brazen?—and told him to "Do it again next week," as if she'd known him her whole life. As if she actually understood the game he played.

Peg!

"Our hero." Uncle Fred offered Jimmy a heaping bowl of ice cream. "Quite a run tonight, son. You looked All-State."

"Thank you, sir, but it's only the fourth game of the season." Jimmy glanced back at Colette and a smooth blush warmed her cheeks.

"Sweet pea, you sitting here without ice cream?" Aunt Jean patted Colette's hand. "What do you want? Vanilla with caramel or chocolate? No strawberry, sad to say."

"Chocolate. Please, I'll get it." She started to get up, but her knees melted on her and she buckled forward, her legs caught in the picnic bench. She had nothing to grab but air. "Aunt Jean—"

She collapsed forward, falling . . .

Jimmy stepped round, his hand outstretched. "I got you."

Colette hopped one-two, trying to steady herself and free her leg. Her hand landed smack inside his large, hero's bowl of ice cream.

The sound of the clay dish shattering on Aunt Jean's patio silenced the party.

"Oh, mercy, I do apologize, I do. My leg . . ."

"It's okay." Jimmy jutted forward, wrapping his arm about her, lifting her free from her encumbrance.

"M-my leg . . . fell asleep." Colette braced herself to gain her balance, her palm pressed against his thick chest and plaid shirt.

He smelled of soap and starch. When she stepped back, he seemed like a giant, watching over her, protecting her.

"Ah, it's all right." He gently let her go. "Steady now?"

"Colette, goodness, child, what happened?" Aunt Jean bent down, collecting the pieces of broken bowl.

"Please, Aunt Jean, let me. I'll clean it up." Colette dropped to one knee, ducking under her rising embarrassment.

"Sugar, why don't you go inside for the broom? And, Jimmy, run round to the utility room and get the bucket. Fill it with water. We'll splash this mess right out into the yard."

In the kitchen, Colette pressed her back against the wall, hand to her thudding heart.

"Humiliating, isn't it?" Peg stepped out from the kitchen shadows. "Being a clumsy oaf."

"You scared me." Colette opened the kitchen closet for the broom. "What are you doing hiding in here?"

"Are you trying to steal him from me?"

"Steal who?" Colette glanced toward the porch. "Him? The shy chap with the football? And I'm not clumsy. My leg fell asleep."

"*Sure* it did. You've always been rather awkward. And yes, Jimmy. I saw you smiling at him, flirting, then falling into his arms."

"Peg, what on earth? Have you at last gone mad? I told you my leg fell asleep." She snatched the broom from its hook. "Besides, I didn't know he was your chap. Did you inform him?"

"I've liked him since the first day I set eyes on him. You knew that, Colette."

"How would I know such a thing? Have you had a conversation with me in your mind again? Not bothering to speak your thoughts aloud?"

It was something Peg did. Hold whole conversations with Colette in her mind, determine the outcome, and respond accordingly. Colette never knew in what mood she'd find her sister.

"You've seen me with him, talking to him."

"I've seen you kiss his cheek, and if you don't mind, what in the world? Besides, you flirt with all the boys." Colette started out to the patio where Jimmy waited with the bucket of water. "Not everything is a competition, Peg."

She said it more for herself than her sister. Only eleven months apart, Peg had always considered Colette her competitor. As young girls, they were often confused as twins, and nothing flustered Peg more.

"I am the oldest."

When they shipped to the country, the school headmaster decisively enrolled the sisters in the same grade. Colette thought it lovely to have her sister as a classmate. Peg considered it humiliating.

In London, they had their own rooms. But at the Morley farmhouse, they had to share. Line upon line, brick upon brick, and the wall between them was built.

Then their mamá died and they bonded in the mourning process. But not for long. When other children were being let home, back to their families, and they were not, Peg became surly. When Papá came for his rare visits, Peg demanded his attention first, and always.

The ravages of war knew no boundaries.

Colette longed to be her sister's friend, but Peg saw the world one way—hers. Even Father Morley could not manage her when she was in a mood.

Then she'd turn on a dime, calm down, and repent with tears. Colette had no choice but to forgive her. Over and over.

Colette thought Peg would never change. Then Papá died, and they had a season of peace.

But when they sailed to America, the jealous, competitive Peg emerged.

"Be forewarned, my sister, I'm going to marry that boy."

Colette chortled. "You can't possibly know who you're going to marry, Peg. And don't you think the boy should have a say? Have you even spoken to him face-to-face? Not just a congratulatory kiss on the cheek."

"Mark my words, I'll marry him. Mamá knew she was going to marry Papá well before he did. She even told Aunt Jean, 'I'm going to marry Harold Greer, mark my words.'"

"So are you Mamá in this story? Telling your sister who you will marry? You don't even know Jimmy. Not been on a date. At least Mamá and Papá had been on a date. Besides, they knew each other in grammar school."

"I know what I know."

"Have you been having conversations in your head again? Working out everyone's life for them? Making decisions they know nothing of?"

"Hush up." Peg's tone wrapped her words in fire. "I *like* Jimmy. He's sweet and handsome. He's mine so don't even think . . . You can't win, Colette."

Colette held up the broom, unable to contain her weary sigh. "I've got to get on, they're waiting for me. But for the record, I'm not interested in Jimmy."

"Shh, keep your voice down."

"Have a go at him. I'm not getting married to him or anyone else. Ever."

Colette pushed through the screen door, fury burning up her bones. In times like these, she missed Mamá. She would have warned Peg to mind herself and stop acting so spoiled.

Jimmy smiled as Colette approached, and she felt his charm through to her backbone.

"Ready?" he said, poised to wash the paving stones with bucket water.

"Ready." Colette swished the broom over the ice cream as Jimmy poured, peeking once, then twice at Jimmy. He was sweet. And very handsome.

"Good as new, I see." Aunt Jean slipped her arm around Colette, smiling.

"I do apologize, Aunt Jean. It was my fault."

"Mercy, no one is accusing you. Your leg fell asleep. Run along and have some ice cream. Help Jimmy scoop another bowl." Aunt Jean pressed between them toward the sliding doors. "You're still the man of the evening, James Westbrook."

Then they were alone. Colette wasn't sure what to do with her hands or where to look.

"You want some ice cream?" he asked.

She nodded, looking up only to trip again into his soft grin and blue eyes.

"Come on, I'm an expert at dishing out ice cream."

"All right, let's see if your ice-cream dishing matches your skill on the pitch." Colette followed, a pluck of happiness on her heart.

"Two or three scoops?" Jimmy held up a clean bowl.

"Just one."

"Okay, then, two it is." He dug into the ice-cream bucket with grandness, making her laugh.

"I said one."

"Girls can never enjoy ice cream, all worried about their figure." When he glanced back, his gaze roamed subtly down her figure, then back up to her face. "You don't got nothing to worry about."

Colette fanned with embarrassment. "Because I don't eat two scoops of ice cream."

"All right, you win. One scoop."

"No, make it two." She inched forward, testing her confidence, feeling comfortable in his presence. "I'm hungry tonight."

"Now you're talking." Jimmy heaped a large dollop into her bowl—surely the equivalent of four scoops—then another. "I see you every day after lunch," he said, handing Colette the bowl along with a spoon.

"You see me? Where?"

"In the north hall. On my way to trig." Jimmy took up another bowl and filled it with the creamy vanilla.

"I never see you." Colette drizzled chocolate over her massive serving. She'd not be able to finish this but she'd do her best.

Beyond the patio, the kids gathered around a fire pit Uncle Fred built. Orange flames burned up the night, crackling, delighting.

"Funny," she said. "To eat ice cream while Uncle Fred arranges a fire."

"Welcome to Tennessee." Jimmy doused his serving with a liberal amount of chocolate and peanuts, then motioned to the picnic table. "I-I saw you . . . tonight. At the game."

"Me?" She sat next to him and spooned a bite of ice cream. Oh, it sent shivers to her brain.

"In the stands." Jimmy reached for the football he'd set off to the side and tucked it under his arm as he balanced his ice cream and straddled the old wooden bench. "I thought you saw me too."

"Oh, there were so many people." Colette fixed on her icy treat, fearing that if she gazed into his blue eyes, she might swoon backward off the bench. She did see him. But not on purpose. Though this chap bothered her, messed with her starched reserve.

"How do you like it here? In Tennessee?"

"Lovely. Aunt Jean and Uncle Fred are simply grand. Peg and I are grateful for their kindness, taking us in and all."

"Why wouldn't they? You're family."

"Yes, I suppose that's true."

"Sorry about your folks. Clem told me they were killed."

"Yes, long ago now, and far away."

"But you miss them?" He swirled the contents of his bowl, blending the chocolate syrup with the vanilla and peanuts.

"Always. Yes."

"How old are you? Fifteen, sixteen?"

"Sixteen." Colette sat up straight. "But I'm in the same grade as Peg. I believe you say 'a junior' here in America."

"Yep, that's what we say." Jimmy smiled, his voice rolling through Colette like a peaceful breeze. "Same as me."

"Well, hello." Peg plopped down on the other side of Jimmy, flipping her shiny curls over her shoulder in a practiced, perfected motion. "You were fabulous tonight, Jimmy."

Colette winced.

"Thanks." Jimmy scooted around to face Peg. "Do you like football?"

"I'm new to the American way of playing football,

but indeed, I find it exciting. Especially when you ran for the score."

"Guess all the practicing paid off." Jimmy laughed, glancing between Peg and Colette.

"Well, bravo you." Peg propped her chin in her hand and fashioned a gaze just for Jimmy.

Colette swallowed a cold gulp of ice cream. Peg was too much. Too *much*!

"Peg," the chap Spice called from the fire. "Come sit."

"Oh, go on, Spice." She giggled, waving him off. "I'm talking to Jimmy."

Oh, Peg . . .

Uncle Fred passed by with his upright bass. Clem and two other boys followed with guitars and a banjo.

"There's going to be music," Colette said, rising up, watching everyone get situated around the fire. In a few moments, the air twanged with the sound of their tuning.

Peg kept her attention on Jimmy. "You're in my mathematics course."

"Right, I've seen you. How do you like Mr. Harrison? Tough nut, isn't he?"

"I've an A grade so far. So I like it just fine."

The music started, a lively two-step tune. Aunt Jean grabbed one of the boys' hands and started box-stepping. The boy ducked his head, enduring the hoots of his friends. Aunt Jean kept him stepping right round the patio.

Peg stood, offering her hand to Jimmy. "Would you like to dance?"

"Um, I"—Jimmy glanced back at Colette—"guess."

"Jimmy," Clem called from the music circle. "Come play the fiddle." He held up a dark, very worn case.

"Y-yeah, sure." In one elegant move, Jimmy jumped the expanse between the picnic bench and fire pit and reached for the instrument.

Peg snatched Colette's arm. "I told you he was mine."

"He sat next to me. What would you have me do? Get up and walk away?"

Clem led the next song, the boys gathering around the fire singing, nearly shouting, "Mule Skinner Blues."

"Yes, Colette, walk away."

"I don't understand you, Peg. What are you doing? Asking a boy to dance, kissing him on the cheek?"

"It's 1948, the war's over, and times are changing, Colette."

"Well, politeness and manners do *not* change with wars or ends of wars."

Colette's gaze met her sister's and there she saw the truth—Peg was scared. As bound as ever. Her wounds from England festering beneath the surface. Colette softened, brushing her hand along her sister's arm.

"I'd never hurt you, Peg. Jimmy and I are barely acquainted. If you fancy him, give him a go."

"Thank you, Lettie. I knew you'd understand."

Colette remained at the table as Peg joined the songs by the fire, squeezing in next to Jimmy, swaying to the rhythm, her lips stumbling over the lyrics.

A chill of recognition ran through Colette. They'd never be free. She and Peg had been molded by war and those experiences had become their father, their mother, and their guiding force.

CHAPTER NINE

TAYLOR

Thursday morning the September sun fell in golden pools on the apartment hardwood. There was so much to do before catching a three o'clock to Nashville from LaGuardia.

Addison, Taylor's trusty-dusty part-time assistant, packed up camera lenses, blaring "Happy" from the speakers hooked to Taylor's laptop.

"*AQ* sent directions to the chapel. I e-mailed them to you." Addison set copies of *Architecture Quarterly* on Taylor's desk. "For your plane ride."

"What would I do without you?" The girl was a genius.

The melody of "Happy" matched the sunlight, the rhythm, the floating beams.

"*. . . feel like a room without a roof.*"

Yes, please, let her feel like a room without a roof instead of all closed up and dug in.

The week had passed quickly, both she and Jack working. He came home one evening with purchases from Saks. Shoes he didn't need, slacks and shirts.

She challenged him. He defended the purchases by

saying he needed to blow off steam. Round and round they went, no one winning. Both losers. And the tone was set for the weekend.

For a moment last week she thought maybe they could get back to the Jack and Taylor who leapt into love. But Jack worked late and twice fell asleep on the couch with the Buckeye blanket.

Taylor fixed on her computer screen. No time for regrets.

She had photos to deliver to Colette from the *Always Tomorrow* shoot before catching her flight. Ms. Greer got a first look at all images, choosing the ones she preferred before Taylor could make any final selections. Before any editing.

Fine by Taylor. Save her time. She copied a selection of photos onto a thumb drive.

The music ended, then started all over again, the bass vibrating through Taylor's soul.

"Addison, did you set this song on repeat?"

"Don't you just love it?" She wiggled around, waving her hands in the air. "Okay, lenses packed. What do you want to do about lighting?" Addison trained her hazel eyes on Taylor.

"Call The Video Company in Nashville. Ask for Ryan. Tell him I need two softboxes, two umbrellas, a power source, and some reflectors for an indoor-outdoor shoot. I'll pick them up tonight. Around six, seven if traffic is bad."

Addison pulled out her phone. "What if he doesn't have them?"

"He will. If not, he'll find them. He's an old friend."

"An old *friend*?" Addison sang her reply to the "Happy" melody. She was young, but the second-best thing to happen to Taylor since she landed in New York. Barely twenty, Addison was a New York City native—savvy and in the know. The perfect girl Friday.

She worked as an assistant for another photographer yet somehow found time to audition for off-Broadway shows. Her goal? "Have fun!" Neither fame nor fortune mattered to her.

But it did to Taylor. She wanted to make a living at her craft. She wanted to be a *name* in the business.

It was her dream since she was a teen. Though it was a wonder she stuck with it after that incident with Daddy. She had needed a candid shot for her black-and-white photography class with Mr. Ellison. Well, she'd gotten one, all right.

So candid she flunked the class.

"You're all set to work on your granny's place?" Addison said. "Are you going to sell it?"

"I don't know."

"What's Jack say?"

Taylor shrugged. "We've not really talked about it."

"What? You're kidding. What do you two do all the time?" Addison slammed her palm in the air. "Never mind, I don't want to know."

"Please. We work, we shop. Well, some people shop."

"I noticed a new shoe box in the trash."

"Only one?"

"Okay, three. Italian leather. Very nice."

"He has expensive taste."

"Then it's a good thing you're so cheap."

"Ha-ha, very funny. Did you call Ryan yet?"

"On it." Addison perched on the edge of Taylor's desk, listening, waiting. "Funny thing just now. As I was about to tell him who I was calling for, I tripped over your last name. Are you Branson now or Forester?"

"I-I haven't decided." Taylor dropped the thumb drive in her bag. Addison had a way of slicing through the façade to the bare naked truth.

Was Taylor a Branson or a Forester?

Addison pooched out her lower lip. "Okay . . . you're keeping Branson. Very hip. Though I pegged you as one of those take-her-husband's-name types."

"We've only been married six months." Taylor reached for her flip-flops under her desk.

"Only? My sister stopped by the courthouse on the way to her honeymoon. Hello, can I speak to Ryan, please? Taylor Branson's office calling."

Taylor listened as Addison dealt with Ryan, a twisting sensation in her chest. So she'd not changed her name yet. Fine. She was waiting. Waiting to see how things turned out. Jack didn't seem eager to make her a Forester. To be honest, she wasn't sure she wanted to be linked to the Forester name.

Rise Forester's shenanigans were legendary in Heart's Bend. It's a wonder he could hold up his head around town. Even worse, he was horrid to his own son.

Addison finished her call, reaching for Taylor's phone. "Ryan said he'd have the stuff ready. I'm putting his cell in your phone just in case. Is there anything you want me to do while you're gone?"

"Check e-mail. Follow up on potential clients and the jobs we have in the queue."

"What jobs in the queue?"

Taylor made a face. They didn't have any jobs in the queue. "Fine. Let's *get* some jobs. I'll follow up with Melinda House. Maybe we can shoot the spring collection. Oh, and check the PO box. Deposit any checks that come."

"What about the Emmys? Doug Voss sent you an expense voucher," Addison said.

And there was that . . . Taylor didn't bother mentioning the voucher to Jack. "I saw it." Taylor reached for her wristlet, slipping her phone in the front zip pouch. "But no."

"It's a job."

"Not one I want."

"Have you seen our bank balance?"

"Addison . . ." Taylor leveled her best I'm-the-boss voice. "No. Besides, Doug doesn't need me. He can hire anyone he wants out in LA."

"He says no one captures people like you."

"Doug likes to win. Get what he wants."

"Does he want you?" Addison's voice mellowed from assistant to friend.

Taylor started for the door, ignoring the question. "I'm heading to Colette Greer's place. Should be back in a few hours."

Then she'd grab her gear and head to LaGuardia.

At the elevator, the doors opened to reveal Doug waiting.

"What are you doing here?" Taylor backed toward the stairwell. It was only five flights down.

"Where're you going?" Doug followed. "I heard the *Always Tomorrow* shoot went well. And you're welcome."

"Don't you have a magazine to run?" Taylor jogged down one fight, then the next.

"Put it to bed last night. Starting fresh this morning." Doug's footsteps hammered behind her. "So you'll go to LA?"

She stopped, whirling around to him. "I'm not going. Good grief, don't you ever take no for an answer? Hire a photographer in LA, Doug."

"I want *you* to go." He'd eased down the steps toward her, lowering his voice, intensifying his words. "Whatever job you're doing in its place won't get you what you want."

"And how do you know what I want?"

"I know you. I used to share a bed with you."

She shivered. "Don't, Doug. Don't." There was no taste as bitter as regret.

He stepped down to where she stood, reaching for her hair, but lowering his hand as she flinched and curled away. "You want influence, a name, a reputation in the business. You're ambitious and hungry, Taylor."

"And look what it netted me. You." She started back down the stairs.

When she had first met Doug on Ocean Beach during a volleyball game with friends, he was witty and charming, the big-time New York publisher hobnobbing with lowly photographers. He was generous with his money. And his compliments.

Thinking she could manage his advances, Taylor never calculated she'd fall for him.

"Come on, Tay." Doug grazed her arm with his fingertips. "Come to LA. It'll be like old times. And if you want, no one has to know—"

"That suggestion is beneath even you, Doug." She rounded down the final flight of stairs.

"Come on, you can't be in love with this guy. You were with me for a year and never once hinted for a commitment. You leave me and—"

"*We* were a mistake."

"—two months later run off with this *ad man*." He scoffed. "I'm telling you I don't believe it."

In the building vestibule, Doug cut off Taylor's exit. "You're too cold to warm up to another man so quickly."

Jaw tensed, heart careening, she shoved him back one step. "Get. Out. Of my way."

"Fine," he said, using his velvet bass, brushing his fingers through the ends of her long, loose curls. "I'm not giving up."

"You should. You really, really should."

"Look me in the eye, Taylor. Tell me you don't have feelings for me. That you're not bored with this up-and-comer. He's too consumed with his career, his own upward mobility, to care for you. I know you, and being noticed is what you need, what you want."

Taylor glared at Doug, wrestling with an irritating awe over his boldness. "If I leave him, how do you know I won't do the same to you?"

He grinned as if he'd won. "Because I can give you what you want, what you need. I'm set in my career. I've made my money. *Gossip* runs like a well-oiled machine. I could honeymoon for a month in Bora Bora and come home to find sales had increased. I have room for love. Room for you."

The silk thread of his confession slipped right through her. "You don't have room for love or me. For anyone but yourself. This is about you getting what you can't have."

"So you think he loves you? Really?"

The fragrance of Doug's cologne trapped her in their past and she couldn't breathe. But it was the lingering truth in his question that made her tremor.

Did Jack really love her? Try as she might, she could not recall one profession of love. Desire, yes. Want, certainly. But love?

"You don't know whether he really loves you, do you?" Doug's arrogance rained on her doubt.

Taylor sidestepped him and exited the building. In the street, she hailed a passing taxi.

He loves me. He does. In his way.

In the moment, that one small confession brought enough confidence to keep her back to Doug, not venturing a response to his accusations as she slipped into the taxi and headed to Colette Greer's.

. . .

"Taylor, come on in." Zoë, Colette's assistant, led her through the penthouse, her ponytail swinging from side to side. "She's expecting you."

On the ride uptown, Taylor had composed herself, mentally scrubbing Doug from her psyche. But she could not so easily dislodge her own words.

"How do you know I won't do the same to you?"

The notion pinged around, looking for a response. Was that it? Did she fear she'd be like her father? That she couldn't go the lifetime-commitment distance? Jack deserved better. Despite his flaws, he didn't deserve his wife abandoning him.

He'd had enough of that in his life.

It was a mistake to marry him when she had so many unresolved issues in her heart.

"Ms. Greer, Taylor Branson to see you." Zoë ushered Taylor into a study where elegant wood floors met with clean, white walls.

"Taylor, lovely to see you." Colette sat behind a heavy, dark wood desk, neatly arranged with a laptop, a pencil tin, and a small Tiffany lamp.

"Here are the proofs." Taylor handed over the thumb drive. "I hear you get first dibs."

"I like to look before some poor photographer wastes his, or her, time editing. Invariably, the network picks all the wrong pictures. Do have a seat."

Taylor picked the closest chair and sat, legs crossed. "This is a beautiful room."

"I think so. I spend most of my time here." Colette studied the photos through narrowed eyes. "You're quite good. I've never seen so many good shots in one setting."

Taylor smiled. "It's a knack."

"You capture expression well."

"So I've heard." It was more than a knack, it was a gift, to make the lens see what she wanted it to see. "Of course, I had experienced subjects."

Colette laughed. "We've been through a lot of photo shoots together, the cast and I. Though I daresay yours was one of the better ones. All sentiment aside, mind you." She carried a hint of her English childhood in her voice.

Taylor's eye drifted to the mantel over the fireplace, the red brick another sharp contrast to the walls. Framed photos watched the room. From the colors and composition, Taylor knew they were personal, private images.

"Who is in these pictures?" She scanned the faces, recognizing none of them.

"Friends, my TV family." Colette continued to inspect the digital contact sheet.

Taylor examined each one, noting there was not one shot of the family on the mantel. "We missed you at Granny's funeral."

"Yes, well . . ." Colette's expression contained no regret or sorrow. Or emotion. "Peg and I said our good-byes quite a long time ago. Taylor, these pictures are splendid. I'm happy with all of them."

"All of them?"

"The network can choose whichever one they want." Colette offered back the thumb drive and pressed a button on the windowsill behind her desk. Standing, she smoothed the lines from her skirt. "Shall we have some tea?"

"I'd love to but I can't stay. I'm flying to Nashville this

afternoon." Taylor scanned the mantel photos one last time. So very different from the images Granny had in her home. Two sisters, with the same blood in their veins, lived very different lives. "Can I ask you something?"

"Go on . . ."

"What happened between you and Granny?"

"We chose different paths." Colette's assessment was quick and purely matter-of-fact.

"But you never visited. Didn't you want to be near her, reminisce about your childhood in England? Or Heart's Bend, for that matter. My sister, Emma, and I have our moments, but at the end of it all, we're the only ones who can remember our childhood, our parents."

"Peg and I did not get along."

"Are you telling me all the space between you and Granny was simply because you didn't see eye to eye on a few things?"

"Peg and I rarely saw eye to eye. So, you're off to Nashville?"

"Actually, to Heart's Bend. I have a shoot there. Colette, Granny's left her house to me." Taylor hesitated. What was that dark shadow flickering across Colette's features? "Is there anything you want from her house?"

Zoë interrupted, and Colette ordered tea for one. Then . . .

"I need nothing from Peg's home. I've got everything I need right here."

Taylor would never classify Colette Greer as warm, but in the moment she seemed to drop one cold degree.

"Well, if I find a childhood memento, I'll let you know. Maybe a photo or teacup."

"Taylor, mark my words, there is nothing in your granny's house for me."

CHAPTER TEN

JACK

He had forty-five minutes to pack and get to the airport. Jack tossed his laptop on the counter and made a beeline for the bedroom, bumping into his wife as she exited the closet, rolling her carry-on behind her.

"Jack? What are you doing here?"

"Heading to Nashville. I have a meeting tomorrow with the FRESH team. I got them to all come in on a Friday, so I need to be on my A game. Despite what Hops wants."

"What did Hops want?"

"He wants me on another job." Jack yanked open the closet doors and pulled his roller bag from the top shelf. Hops could go to London himself if he thought that job was so important. But Jack didn't want to run a foundation for WhiteWater Media, a cutting-edge social media group. The CEO was two years younger than Jack.

He wanted his own client back. FRESH Water.

"How long will you be there?" Taylor asked.

Jack tossed his suitcase to the bed. He didn't need much. "Until Sunday. Getting in a game of golf with the

CEO, Lennon, on Saturday." Socks, underwear, T-shirts, jeans, a nice button-down, and some golf gear.

"What about seeing Sam and Sarah? We told them we'd visit when we called to tell them we eloped."

Sam and Sarah were Jack's last foster parents, who treated him more like a son than anyone ever had. They were his mentors, saviors, guiding light. But he didn't like going home. Even to see the people he loved most. Because there was always the off chance he'd run into his father. And that he would avoid at all costs.

"Let's plan another trip to see them. No time this go-round."

"Your call." Taylor leaned against the door frame. "So how do you plan to win back the account?"

Jack slipped his phone out of his pocket. "Taylor, could you put this on the charger for me? I don't want to lose juice on the trip."

"Y-yeah, sure."

Her quiet hesitation raised his attention. Was she all right? "A-are you ready for your trip?"

"I think so. Hey, why don't you come down to Heart's Bend and stay with me for a few days? I'll be at Granny's. Emma insists we finish with the house."

"No can do. If I win FRESH back, no, *when* I win FRESH, I've got to get back here and roll up our corporate sleeves. We've got work to do. Not to mention hiring Carmen's replacement and showing some love to the accounts I've neglected this week." Jack tossed his Dopp kit on the bathroom counter. Toothpaste, toothbrush, shaving cream . . . "What time is your flight?"

"Three."

He glanced over at her. "I got the last seat on a two forty-five direct flight."

"LaGuardia?" Taylor ducked into the bathroom, taking a small packet of Dramamine from the medicine cabinet.

"No, JFK." Jack wedged his toiletries in the suitcase. "Otherwise we could've shared a cab."

"I've got a cab on the way, Jack. There's plenty of time to drop you off and get me over to LaGuardia. I'm prechecked so it'll save me time." Taylor tapped his shoulder. "Don't forget your Dramamine or you'll get motion sickness."

His fingers grazed over hers. "Th-thanks, babe." Their gazes locked. "Hey, why don't you come up to Nashville? Stay with me at the Hermitage."

She shook her head. "You'll be working and golfing. I have the chapel shoot tomorrow, with time reserved on Saturday in case I want to go back. And I'm working on the house. Speaking of . . . what should we do with Granny's house?"

"Whatever you want." Jack glanced around the room. Taylor could see him running through a mental checklist. "When do you come home?"

"Saturday next. Jack, we need to talk about Granny's house. Are we keeping it?"

"Why would we?" He zipped his suitcase. "It's not like we want to live in Heart's Bend ever again."

"Look, I know we both had to escape for a while, but never?"

"Not in the big-picture plan, Taylor. I thought you knew that."

"Then why'd you marry me? I'm Heart's Bend, a piece of what you want to forget. We have to go home sometime. To see my mom, my sister and her girls, Sam and Sarah."

"Okay, fine, but we don't have to do that now, do we? And you're *not* Heart's Bend. You're"—he shrugged—"*different*. A New Yorker."

He couldn't tell her because the words were all jumbled in his chest, but knowing her, watching her in high school, made him believe the world was a better place. He couldn't explain it. But he'd always been drawn to her.

"A Yankee?" Taylor grinned. "Granny would roll over in her grave."

"Like she was a true Southerner? Coming from England?"

"She adapted. Hey, by the way, I saw Colette today. She had some deal where she approved the photos from the shoot. I tried to get her to talk about Granny, but . . ." Taylor waved her hand past her face. "Ice."

"You're surprised?" He brushed past her for the kitchen. "Did I see Pop-Tarts?"

"Yeah, I guess. I mean, I know they didn't see each other much, but I thought she'd wax sentimental or something."

"My gut tells me whatever went down between the two of them left no room for sentimental waxing." Ah, cherry. His favorite. Jack tore open the foil wrapping. Creative work and dashing to the airport made him hungry. This would hold him until he arrived in Nashville. "How did Colette like the photos?"

"She liked them. All of them. Which is weird. No one ever likes *all* the shots."

"You're good. I've told you that before." Didn't she believe him? He'd told her before. "Why do you think I gave you the *AQ* job?"

"To one-up Doug."

"What? No." Did he sound convincing? Because he refused to be *that* kind of husband. Motivated by jealousy. "Because I thought you'd do a good job." Jack consumed the Pop-Tart in a few bites. Eating fast was practically his superpower.

Growing up, moving from house to house every year, and from family to family, he'd learned to eat fast. At twelve, he did a few odd jobs for neighbors and earned enough money to keep a food stash under his bed. It was a good plan until that particular foster mother discovered a trail of ants leading right to it. When Jack came home she was waiting. Popped him in the face before he could offer one word of explanation.

"Well, either way, I'm on my way." Taylor brushed her hand down his arm and his desire for her stirred. "You never told me your great plan for FRESH."

He pulled another Pop-Tart from the box. "My plan is brilliant. Begging."

She laughed, and the melody loosened the tension in his gut. He loved eliciting her laughter. He didn't know he possessed such a power until they started spending time together. He had never laughed so much as their first month together.

"At least my idea was better than begging," she said.

"Your idea?" Jack poured a glass of milk and glanced

at his phone, checking the charge. "I'm going to appeal to our relationship with them. I'm not going to overwhelm them with ideas, just sincerity about our history together. Besides, it was all I could do to talk Lennon into letting me address the team." Jack swigged down a gulp of milk. "So what's this idea of yours?"

"Don't you remember? Last week, when you were falling asleep on the couch, I landed on an episode of *Always Tomorrow*, and Colette, I mean *Vivica*, splashed some dude in the face with water. Right in the courtroom. It's her infamous move. I said Colette would be a great spokeswoman for FRESH—"

"You said that to me?" Jack sobered, trying to remember.

"Yes, right after you muttered something about me being hot."

He wrinkled his brow. "When I was asleep? Because hiring Colette is actually a great idea."

"Of course." Taylor flirted over her shoulder as she slipped back into the bedroom.

Hey, and for the record, you are hot. He'd shout it from the rooftops if she asked him to. But he wasn't good at intimate confession, at sharing the deepest feelings of his heart. When he was awake. A year ago he'd added "work on compliments" to his personal to-do list.

But it was hard to harvest words that were never sown.

Jack finished off his third Pop-Tart, walking back to the bedroom. "Do you think she would actually do it?"

Taylor shrugged. "Now that she's retired, she might want a new project."

"Hmm . . ." He'd thought about Taylor all day, whispers, impressions, fleeting images drifting across his heart. And he missed her. Missed the light in her blue eyes. Missed the floating sensation she inspired in his middle, like drifting across a glassy sea, baking in the sun's rays, his fingers intertwined with hers.

When she looked at him, he was free, his cares floating away on her current.

"Do you want to call Colette?" Taylor stood in the doorway, holding up her phone. "Ask her before you go down there? Just in case." Taylor tossed her phone to him.

"Really? Yeah, why not. Let's see what she says." Jack caught her phone. "Thanks, Tay."

He'd not considered an aging soap star for his pitchwoman, but why not? Colette Greer was an icon. A legend.

He tapped the screen to navigate to Taylor's contacts, pausing when her display showed five missed calls from Doug Voss. He glanced up at her, the familiar dark wave crashing over him. "Taylor, what—"

"Yeah?" She looked up from where she packed her laptop, her gaze clear. Innocent.

"N-nothing." He smiled. If she intended for him to see Doug's calls, she was a better actress than her aunt.

He found Colette's number and dialed, walking over to the window, peering out, a gnawing in his gut. He hated that Doug Voss was in her world. Even a little bit. Colette's voice mail answered and Jack fumbled for words.

"Colette, Jack Forester, Taylor's husband." The word

resonated through him. He liked that word. He liked all it implied. "I was wondering how you'd like to be a spokeswoman for FRESH Water? Let me know." He rattled off his number, then handed the phone to Taylor.

"Did you get ahold of Colette?" Taylor dragged her gear to the door, her shoulder loaded with her laptop and camera bags.

"Voice mail."

"Keep it. Try her again on our way there." She fumbled to open the door, catching her laptop case as it slipped from the top of her suitcase. "Let's go down. The cab will be here any minute."

"Here, let me help you." Jack tucked Taylor's phone in his pocket, reaching for her suitcase. "You get the elevator. I'll grab my stuff."

"Jack, don't forget your phone. You'll go crazy without it."

"Right, right." He came from the bedroom, unplugged his phone, and coiled the cord in his laptop case. His phone slipped from his hand, banging on the floor. Taylor jumped to pick it up. "Hold on to that for me." Jack reached for her suitcase, adjusting the strap of his bag on his shoulder. "Can you do that? Do you mind?"

"I can hold on to anything you want, Jack." Taylor regarded him for a moment, then disappeared into the hall. "Elevator is here."

He followed her out, locking the door, his heart on fire. About to lean in to kiss her, the elevator doors pinged open and she stepped in.

"You coming?" she said, a soft laugh in her words.

"I promise to give you back your phone before the airport."

Jack swallowed, stepping into the elevator. "I wasn't worried about my phone."

"Then what?"

"J-just thinking."

He wanted to bonk his head against the side of the elevator, frustrated at his inability to say three simple words, "I love you." Words he longed to say but couldn't.

As the car descended, he rode to the bottom of his heart, to where his thoughts settled in the sludge of his own truth.

He loved his wife and if he didn't find a way to tell her, he could very well lose her. And he could blame no one but himself.

CHAPTER ELEVEN

JIMMY

For more years than he cared to remember, Jimmy had started his Friday mornings in the same corner booth of Ella's Diner. With his date. The doc.

Sipping his coffee, he stared out the window, monitoring traffic—what little bit still came through downtown these days.

He hoped the city council's plan to beef up the old city center panned out. He had a great affection for the old town. Spent many a happy weekend at Millson's drugstore and soda fountain.

But those days had long passed. Time was like spilt milk. It could never be put back in the bottle.

"Refresh your coffee, Jimmy?" Tina, owner of Ella's, stood poised over the table with a full pot of black brew.

"Naw, I think I'll wait for the doc. But if'n you don't mind, I could munch on a donut."

"Plain or chocolate?"

"Got a plain with chocolate icing?"

"Now, you know I do." She turned to go, saying over her shoulder, "Doc's late, isn't he?"

"It's all the rain. I told him to pave that road out to his place, but *noooo*, he never listens."

It rained a gully washer last night, thunder clapping, lightning flashing. Power went out for a good hour or two. But it didn't bother Jimmy none. He just went to bed, the evening song of rain on the rooftop his favorite lullaby.

The sun glinted off a passing car windshield and Jimmy squinted through the brightness. Thunder in the night, but sunshine in the morning. Wasn't that a metaphor of life?

The whole town looked washed. Clean. And the Cumberland flowed with gusto.

"Here you go." Tina set two donuts in front of him. "One's on me." She freshened Jimmy's coffee without asking and moved to the next table.

With a chuckle, Jimmy took a bite of his sweet breakfast. Tina was a good gal. She'd taken over after Ella died back in the early 2000s. She kept this place going like Ella would've wanted.

That tough ole broad survived the postwar construction boom, staying put when all the other businesses were bugging out and taking up residence in suburban strip malls and shopping plazas. Ella alone could be credited with keeping the center vein of Heart's Bend pumping.

As for Jimmy, he'd been coming here for sixty-five years. He stored a lot of good conversations with Dad, the doc, and others within these walls.

"You'll live to be a hundred." Dr. Nick Applebaum tossed a manila envelope on the table, slid into the booth across from Jimmy, and waved to Tina, pointing to the spot in front of him. "Black coffee, please."

"A hundred?" Jimmy emptied the envelope's contents onto the table. "Have trouble getting out this morning, Nick? Was your drive washed out?"

"Don't start with me."

"I told you to pave the road back to your place."

"Tina," Nick said, reclining against the booth as the fifty-something redhead set a cup and saucer in front of him. "Tell me why I've been having coffee with this know-it-all for the last twenty-five years."

"Don't drag me into this." Tina gave Jimmy a wink. "Besides, I agree with him. Pave that ole road, Doc."

"Oh, I see where your loyalties lie." Shaking his head, Nick leveled a spoonful of sugar into his coffee, then tapped the papers in front of Jimmy. "Your cholesterol is good, your blood pressure, sugar, heart. If I didn't know better, I'd think the lab mixed up your blood work with that of a younger man."

"All those TV dinners Dad fed me as a kid preserved my insides." Jimmy reviewed the numbers that didn't make a lick of sense, so he'd trust the doc's word.

Nick sipped his coffee. "Whatever you're doing, keep it up. No need to resign yourself to the retirement home yet."

"I'm going to die in my place, Nick. I've kept it up. Don't see a need to move. I'll hire a nurse to come in to change my diapers if I have to, but I'm staying put."

"That so? Rumor is you're selling your place. Heard

Keith Niven talking something about it at church Wednesday night."

"Did you now?" Big mouth. "He weren't talking about the house."

Nick regarded him over the rim of his coffee mug. "Selling some property?"

"I thought I might."

"You hitting the skids? Running out of cash? Don't know how, since you've worn the same shirt to breakfast since I can remember."

"What?" Jimmy smoothed his hand down the front of his blue plaid snap button. "This ain't more than ten years old."

"Jim, buy a new shirt. What's an old bachelor got to spend his money on?"

Jimmy squirmed under Doc's honest observation. He'd tried not to imagine how the townsfolk saw him. An old bachelor, living alone in the house he grew up in. It might seem kind of sad to those on the outside. But he'd made his choices. He was used to the way things were, right or wrong, good or bad.

"I don't need to spend money and I'm far from hitting the skids. This is just a square of land I don't need no more."

"With all the development going on around here, you should get a good price for it."

"Well, it won't be going to any development group. It's got a right nice building on it."

The doc made a face. "Buildings can be knocked down, Jim."

"Not this one." Selling his chapel was one thing, but

destroying it was another. No, no, no, he'd never let someone knock it down. "So I'm in good health?" He slipped the papers back into the envelope and set them aside. "I was thinking of taking up golf. Seems like all the fellas are playing."

"Come on down to the club. I'll teach you—"

"Good, you're still here." Keith Niven beelined for the table, interrupted Doc, and slid in next to Jimmy, taking a bite out of his donut. "Coach, I've got great news."

Jimmy made a face, raising his hand to flag down Tina. "Need another donut over here." Then he glared at the interloper. "Keith, I'm having coffee with the doc."

Jimmy arched his brow and tensed his jaw, trying to communicate without words. *Later.*

Discussing the chapel felt personal, though once it hit the market his secret would be out. Nevertheless, he didn't feel like chatting in front of the doc. He was a clever man. And being as he was Jimmy's doctor and had seen him naked, Doc would not hesitate one wink to pry into his personal life.

"Of course you are. You always have coffee with the doc on Friday mornings," Keith said, reaching for a napkin. "We listed the place online yesterday and *bam*, we've had over two dozen queries."

"Well, fine. I'll meet you at your office in an hour. How's that?"

"We don't have an hour. We need to move fast." Keith smiled up at Tina as she set a fresh donut in front of Jimmy. "Could I get some coffee and a donut?"

"You sure can." Tina slid Jimmy's former donut in front of Keith before walking off.

Jimmy grinned at the doc.

"Listen, Coach, the pictures Lisa Marie took with her phone are okay, but we can do better. Didn't you say you had a photographer coming?"

"Meeting her around ten." Jimmy peeked at Nick, who was watching the whole thing rather amused.

"Perfect. Mind if I tag along?" Keith rubbed his hands as Tina set down his coffee. "Thank you, darling, you're the love of my life."

"Shall I tell your wife or shall you?"

Jimmy laughed. That Tina. She'd held on to more than Ella's the last fifteen years. She'd held on to her spirit, her gumption. Raised three boys alone while working here as a waitress, then as owner. Just sent the last one off to college.

Keith slurped his coffee. "So, what about the photographer?"

"No, you can't come. Don't go posting a For Sale sign on the property until she does what she's got to do."

"Why not? You're killing me here, Coach. I'm trying to make a sale, land us a pot of gold. Besides, it's too late. Put up the sign last night before the rain set in. Shew, that was something. Had my dog trembling like a reed."

"What this about?" Nick asked.

"Doc," Keith said. "You've not seen it? Ole Coach here has a wedding chapel tucked away up north off River Road. Like it was some kind of fairy-tale secret."

So the truth was out, from Keith's fat lips straight into the air they breathed. Doc scrunched up his sun-leathered expression.

"Is it a secret?"

Jimmy set his cup down with a clank on the Formica table. "I reckon it ain't no more."

"Anyway, I need to talk to this photographer. Get some better shots, show off the chapel's charm." Keith set his business card down, then threw a five on the table as he gulped the last of his coffee and reached for the bitten donut. "Don't tell Lisa Marie, but she is one bad iPhone photographer. Yikes. Didn't think it was possible. But, Coach, I'm counting on you. Have the photographer call me." Keith slid out of the booth. "See you, Doc."

"Not if I see you first." Nick snickered into his coffee, hiding behind the white china, elbows on the table.

"Well, go on," Jimmy said. "I can see you're dying to ask."

Doc sobered. "How long have I known you? Thirty years? You've never once mentioned owning a wedding chapel."

"Well, now you know."

"When? Where? I never heard of such a thing in Heart's Bend."

"Because there ain't a wedding chapel in Heart's Bend. There's my chapel, on my land, and I happened to build it for a wedding."

"Whose?"

Jimmy drummed his fingers on the table. Well, that was the million-dollar question. But the answers in his head didn't form easily into words. Because they required pieces of his heart. He shifted in his seat.

"Well?" Nick said.

Darn. This should be a piece of cake. He'd coached high school boys for crying out loud. Fought in Korea.

Jimmy cleared his throat. "Mine." There, he'd said it, blunt, with no fuss.

Nick reared back, frowning. "Yours? You were married?"

"No, I didn't get married. So, I'm selling." Jimmy stared at his coffee, twisting his cup between his hands.

"You built it but never used it? When? How long ago?"

"A good while. Years." Decades.

"More than thirty, I reckon, since you never mentioned it to me."

Jimmy exhaled and sat back against the red vinyl booth. "Started it the summer of 1949, if you must know. I worked night and day on it 'cause I wanted four walls, a floor, and a roof by the time I proposed. I didn't make it, but at least I had the walls."

"You had a girl?" Nick couldn't look more confounded.

Jimmy sipped his coffee. "Yep, I had a girl."

"And this never came up? In all of our Fridays? In all of our conversations?"

"You never asked."

"I'm asking now. Who was this girl who inspired you to build a wedding chapel?" Nick leaned forward on his elbows, his steely gaze locked on Jimmy.

Jimmy peered out the window. "I'm not sure I know where to start."

"How about the beginning?"

"Better yet, how about the end?"

• • •

OCTOBER 1954

He stood in the middle of the chapel, a gas can and sledgehammer in hand, his boots dusted with dirt from the floor.

Over his shoulder, the drifting sunlight warned him that time was running out.

Jimmy assessed the rafters, the walls, and formed a plan. The rafters would ignite easily enough. They were gray and dry from three years of exposure. But the walls? They'd need help. He couldn't make a fire hot enough to burn limestone.

Jimmy settled the sledgehammer by his feet as he knelt down to loosen the cap on the can. The bitter fragrance of gasoline stung his nose and soured the perfume of fall in the air.

Standing, he drew a clean breath to clear his nostrils. Did he really want to destroy this place? Because if he did, his dream would *really* be over. And he'd never rebuild it.

Closing his eyes, Jimmy plowed through his feelings and examined whitewashed memories.

Before Korea, he'd brought Colette to the unfinished chapel to tell her he loved her—and that he'd been drafted. Over their heads in love, fueled by intense emotions, they did things that night, said things, made promises that didn't last the length of boot camp.

When he came home from the war restless and angry, Dad, in all of his quiet wisdom, nudged Jimmy to enroll in school, take advantage of the GI bill. Get an education.

"*You've earned it, Jim.*" Dad had started calling him Jim since he'd been a soldier.

Reaching down for the gas can, Jimmy scanned the unfinished chapel one last time. The idea to burn it down had hit him during dinner tonight.

Dad dished out pot roast while asking about college. How were his classes? His professors? Did he make any new friends yet? Meet any suitable young ladies? And it occurred to him that as long as the wedding chapel still stood, Jimmy would never move on.

It had to go. *She* had rejected him. Now he would reject her.

About to douse the perimeter with gas, Jimmy patted his pockets for matches. Ah, he left them in the truck.

When he turned for the door, Peg Branson stood there with a young boy on her hip.

"She's not coming back, Jimmy. You know that, don't you?"

"You drove all the way out here to tell me that?"

She entered farther, her blue housedress swishing about her legs, her white sneakers no match for the layers of dirt on the chapel floor. Her clean cotton scent defied the odorous gasoline. The boy, about two, maybe three, clasped his hands around her neck.

"I was heading home from my mother-in-law's when I saw you turn in here. I kept going but I couldn't help it—I had to turn around."

"To tell me your sister wasn't coming back?" Her presence irritated him, but he shouldn't be angry with her. It wasn't her fault that Colette ran off with another man. At least Peg had the decency to tell him the truth.

"What are you going to do with the gasoline?"

"What do you think?"

"I'm guessing you intend to burn the place down." The boy squirmed, struggling to get down.

"So you best be getting on home. It's going to get hot and dangerous around here real quick."

Peg lowered the boy to the floor. "Why you burning it down?" She took a slow turn, studying the rough build. "What is this place?"

"A chapel. A *wedding* chapel."

Peg's gaze narrowed, darkened. "You didn't! For Colette? Did she know about this place?"

He nodded once. "I brought her here."

"And she still ran off? Really, Colette can be the most selfish . . . Now, you're not mad at me for telling you, are you? Because I couldn't take it, I couldn't take it." She stepped around the boy as he gathered tiny fists of dirt, and reached for Jimmy's arm, a pleading look in her eyes. "I-I'm just going to say it. You know how I felt about you, don't you? How I still feel."

Her confession washed him with uneasiness and he freed himself from her grasp, stepping back. "Don't say such things. You're married. I'm not mad at you, Peg. You did right by telling me. But don't—"

"I'm glad." She exhaled, smiling, pressing her hand to her chest. "I couldn't bear it if you were angry with me. But, Jimmy, you never saw it in her . . . how selfish she was, caring only about herself. She ran off with Spice the first chance she got."

"What do you care? You ran off with Drummond Branson. Had a kid." Jimmy nodded at the boy now tossing dry dirt into the air. "Don't come in here telling me how you feel about me. It's not right."

"But I still care about you, Jimmy. Colette had no business treating you the way she did. I'm sure our mamá is turning over in her grave."

"She can turn all she wants. Won't change a thing. I just want to get on with my business." Jimmy reached for the sledgehammer. He needed to hit something, knock out a few walls, then light his fire.

"Well, wait, you haven't met DJ yet." She swung the kid up in her arms, which made him none too happy. He screamed, kicked and squirmed, soiled Peg's pretty dress with his dirty hands. "DJ, meet Uncle Jimmy." She grabbed his hand and waved it at Jimmy, then kissed his smudged cheek. "Isn't he divine? Just the cutest thing ever?"

Jimmy gave the kid a good solid look. Not being around little ones all that much, he wasn't quite sure how to gauge their cuteness. But this guy was right handsome with his thick blond hair, rosy cheeks, and bright blue eyes.

"You sure this is Drummond Branson's kid? He's mighty fine looking."

A few years ahead of Jimmy in school, Drummond missed Korea because he was in college. Now he had his own appliance store, a pretty wife, and a fine son.

Peg laughed. "Oh, Jimmy. I see Korea didn't kill your sense of humor." She stepped closer, angling the boy in Jimmy's direction. "So what do you think?"

"I said he was fine, didn't I?"

"I just love him. Just *love* him."

She shoved the boy toward him again. Peg could be pushy. So Jimmy shook the tyke's hand, surprised at how buttery his skin felt against his calluses. When he looked up, Peg was watching him. A tad too close.

"You're a good man, Jimmy Westbrook."

"So's Drummond, Peg." He raised the hammer to his shoulder.

"Jimmy, you know I'd do anything for you, don't you? *Anything*."

He regarded her for a moment, hearing something between her words. Something sharp and shaded. "Anything?"

She gripped his arm, her warm breath brushing his cheek. "Anything, anything."

"Will you talk to Colette—"

Peg released him with a slight push. "Colette, Colette, Colette. I declare, you've a one-track mind. Forget about her. Colette, indeed. You build her this chapel and how does she thank you? By spitting in your face and running off."

"But I'm home now." The desperation in his voice set him a bit off kilter, but he wasn't above begging. "She was afraid. Afraid something might happen to me. I don't blame her after what she went through in the last war, losing your parents and all. I just sense if we could talk, we'd clear up this whole thing."

"No, Jimmy, *no*." Peg's insistence drove through him. "She left because she loved another man. Have some pride. You fought for your country. She doesn't deserve you. She never did. Spoiled child."

"Don't speak about her that way, Peg. I mean it."
Defending Colette came easy.

"Look at you, taking up for her when you're about
to set this place on fire." Peg snatched up the gas can,
waving it around. "Do it!" The raw tension in her voice
and frantic passion pressed against him. Scared him.
"Let the symbol of your love go up in smoke. You didn't
know her. You only knew what you wanted to know.
She doesn't deserve your devotion."

"She was kind and decent. Beautiful. Perhaps it was
you who didn't know her."

"I knew her, better than anyone." Peg stepped back,
her intense expression suddenly softening into a smile.
"You can do better, Jimmy. Find a woman who loves
you." The traces of her English accent bent the vowels
of her otherwise Southern charm.

"Who would that be? You?"

"You just have to ask."

"Go on home, Peg. Consider your son." Jimmy
adjusted the weight of the hammer on his shoulder.
"Think of Drummond."

"I'd leave him—"

"Go on, Peg. Get home to your husband. Be a good
wife and mama. Don't let DJ here grow up without his
mama. Trust me, it ain't no fun."

"Now you're angry with me." She stamped her foot,
stirring a small puff of dust.

He sighed, sweeping his gaze upward to the fading
fall day. The short breeze whistling through the pines
cooled the heat rising on his cheeks. "I'm not angry, Peg.

Just don't want to ever be a party to a woman leaving her man, leaving her kid. Besides, I don't feel for you—"

"All right." Her tone was too sweet, her smile forced and unnatural. "I'll go. But you burn this place down. To the ground. Hear me? Don't waste your life pining for her, Jimmy."

"I'll be seeing you, Peg."

"Don't be a stranger. Come around, we'll talk about old times. Drummond would love to see you." Just like that, she flipped the switch from jealous sister to sweet Southern housewife. "We can remember Clem. Dear Clem. We all miss him."

"How's your Aunt Jean doing?" He'd been meaning to go around to the Clemsons' place, sit a spell, and remember Clem. But he couldn't bring himself to do it. The hurt was too raw. The memories too dear.

"She's hanging in there. Little DJ here seems to help. Brightens her up. What a blessing he is to us all."

"Give her my love. And your Uncle Fred too."

Jimmy watched her go, an echo rising in the hollow in his chest. When he heard her engine fire up, he picked up the sledgehammer and with every ounce of muscle, sorrow, anger, and fear, he swung at the wall.

For Clem. Killed in action after one month in Korea.

The steel head pinged against the stubborn stone, the pressure vibrating through Jimmy's grip and up his arms.

For Colette.

Another resounding ping sending a vibration through Jimmy. He swung again.

For Colette.

For Clem.

For Colette, Colette, Colette.

Sweat beaded on his brow and cheeks as each hammer blow knocked a small piece of rock from the wall. He swung again, plumbing his emotions, tears seeping to the surface.

A blow for *lame* war.

For his dad, living alone, pining away over a worthless woman who weren't never coming back.

Jimmy paused long enough to fill his lungs and strip away his shirt. Then he swung again, crashing the hammer into the unyielding wall.

"Oh, Jimmy, one more thing—"

He whipped around to see that Peg had returned with DJ in tow. "What? I thought you'd gone." What was she doing here?

"I-I just remembered . . . Are you all right?" Her eyes roamed Jimmy's face, down to his bare chest and the hammer in his hand.

"What do you want, Peg?"

She jerked her hand toward him, holding a small box. "Drummond . . . he, well . . . purchased this Argus camera for me." She held up the black device. "You know, to take pictures of DJ. I'm having a dickens of a time finding things to take pictures of so I can practice. Then it occurred to me to get a snapshot of DJ with his Uncle Jimmy."

"I'm not his uncle." What was her angle? Rubbing in that he'd lost Colette?

"For Clem. Be his uncle in place of Clem. You know how he would want that, Jimmy."

He faced the wall and brought down the hammer.
"You were his cousin, Peg."

"You know Clem was more like a brother than a
cousin to me. Now, what do you say?"

The last thing he wanted to do right now was pose
for a picture.

"Jimmy?"

He dropped the hammer and swooped up his shirt.
"Make it quick."

"Thank you, thank you . . . DJ, here, go to Uncle
Jimmy."

He reached for the kid, anchoring him in the crook
of his arm. "What're you feeding him? He weighs a
ton."

"He's a good eater, my boy. Takes after his daddy.
Now . . ." Peg raised the camera to her eye. "Jimmy, just
plop him on your hip . . . yeah, like that . . . Why're you
holding him like a sack of manure? He don't stink, and
he won't bite."

Peg could be exasperating, and her timing needed
work. But now that he'd calmed down, Jimmy understood that Peg was the closest he'd come to Colette in
a long time.

The kid fussed and squirmed while Peg figured
out her new apparatus. "Hold on, DJ. Mamá wants a
picture."

Jimmy adjusted the boy for a better grip. There. He
glanced down to see the boy peering at him with wide
curiosity.

"How're you doing, kid?"

He grinned, reached up, and beeped his nose. *"Beep!"*

And Jimmy laughed.

"Perfect." Peg's skirts swirled as she walked around to take another picture. "I snapped that one just right. DJ, you *are* the cutest thing. Jims, you should see him dance. He's a savant, I tell you. DJ, look at Mamá."

"How old is he?"

"Th-three," Peg said, clicking away, circling like a beast on the hunt. "Well, he will be in a few weeks."

Peg continued to take pictures, trying different angles and light, even using a flash. But then Jimmy had enough. "Here you go, DJ. Back to your mama."

"All right, I suppose we're done." Peg kissed her boy, letting the camera dangle from a wrist strap. "I guess I'll go."

"Peg, I'd appreciate if you'd not flash those pictures around. Kind of embarrassed to have built a wedding chapel when there was never going to be a wedding."

She hesitated, then turned to go, glancing back from the door. "You could've had me, Jimmy."

"Listen to yourself, Peg. Your mama is rolling over in her grave."

"Yes, I suppose she is—"

"Go on home. Let's forget this conversation." He wanted to like her because she was Colette's sister. But if she spoke one more word about leaving Drummond, he'd despise her, sure as he was standing here.

"You know I loved you." Her words hung in the silent space between the barren chapel walls.

Realization dawned. He stepped toward her, swinging the hammer over the dirt. "Peg, is that why she left?" His adrenaline rushed, leaving him winded, out of strength. "Did you do it, Peg?" He stepped toward her. "Make her leave? Tell her some lie?"

"No, no. Is that what you think?" She started out of the chapel. "I might have spoken my heart just now, but my sister made her *own* choices. I tried to warn her, talk her into waking up, but she made up her own mind. She chose Spice and fame over you, Jimmy. And she's never coming back."

Jimmy followed her to her car. "Sisters fight, Peg. Say things they don't mean. That's all I'm saying. Maybe you said something that made her think she had to go. Let you have me instead."

"No, never."

"Then talk to her. 'Cause I never felt for you that way."

Peg slipped DJ through the open passenger window onto the seat, then walked around to the driver's door, angry and pouting. "What was I thinking? If I lived with you I'd be haunted by Colette's ghost. With that fairy-tale notion you have of her stuck in your head."

Dropping behind the wheel, Peg fired up the engine and reversed down the road with such force that little DJ fell backward in the seat, his little hand grasping at the top of the door.

Darn that Peg. What was she thinking coming round, spouting of love, making indecent propositions? Jimmy glanced back at the chapel. But she got one thing right. He was living with a fairy tale.

Striding toward the chapel, he figured he had just enough light to do what he came to do.

He snatched up the gas can and was about to pour when he heard it. The push-thump, a syncopated *whoosh-thump, whoosh-thump*.

He faded to pale. "Peg?"

He scanned the perimeter, raising his gaze skyward from the ground, searching for the source.

"Peg, is that you?"

He waited. When he didn't hear the sound again, he took up the gasoline. But when he was about to pour, he heard it again. A thrumming, whooshing, throbbing that went clean through him.

Jimmy scurried to the door. "Who's here?"

But the torn-up yard, littered with chipped limestone and wood shavings, was empty save for the song of the evening birds.

Though the army doc gave him a clean bill of health, and he'd not had a nightmare in months, this had to be shell shock, kicking in a bit late. What else could it be?

Back to the gasoline, Jimmy tipped it to pour when the *whoosh* echoed over the chapel, raising gooseflesh down his neck and arms, clean to his toes.

He tipped his face to the patch of blue exposed between the trees. "I'm burning her down. To the ground. You can't stop me."

The hollow, haunting *whoosh* settled on and over him with an even *whoosh-thump, whoosh-thump*. He knew that sound. A beating heart.

Jimmy stretched to his full height, squaring up his shoulders and hanging on to the gas can. He had fought in a war, but this moment carried more power than guns and ammo. It settled over him with its own brand of fear. Of reverence.

The rhythm beat strong and clear, all around him. In him. Through him. Soon his senses lost all bearings. Where did the sound begin and Jimmy end? He had no gauge.

Moment by moment he lost all strength and slowly sank to the hard, red dirt ground.

CHAPTER TWELVE

Taylor

At Granny's, Taylor woke when light broke through the back bedroom windows where she slept.

Siting up, she reached for her phone, well, Jack's phone, and checked the time through bleary eyes. Eight o'clock. She'd better get a move on.

But she couldn't quite kick out from under the blanket yet.

Flopping back on the pillows, she stared at the familiar swirls in the ceiling plaster. She'd spent a good number of happy childhood days in this room, her refuge as a teen when Mama and Daddy divorced and she didn't want to pick sides. Granny declared herself Switzerland and Taylor transferred her citizenship there.

Though Mama was innocent, a victim of Daddy's wandering ways, Taylor refused to be mean to his face. As mad as she was at him, the daddy's girl in her couldn't do it. So she just avoided him. And over the years she got pretty good at it.

The trip to Nashville last night was crazy. Flight delays due to a storm in the Midwest were compounded by the fact that Jack got out of the cab with her cell phone, leaving her with his.

And since he didn't have Emma's number in his contacts, she had no way to call her and let her know the flight would be late.

She also missed connecting with Ryan for the equipment. She'd have to make do without.

Thankfully, Emma checked the flight online and was waiting for Taylor when she arrived, exhausted, after midnight.

"I take back every bad thing I said about you when we were kids," Taylor had said as she crawled into the passenger seat.

But now it was Friday morning and time to work. Time to see this secret wedding chapel.

Taylor snatched up Jack's phone and texted him, well, texted herself.

HEY! DID YOU NOTICE YOU HAVE MY PHONE? NEED TO SWITCH.

She waited for him to text her back, but when he didn't she showered and dressed.

Still no response.

Gathering her gear, she tucked his phone in her pocket and headed downstairs, the nearly empty house eerie, echoing her footsteps.

While Granny left the house to Taylor, she left the contents with Emma. As if to ensure they'd have to work together.

But unlike Granny with Colette, Taylor and Emma got along. So far anyway.

Emma had done a great job of clearing out most

of the furniture, going through the interior, lining up Granny's dishes on the dining room table, ready for someone to take. Otherwise, Emma wanted to sell them at an estate auction.

Pausing in the doorway to the kitchen, Taylor looked back through the living room, a small ache in her heart. *Miss you, Granny.*

She'd died so suddenly. An aneurysm.

But Taylor didn't have time to linger. From the hook by the back door, she snatched Granny's keys and headed out.

Unlocking the detached garage, she slid open the wide door, smiling when the chrome of Granny's old Lincoln Continental convertible glinted in the sunlight.

Setting her gear in the trunk, she glanced around the garage for items she might use for lighting.

Finding nothing, she went back inside and Mac-Gyvered a reflector using pieces of cardboard covered with tinfoil. Then collected two lamps from the living room.

Back out to the car, she settled her makeshift gear in the trunk, slipped behind the wheel, and powered down the top.

It was a beautiful day, and despite the bumpy beginning to her weekend, she was going to have the Tennessee sun warm her skin this morning. And have fun. Yessiree, fun.

Later she'd figure a way to exchange phones with Jack. He was only an hour up the road.

Spotting the street just before the turn for the

chapel, she slowed the Lincoln, narrowing her gaze at the For Sale sign along the roadside.

The tires crunched over the gravel as Taylor steered down the narrow lane toward the chapel, low-hanging tree limbs reaching for her. She gasped when she emerged into a small, open grassy area full of light and serenity.

She eased the car behind the truck parked under a patch of blue sky, then popped the trunk, surveying the chapel and the grounds.

"No wonder *AQ* wanted pictures."

But from the golden beams dancing in the air about the chapel, backed by an umbrella of white light, Taylor thought she might just have her first, perfect, natural lighting job.

Way to give a girl a break, God.

Maybe it was her imagination, but as she pulled her makeshift reflectors out of the trunk, she thought a bass *You're welcome* buzzed through her.

"Taylor?"

Taylor peered around to see Coach Westbrook heading her way. He looked pretty much the same as the last time she saw him—white haired with lively blue eyes, a bounce in his step, and squared-back shoulders.

"Coach?" She shook his hand. "I think you look younger than the last time I saw you."

He laughed. "Don't know about that." He reached to help her with one of the lamps. "Sorry, but I don't rightly remember you."

"Don't see how you should. I was the yearbook and newspaper geek in high school. Always hiding behind my camera."

"Well, when you hold your camera to your face, I guess I'll recognize you then." He laughed at his own joke, drawing her in immediately.

Okay, she liked this man. A lot.

He held up the lamps. "Don't know what you had planned for these, but there's no electricity out here."

"What? Really?" She sighed and opened the trunk, stepping aside for Jimmy to lay the lamps back on the fuzzy lining. "How do you see for ceremonies and stuff? Candlelight?"

"Ain't never had a ceremony, but yeah, candles, lanterns." He rattled his keys and headed for the chapel steps. "The cupola up top lets a lot of light in. Like a funnel of sorts. This time of morning is good too. Not that I know anything about taking pictures."

"So, Coach, you've never had a ceremony or service out here? Ever?"

He slipped the key in the door. "Nope."

"Can I ask why? And is that why you're selling the place? I-I saw the sign."

"Just never got around to it. Keith Niven called, wondering if she were for sale, and I thought, 'After sixty-four years, why not?'"

Taylor followed him inside, looking for a staging area, pausing when the beauty of the interior captured her. "Coach, this is incredible." She lowered her voice. "Serene. Beautiful."

The light falling through the cupola fanned through the tiny sanctuary like illuminated ribbons, creating a sense of floating. Of moving. She assembled her camera, eager to capture the light before it moved.

"She's an old friend, I guess."

"Then why are you selling?"

Coach eased down into the last wooden pew, his hands cupped over his knees. "Like I said, I guess it was time."

With each word, Taylor *felt* him. Kindness wrapped in sorrow and regret.

A beam draped over his shoulder as he stared toward the window and Taylor aimed her camera, capturing the vulnerability of the moment.

He glanced her way. "Ah, now I recognize you. *Girl with Camera.*"

Taylor lowered her Canon and regarded him. "Yes, *Girl with Camera.* How did you know?"

"You entered a black-and-white of yourself in a county art show. Called it *Girl with Camera.*"

"That's right . . . You remember?"

"I was one of the judges. Made an impression on me. Reminded me of someone I used to know."

"My granny? Peg? You went to school with her."

"That's right. Peg."

"You coached my dad in football. Drummond Branson Jr. Only they called him DJ when he was a kid."

"I remember your daddy. He was a solid player."

"You must remember my aunt Colette too." Taylor captured two more shots of Jimmy. He was interesting. The sanctuary was gorgeous, but there was more, beneath the surface. The room almost seemed to respond to Jimmy. As if it knew . . .

"Have you been keeping this place a secret?" Taylor

checked the camera's display, paging through the shots she'd taken, her excitement rising. They looked perfect. It was odd that such flawlessness had come with so little effort and no artificial lighting. She wondered if editing these images might be altering something sacred.

"A secret? No. Just never told no one. Being out of town, back off the road, hid by the trees, I didn't get many inquiries."

Taylor walked the length of the center aisle, brushing her hand over the top of the pews, her footsteps soft against the slate floor. "You built this yourself?"

"My father helped. A few friends. Mostly me."

At the kneeler, Taylor paused, running her hand over the smooth, carved wood splayed with a prism of colors. She raised her gaze to the large stained glass window behind the altar and stepped back, aiming the camera. Any other time, this would be a cover shot, but today the source of beauty in this room was Jimmy himself.

"The stained glass is beautiful," she said.

"I rescued it from an old church in downtown Nashville when the postwar construction commenced."

"And the pews?" She dropped to one knee and aimed for a shot down the main aisle, giving the image movement and depth.

"Built them myself, from the wood I rescued. What's it called today? Reclaimed?"

"You're quite the craftsman." The side windows, with their square panes, let in a blend of light and shadow that shifted when the breeze swayed the tree limbs.

"How long did it take to build?"

"Ten years, give or take. Got interrupted by Korea. Then college."

"But you never married? Here or anywhere else?" Taylor made her way back toward Coach, trying to identify the unseen feeling that drew her to this place.

"You married, Taylor?"

"I am. To Jack Forester. He grew up here."

"I know Jack. Know his daddy too. Rise Forester."

"Don't let Rise hear you call Jack his son."

Coach harrumphed and she knew she'd just found a comrade.

Their conversation faded as Taylor captured the room, finding the shots she wanted, already eager to review the proofs. *AQ* wanted them by Tuesday.

"There's a feeling here . . . I can't put my finger on it." The sound of a distant *whoosh-thump, whoosh-thump* passed through the chapel, through her, electrifying the hair on her arms. What was that? "Coach?"

But he was gone, the chapel door wide open.

"Coach? Did you hear that sound?" Taylor moved to the door, glancing around for where the sound might have originated.

He stood in the yard in a dome of light, facing his truck. "You about done?" he said.

"Yeah . . . I thought I . . . I'm about done. Are you all right?"

"Fine, just wanted some fresh air, is all."

Taylor glanced back at the chapel. Did she expect to see someone, *something*, chasing after her? "M-maybe I could come back tomorrow?" The *whoosh-thump* echoed through her, familiar yet disconcerting. She'd heard God's heart before but never like that, so loud and powerful.

"Sure, if you need."

Back in the small, square sanctuary, Taylor packed up, her hands slightly trembling as she listened. Would she hear it again?

Just as she got to the door, she heard it. *Whoosh-thump.* She stopped, breathing deep. *Whoosh-thump.* The rhythm timed with her own pulse, resonating through her.

Lord?

"Let's get a move on, Taylor." Coach motioned for her to exit, swinging the door closed behind her and locking the chapel.

"What time tomorrow?" he said. "My real estate agent wants to talk to you about taking pictures, but you ain't obligated."

Coach brushed past her down the steps. Taylor reached out, grabbing his arm. "Coach, you can't sell. There's something special about this place. Something . . . alive."

Coach stared off, shaking his head. "Whatever was alive is dead now." He peered back at her. "Trust me now. Come on, let's head home."

Taylor settled her camera in the trunk, eyes on the chapel, feeling her way through her thoughts, through what just happened in there. Did Coach hear it too?

Either way, she felt changed somehow. As if encountered by the Divine.

. . .

JACK

Standing at the head of the conference room table, Jack gathered the attention of the FRESH drinking water executive team. Directly facing him, at the other end of the table, sat Lennon MacArthur, drumming his fingers with expectation.

Next to him sat Karli Jackson, FRESH Water's dynamic head of marketing. She was beautiful, hip, and a marketing whiz kid. The exact kind of partner 105 thrived on. In fact, 105 might need FRESH as much as FRESH needed 105.

Forgoing mundane introductions, Jack launched into his pitch.

"A friend of mine is a triathlete," he said. "He trains six mornings a week." From the conference table, his phone buzzed.

He'd known since last night that he had Taylor's phone, but he didn't mind because he'd hoped to hear back from Colette. Still talking, he read Taylor's screen.

"Health is more than just a passing fad for my friend. It's his life." Doug Voss's name blazed across the phone. Jack dropped it to the table, his fingers burning. "My friend can't win, can't excel—" The phone buzzed again. "Unless he's fueling his body with clean, natural foods and—"

. . . MEET ME IN LA. AFTER THIS PHONY SHOOT

"Jack, are you all right?" Lennon leaned forward, his expression impatient.

"I'm good. All good." But sweat trickled down his sides and the churning in his chest made him feel as if he just might explode.

"FRESH Water has been the icon of clean living and clean drinking. Aubrey James brought your mission of clean to the world with her commercial, 'Please make mine FRESH.'"

Jack sang the little ditty as Taylor's phone vibrated once more. He restrained the impulse to fling the thing against the wide, thick window.

"Jack, do you need to get that?" Lennon's firm tone lacked graciousness.

"As a matter of fact . . ." Jack swiped open Taylor's phone for a reply text.

THIS IS JACK.

He hit Send. No need to say more.

"Let's all take five," Lennon said, pushing away from the table.

"Colette Greer." The words fired out of his mouth without regard to what he would say next. But he had to do something. If he let this team take five, half of them wouldn't return. He took a slow breath. "Colette Greer."

"The soap actress?" Jack had earned Lennon's attention.

"One and the same. She's iconic, just like FRESH. Instead of narrowing FRESH's market to the health conscious, let's go for the *semi*–health conscious. The busy mom, the businessman shuffling through the airport. He stops at a kiosk and says, 'Make mine FRESH.'"

"All right, you have me. How does Colette Greer play into this broader brand?"

"She's an adjective. An instant image comes to mind when we say her name. 'She's the Colette Greer of our family.' Immediately we know that means a tough broad who's also a refined woman of taste." He'd found his stride, no thanks to that blowhard Doug Voss. "A friend of mine won several awards last year. She said, 'It's a Colette Greer kind of year.'" Jack snapped his fingers. "I knew instantly what she meant."

"Your friend needs a new shelf to display her awards," Karli said.

"Exactly. Colette is also widely known in the demographic you want to reach. Aubrey brought in the youth and health conscious. Colette will bring in the middle-agers and seniors, not to mention that her name and fame extend to Latin America and Europe." Now he was cooking with gas. He loved this idea. He hit the button on the projector and displayed his first slide. The presentation was rough, but solid. It was the best he could do on the airplane. He really owed Taylor for this plan. "Colette's character, Vivica, is famous for tossing water in people's faces." Jack launched the Internet on his laptop, bringing up images of Colette-Vivica splashing water in people's faces. Colette's face launched on the screen. "We have so many options to explore. Serious, humorous, parody—"

"Jack, we want people drinking our water, not tossing it in people's faces." Lennon chuckled. His team echoed, laughing in harmony.

"Exactly. She *almost* tosses FRESH Water, but—" Jack peered around the table, controlling the pace of the discussion, giving himself time to think. "When she realizes she's about to toss FRESH, she puts it down and goes for the stale drink on the bar or the fizzed-out tonic water on the end table."

Lennon grinned. "Go on."

Next slide. "Colette winks at the camera. 'I'd never waste FRESH on a face like that.'" Okay, corny, but it was a start. "Maybe we get one of the other cast members to play the part."

"Jack, this is great, but Colette is . . . *old*. Won't that date the product?" Karli said. "Date us?"

"No." Because maybe or even possibly was not an option. "Because we already have the youth up to thirty-something." He rattled off data they already knew. "Now we go for everyone else. Americans are sentimental. We're tired of losing our favorite shows to reality programming. Tired of media and whoever telling us who we are is not good enough. Colette embodies what we love about ourselves. Karli, she was the number one personality on daytime television for three decades."

"Well, her character Vivica most certainly was."

"The anniversary of the show is coming up and there's word that Greer is writing a memoir. There's a tie-in right there. Buzz and built-in media without FRESH spending one extra dime."

Lennon exchanged glances with Karli. "I like it."

"You sold me, Jack," Karli said. "You and 105 think on your feet. Literally."

"It's the way we roll. Hops and I value you as a top client." That wasn't entirely true on Hops's part, but Jack wasn't here to discuss London and another client's foundation, was he? "105 and FRESH are a great team."

"Okay, let's wrap this up. I've a tee time." Lennon took command of the meeting. "It's Alpine or 105. Karli?"

"105."

"Anderson?" Anderson Ladd was head of production.

"Lennon, our CFO isn't here," Anderson said. "We weren't supposed to have a pitch, be taking a vote. We made our decision."

Note to self: Buy Anderson a nice set of golf clubs. Win him over.

"That's not an answer to the question, Andy," Lennon said. "105 or Alpine?"

Anderson sighed. "Jack, are you sure we can get Colette Greer?"

"She's my wife's aunt. What do you think?" So he stretched perceptions. She was Taylor's aunt. That part was true.

"I don't know—" Anderson pushed away from the table. "I'm not sure I see this Colette Greer thing. Is this the campaign we want? I liked what Alpine brought to the table."

Jack launched into sales mode, the place he soared, where he found his passion. Convincing clients he was worth the risk. It was the only time he felt he was worth anyone's trust.

Except that day on the beach with Taylor.

The debate spiked among the team members until Lennon raised his hands for silence and called for a vote.

One by one, each person at the table voted for Jack.

Lennon came around to shake Jack's hand. "It's good to be back in business with 105."

"You won't regret it."

As the room emptied and Jack packed up his computer, the joy of his victory quickly faded. So Doug Voss was still going after Taylor. She seemed to stop him in his tracks when he came to their apartment, but what if she had encouraged him privately in some way?

Otherwise, why was he pressing her?

At his rental car, he tossed his gear into the trunk and scanned the messages from Voss. Every one of them tried to entice her to join him in LA.

No one has to know

It'll be like old times

Getting in the car, Jack sat back, thinking, his waning adrenaline leaving him exhausted. He ached to just sit and be, eat a sandwich at Bread & Company, and think.

But he needed to swap phones with Taylor. More than that, he needed to see her. Talk to her.

Are you having an affair with Doug Voss?

Freedom to share his heart, his fears, was not his bailiwick. But if he truly loved Taylor, he'd have to learn. Or he just might lose her.

Jack wrestled against the sting of tears. He hated crying. Worse, he hated this feeling in his gut, the free-falling sensation of rejection with no emotional limbs to grab onto.

Yet he *knew* from experience that if he acted rejected, Taylor would reject him.

How he'd learned to deal with devastation in the past was to play in the neutral zone. Be cool. Act casual, as if he didn't care his father didn't want him. Or that the older he got, the more he moved from foster home to foster home. Until he landed at the Gillinghams'. But that, too, was not without its hurdles.

But Taylor? He couldn't pretend he didn't care. Couldn't be his own island. Because he loved and wanted her. Needed her. And deep down, he believed she felt the same way.

Firing up the Mustang rental, Jack aimed for Heart's Bend, the morning sun behind him. He'd have to come back tomorrow for golf with Lennon, but if he wanted to change, to stop running from fear of rejection like he always had, why not start today? With his wife. The love of his life.

CHAPTER THIRTEEN

JIMMY

So, he'd met Taylor. The granddaughter of Peg and the daughter of DJ, the little tyke he'd told Doc about this very morning over coffee.

The boy grew up to be Drummond Branson Jr. A fine kid. A good football player. An upstanding Heart's Bend citizen as far as Jimmy knew.

Jimmy slowed for the turn home, resting his hand on the gear shift. Seeing that girl did something to him. He'd not seen Peg for some years before she died. Taylor was the closest he'd come to the Clemsons, or to Colette, in a good long time.

Now folks' sudden interest in his chapel jarred his memories. Awakened his sleepy ole ticker.

He'd heard the *whoosh-thump* again this morning and the sound rattled his bones, shooting him out of the chapel into the open air and sunshine.

Lord, have mercy. What was that sound?

He didn't know if Taylor heard it, but he could've sworn she'd lost some of the rose from her cheeks by the time she came out.

Jimmy hoped it wouldn't scare off the buyers. Or

that if Taylor *had* heard it, she had the brains to keep it to herself. Just like he'd done all these years.

No one would want a haunted wedding chapel.

At the turnoff to his place, he just kept on going, cresting at the next hill, taking the bend in the road, and driving from his present into his past.

. . .

November 1948

Friday night under the lights

The cold complicated things. Jimmy couldn't hang on to the ball. His numb fingers refused to cooperate no matter how much he warmed them between plays.

The Rocket defense was on the field now giving it to Lipscomb. At the referee's whistle, Jimmy braved a glance into the stands, searching for Colette through the glare of the lights.

Since their first conversation at Clem's house two months ago, Jimmy found it nearly impossible to speak to her. The fellas—Spice, Bradley, the Greaves brothers, and the rest—all vied for her attention. Peg's too. They were a shot of life to the same ole Rock Mill High crowd.

Then today, after lunch, he had spotted her alone in the hall. Blessed be. The Great Divine had parted the sea of male attention to give Jimmy half a chance.

His heart doing the jitterbug, he approached, asking if she would be at the game tonight.

"It's our last one."

"Of course." Her smile made him weak. "We wouldn't miss it."

"Will you root for me?"

"S-sure. We'll all be rooting for you."

With her confession tucked into his heart, Jimmy felt like he could do anything.

But much like the rest of the football season, tonight did not go his way. The hero he'd been in the opening game was a distant memory. If he didn't possess the game ball as proof of that magical night, he'd doubt it ever happened.

"Westbrook, you playing in this game or what?" Coach nabbed him by the shoulder pads and shoved him toward the field.

With one last sweep through the stands, Jimmy spotted her in the middle section. When she waved, his heart moved against his mountain of doubt.

"Westbrook! Get me a touchdown and end this thing."

"Yes, sir." He tried to contain his smile but failed. So what? He didn't care. This play was for her.

Jimmy bent into the huddle as Clem called the play, but his mind was on Colette. He didn't know how empty he was until he met her. She touched him. Filled him. Made him understand all those silly songs. Sometimes when he saw her in the hall, he couldn't breathe. He daydreamed about her over breakfast. So much so Dad popped him on the side of the head just the other day.

"What's wrong with you? Did you hear what I just said?"

"Yeah, Dad, you're working late. Stop with the head hitting. I need all the brains I can get."

He'd heard talk of *love* in the locker room, though it sounded more like lustful shenanigans. Boys bragging about getting under a girl's blouse or making their way up her thigh.

Jimmy wanted those moments too. He sure did. But he wanted them with Colette, and only Colette. In the right way. He wanted to talk to her, hear her voice, sniff her perfume, ask her a million questions. Then he'd taste her lips and feel the curves of her body against his.

"Listen up, fellas," Clem said to the huddle. "This is it. No time left on the clock. Coach called a left side sweep, blue nineteen." He put his hand on Jimmy's shoulder. "You got it? Left side sweep—"

"Blue nineteen. Got it."

"Break!"

Jimmy lined up behind Clem feeling alive, ready to go. They knew this. They'd practiced it a hundred times. *Easy as pie.*

Down by four with six seconds remaining, once more he had a moment to shine.

Try to end the season the way you started.

Clem called "blue nineteen" and Jimmy went into motion, his breathing deep and even. Despite the cold he moved with speed and precision.

Sweeping around Clem, running to the left side, he raised hands up, reading for the ball. He had space in front of him, a gaping hole in the defensive line. He was open. Wide. Open.

But the offensive line didn't hold and Clem scrambled away from the defense. The play was busted. Clem looked down field to pass, but every receiver was covered. Jimmy broke from his route, running for the end zone, waving his hands in the air.

I'm open, Clem. I'm open.

Clem spied him and released the ball, spiraling it perfectly toward Jimmy, placing it right over his shoulder. Jimmy reached for it, exhilarated when the cold leather hit his palm.

The rest was a blur. The ball bounced from his hands and he swore a blue streak as the Lipscomb safety slammed into him. He went careening down to the field.

The ball . . . the ball . . . His hands flailed in the air. But he couldn't . . . grab . . . hold.

As he crashed to the ground, the safety scooped up the ball and started to run. From his prostrate, humble position, Jimmy watched the player from the other team become the hero, running down the sidelines, a horde of Rock Mill purple jerseys chasing him while he scored a touchdown.

The visitor stands exploded. The whistle blew. Lipscomb had won.

Jimmy rolled onto his back and stared up at the lights. His humiliation was complete.

Clem angled over him, offering his hand. "My fault."

"How you figure? You threw a perfect pass."

Refusing his friend's hand, Jimmy shoved up on his own. He didn't want help. He didn't deserve it. He'd let the team down.

"Come on, let's go get warm. Hear the coach yell."

But Jimmy didn't follow Clem to the locker room with the rest of the head-hanging team. Instead, he sat on the bench, hiding under his helmet, as students, parents, friends, and fans funneled out of the stands, disappointed.

Over and over, Jimmy replayed the pass and the drop. How did he not catch it?

The stadium lights went out. Still Jimmy sat, unmoved.

"Hello?"

He jumped at the sound of her accented voice, swerving around to see her standing behind him. "C-Colette. What are you doing here?" He gazed at her through his face mask, his heart sinking. She had seen his failure.

"Bad luck on that play. That bloke ran straight into you," she said with her long vowels and lyrical consonants. "I don't understand much about this game, but surely that must be a penalty." She lowered herself next to him, hooking her hands over the edge of the bench, a touching intensity in her expression.

Jimmy laughed. "He's allowed to do that, and if anyone deserves a penalty, it's me. I should've seen him coming. I should've caught the ball."

"What of your teammates? Shouldn't they run him off or something? Do they call it tackling?"

"Yes, tackling, blocking . . ." He peered at her. "What are you doing here?"

"Keeping you company. No lad should sit alone after such a blunder."

"Blunder? That's putting it mildly."

"Your shoulders are all rounded and sad looking." She smoothed her hand down his arm, igniting an inferno in his chest. "It's awful to be alone when you're blue."

"If feeling sad gets you next to me, I'll be sad every day. All day."

Her light, airy laugh nearly made him forget his *blunder*. "Jimmy, I'm not worth all that, now, am I?"

"You should be getting home. It's late and cold. And yes, you are."

She leaned to see his eyes behind his helmet. "Are you going to take that contraption off? Or will you sleep with it on? It won't change anything, you know."

Jimmy tugged off his helmet and smoothed his hand over his wild, sweat-soaked hair. "Where's the gang? Shouldn't you be with them at your aunt and uncle's?"

"Aunt Jean's making hot cocoa. Wouldn't you care to come?"

"I was thinking of making popcorn at home, maybe listen to the hi-fi."

"Oh—" Even in the darkness, Jimmy could see the sparkle in her eyes dim with his subtle put-off. "I was rather hoping you would come."

"How about you come to my place? It's just me and my dad, kind of quiet, but—"

"Will there be hot cocoa?"

Hot cocoa? He had no idea. Did they have chocolate in the house? Dad was turning into a pretty good cook, but chocolate? "Yes, absolutely there'll be hot cocoa."

"Then I'd love to come."

Jimmy stood, offering her his arm. "Shall we? And sorry, I'm a bit smelly."

She laughed softly, hooking her arm into his. "Clem's taught me that most boys are a bit smelly."

"I'll get my gear from the locker room and get cleaned up, promise."

"No worries, Jimmy."

Jimmy. She'd said his name. *Jimmy.* All his failures faded away with the sound of her voice.

CHAPTER FOURTEEN

TAYLOR

A little before noon, Taylor slipped into Granny's driveway with a bag of fries from the Fry Hut, a fifty-year-old Heart's Bend icon, like Ella's and Donut Haven. A large Diet Coke sat on the seat next to her, buckled in because old cars with bench seats had no cup holders.

Her big sister, Emma, waved to her from the front porch steps.

"What are you doing here?" Taylor stepped out, fries tucked under her arm, grabbing her soda from the lap belt. She hadn't eaten all morning, and by the time she left Jimmy's no-wedding chapel, still a bit awed by the place yet shaken by the sound she'd heard, she was beyond starved, craving a fast-food fix from the Hut.

Simple name, great food.

"Can't I play hooky from work to see my sister?" Emma sat against the left side column supporting Granny's veranda. "How'd it go?"

"There are no words. Have you seen that place? Incredible. It has this vibe about it." Taylor omitted what kind of vibe. She didn't want to endure Emma's questions. "The natural light was amazing. Didn't use any lamps or reflectors." Taylor hesitated at the trunk, deciding to haul her gear in later. She had hot fries in hand that needed devouring. "The inside was breathtaking. Slate floor, arched, wood-trimmed ceiling. But Coach was the one who . . ." What? "Gave it life."

She'd convinced herself the *whoosh-thump* came from tree limbs bouncing against the slate roof. Now, she wasn't sure.

"I can't wait to see the shots." Emma reached for a fry before Taylor's backside hit the clapboard step.

She settled the fries between them. They were hot, salty, and fabulous.

"These have to be in heaven." Emma waved a long, golden fry at Taylor.

"I thought we didn't eat in heaven."

"What about that supper, at the wedding?"

"Where's that again?"

"I don't know, end of the Book somewhere." Emma waved her fry around. "I think we won't ever be hungry."

"That would be nice."

"But these fries have to be there. They are *heavenly*."

"Your logic confounds the wise men." Taylor munched on a few fries, doing a bit of emotional sorting, thinking through the morning, deciding the things she loved about the chapel. Wanting to go back.

"Heard from Jack?"

"No."

"Hmm. Makes me wonder. I think he'd be dying to get his phone back."

"Makes you wonder what? He's busy with a meeting this morning."

Fresh off a divorce, Emma's favorite sport these days was marriage-bashing, and Taylor didn't want to play. Especially not after experiencing the goodness of the chapel.

"My one and only date with Jack in high school was at the Fry Hut." She grabbed a few more fries, savoring each bite, then taking a long sip from her soda straw.

"Javier took me to Nashville for a concert." Emma reached for more fries, staring out at the lawn. "But he's gone and I'm over crying about how I thought divorce would never happen to me. You know how families have traits? Like everyone is overweight, or everyone is skinny, or they all play an instrument? Our family trait is everyone divorces."

"Shut up. That's what you want our legacy to be?" However, the truth in Emma's claim rattled Taylor. As far back as she knew, both sides of the family were wildly successful at divorce.

"Doesn't matter what I want. It's true. Makes me wonder what you were thinking when you eloped with Jack."

"I don't know . . ." *He swept me off my feet.*

"Well, 'I don't know' is as good a reason as any."

"Hush. Eat your fries."

You ready?"

"Are you?" Three days she'd waited to marry him. Even on Martha's Vineyard, a romantic elopement required due legal process. But with each day, she envisioned a life with Jack, and it was a beautiful one.

"More than."

He brushed the dangling curl of her updo from her neck. They used the three-day waiting period to get ready. They both bought something to wear. Jack bought plain platinum bands and got a haircut. Taylor got a mani-pedi and a facial. This morning the stylist swept her hair up in ringlets and curls.

"Are we crazy?" she said.

"I like crazy, don't you?" He swept his hand around her neck and drew her into him for a kiss.

Yeah, she liked Jack's kind of crazy. "I can't believe the Jack Forester of Rock Mill High is marrying me." The brooding scholar-athlete with the wounded past had dumped her after one date. But there were plenty of girls waiting to take her place. "All the girls wanted to rescue you in high school."

He grinned. "Well then, here you are, rescuing me."

She sobered. "Do you need to be rescued, Jack?"

"No, but I'll admit to whatever you want to make you stick by me."

"Jack, I want to say I—"

"We're ready for you now." The officiant beckoned for them to follow him to the beach.

Jack took her hand. "Let's go."

Taylor squeezed his hand. Like a couple of crazy kids, neither had said "I love you" yet.

Getting married felt like it deserved some kind of love confession, didn't it?

"Jack, you know we should—"

"I know, have a back door." He stopped and peered right through her eyes and down to her soul. "If it doesn't work out we can walk away, no fuss, no muss."

If it doesn't work out . . .

She wanted to say "I love you" and he instituted an escape clause.

"—so, the chapel. It's nice? I need to drive out there." Emma frowned at the empty fry bag.

"You should wait until you're in a more pleasant state of mind concerning marriage," Taylor said, still trapped between Emma's conversation and her memory.

She should have stopped Jack right then and there with a "What do you mean 'If it doesn't work out'?"

But she was committed to and caught up in the moment. She believed she could beat the odds. That's what crazy people did—the same thing as everyone else, only expecting different results.

"How was Coach? I see him downtown once in a while. At Ella's."

Emma had taken after Granny and gone into banking right there in Heart's Bend. She claimed the smell of money was her favorite perfume.

"Fine, I guess. Doesn't seem like he's in his eighties. He's as old as Granny was but looks like he's got a lot of living left to do." Taylor sipped from the soda, listening to the sounds of the street. A screen door clapped shut. The hint of a country melody. A car starting. "Here's what's weird. Coach spent ten years building this chapel, and for whatever reason, he never used it, and is now selling it."

"People are crazy. Did he give you the story?"

"Not really."

"Maybe some girl broke his heart and he never recovered."

"I suppose." Taylor chewed on the end of her straw. "That would be sad."

"Oh my gosh, I want more fries. See what you did to me. They definitely have to be in heaven. Or I won't go," Emma said.

"So hell is a better option? I'm pretty sure there will be no fries in hell."

Emma laughed. "Then that settles it. No hell for me."

"I don't think heaven is intended for our carnal satisfaction, Em."

"Well, one morning in a chapel and look who's got a sermon."

"I'm just saying." Taylor wadded up the fry bag, feeling full. And a little queasy. Ever since rushing to the airport yesterday, her system was off.

Stress. Just stress. She thought the fries would be the perfect comfort food. Yet here she was with greasy, salty fingers and a gurgling belly.

"So, how *is* married life?"

"Adjusting."

"Could've knocked me over with a feather when you called to say you'd eloped." The warm edge of the noon sunlight fell over their legs. "With Jack Gillingham."

"Forester. He's using his real name now."

"There's a brave soul."

"No one in New York knows his dad is a scalawag. Besides, it's his legal name."

"And is it yours? Are you a Forester too?"

"A Branson."

Emma made a face. "Why? You never struck me as a feminist, keep-your-own-name kind of girl."

"Haven't got around to it, is all."

"You eloped and I got divorced." Emma raised her hand in a mock toast. "To us."

Emma leaned back, propping her elbows on the step behind her. "I didn't want the divorce, you know."

"I know."

"I know you know. So, Taylor, be careful, okay? Don't let Jack get away."

Taylor nodded, shaking the empty soda cup. "I'll do my best."

But it wasn't solely up to her. Jack had a say in things. Like an out clause.

"If it doesn't work out we can walk away, no fuss, no muss."

. . .

JACK

The day remained all sunshine and blue sky as Jack cruised across the Heart's Bend town line. He'd grabbed lunch at a diner outside of Nashville and called Hops, delivering the good news that FRESH Water was a 105 client again.

But Hops didn't care about FRESH. He cared about Jack accepting the job in London. "You're the best man for the job," he said.

The whole exchange made Jack anxious. And now that he was on his way to Heart's Bend to exchange phones with Taylor, he knew he had to ask her point-blank about Doug. If any confidence remained from winning FRESH, it was leaking out of him fast.

He didn't even mind visiting the old hometown if it ensured him he'd not lose his wife. A quick stop-off would make it easy to avoid Rise Forester's neighborhood.

If he didn't have the golf game with Lennon, he'd visit Sam and Sarah. Meanwhile, he rehearsed what he wanted to say.

"Aha! Confess. You're having an affair."

No, too reality TV.

"So, what's really going on with you and Voss?"

Too casual sounding.

"Listen, do you want to be married? To me?"

But if he could peek over the edge of his insecurities, he'd admit Taylor seemed frustrated when Voss showed up at the apartment unannounced. She didn't want him there any more than Jack.

What a moron. Doug had to manipulate to get what he wanted. The accusation boomeranged, popping Jack right in the heart.

And are you any better?

He squirmed in his seat, not enjoying the scrutiny of being under his own microscope.

He wanted to say things to her, he did. It bothered him that intimate words were so hard to speak. Even when he felt them, his heart bursting, he couldn't *say* them.

I love you!

Taylor had whispered the words a few times while making love, but he didn't exactly repeat it so she quit. He didn't blame her for that, or even for maybe falling out of love with him altogether.

He'd married an amazing woman one lucky weekend, when the demons of rejection and heartache were on a vacay from his soul.

And just when he believed his rash, impulsive proposal might turn into the best decision he'd ever made, *wham*, those nasty devils returned and crushed him with the boot heel of "Reject!"

Whether or not Taylor encouraged Voss was one thing. But another man—a good-looking, rich, well-connected man—was trying to steal his wife, and Jack knew sure as shooting he couldn't compete.

So did he let go or fight? He had perfected letting go by the time he was ten. He had the emotional stickiness of used tape.

The Fry Hut popped onto the horizon and Jack gave the place two horn toots as he passed by. He'd taken Taylor there on their first, and last, date in high school. His buddy Bryan had promised Jack the use of his employee discount. Of course the Fry Hut didn't *have* an employee discount . . .

But the fries he shared with Taylor that night were about the best food he'd ever eaten. It'd been a cold fall Saturday and Jack drove them out to a plot of land off River Road. They climbed onto a love seat he'd wedged in the bed of his truck, snuggled under a blanket, and counted the stars.

Jack felt like the King of the World that night. He had plans and dreams. But after one date, he felt those strange gurglings of affection for Taylor and backed off. Whenever possible in his life, he did the leaving. Because just when he thought everything was good, he'd walk through the door to see somber faces.

"Jack, this is your last day with the Feltons." Or the Crandalls. The Horches. The Arguses. The Taggs. Just when he started feeling settled, off he'd go to another foster home.

But that was then. This was now. He was in command of his destiny. Aiming the Mustang through familiar hometown streets, Jack slowed, turning onto tree-lined Chelsea Avenue where the wealthy in town lived fifty years ago. Now the rich lived north, on the edge, closer to Nashville.

But the south side was now part of the historic district.

He parked along the curb in front of house number 828, a three-story Tudor once featured on HGTV when it was lit up for Christmas.

He didn't need to wonder if Taylor was here. She sat on the front steps with Emma. His heart raced as he stepped out of the car, his pulse thick in his ears, catching the sheen of her golden-brown hair in the light and the lean cut of her long legs. Shew, she made him want to shout to the world, "I love this woman!" She made him all twisted up with love.

"Jack." She jumped up, brushing her hands over her shorts as he made his way up the walk. "You're here. Did you call?"

"I called my phone and left a voice mail." He held up her phone. "Have you been missing this?"

"Actually, no." She squinted at him through the sunlight, pulling his phone from her pocket. He wanted to grab her, hold on to her, never let her go. "But I know you're missing this. You have some calls from Hops."

"Thanks, and you . . . you"—he cleared his throat— "have some messages too."

"Addison?"

"No." *Just say it. Doug Voss!* "Hi, Emma."

"Hello, Jack. Welcome to the family."

"Th-thanks."

Taylor unlocked her phone. "H-how did it go? Did Colette call?"

"No word from Colette yet, but I got the account back."

"Yay, Jack, way to go." She raised her hand for a high five. Which he returned, wrapping his fingers around hers and drawing her to him, leaning his lips to her ear.

"Doug Voss texted you a dozen times."

"What?" She pulled away.

"He wants you to meet him in LA." When he released her, she examined her messages, avoiding his gaze.

"Well, I don't want to meet him."

"Then why does he keep texting?"

She raised her gaze to his. "You think there's something behind his insanity? Like me . . . encouraging him?"

"I don't know. Are you?"

"Oh my gosh, Jack. Did you see me refuse him the other night? And did you have this jealous streak when we got married?"

"When we got married you weren't texting with Doug Voss."

"I'm not texting him. He's texting me." She flashed the face of the phone to him. "But apparently you're texting him."

"I had to respond. He was disrupting my meeting."

"I told you, he likes to win, get what he wants." Taylor started up the walk toward the steps where Emma sat watching. "I'm going inside."

"Jack," Emma said. "Come on in. Granny has a ton of books, LPs, photographs. Go through them and take what you want."

"Thanks." But he didn't want anything but Taylor. He skipped up the steps after his wife. "How'd the shoot go today, Taylor?"

She raised her nose from her phone where she'd been typing and scrolling. "Fine."

"She said the place is unbelievable." Emma, filling in details, was trying to be the soft center between them. It bode well for Jack that Emma seemed to be on his side, or at least not against him.

"Then *AQ* should be happy."

"Jack," Emma said. "Are you staying for the week-end? Getting to know your new kin?"

"Actually, I need to get back. Lots of work to catch up on and I have a golf game in the morning."

"Really? You can't stay?"

"Emma, leave him alone. If he has work to do, then he has work to do." Taylor's stubborn glare locked with Jack's. "Besides, he hates it here."

"What? You hate our sweet town?"

"No, I'd just rather be somewhere else." Jack stepped over to Taylor, shoving aside Emma's words and the accusation her town was not good enough for him. He might like HB more if Rise Forester didn't dwell here. "Say, Taylor, I used your idea, you know, Colette Greer tossing water on folks. They loved it."

Her eyes widened. "But you don't have Colette on board yet."

"No, and that is the kink in the works. Do you think you could call her? I could stop by her place Sunday, or Monday, any day, and see if she'll join us." This was rare for him. To be so reckless with an account.

"I don't have any clout with her."

"You can try, can't you?" He took Taylor by the hand and led her away from Emma's eager ears. "Look, Colette aside, I'm sorry about what I said, about you and Voss. But what am I supposed to think?"

"Just because everyone else has let you down doesn't mean I will. See, Jack"—she rapped softly on his forehead—"the ghost of Rise Forester clouds every-thing you believe."

"Like it or not, this is who I am. I'm trying here."

"Me too, but you make it so hard." Taylor pursed her lips into a thin line. "I'll call Colette."

"Thank you. And Doug Voss . . ."

She sighed. "Please forget about him."

Jack exhaled, the dust of his past swirling in him, coating his thoughts, emotions, and marriage. "I-I can stay for a while if you want. But I do have work to do."

"It's okay." Taylor smoothed her hand over his chest. "I've got stuff to go through here with Emma. I'll see you next week." She leaned forward, inviting him into a kiss.

Jack pulled her close, pressing his lips to hers, loving her, tasting her, letting his touch say what his words could not.

CHAPTER FIFTEEN

COLETTE

Justine insisted on working Saturday afternoon, claiming they needed a jump on their deadline. So Colette gave it her all, but she was tired and moving slowly.

Nevertheless she'd dressed, fixed her hair and makeup, and brewed a pot of tea the way Mamá used to. Zoë was off on weekends so she had to fend for herself.

"I know I've been sort of random in collecting information, Colette, but I'm trying to get a feel for how your story should flow."

Across the study, Justine twisted the cap from her Diet Coke and took a big gulp.

"Eclectic is fine." Though Colette preferred stability, predictability, boundaries, and consistency. Routine. Everything working on a soap like *Always Tomorrow* provided.

"Tell me about Peg." Justine read from her computer. "She seems to be a bit witchy. What kind of relationship did you have with her?"

"I loved her. We'd endured a lot together, Peg and I. But she was always a jealous one. In Heart's Bend it boiled down to the fact that we loved the same boy."

• • •

February 1949

Rock Mill High

The end-of-school bell pealed through the concrete and metal hallway, voices rising, bouncing with laughter, the exterior doors opening to the crisp cold, the air swirling with tiny snowflakes.

Colette arranged her books in her locker, covertly peeking toward Mr. Kirby's shop class. Jimmy and Clem would emerge at any moment.

Slowly she rearranged her books, moving trigonometry to the left and chemistry to the right in a reverse alphabetical order. But tucked in her hand was the winter dance flyer.

Saturday, February 12th
six o'clock

Less than a week away and no one had invited her to go. But she'd made up her mind. If Jimmy didn't ask her, she was going to be forward and ask him. Well, maybe she would hint very strongly.

After all, Peg had been saying for months now, "Girls can be bold. It's nearly 1950."

Ever since that cold Friday night on the football field, when Jimmy's dropped ball lost the game, he'd been coming round Uncle Fred and Aunt Jean's almost every evening, pretending to visit Clem after supper.

Then he started showing up before supper and Aunt Jean instructed Colette to set a dinner plate for him.

A week later, he popped round right after school and did his homework at the dining room table with the rest of them. He even got roped into helping with Clem's chores.

By Christmas break, Colette's crush was complete.

Male voices resonated behind her and she gently closed her locker. A shiver surfaced as she leaned against the metal door, clutching her coat to her chest, watching the boys come down the hall.

"This way, y'all." Peggy led a band of girls past Colette, her perfume swarming, her Southern accent practically perfect. The sad orphan girl from England had become a true American beauty.

Colette looked askance at her big sister, the one who'd blossomed in the six months they'd lived in Heart's Bend. She was popular. Even the head cheer-leader, Christy Eames, doted on Peg. But Colette knew it was based on fraud and fakery.

As she'd promised, Peg showed Christy a letter from Princess Elizabeth, inviting her to tea with her and Princess Margaret at Buckingham Palace. Peg invented a life for herself that was very far from her reality. Christy told the whole school and now every girl treated Peg as if she were a princess herself.

When Colette was asked if she too had tea with the princesses, she had no choice but to say, "No, only Peg." And in one sense it was true. In Peg's mind she probably did have tea at the palace. Who knew what reality she'd created in the space between her ears?

"They're coming, girls." Peg adjusted the stack of books she carried on her hip, fixing her smile on Clem and his friends as they walked through the hall like the four horsemen.

Colette shivered again. Weren't boys marvelous? So powerful and rugged. But Jimmy was head and shoulders above them all with his football stride, thick chest, and big shoulders.

"Hey there, Cousin Clem." Peg joined the stride of the boys, tossing her hair and flirting over her shoulder at the others. "Jimmy . . . Spice . . . Mike."

Christy and the other girls joined in, batting their eyes. "Hey, boys."

"You're looking pretty, Peg," Spice said.

"Why, thank you."

Colette remained against the lockers, the cold stain of disappointment on her heart. Jimmy walked right on by, talking and laughing, before disappearing through the steel double doors, hiking his collar against the cold and tugging on his cap.

Colette dropped her books in her locker and slipped on her coat. *Forget it.* She was through with Jimmy Westbrook.

Tugging on her gloves and hat, she gathered her books again and slammed her locker door. *Take that!*

At the end of the hall, she burst into the cold, startled to find Jimmy leaning against the bricks.

"Better hurry, you'll fall behind step with the others." She skipped down the steps, eager to be away from him, eager to hide her wash of tears.

"I wanted to wait for you."

"You just walked past me like you didn't know me." Her foot slipped on a patch of ice and Jimmy steadied her with a firm grip.

"Whoa, careful. Can't have one of Rock Mill's best dancers breaking her leg."

Colette leaned into him a bit, taking longer than necessary to steady herself. Never, *ever*, did she imagine she'd feel this way about a boy. Or *want* to feel this way. Not after Papá died.

She missed him. Sometimes she pretended to see him walking toward her from the shadows.

"Lettie, love, I'm here to take you home. Have you missed me?"

"Terribly, Papá."

But Jimmy, with his square jaw, kind blue eyes, and thick dark hair creamed into place, was a man to be admired. Like Papá. He made her feel warm and safe.

Peg, on the other hand, held herself in reserve when Papá came to the farm. Angry at him for sending her away, she punished him by refusing his kisses and attention.

"G-guess we'd better catch up to the others." Colette found her footing, slipping free of his hold.

In the distance, the gang straggled in pairs. Boy, girl, girl, boy.

"I reckon so."

Since that one night on the field, they'd never been alone. Colette liked having him to herself.

"Come on, slowpokes." Peg ran back to them, her

silky brown curls bouncing against her rosy cheeks, the roundness of her breasts showing beneath the thick coat.

Colette hesitated. When did her sister become a beautiful, alluring woman while she still felt like an awkward girl?

Peg had been somber in England, angry and bitter. Especially after the business with Mamá dying. Colette shuddered. Peg was enraged when Papá came to tell them she'd died. Even more so when he confessed six months had already passed.

Peg was young, but that moment changed her. Colette could see it now.

Peg wrapped her arm with Jimmy's. "Come on, you two. What are you talking about? Who is going with whom to the winter dance?"

Jimmy smiled, the red hue on his cheeks deeper than the cold. "Who are you going with, Peg?"

She shrugged, giving Jimmy a grin that Colette felt through her middle. Her sister, the bombshell, a brunette Betty Grable. "Depends on who's asking me."

Colette flared with a jealous spark. She'd like to kick Peg in the shin. If she had the courage.

Spice, *the* most popular boy in school, mooned over her daily. But Peg ignored him.

Oh, Peg . . .

Colette slowed, letting Jimmy and Peg walk ahead. If Peg wanted Jimmy, then Colette mustn't stand in her way.

"I declare, I'm freezing," Colette said, suddenly skipping ahead. "I'll catch up to the others."

"Wait, Colette—" Jimmy's voice iced on the breeze.

"Run, sweet Colette. Tell Aunt Jean we're on our way, frozen and starved."

Colette brushed away the burn of warm tears. "Cousin Clem, wait up."

"Hurry up, Lettie." Clem waved her on.

Before she could reach him, a firm hand caught her shoulder. Colette looked around into Peg's eyes.

"He's going to ask me to the dance."

Colette stopped. "Are you sure? Peg, everyone knows Spice wants to ask you."

"Then why hasn't he?"

"Perhaps because you keep flirting with Jimmy."

"Then phooey on him if he can't endure a little competition." Alone with Colette, Peg relaxed into the familiar accent of home. Of England.

"Competition? Between men? You're only seventeen. What do you know?"

"I read the romances in Aunt Jean's *Cosmopolitan*."

Colette gasped. "Let Aunt Jean hear you and see what comes of your worldly ways."

"Listen to you. She wouldn't care. She lets me wear makeup, doesn't she? Even when Pastor Brown preaches against the evil of a woman's paint."

Peg laughed, a sound Colette rarely heard in England, and offered a flirty wave to someone. Colette traced the length of her gaze to find Jimmy square in Peg's sights.

"If you chase him too hard, he'll never let you catch him."

"Chase him? Naive Colette, I'm luring him in, setting my hook. I'm going to make Jimmy Westbrook my man."

"Why, Peg, when all of the other boys beg for your attention?"

Peg shrugged. "Because I like him and—"

"Come on, you two," Clem called from the porch, leaning over the rail. "Mama's got hot chocolate and cookies."

"—he's the only boy *not* chasing me." Peg hurried inside while Colette hesitated, debating her sister's motivation. She had half a mind to warn Jimmy.

But ratting out her sister felt like the worst sort of betrayal. What would it hurt if she wooed Jimmy? He was smart and clever, man enough to look out for himself.

The kids piled their coats on the dining room table and gathered in the kitchen.

Colette slipped into the downstairs bathroom, checking her hair, smoothing down the fly-aways electrified by the cold.

She regarded her heart-shaped reflection, jutted out her chin with a harrumph, then jerked open the door. If Peg wanted Jimmy, then she could have him. But at the notion, sadness pinged her heart.

Around the door she bumped square into Jimmy.

"I need to talk to you," he said, low, his warm breath tickling her ears.

He shuffled her through the living room, out to the porch and down the steps, into the first flakes of an afternoon snow.

"Jimmy, what's wrong?" Colette shivered, gripping

her hands at her waist. In his haste, Jimmy had forgotten she had no coat. "Is this about the dance? You know if you ask Peg, she'll go."

"You think I want to take Peg? Colette, don't you know? It's you. It's always been you."

"Me?" The chill on her skin manifested in her voice.

"Colette, sorry, here—" Jimmy shifted out of his jacket and draped it over her shoulders. "Now what's this about Peg?"

"She's the pretty one. All the boys are moony over her."

Jimmy laughed. The look in his eye was one she'd never seen before and it made her shivers sink deeper, making her giddy and weak at the same time.

"Girls like Peg are a dime a dozen. No offense. I know she's your sister, but, Colette, you're . . . I don't know, special."

She could no longer feel the ground beneath her feet. Only the power of his words.

"The first day I met you I knew you were special. I even told my dad about you. Then you sat with me on the field after that awful game." He stepped closer. "I wanted so badly to kiss you."

"*Wanted* to?" Colette could swoon at his nearness, at his electric confession.

The snow thickened, padding the air with a white calm, turning the everyday lawn and house into a magical kingdom. Colette was the damsel and he the handsome prince.

"Are you shocked?" He reached for her hand and gently guided her around the giant fir, out of view from the house. "I still want to kiss you." Jimmy pressed her hand to his chest where his heart thumped beneath her palm.

"Your heart is a drum." She withdrew her hand, smiling, her palm vibrating with the reverb of his heartbeat.

"So, will you?"

She pressed her lips into a tight line and nodded. She might just scream otherwise.

"You will?"

"Yes."

Jimmy scooped her up, spinning her around. "You've made me the happiest fella." He set her on her feet and swept the back of his hand against her cheek, then lowered his lips to hers, warming her with love's first kiss.

In that moment, Colette unlocked the inner door of her heart and invited Jimmy in. Such a sensation, his lips on hers, hot tingles rushing over her cold skin. What choice did she have but to love?

When the kiss ended, he wrapped her into him and she rested her head against his chest.

"Want to tell the others?" he said, kissing the top of her head.

She shook her head. "For now, let it just be between you and me."

After he kissed her again, Jimmy led her from behind the tree, cutting a path through the fresh snow toward the house where Peg watched from the porch, a silent fury exploding all around her.

CHAPTER SIXTEEN

TAYLOR

Saturday morning Taylor woke late, to a big glob of sunlight heating her room. Kicking off the covers, she fought through a sleepy fog, shuffling from the bedroom to the bathroom.

She'd stayed up late playing around with the chapel pictures. As she thought, most of them miraculously did not need editing. Each one possessed an ethereal, magical quality she did not want to tamper with.

So she uploaded the best raw images to *Architecture Quarterly*'s Dropbox and sent an e-mail. Job done.

Nevertheless, she'd made up her mind to go back to the chapel for more photos. Or to just sit. Think. Try to figure out the fractured pieces of her life. Try to understand what made Coach's place so special.

The image of him sitting in the back pew, staring out the window, lingered with her. Played a melody within her heart. A song she felt but did not hear.

But first she needed to shower, to wake up. Man, she was tired. Now that the pressure of travel and work was off, she deflated like a cheap balloon.

The warm shower water cleared the sleep from her head and thoughts of Jack surfaced. He left soon after their phone swap last night, and while she encouraged him to return to Nashville, she wanted to run after him, calling for him to come back.

Argh! They seemed caught in a cycle of pulling each other near, then pushing away.

But if she thought about it, his first promise to her was not to love and cherish, but "*If it doesn't work out . . .*"

"Hello? Tay?" Emma's voice climbed the stairs. "I brought breakfast."

Taylor leaned out the bathroom door, dripping on the white tile. "Just out of the shower. Be down in a minute."

"I brought fresh bagels from Ella's."

Taylor grimaced. Bagels? Ever since her Fry Hut binge, she'd not been hungry. In fact, she felt sort of queasy, with a heavy stomach.

Taylor dried her hair and turned to hang up the towel. The quick movement caused her to lose her balance. She reached for the sink, the porcelain cooling her warm hand.

"Mmmm," she moaned, sinking down to the toilet, her head spinning, her stomach roiling.

Breathing deep, she swallowed a small sting of bile. The bathroom walls inched closer and heat beaded up on her forehead.

"Hot . . . in here . . ." Another deep breath and the dizziness waned. Taylor steadied herself, reaching for the flimsy cotton robe on the back of the door, and moved to her room.

But the room spun around and she stumbled to the window. Shoving it open, she pressed her face against the screen for a pure, cleansing breath.

"Taylor?"

"Yeah, coming." *Don't come up here, Emma, don't come up.*

Taylor moved to dress, holding steady, breathing deep. Please don't tell her Fry Hut fries made her sick. She might just have to mourn if true.

"What do you want to do today?" Emma called.

"I-I don't know." She fell back on the bed to slip on her jeans. "I want to go back out to the chapel. Where are the girls?"

"Javier has them. Welcome to divorced life."

Taylor tugged on her top. Emma's bravado didn't fool her. "Sorry, honey."

"Ah, forget it. What can I do? Let's shop."

"Maybe." Man, she was warm. Still sweating from her shower and the Fry Hut crud, Taylor wandered down the hall to the bum room, searching the closet for an oscillating fan. "We need to finish going through the house."

Taylor plugged in the fan and dropped to the sofa, letting the breeze swish through her. She was too tired to answer. Closing her eyes, she waited for a wave of dizziness to pass. It was then she remembered her weird Jack dream.

She saw his face over and over, morphing into weird, distorted images, cackling at her, pointing and shouting, "I don't want you!"

Shaking off the memory, Taylor leaned close to the fan.

"What are you doing?" Emma's question came from the doorway.

"Cooling off. Shower made me hot." The fan stirred the settled air of the bum room, raising the scent of Granny. "Smells like her, doesn't it?"

"Yeah, it does." Emma entered and curled up on the couch next to Taylor. "You miss her?"

"I do. Sorry I didn't see her more before she died."

Taylor ran her hand over the top of an antique mohair sofa facing the old boxy analog TV with its VCR hookup. Granny's "hi-fi" stereo took up the front corner and a portion of the wall on either side with its giant faux panel speakers.

One wall of shelves was filled with vinyl LPs.

"Remember how she used to play Glen Campbell over and over?"

Emma's soft laugh sealed Taylor's memory. "'Get on up, shug, turn the record over for me.'"

Taylor glanced at her sister. "Pretty good imitation."

"Ever wonder why she gave the house to you but the contents to me?"

"Keep us friends, maybe? Maybe she had her relationship with Colette in mind." Taylor stood slowly, feeling better, and stepped over a box of books to the album shelf and started flipping through. "You think these are worth money?"

"The estate appraiser thinks so. If you want any of them, take them now. Otherwise I'm carting them to auction next month."

Taylor stopped at the Fleetwood Mac *Rumors* album. "Em, look, I didn't know Granny was so hip."

But Emma's phone was ringing and she stepped into the hall to answer.

Removing the album from the shelf, Taylor frowned as a white envelope with her name scrawled across the front dropped to the floor.

"Tay, I've got to go." Emma popped into the room. "Javi just called. Alena is sick. Threw up in his car and now she's crying for me."

"Did she have Fry Hut fries?" Taylor held up the envelope. "Did you see this? I found it tucked in with the albums."

"What is it? And no, she didn't have Fry Hut fries. Why? Did they make you sick?"

"Yeah, still dealing with it."

"I ate them and I'm fine. What's in the envelope? Never mind, I've got to go. Tell me later." Emma exited the room, then returned. "If you want, come by the house later."

"And catch whatever Alena has? No thanks."

"Is that your speech for Aunt of the Year?"

"I'm nominated for Aunt of the Year?"

"Not anymore." Emma checked her phone. "I've got to run. But I'll see you at Mama's tomorrow night? For dinner?"

Mama had a standing deal with her daughters— Sunday night dinner at her place. No excuses. Except maybe moving to LA and New York.

Taylor smiled, finally cooling off. Finally feeling herself. "Wouldn't miss it."

As the door slammed behind Emma, Taylor returned to her fanned post on the couch and tore open the envelope. Inside was a letter written in Granny's elongated hand, and a weird old key.

> Taylor,
>   If you're reading this, I'm gone. I hope my funeral was nice but short, and that Mrs. Bath didn't blubber like she did at Carl Bell's service. What an embarrassment.

Taylor laughed softly. "Pragmatic to the end." No one could ever accuse Granny of being overly sentimental.

> So you hitched your wagon to the Forester kid? Here's my advice. Speak up, say what's on your mind, don't assume. Enjoy the bedroom. Ahem. And well, sis, if it ain't working, don't hang around and waste your life.

Granny!

> Anyway, as I'm trying to get into heaven where I will surely see my dear mamá and papá again, I want to right a very deep wrong. I'm not really sure how to go about it, or if I'm even making the right decision. So I'm passing the buck to you. Sorry, Taylor, hope you don't hate me afterward. Then again, hopefully I'll be in heaven and won't care.
>   In case you're wondering, I'm giving this task to you because, well, the others are idiots.

Taylor laughed through her tears. Granny, Granny, Granny . . .

Besides, you're my favorite. You're wise and I like Jack. He seems to have his head on straight despite what his daddy did to him. What a despicable creature, Rise Forester.

Taylor sat back. Jack. Her Jack. He'd be on the golf course with Lennon by now. Taylor embraced a pang of missing him.

You probably know by now that I set your dad as my executor, but I'm leaving the house to you and the contents to Emma. Pretty savvy of me.

Work together with her to ensure everyone gets what they want, and don't fight over anything. It's only stuff and not worth the family being torn apart. I should know. Family is the most valuable thing on earth, though Lord knows I didn't live my life with that conviction. Remember that family isn't just blood kin but anyone who fits into your heart.

The key is for the box. If you find it, make a wise decision about its contents. Consider all involved and, Taylor, if you think it won't help or if it'll cause more harm than good, leave it be. Take it to your grave, as I have done.

Either way I'm sorry. I really, really am. Keeping secrets hardens a woman's heart. I didn't realize how much so until it was too late.

Taylor glanced at the key, then around the room. Was there a box with a lock in here? And what secret?

> All these years I had to keep quiet. But now, death has given me opportunity to speak. Not many folks can say that, can they?
>
> When you were in your teens, I saw how your parents' divorce affected you more than Emma, and I just want you to know, if the saints of heaven really are praying and watching over, and I'm allowed in, bless the name of Jesus, I'll be sure to pray for you.
>
> Taylor, I never said it enough, but I love you. I was always very proud of you. Be well. And if you can, hug Colette for me. Tell her I'm sorry.
>
> Granny

Taylor reread the last lines, trying to discern the unwritten meaning. *"Tell her I'm sorry."*

About what, Granny?

Tears swished across her eyes, spilling to the tops of her cheeks. She felt cheated, like someone had offered her an ice-cream cone, then snatched it away before she could take a lick.

"Love you, Granny."

Taylor brushed her hand over her tear-touched cheeks and slipped the letter back into the envelope and palmed the key. Placing the *Rumors* album back on the shelf, she glanced about the room. Where would Granny stash a mysterious box?

From down the hall, she heard her phone ring. *Jack.* Taylor rose from the couch, the sudden move draining her balance. Grabbing the arm of the sofa, she let the moment pass, then hurried to her room.

"Hello?" She didn't recognize the number.

"Taylor?"

"This is she."

"Keith Niven, Niven Realty. I understand you have pictures of the Westbrook property. I was wondering if you'd like to share?"

"Share?" Taylor set the letter and key on the old dresser, then leaned against it. Seriously, no more Fry Hut fries. "No, um, sorry, I took those for a client."

"How about I hire you to shoot another set?"

Architecture Quarterly didn't ask for an exclusive, so . . . "What do you need them for?"

"Website. We've listed the chapel for sale but the images my associate took don't capture the essence of the place. Do you have time?"

"I do, but I'm not sure I like the idea of Coach selling the place."

"I hear you, but he's ready. We'll get him fair market value."

"I don't think it's about the money." Really, this wasn't her business.

"Listen, are you speaking for Coach or yourself? Because he's the one who gave me your number. So I'm thinking he's a go for selling. So, are you in?"

Taylor rattled off her top fee, which Keith agreed to without a hesitating breath.

"Can you come now? I'm at the chapel with Coach."

"Now? Yeah, sure."

She stared out the window, echoes of Granny's letter

drifting through her head, followed by images of Jimmy staring out the chapel window.

What secret? And why was Coach selling?

Pushing past the waves of queasiness, Taylor grabbed her purse and headed out.

At the Lincoln, she checked to ensure her equipment was still in the trunk, then fired up the engine.

The drive out to River Road cleared her head and relieved the effects of the French fries. By the time she turned down the chapel's lane, she felt strong.

"She's beautiful today, Coach," Taylor said, greeting the old man in the middle of the chapel yard.

"She's beautiful every day."

What's going on?

Accompanying Coach Westbrook was a lean man in what appeared to be a tailored suit. Professional, with eager eyes and an eager gait, he introduced himself to Taylor.

"Keith Niven." He shook her hand with a firm grip.

"Taylor Branson."

Maybe between LA and New York she'd become cynical, but she didn't like Keith. Too slick. Too smarmy.

"Ready to take some pictures?" he said, pronouncing it "pitchers" and popping his hands together.

"Let me get my camera." Taylor raised the trunk lid, reaching in for her camera. "Hey, Coach?"

"Taylor?"

"You sure you want to sell this place."

He glanced away but nodded. Once. "It's time. Ain't getting any younger."

Taylor walked with Keith into the chapel while Coach waited outside.

"We have some powerful interest in this place." Keith paced down the center aisle, hands on his waist, suit jacket shoved back.

"What does that mean? 'Powerful interest'?" Taylor snapped on a lens and took a couple of test shots.

"People with deep pockets wanting to buy."

"Why do folks with deep pockets want a wedding chapel?" Taylor moved through the sanctuary, searching for the angles and light she'd found yesterday. But the air in the chapel was different. Taylor glared toward Keith. She suspected the change was more about the absence of Coach than the presence of Keith.

"I can sell this place within the month," Keith said, his words puffed up. "I've got a group from Nashville and one from Vegas coming for a look-see. Destination weddings in smaller venues like chapels are all the rage. This place will be hopping." He snapped his fingers, one-two-three.

Taylor took a couple of shots, but her heart wasn't in it. She ached for Coach to keep this place. When she positioned herself in the front corner for a wide shot of the sanctuary, Coach walked in.

She snapped the shutter, capturing the old man in his custom space.

Tell me, Jimmy, what's on your mind?

From his expression, it wasn't buyers from Nashville and Vegas.

"Say, Coach," Taylor said, walking toward him. "Ever

think about running the place yourself? You could hire a manager to help coordinate it all." She powered off her camera and removed the memory card. "Here you go, Keith."

"Taylor, Taylor." Keith jumped between them. "Running a wedding venue is mega work. Coach is retired, enjoying life. He doesn't want to run a wedding business."

"Coach, what did you have in mind when you built this place?" Taylor shoved the card at Keith, feeling mama bearish about Coach. Like he needed someone, her, in his corner.

"What did I want? Get married, I reckon."

"So, why didn't you?"

"Listen," Keith said, snatching the card from Taylor. "I hired you as a photographer, not an advocate for my client against me. I'm about to make Coach a lot of money."

Maybe it was the ordeal between her and Jack. Or waking up this morning feeling puny. Or maybe it was because she just believed Coach needed someone to advocate for him, but Taylor had enough of Keith Niven.

"Don't push me or Coach. I only want to make sure he has a choice. That this is really what *he* wants. Can't you see this place means a lot to him? Are you being discreet with potential buyers? Or are you bringing by any ole Elvis preacher who'd marry a chicken to a duck for the right price?"

"You wound me." Keith slapped his hand to his chest. "I'm not a two-bit hustler. I was agent of the year last year. I'm a *professional*. This is my career. It's my duty to sell this extraordinary property to the right buyer for top dollar, making money for everyone."

"Taylor, Taylor, it's all right." Coach slipped his hand into hers. "I appreciate you sticking up for me, but I know what I'm doing. Keith is a good man."

She exhaled, deflating some of her ire, but didn't withdraw her hand from his, not clear whether he held on to her or she to him.

"Fine, but, Keith, do not treat Coach's life's work like a two-bit hotel. And what's top dollar, by the way?"

"Coach," Keith said, laughing. "I thought you just met this gal. But you have a tiger in your corner. Top dollar is top dollar. At today's prices, Coach will walk away with a mighty tidy sum."

Taylor peered over at Coach, who boasted a smile, but his slightly rounded shoulders cracked her heart a bit wider for him.

"Coach." She squeezed his hand. "Are you really sure you want to let this place go? I just feel like there's something more here—"

He squeezed her hand back. "Trust me, kiddo, I let go a long time ago."

A brush of light fell over the pews from the western windows, spreading a gentle wheel of color through the stained glass. A soft red, pale blue, and shallow green puddled across the floor.

Then she heard it. The light *whoosh-thump*. Taylor whipped around toward the door, her middle taut with anticipation. "Did you hear that?"

"Hear what?" Coach said, releasing her hand.

Taylor shook her head. "Nothing. Just the wind." She

turned to Keith. "You have some good shots. Keep the memory card, Keith."

"I need to pay you." He pulled his wallet from his pocket but Taylor waved him off.

"Just find the absolute best buyer for Coach. For this chapel."

"Trust me, I will, but I insist on paying you." Keith pressed a wad of bills in her hand as he headed out. "I hate to be beholden."

I bet you do.

Alone with Coach, Taylor smiled. "Guess that's it for now." Then she heard it—the *whoosh-thump*. The sound of a heart's chambers.

She tossed Coach a visual. Their gazes met and she knew. He'd heard it too.

"Do you think buildings have a soul, Taylor?" He jutted out his square chin where a soft dusting of white whiskers caught the light.

"A soul?" she said, raising her gaze to the ceiling. "I reckon not. Only humans have souls. But I suppose an old building just might have a *heart*." She tossed it out there, waiting for him to respond, to confess he heard it too.

He nodded and turned for the door. "You ready? I'll lock her up."

In the yard, Taylor bid Coach a good day and climbed behind the wheel of the Lincoln.

Coach could not, *must* not sell this place. Because Taylor innately understood any change of hands would end a dream that somehow still yearned to live. And the key of that dream was buried in the heart of one sweet old coach.

CHAPTER SEVENTEEN

JACK

Focus, Jack, focus.

His mission Monday afternoon was simple. Convince Colette Greer to lend her legendary name to FRESH Water.

Karli Jackson from FRESH had phoned over the weekend, gushing about how much the team loved Jack's *fabulous* idea. Then she dropped the hammer.

"No Colette Greer, no deal."

Jack was never so relieved than when Colette called Sunday evening just after he arrived home.

Without any small talk, she agreed to meet with him. "Monday afternoon, one sharp."

Yessiree, he was not going to lose an account to Alpine & Schmidt.

Now, pacing his office, Jack prepared to pitch his A game.

Hops popped into his office. "I still need my best man heading up WhiteWater's foundation."

Jack glanced up from his notes. He liked to jot down his ad libs. "Fine, fine, let me get through this FRESH business and I'll give you an answer."

"Sooner rather than later, Jack."

"Okay, okay."

Rocking back in his chair, Jack stared at his glass wall, watching Hops disappear into his office.

London. He'd not even brought it up to Taylor. What if he wanted, needed, to go to London, but she insisted on staying here? Jack's chest constricted with the idea of leaving his wife in New York while that snake Doug Voss slithered through the streets.

Try as he might, he could not trust. He'd been burned by that match too many times.

He woke up this morning with an odd line running through his head, rocking his confidence.

"If it doesn't work out we can walk away, no fuss, no muss."

Who said that? Taylor? At their wedding? His memory played a recording of her voice saying, *"No fuss, no muss."*

Know what? He didn't have the emotional time to dwell on it. Jack reached for his phone and slipped on his suit jacket.

If he didn't leave for Colette's now, he'd be late.

Grabbing a fourth cup of coffee, Jack stopped by Hops's office. "I'm on my way to Colette Greer's."

"Fine, keep me posted." Hops remained focused on the document he was reading.

"I'm not losing this account to Alpine & Schmidt."

"So you've said."

"Why don't you hire someone who's already in London? To head up the foundation?"

"Because I hired someone in New York who said he'd do anything and everything I asked."

Ah, speared by his own confession. "That was a long time ago."

Hops glanced up. "What's changed?"

"Me. I'm experienced now. Married."

"Which is exactly why you need to be in London. As a photographer your wife must be dying to go."

Jack kicked out one of the chairs in front of Hops. "I haven't told her."

Hops reached for his 105 coffee mug, using it more as a prop than to drink coffee. "Things not going well between you two?"

"We're adjusting."

"Want some advice? From a man who's been married three times?"

"Not really."

"Third time's a charm, Jack."

"I don't want to be married a third time. Or a second."

"You may have no choice." Hops set his cup down and leaned on his elbows. "Jack, if your job is sexier than your wife, then it's time to cut her loose."

"Excuse me?" Where was he going with this?

"You come in early, stay late. Bust your butt to win back an account I'm not all that keen on keeping."

"FRESH has been a key account for ten years. Besides, I'm trying to build a career here."

"So you lose one account, Jack. It happens."

"Do you hear yourself?" Jack jumped up. "Cut the

wife loose, cut a key account. Well, no, I don't want to lose FRESH." Or Taylor.

It wasn't so much that he hated to lose—he hated the . . .

Rejection.

"I've been where you are, Jack. Believe me," Hops said. "I know *exactly* how you feel. So trust me when I say sometimes you have to let things go, move on, scale higher mountains. Before your marriage you'd have beaten down my door for the London spot. Again, what's changed?"

"I have a personal life."

"Yet here you are, at the office morning and night, spending your weekend on a B-level account. If that is more enticing to you than whatever is waiting for you at home, then cut your losses, Jack. Elope *out* as quick as you eloped in."

"That's your sage advice? 'Elope *out*'?"

"Took me three marriages to figure it out, but yes, that's my sage advice."

Jack regarded Hops, searching for a response, finding none. His words felt dry and void, his heart pinging with the buried truth in his boss's odd logic.

From his pocket, Jack's phone buzzed, reminding him to leave for Colette's or be late.

"I've got to go." He backed toward the door.

"Good luck. But, Jack, after you fix this FRESH thing, it's off to London. I'm not asking anymore. I'm telling."

Jack stepped over Hops's verbal gauntlet, tension twisting through him. If he had to choose between

London and his marriage, between his boss and his wife, he'd sink. Drown in indecision.

After riding the elevator to the street, Jack whistled for a cab.

While the idea of losing Taylor stole his breath away, his job meant everything to him. For the past five years, Hops and 105 had been his family, a constant in his life, a place of security and success.

So if he had to choose . . .

Jack scooted into the backseat of a yellow cab and gave the driver Colette's address. He stared out the window at the traffic and pedestrians, grappling with Hops's advice and the churning question—If he had to choose . . .

Squirming in his seat, he stretched his starched collar, trying to inhale deep.

He didn't know. He just didn't know. And in the face of his indecision, a slow-burning fear settled in his soul.

. . .

The famous Colette Greer met him in the middle of a bright, square room where a wall of windows faced Central Park.

"Come in, please." She shook his hand and the power of her grip made him question her age.

"Thank you for meeting with me." Jack sat in the chair she indicated, a bit in awe of the soap legend.

She had a presence about her, a savoir faire he didn't find in most women, or men, for that matter. To his surprise, though, she reminded him of Taylor. Her countenance, her frame, the way she carried herself.

He'd collected himself, stuffed away his conversation with Hops on the ride over, finally feeling composed on the elevator ride up to Colette's penthouse.

"Zoë, bring round some tea," Colette said. "You like tea, don't you, Jack?"

"Yes, ma'am." He'd drink tea until his eyes swam in orange pekoe if it landed Colette for the FRESH account.

She sat on the corner of the sofa, diagonally from Jack, who'd dropped into the nearest big and boxy armchair. Everything in the room was white except the dark furniture.

"So what's this all about? This FRESH Water opportunity?"

"Thank you for seeing me, Ms. Greer." Jack scooted to the edge of his chair.

"How's Taylor?"

Jack moved to the edge of his seat, adjusting his jacket, focusing on Colette. "She's fine. In Heart's Bend, actually. At her granny's house. She went down to take pictures of a wedding chapel."

Colette glanced away. "Wh-what is she doing at her granny's house?"

"Not really sure. Her granny, Peg, your sister, left the house to Taylor but the contents to her sister, Emma. Pretty unique situation."

Colette sat back. "I see. And this chapel?"

"I don't know much about it other than ole Coach Westbrook built it. Did you know him? Jimmy Westbrook?"

"I-I believe I went to school with a Jimmy Westbrook."

"Apparently he built a wedding chapel but never used it. Ever."

"Tragic, isn't it, how love can tumble a soul?"

Tumble a soul. Jack considered the odd conclusion to Coach's building a chapel. "I guess it makes one think."

In a flash, Jack saw himself as an old man, aging and alone, a curmudgeon like Scrooge. Bitter like Rise Forester. And panic kicked in. No! He wouldn't let it happen, but sure as shooting, that would be his future if he didn't learn to speak his heart.

If he wasn't sitting in front of Colette, he'd text Taylor now. No, *call.* He should call. Because Voss liked to text.

"How is Taylor's family? Are they all well?"

"Her mom owns a production company and is pretty influential around Nashville. A couple of movies were shot on location in Heart's Bend and she worked on those. Let's see . . ." Truth was, Jack didn't know all that much about Taylor's family. "Her dad runs Branson Construction & Survey. She doesn't talk much about him. Of course you know him—he's your nephew."

"I've not seen him since he was a very young lad."

Colette's assistant bounced in with a tea tray and set it on the table. She handed a cup and saucer to Jack, then one to Colette, before pouring from a glossy white china pot. She passed a plate of thin cookies.

When she left, Colette sipped her tea, eyeing Jack over the rim. "Well, I suppose you came for some other reason than to discuss my family."

"Yes, ma'am, I did." Jack gulped his tea and burned his tongue. "I'd like you to be the spokeswoman for FRESH Water."

"So you said in your voice mail. Why me, Jack?"

He squared his back and launched his pitch.

You're an icon . . . known around the world . . . infamous for tossing water in people's faces . . . classic actress with drama and comedic skill . . . broad appeal.

"Who do you want treasuring your water product? Colette Greer. The FRESH people think it's brilliant."

"Interesting." She reached to add a bit more cream to her tea. "I do like FRESH."

"And FRESH likes you. No, they *love* you."

"Are your folks in Heart's Bend?"

Jack tipped his head at the sudden change in conversation. "Mine? Um, yeah, kind of. It's complicated."

Colette cradled her cup and saucer in her hand. "We have a few minutes."

Okay, but he was really on a roll with his FRESH pitch. Jack balanced his tea on his knee and shoved a cookie in his mouth.

"My parents married, divorced, and I lived with my mom until she was killed in a motorcycle accident. I was nine."

"I lost my parents in the war."

"It's no picnic, is it?"

"Hardly."

"My dad claimed my mother cheated on him and that I was not his son. She, however, claimed his parents hated her because she was not of their social and economic class. Eventually they pressured my father into divorcing her."

"See? How often love is tragic."

Jack set his tea aside, uneasy at the way Colette's

philosophy mirrored Hops's. Same sentiment. Different words. "Yes, tragic."

"Who's your father?"

"Rise Forester Jr." He tagged the name with attitude.

"Is his father Rise Sr.? I knew him. In high school."

"That'd be the one. I never knew him." They showed no interest in him. Ever.

Colette seemed to ease down further in the sofa. "But you want to talk about FRESH, don't you?"

"This is a great campaign, Colette." Jack surged forward into his racing lane and settled in, describing the youth and vitality of the FRESH Water bottling company.

"And I get to toss water in someone's face?"

"In the way only Colette Greer can."

"Or Vivica Spenser. She invented that move." Colette's laugh floated over him.

Jack's hope slowly rose. "So you'll do it?"

"Why not? It sounds fun. And at my age, a girl never knows how many days of fun she has left."

Jack contained himself enough to offer her a proper handshake and a professional, "It's an honor. Welcome to the fam." He grinned. "You've made my day."

"And you mine." She returned his hearty handshake.

"Thank you for this. You're going to love working with 105, and FRESH." He retrieved two business cards from his wallet. "Here's my card, and one from FRESH. Please call them if you have any questions. Otherwise, we'll move forward. Have your manager call me. We can go from there."

"Will do."

When she didn't reach for the cards, Jack deposited them on the table. "Thank you for your time and the tea."

"No, thank you."

Striding down the wide, grand hall to the elevator, Jack did a jig and tugged his phone from his pocket. That was almost too easy. But if being "family" plied Colette for him, he'd take it.

He never tired of winning an account. It felt like Christmas every time. Joy to the world!

Calling Taylor, Jack deflated some when her voice mail answered. Hanging up, he opted to send a text.

JUST MET W/YOUR AUNT. SHE'LL DO FRESH CPAIGN. ASKED A LOT ABOUT THE FAMILY.

He entered 105 walking a few feet off the ground and informed his team they'd beaten Alpine & Schmidt and won back the FRESH account with Colette Greer as their spokeswoman.

Cheers all around.

In his office, Jack checked his phone for a response from Taylor. Nothing.

Energized, he made calls to the clients he'd been neglecting recently, but by midafternoon, he'd still not heard from Taylor.

He pinged her with a YOU THERE? text.

Nothing.

By the time he made his way home late that evening, through the angles of city shadows and lights, his slow-burn fears about his life with Taylor threatened to become a blaze.

. . .

TAYLOR

The last time she had stood outside her daddy's Heart's Bend office peering in the window, she'd been fourteen, maybe fifteen, and he was her hero.

She'd not intended to stand here now on this Monday afternoon, but all weekend she battled the idea that Coach Westbrook needed her. If not her, then someone.

Despite her personal feelings toward her father, he was the perfect one to look in on Coach. Because no one adored his old football mentor more than her daddy.

She played her Saturday exchange with Keith over and over in her mind all weekend, convinced the man didn't have one sincere bone in his body.

On Sunday she intended to go to church but overslept. She still fought the Fry Hut bug. She slept most of the day, waking up barely in time for dinner at Mama's.

Which brought her to now. Daddy's office in downtown Heart's Bend. The sign on the window read the same as always.

"Branson Construction & Survey—Founded 1977. Serving the central Tennessee area and beyond."

Taylor ran her hand over the thick white-painted letters. These were new. Not the ones she helped him paint on the glass when she was twelve.

Peering through her own shadow, she saw Daddy bent over his desk, working. She might not respect his moral choices, but she could not deny he was one of the hardest-working men she ever knew.

When she was little, they had a little routine when he came home. As he pulled into the driveway, she'd burst out of the house, run down the sidewalk, and leap into his arms. He'd catch her, always catch her, and twirl her around.

Never once was she afraid of leaping. Never once did she fear he'd not raise his arms to catch her.

Then she saw him with another woman and her relationship with him became like papier-mâché. Hardening with time.

Taylor reached for the handle and let herself in. Daddy looked up from his legal notepad, a yellow number 2 pencil in hand.

"Mercy, mercy, if my eyes do tell." Marabelle, Daddy's longtime secretary with the bottle-red hair, shoved away from her desk, approaching Taylor with her arms high and wide. "What in the world? Drummond, you didn't tell me Taylor was in town."

She braced herself for a face-smothering grand-mama of a hug.

Daddy slowly rose to his feet. "Guess not, Marabelle." How could he? He didn't know.

"Hey, Daddy." Taylor waved at him from under Marabelle's plump, ample arms.

"Taylor." He nodded her direction. "What brings you around?"

"I need to ask you something," she said, wiggling free from Marabelle's embrace.

"You want a cup of coffee?" Marabelle pointed to the

coffee cart. "We've got a couple of those fancy creamers. And there're some donuts from Donut Haven." The red-lipped secretary pinched Taylor's side. "I see you can afford to put on a few extra pounds. Drummond, I don't think they have food up there in Yankee land."

"Now, you know they do, Mara. Some of the best restaurants in the world are in New York City."

"Well, sure, they charge you a hundred bucks for an ounce of pâté and call it a meal." She tsked and loaded up a paper plate with a selection of donut holes.

But really, Taylor wasn't hungry. Even if she was, nothing sounded appetizing this morning.

"You all right, Tay?" Daddy sat back down at his desk, propping his hands on its computerless top. Daddy still worked with paper and pencil and the old-fashioned telephone. Last year Emma talked him into a smartphone, which now sat to one side of his desk, the screen dark.

"Sweetie pie, eat, you look green." Marabelle set the plate of sweets in front of her.

"I'm fighting the flu bug, I think. Catching what Alena had. Mara, do you have any bottled water?"

"Sure do. Sit tight." She hurried around the wall to the kitchenette. "You know I heard on the news something was going around."

"So, how can I help you?" Daddy said. "Everything all right with Jack?"

Not really, but that was the last thing she wanted to talk about. "Do you know anything about a wedding chapel out on River Road? Coach Westbrook built it. Started it in the fifties, I think. Took him years to build." Where was Marabelle with that water?

"I've not *heard* of it, no, but I actually saw it a few years back." Daddy leaned back, calling over his shoulder, "Mara, when did we do the surveying for the county off 251, River Road?"

"Ninety-two."

Daddy grinned. "Who needs a computer? I got Mara."

"Yeah, but can you back her up in case she crashes?"

Daddy's laugh burst from his chest, a confetti of colors and tones. It hit Taylor in a familiar yet dry place and slaked the edge of her thirst. "She keeps meticulous records, but if you mean this place would be lost without her, you got that right."

Marabelle hurried toward Taylor with a bottle of water. "What's got y'all so tickled?"

"Taylor says I can't back you up. You're not a computer," Daddy said.

"Darn right." Mara huffed, digging her fists into her round, wide hips.

"So if you crash . . ."

"It's called job security, Taylor. Don't forget it." Marabelle returned to her desk. "Drum, I'm heading to the bank. They messed up the automatic draws again. Looky here, Taylor, this *human* has to go fix what *their* computer did."

Taylor saluted the woman with her water. "Give 'em what-for, Mara."

"So, what about this chapel?" Daddy focused in on Taylor.

She shrugged, picking at the water bottle label. FRESH. "Coach Westbrook built it. Did you know about it?"

"I might have. How'd you find it?"

"I came down to do a shoot for *Architecture Quarterly*."

"No kidding?" Daddy nodded, impressed. "That's one of my regular reads."

"*AQ* heard about it and wanted to feature it in their Chapels of America edition."

"Well, I've seen the chapel. On the outside." Daddy whistled, shaking his head. "It was impressive. I came on it out of nowhere, traipsing through the woods. I knew the land belonged to the Westbrooks, but that chapel wasn't on any of the drawings or specs I ever saw." Daddy tapped his pencil against the desk, his gaze shifting between his yellow legal pad and Taylor. "What's going on? Did the shoot not go well?"

"No, it went great. Beyond great." Their eyes met for a second, then Daddy looked away.

He wasn't comfortable. But could she blame him? She'd kept him at arm's length for fourteen years. But today she chose to lower her arms. For Coach. And if she was honest, it was good to see him.

"Listen, Daddy, Coach is selling the chapel. Keith Niven is the real estate agent. Do you know him?"

"I do. He's a good man. Knows his business."

"He told Coach he would get him top dollar, but I have this feeling in my gut Coach shouldn't even be selling. He built that chapel for a reason, but something happened and he never used it."

"Then maybe it *is* time to sell. Coach is getting on in years. He might think someone could get use out of it."

"I know, but something doesn't seem right to me. Not only is the wedding chapel a masterpiece, but it's on all that land. The land alone is worth a lot. I have a feeling Keith is going to lowball him."

A *feeling* was not a good argument. Or even a reason. Not logically, anyway. Not to mention she was going to bat for a man who didn't ask for, or want, her help.

"You realize the higher the price, the more commission Keith makes. I'd trust he's pricing it for the current market."

"I guess so." Taylor twisted the cap from her water and took a glorious swig. The cool water eased the flashes of heat spiking beneath her skin. "It's such a beautiful place. I hate to think of him selling. It's as amazing on the inside as the outside. The light is almost otherworldly, if that doesn't make me sound crazy. I didn't even have to edit any of the photos I sent to *AQ*."

The twist in her gut told her Coach put more than time and sweat into the chapel. He'd left his heart and soul there.

The walls, the windows, the floors, and the light all reflected him. His love for whoever . . .

"What do you need from me?"

Taylor peered at her father. *Thank you.* He could've told her he was busy, to get lost, to not stick her nose where it didn't belong. Because that's more or less what she'd done to him for the last half of her life.

"Will you look into it?" she said. "Find out what Keith's up to? Maybe figure out what the land and the chapel are worth. If anyone knows the value of land and a building, it's you. Besides, Coach is one of your favorite people in the world."

Daddy tapped his pencil against his palm. "All right, if it means that much to you."

"It does." She sat up straight, relieved, smiling. "Thank you."

He regarded her for a moment. "Ardell is making her famous sloppy joes for dinner. She'd love to see you, Taylor."

"I can't."

Daddy nodded, clearing his throat. "Well, if you change your mind—"

"Emma and I are going through the last of Granny's stuff. If there's anything you want—"

"I got everything I want."

Taylor stood to go, tapping her leg with the water bottle. "You know, I found a letter addressed to me hidden among the LPs. She wrote it not long before she died. Like she knew her time was near. Did she say anything to you about it?"

"No, sorry, Tay. What did it say?"

"Funny things . . . You know Granny. But she claimed she had a secret."

Daddy laughed. "Now, why doesn't that surprise me? Mom embodied secrecy. Did she tell you the secret?"

"Sort of. She left me a key, said to find a box, and if I felt like it was worth sharing . . . whatever I found . . . I could share it. Otherwise she said to take it to my grave like she did."

Daddy stiffened, making a face. "Oh, my mother. Cold in the ground and trying to pull strings. Taylor, listen, don't get wrapped up in her shenanigans."

"Do you have any clue as to what the secret might be?"

Technically Taylor was breaking one of her five "Dad Rules" by sitting here, talking personal business with him, but rules were made to bend from time to time.

"Not one."

"Why did she and Granddad divorce?" Taylor never knew her paternal grandfather, nor the stories behind his romance with Granny and subsequent demise.

He died at sixty-two of a massive heart attack when Taylor was a baby.

"He and Mom fought a lot. That's all I know. I asked her about it once after your mom and I were married. She mumbled something about Dad being jealous and pigheaded."

"Was he?"

"Not that I could tell. If you ask me, she won the coin toss on being pigheaded. He was always good to me."

"Do you think Granny really had a secret?"

Daddy shook his head, arms propped on his desk. "No, I think she had a lot of secrets."

"Hmm . . . Maybe to do with Colette? I saw her last week, by the way. I did a shoot with the *Always Tomorrow* cast."

Daddy arched his brow. "You're getting some good work, kiddo. Did I ever tell you I didn't even know Mom had a sister until I was twelve or thirteen? I met

Colette in the seventies when she was a parade marshal." Daddy shook his head, tapping his pencil on
the desk. "If Mom has a secret she's passing on to you,
wouldn't surprise me if it had to do with Colette."

The push-button phone on Daddy's desk rang out.
"Branson Construction—"

Taylor got up, waving, and started for the door. The
water had helped ease her wooziness. Daddy held up
his hand, signing for her to wait.

"Hold on, Ralph." Daddy pressed his hand over the
mouthpiece. "Will I see you before you leave?"

"I want to finish with the house and—"

"All right, then. Have a good trip home, Taylor."

"Yeah, and thanks for checking on the chapel
for me."

"You still have the same cell number?" Daddy
shoved the yellow legal pad her way, offering his pencil.

"Same one." But she wrote it down anyway.

"I'll call when I find out something."

"Thanks."

"Taylor?"

She paused at the door.

"For the record, you're one of my favorite people. If
not my most."

Taylor shoved outside, speed walking to her car, her
eyes flooding. Why did he say that? Why?

Behind the wheel of the Lincoln, she slammed the
door shut and fired up the engine. As she placed her
hand on the gear shift, a rolling sob broke her strength.

She folded forward, resting her head on the sun-
warmed wheel.

She'd never articulated to him what she saw in the family room that day. But by now the image was buried so deep, she wasn't exactly sure how to dig it up. How to frame it with words.

But his raw moment of kindness challenged her. Did she want to live the rest of her life without her daddy? Perhaps it was time to roll away the stone from her heart and let love out again.

CHAPTER EIGHTEEN

JIMMY

He'd gotten an unexpected call from Drummond Branson asking to see the chapel. He'd be jigged if he and his chapel weren't suddenly the most popular things in Heart's Bend.

Taylor told Drummond about it and he said he was curious, so Jimmy agreed to meet him Wednesday morning.

When he woke up that morning, he had the idea to swing by the nursery for a few morning glories and purple asters.

Even though he was selling the old gal, it wouldn't hurt to spruce up the chapel garden a bit.

But he'd be glad when things settled down. All this chapel business was messing with his nap schedule. A man his age needed his beauty sleep.

More than that, it messed with his memories. With his heart, making him want things he could never have. It was too late. The ship had sailed.

Parking in the chapel shade, Jimmy popped the truck gate and pulled the flower pots to the ground. Carting them to the bed on the eastern wall, he set them where he wanted.

Returning to the truck for his shovel, he paused to unlock the chapel door. Easing it open, he stuck his head inside, tentative yet expectant.

"Hello?"

Was it here? The *whoosh-thump* of a beating heart? He'd heard it Saturday with Taylor. He was ninety percent sure she heard it too—if the look on her face was any indication. He imagined he wore the same one.

He didn't feel right bringing it up, but it was comforting to know he wasn't crazy. The trick now was to figure out *why* Taylor heard it. What did it all mean? The beating heart only he and Taylor heard? Chills rushed over him just thinking about it.

Yet he had no idea what it was or where it came from. He was willing to believe things happened that made no sense. Things that had to be left up to faith. To God.

Backing out of the chapel, he moved on to the flower bed, dropping to one knee, his old bones complaining. When he reached for the weeds and pulled, a dark memory surfaced and flooded his senses.

· · ·

OCTOBER 1954

AT THE CHAPEL

"What are you doing, son?"

Jimmy wheeled around to see Dad stepping through

the open stone doorway. It was too late to hide the gas tank at his feet.

"I thought you were sleeping through *This Is Your Life*."

Dad had finally broken down and bought a TV while Jimmy was in Korea. He had a steady schedule of programs he liked to watch.

"What you got going on with that gas can?"

"Dad, this doesn't concern you."

"I think it does. I put some backbreaking work into this place, helping you cut stones and raise the walls, trim the beams."

Jimmy glanced back at his father who stood just off his left shoulder. "Peg stopped by. Said Colette's not coming back."

"So you're going to burn this place down like it's the end of the world?"

"It is the end for me. I loved her. I've always loved her. Since before I met her."

"How could you love someone—"

"I saw her in a photo."

"Fine, you love her. But if she's not coming back, Jim, then let her go. You're twenty-two, almost twenty-three, with your whole life ahead of you. You'll meet another gal."

"Did you let my mother go? You've never loved anyone else."

"Don't be like me."

"I'd be proud to be like you, Dad," Jimmy said quietly. "You're a good man."

"Then don't be like me when it comes to love. Find a nice girl and make a life for yourself."

"But I built this place for Colette." Jimmy scuffed the dirt beneath his boot. This exact spot was where he'd declared his feelings for her, and she for him.

Where he took her as his own.

"When your plans don't work out, you make new ones. You can't imagine being in love with another woman right now, but you will. And you'll want this place. You've done so much work on it." Dad walked along the dusty wall, knocking some critter's nest from the stone. "You'd be foolish to burn it down."

"What about the part of me that feels foolish to leave it standing? All those hours of work for nothing." He nailed his sentence with a spike of bitterness. "It's not a monument to love but to foolishness."

"Don't be that way, Jim. Life has a way of coming around. You don't know what tomorrow will bring."

"I know life brings war and people skipping out on their promises. Life *takes* as easily as it gives." Jimmy snatched up the gasoline can. "You'd better go if you don't want to see it burn."

Dad clapped a hand on his arm. "What if she comes back? Ever think of that?"

"She's never coming back, Dad. Three years of nothing except a Dear Jimmy letter." After which he tried to write to her, even call her when he was on a twenty-four-hour pass, but she'd already taken off for New York. With that son-of-a-gun Spice Keating.

And he'd called Spice his friend.

So Jimmy drank too much, gambled too much. Risked too much. He was lucky he didn't wind up in the brig. Lucky he didn't get shipped home in a body bag.

"She's young, got her head full of ideas. But she'll come around."

Jimmy made a face. "Did you not hear me? Three-plus years, Pop. Peg's right, she's not coming back." How did Dad, of all people, not get it? "Besides, she's on that soap opera." What a load of malarkey. A drama about small-town American life starring an English girl.

"Yeah, I watched it last winter when I took a few days off."

Jimmy crinkled his gaze at his dad. What? He never took a day off. "Were you sick?"

"No, I just realized in thirty years of working, I never took a vacation to just sit. So I thought, 'Why not?' Ended up watching a couple of episodes of *Always Tomorrow*."

"I don't want to hear about it."

"She was good. Looks pretty on the TV."

"Dad, please." Jimmy reached for the can, the loose cap rattling. "Better step back because I'm dousing this place."

"You got water in case the fire gets out of hand?"

"I filled a few buckets. And I got all the dirt I need right outside the door."

"So you've been thinking of this for a long while."

No, not really. "I have to do it, that's all."

"You fought a war, Jim."

"And?" The gas can banged against his leg.

"I'd think you'd have gained some courage."

"Don't talk to me about courage."

"Then don't be a coward." Dad leaned into him, his jaw tense, his eyes like steel. "Finish what you started."

"For what reason?"

"You remember when you first tried out for football? And you fumbled on your first carry? Did you quit? No, you got back in the game."

"This isn't football, Pop. This is my life. This is about Colette making me promises and then running off the moment I left for boot camp." She played him for a fool. Oh, boy howdy, how she played him.

"You finish what you started, Jim, or you'll quit everything."

"No, I won't. How can you say such things?"

"Because I've lived it. You said it yourself. I never got over your mother. Mark my words, by the time you realize you're a quitter, it will be too late. You think fighting a war tested your mettle? Well, this right here, in matters of the heart, is where real men are born. Finish the wedding chapel. See what kind of man you are then. And when you can look yourself in the mirror with a steady, clear eye, you'll know real courage. Then, if you want to get rid of this place, do so. But finish what you started."

Jimmy gazed up at the open ceiling, at the canopy of descending twilight. "I went to New York." The confession felt good. "On my way home. She wouldn't see me."

He'd waited outside her studio in the cold until his legs were numb. A hundred people must have exited that door, but never Colette.

Finally, an older gentleman came out.

"Go on home, son. She's not going to see you."

"Did she say why?"

He shook his head. "Just go on home."

Dad clapped his hand on Jimmy's shoulder. "Then you have your answer. Marry a Heart's Bend girl. Make a life for yourself. This chapel ain't your problem. Your heart is your problem. Your expectations." Dad tapped his finger against Jimmy's chest.

"A broken heart is a force to be reckoned with, Dad."

"Then reckon with it." He gently released the gas can from Jimmy's hand. "But not with this. Not with burning this place down. Reckon with it by finishing."

Jimmy didn't bother to hide the swell of tears. "I got a long way to go to finish."

"You in a hurry? Got somewhere else to be?"

He shook his head as his tears tracked down his cheeks. But Dad didn't seem to mind at all.

"I'll help you."

"You think I'll meet someone else like her? Really?" He didn't bother to spell out Peg's offer. Even if she wasn't tied to Drummond, Jimmy could never take her. He'd see Colette every time he peered into her eyes.

"I do. Let me predict you'll marry the love of your life right here in this chapel." Dad pointed to the floor, then walked the gas can out through one of the unframed windows. "Now, if you don't mind, I'm a bit low in my tank."

Marry another woman here? Jimmy surveyed the unfinished walls and floor.

His last night with Colette had been spent here. And in truth, he'd given the chapel to her.

"I built it for you, Lettie. It's your wedding chapel."

"How about dinner at that new diner? Ella's?" Dad poked his head through the window. "My treat."

He wasn't hungry but he hated to let Dad down. "Yeah, sure." Heart still heavy, if not slightly relieved, Jimmy gathered his tools and headed for his truck.

Dad was right. He had to finish what he started. Colette might have run out on him, but he would never run out on her.

Because keeping no record of her wrong was in fact the definition of love.

CHAPTER NINETEEN

COLETTE

She needed an excuse to go to Tennessee. To see *that* chapel. Jack's news that Jimmy was selling it jarred her. In a way that both surprised and angered her.

Jimmy could not sell the chapel. It wasn't his. He had no right.

When Colette reached for the phone, her eye glanced over the business cards Jack left on the table. One of them had a familiar skyline faded into the background behind the embossed word FRESH.

Nashville. Of course! FRESH was in Nashville. If she ever doubted God cared about the little things in one's life, her faith rose a bit today. Or perhaps fate merely showed its hand.

Either way, she was Nashville bound.

Colette dialed Ford.

"My favorite client, what can I do for you?"

"I've just agreed to be the spokeswoman for FRESH Water."

"You what?" Slow, hesitating. "Don't you think you should talk to me first?"

"What do you think I'm doing now?" In truth, Colette

never made a move without Ford. But when that handsome Jack, married to her beautiful Taylor, sat before her today, well, she just couldn't refuse. "But I've already agreed. You need to phone Jack Forester over at 105." Colette rattled off his phone number. "When you work out the details, tell him I *must* visit the FRESH offices."

"Because? Colette, what are you up to?" Ford lowered his voice, digging for the truth.

"Nothing. I just want to see their offices." Colette flicked the FRESH card against her leg, her heart racing a bit at the idea of traveling to Nashville. To Heart's Bend.

"Hmm, I know that tone. You're up to something." Now he sounded amused. And patronizing.

"Just do as I ask, Ford. Please." Mercy, she felt a headache coming on.

"Does this have anything to do with your sister dying?"

Colette sat forward. What a perfect alibi. *Ford, you lovable coot. You're not as clever as you think.* "Yes." She cleared her voice. "Yes, it does."

"I told you—"

—to go to her funeral. "And I didn't listen. You said I'd regret not saying good-bye, and you're right. I want to visit her grave, see her family."

"Does this have anything to do with your great-niece, the photographer?"

"No, no, not at all."

"Or talking with Justine?"

"Ford, why the third degree? You wanted me to go home and now I want to go."

"Fine, but you don't need an excuse, or to be a bottled water spokeswoman, to visit your sister's grave."

"But I do, Ford." There was more truth in those four simple words than any conversation she'd ever had with him. "I do."

She'd been running for so long. Running from her troubles since she and Peg were girls in London. Running from war. Running from danger. Running from death. Running from fear. From shame. From Jimmy. From love.

From the devil's deal she made with Peg.

"Fine, you win."

"Of course I do." Colette exhaled with relief.

"I'll never understand how your mind works. But I'll request an on-site visit."

"Soon." She squeezed her hand into a fist. She sounded too eager, but she was determined not to shrink back this time. She was not a girl of twenty any longer.

"How soon?"

"This week."

"This week?" Ford's voice rose at the end when he was excited. Or stressed. "Why this week? Let's take our time, hammer out the details."

"I don't care about the details."

"Don't care? Do you remember the dishwashing product that had you so tied up you practically had to get permission to go to the loo?"

"Well, I did go to the loo, and frankly, at eighty-two, I don't rightly care how much they tie me up."

"Well, I do. Colette, you have a book coming out next year and the publisher is expecting you to promote it on the talk shows. I can't have FRESH throwing a flag on us, calling breach of contract."

"Then get busy. Call Jack. Work it out to your liking. But, Ford, I want to visit FRESH this week." Before Jimmy sold her chapel, her last fond memory of love. "It's a deal breaker if they can't see me this week."

"Deal breaker? Colette, what are you not telling me?"

She sighed. "That you're fired?"

Ford's laugh burst the tension. "Fine, this week. Any contingency if for *some* reason they *can't* see you?"

"I don't care if I meet with the janitor. I want to be at FRESH this week." The urgency in her bones fortified her with each passing moment.

"How's the book coming?"

"We're keeping on schedule, if that's what you mean."

"It's not, but that's good to know. Do you like Justine?"

"I didn't think I would, but I do."

"Are we going to have a bestseller at the end of it all?"

"Now, that I cannot tell you." Colette changed the conversation and asked about Kate, Ford's wife, and about their darling new granddaughter, then rang off, sinking into the sofa, zapped of all energy.

Jimmy was selling *her* wedding chapel. But when she paused to really consider it, his selling the chapel didn't surprise her.

It was the fact he'd actually *kept* it for all these years.

She reached for the tissue box. After all these years, tears surfaced for him.

What was it Jack said? The chapel never saw a wedding. Last she'd heard Jimmy wasn't married, but that was eons ago. Over forty years. Surely he'd married along the way.

But she didn't marry, did she? Though she'd dined with her fair share of suitors. Besides Luciano Diamatia, Spice Keating, and Bart Maverick, Colette had rejected a marriage proposal from a Wall Street broker. She must remember to tell Justine about him. Years later she declined a quick proposal from a younger actor she met ten years into the show. He didn't love her. He loved what he could obtain with her, from her.

But she could see the past so clearly now. It had been Jimmy. Always Jimmy. A nervous jitter brought her to her feet. She had to see him. More than the need to breathe. She had to see him.

When she agreed to the autobiography, she felt sure that all of her sins and secrets, her truest feelings, were tucked away.

But the journey with the book, along with seeing Taylor and hearing the news of the chapel, excavated her true past.

Thick tears salted her tired eyes. Then one sob followed another, pressing Colette forward until her forehead rested on her knees.

Her body tensed with the exorcism of remorse, of pent-up pain.

For Mamá, for Papá, for Peg, for Jimmy. For herself. For every heartbreaking decision.

She gave way to the sorrow, sinking from the sofa to the floor, sobbing until she was exhausted.

"Ms. Greer?" Zoë. Of course she must have heard her. "Are you all right?"

"I'm fine." Colette pushed herself up, collapsing on the sofa.

"A-are you sure?" Zoe's tentative voice came from the doorway.

Yes, she was quite sure. "I'll have some tea. Ring Justine and ask her to put off for an hour."

"I-I'm here . . . if you need me."

"I know, love. Thank you."

With Zoë off to make tea, Colette made her way to the window where the sun sat high and glorious over the city. The row of red-tipped trees in Central Park put her in mind of Heart's Bend, and being with Jimmy, her hand clasped with his.

She decided. She would tell Justine the whole lot. Because somewhere in the mess among the buried things, among the twists and turns, Colette Greer had become the woman she was meant to be. And she wasn't done with living yet.

. . .

FEBRUARY 1949

WINTER FORMAL

Colette hurried alongside Jimmy through the cold for the gymnasium door, her hand warm and secure in his. Her high heels caught on the parking lot pebbles, and she laughed, steadying herself with a good grab of his arm.

"Aunt Jean insisted I buy these shoes. I feel like I'm walking on stilts."

She'd taken the sisters shopping, declaring that at last she had *her girls* and was treating them as their own mamá would have.

Peg also wore a new dress and new shoes. Spurning Spice's advances, Peg attended the dance on the arm of a Vanderbilt college graduate and a Rock Mill High alumnus, Drummond Branson.

Colette had no idea how they met, or why in the world a chap of twenty-three had agreed to attend a high school formal, but that was the power of Peg. Aunt Jean teased her, saying Peg could talk the devil into attending a revival meeting.

Nevertheless, Peg's dashing bloke provided a good distraction. She'd not be bothering Colette and Jimmy.

"Come on, get in here." Clem popped round the gymnasium doors, waving for them to hurry. "They're playing the boogie woogie, Lettie, and my date can't dance to it, so—"

"I'm not dancing my first dance with you, Clem. Boogie woogie or not. Oh, gee whiz, these shoes—" Colette stumbled to the door leaning on Jimmy's arm.

"Hold the door, Clem!" In stride, Jimmy scooped Colette into his arms, cradling her against his chest, and carried her across the gymnasium threshold into a rainbow of light reflecting from a twirling mirror ball.

The winter wonderland–themed gymnasium swarmed with bejeweled young women who oohed at Colette's grand entrance. The chaps in suits hooted and cheered.

"That's the way to handle your girl, Jims."

Colette squirmed, embarrassed. "Put me down,

Jimmy." But when she looked at him, Jimmy's expression captured her and she knew then she never wanted to touch the ground again.

"How'd I get so lucky to be with you?"

"Jimmy—"

She was about to let him kiss her when Clem stuck his face in between them and ruined everything, tugging Colette out of Jimmy's arms, dragging her onto the dance floor.

"You can swoon later. The song's nearly half over." Clem spun her out of her coat, tossing it to the floor.

With a backward glance at Jimmy, who gave her a thumbs-up as he stooped to pick up her coat, Colette called, "I shall return."

He was simply the best. And she the lucky one.

But for now it was time to boogie woogie. The hours she spent dancing with Clem in the basement made this dance all the more fun. Together Clem and Colette cleared the floor, their classmates standing back, astonished.

"Go, cats, go!"

For Colette, the music was a release. A way to *speak* the unspoken—the words Peg refused to hear, the feelings she refused to express. Colette's moves practically shouted all of her sorrows and no one was the wiser.

So she kicked off her shoes and danced, the folds and flounce of her full, cream-colored skirt twisting one way while her legs went another, creating a taffeta and tulle wave.

Clem brought her around and back, under his arm

and out again. Colette's gaze met Jimmy's. He grinned and winked, and Colette soared.

She'd finally found her place. Her home.

When the song ended, she collapsed in her cousin's arms. The kids swarmed them, applauding, cheering.

"You're the best, Lettie," Clem said, breathless, returning her to Jimmy, swiping his loose bangs into place. "You cleared the deck."

"No, *we* cleared the deck."

"You dazzled them, Colette." Jimmy drew her in, kissing her cheek.

"It was Clem. He's the showman."

"But you're the star."

Colette regarded Jimmy, catching her breath. "If I'm a star, then you're my sun."

"I'll take it."

From the bandstand, the bandleader crooned into the mic. "All you lovers, on the dance floor. This is your song." He began to intone the sound of Perry Como's "Because."

Jimmy held up Colette's shoes, then bent to one knee, cupped her ankle, and slipped them on. Standing, he gathered her close. "They're saying this is our song."

"So I heard. Oh, Jimmy, are you real? You're so wonderful."

"I'm real. And only for you." He kissed her and began a slow, purposeful dance. Colette cradled her head against his shoulder, hearing his sweet tenor vibrate through his chest as he sang to her.

"Because you speak to me in accent sweet."

"I love your accent sweet, Colette," he whispered.

"And I love yours."

Laughing low, he tightened his arms around her waist. "I guess I would have an accent to your ears. But you have the corner on smelling sweet."

"You smell like clean soap."

"Is that good?"

"It's very good."

As the song played on, there was no need to speak, just sway and move and understand what it felt like when heaven came to earth. She never wanted to leave this moment. Or Jimmy's arms. Even as the bandleader's song faded away, Colette remained molded against him.

With a trumpet blast and drums pounding, the romance ended and the gym hopped with a lively jive.

Colette shouted over the music, "I liked the last song better."

"Me too." Jimmy cupped his hands around his mouth. "Bandleader, play 'Because' again."

"Why can't we dance the way we want?" Colette said, snuggling against him.

"Fine idea, Miss Greer."

With the rest of the kids bopping around them, Colette and Jimmy danced to the song in their hearts.

Then Peg appeared, dragging Spice Keating by the hand. Oh, bother. "Y'all, the music's changed. Come on, dance." She pressed her hands to their shoulders, prying them apart.

"Where's Drummond?" Colette asked. What was her sister doing?

"Out back getting a smoke." Peg slipped her arm through Jimmy's. "Let's dance."

Before he could protest, Spice stepped up, took Colette's hand, and led her onto the floor.

"Come on, trip the lights with me. You're the heppest gal here." He twirled her away and started the jive. "Come on, doll, relax."

She tried to dance, trembling, missing Jimmy, missing his warmth, his heart.

"Come on, get with it." He spun her about so fast she had to start dancing or fall off her heels and break an ankle.

But all she could do was go through the motions. Because somewhere among the kids, Jimmy danced with conniving Peg.

At the song's end, Spice trapped her, wrapping his arm around her and walking her toward the punch bowl. "Ever think of dancing onstage or TV?"

"Not really." She scanned the room for Jimmy.

"I'm getting out of here as soon as we graduate. I have big plans for my life."

"G-good for you." Where did Peg get off to with her date?

The microphone squealed across the gymnasium. "All right, everyone. It's time for the dance-off. On the floor with your partner. If you get tapped on the shoulder, you're out. Move off to the side."

Colette excused herself. "I'd better find Jimmy." There were only a couple hundred juniors and seniors, but in the small gymnasium, it seemed like thousands.

"No time, doll." Spice held on to her hand. "The dance

has started." He nabbed her at the waist and started swinging and singing, twisting and twirling, pressing the tip of his tongue beyond his lips.

Really, Spice was as comical as he was handsome. So Colette gave it a halfhearted go, glancing round when she caught the scent of soap. But it wasn't Jimmy.

"Hey, what's that cool move?" Spice mimicked her head jerk, grinning, looking so ridiculous she had to laugh. "I like it, doll. Here's a new move." He snapped his head around, then his body, his feet tapping the entire time. "They can't tap *us* off the floor now."

"You're crazy, you know that?" Hesitating, Colette figured the move in her head and mimed Spice just as the judges came around. They nodded their approval and moved on.

"What'd I tell you? I got a nose for what's good."

Colette continued to jerk and jive, scanning the dancers for Jimmy. She finally spotted him dancing with Peg. He waved, giving her a thumbs-up.

"Want to win this, Spice?" She would win for Jimmy, and to spite Peg.

"You know I do, doll face."

"Then shall we?" Colette kicked her shoes to the side and took his hand, adding flair to their new signature move.

One by one, the chaperones tapped couples off the floor. But Spice and Colette remained, creating new moves out of the boogie woogie, the Charleston, the jive, and the jitterbug, with a little bit of the catwalk thrown in.

When they were the last ones on the floor, the

bandleader rang a bell. "Ladies and gentlemen, we have our Winter Formal Dance-off winners." He read from a card. "Come on up here . . . Colette and Spice. Let's give them a round of applause."

Spice led her to the bandstand, hand on her waist. After hoisting her up onto the stage, he joined her, both of them breathless.

"That's *my* girl. The winner of the dance-off!" Jimmy's voice powered across the gymnasium as he stood on top of the bleachers.

The bandleader awarded them pint-sized trophies, inviting the kids to applaud one more time. Then just like that it was off to the next song. "Here's a song made popular by the great Doris Day."

Spice tried to help Colette off the stage, but she brushed past him and ran up the bleachers into Jimmy's waiting arms. "You showed 'em, Lettie."

"I did it for you."

"Good, 'cause you know I couldn't help you win the dance-off." He led her back onto the dance floor, spinning her around under a shower of sparkling stardust.

"Would you be mad if I said I think I love you?"

Colette peered at him through the lights, through her own vision of love. "It's not just the night? The music, the mirror ball?"

"No, it's not. It's you." He brushed his finger along the curve of her jaw. "I have a confession. Before you moved here, Clem showed me a picture of you and Peg."

"What picture?"

"You were with a bride by a stone chapel."

"Ah, the wedding of our friend in the village. It was such a happy time in the middle of war."

"You looked so happy and, well, I think I fell in love with you that day."

"Jimmy, you can't really mean it." But when he stepped toward her, she knew his intention. "No one falls in love with a girl in a photo."

"I knew you'd be swell, Colette. And I was right. I love you."

"Well . . . I mean . . ." His confession burned away her fears, her walls. "Y-you're only seventeen. We're kids."

"I don't care." He lowered his face to hers. "When I'm eighty-three, I'll love you. What I need to know is if you think you could love me someday. D-do you think you could? Someday?"

So vulnerable. So sweet. "Yes." She smoothed her hands over his stiff blue suit jacket. "Perhaps someday. Perhaps today."

He touched her chin, lifting her face to his, looking at her in a way that inspired all sorts of delicious, romantic feelings. Then lowered his lips to hers, kissing her so sweetly that it sealed everything that was right and lovely about this night in her heart.

CHAPTER TWENTY

TAYLOR

Seriously, Taylor, what are you going to do with this place?" Emma came into the bum room carrying a box and dropped it to the dull, thirsty hardwood.

"You keep asking and I keep saying 'I don't know.'" Taylor turned from the record shelf, a stack of vinyl LPs in her arms. "Do you want to buy it?"

"No, I like my house. It's new, modern . . ."

Emma took off work Wednesday to spend time with Taylor going through the bum room. The one room she'd not really cleared out. And the attic.

I wanted to wait for you.

Otherwise, Emma had taken care of her duty, ridding the house of furniture and clothes, cleaning out the cupboards, stacking the remaining dishes in the dining room, contacting estate sale agents.

"Why don't you and Jack keep it?"

"He says he never wants to live here. Doesn't want to see his father. So, what about the attic?" Taylor flipped through the albums. Jack might like some of these. He bought a turntable on a whim a few months ago but had nothing to *turn* on it.

"I went up there, but it's hot and dusty so I've been putting it off."

"Yeah, well, if I sell, you know the attic goes with it." Taylor didn't like the attic either. Emma turned it into a haunted house one Halloween when they were kids and Taylor hadn't been up there since. "And by the way, you need to clean out Granny's kitchen drawer by the fridge." Taylor opened it last night to find it full of nothing but sauce packets from every restaurant in town. There had to be a thousand of them.

"I know, I saw it." Emma brushed dust from the book in her hand. "I sort of hate to throw them away. They remind me of Granny more than just about anything."

Taylor laughed. "She was a hoarder."

"Either that or forgetful."

Taylor set the albums in the box, then faced Emma. "I'm hungry. I'm going to get last night's leftover sub."

"Hungry?" Emma made a face. "We just ate lunch two hours ago."

"I know, but we've been working like dogs. You're not hungry?" Taylor jogged downstairs and retrieved last night's leftovers from the fridge, then grabbed the bag of chips Emma brought over this morning.

Sitting at the kitchen table, she glanced up at her sister, sinking her teeth into the delicious London broil on wheat. "You should keep this table." She knocked on the Formica table trimmed in fifties chrome. "It's vintage."

"I might. Mama had her eye on it last time she came by." Emma sat in the chair opposite Taylor. "So, you're feeling better, I take it."

"Much." Taylor shoved the sandwich at her sister. "Want a bite?"

"No thanks." She got up for a bottle of water. "I'm single again. Have to watch my figure."

Taylor motioned for Em to grab her a water too. "Hey, one of the benefits of being married. I can eat whatever I want."

"Ha! That's what I said when I was pregnant," Emma said, passing Taylor a water. "Then I had a heck of a time dropping sixty extra pounds."

"I'm not gaining sixty pounds. Besides, I didn't have breakfast so two lunches is allowed." Taylor twisted the cap from her water and took a long swig. "Hey, do you want to go to Taco-Taco tonight? Bring it back here and watch *Frozen* with the girls in the bum room?" She'd been craving tacos, like, all day.

"How are you thinking of tacos with half a sub stuck in your mouth?"

"You know me, I plan ahead."

"Said the girl who eloped." Emma weakened and snuck a handful of chips. "So, did you find the box belonging to the key? I wonder why Granny didn't write me a letter."

Taylor shrugged. She'd keep Granny's "idiot" remark to herself. "Not yet. I haven't looked that hard. If it's in the attic then I'll never find it."

Emma sighed. "Okay, fine, I'll look when I go up there next."

So far this week Taylor had learned *AQ* loved her shots of the chapel. Addison had deposited checks from the weddings she'd shot and from Melinda House. She'd also texted with Jack, who said Colette had agreed to do the FRESH job.

Woo hoo.

Woo hoo? Taylor smiled. Jack never said woo hoo. He must be excited.

"Seriously, Taylor, what are you and Jack going to do with this place?"

Taylor swallowed her bite, reaching for her water. "It's not his decision."

"In part it is. You're married now, Tay. Not a lone sailor at sea."

She frowned. "Sailor? Sea?"

"You need to start thinking like a married woman. You still have a single gal's mind-set. I may be divorced, but I know what it takes to be married."

"He still thinks like a single man, so consider my side of things self-preservation." Taylor took a final bite of her sandwich. After this, she definitely wanted something sweet. "Hey, you want to go get ice cream?"

"Are you serious?"

"Is Del's still open? I'd love one of their blizzard things."

Emma patted the tabletop. "Yeah, let's go get ice cream. I'll drive." She snatched the Lincoln car keys from the hook before Taylor could get up.

"Hey, that's my car." Taylor wiped the mayo from her lips, running after her sister, shutting the back door behind her.

"Granny left it to both of us." Emma slipped behind the wheel, firing up the old classic before Taylor could protest further. She jumped in the passenger seat and shot her hands over her head.

"Let's go."

It was a textbook fall afternoon, the sun brilliant in a blue sky. The breeze was gentle and thin, with an edge of cool between sun-warmed layers.

Switching on the radio, Taylor tuned to 101.7 for some oldies.

"Wonder what's in here." She popped open the glove box.

"Probably more sauce packets," Emma said, laughing, the wind whipping her short auburn hair back from her face.

"Yep, you're right." Taylor held up several packets of ketchup. "Granny, what love affair did you have with ketchup and soy sauce?"

But underneath the fast-food packets and stacks of napkins she found a buttery-soft pair of Aigner leather gloves. "These are *nice*." She slipped them on, peeking at Emma. "They fit. Are we going to fight over them?"

"Nope. Take them. Wear them in good health."

Taylor made a face. "Why? What did you find? Something better?"

Emma winced. "Gucci gloves. In her room."

Taylor gasped. "Cheater . . ."

"Hey, she left the contents to me." Emma barreled toward the light, braking hard when it clicked red.

But the *real* treasure came last, when Taylor burrowed to the bottom of the compartment and removed an old black-and-white three-by-five photograph.

"What is it?" Emma said, leaning to see, pushing Taylor's arm down for a better look.

"Looks like Granny when she was a teenager." Taylor flipped it over.

April 1950. Me, Spice, Jimmy, Colette.

"She was what? Nineteen." The light flashed green and Emma hit the gas, surging the big Lincoln forward, slowly picking up speed. "Looks like they're sitting down in the dip below the grassy knoll. River Road Park. We had our senior pictures taken there."

"Yeah, I remember. It rained my year. My hair was like . . . frizz city." But Taylor's attention was captured by the image of the four sitting in the basket of the knoll. "When'd she marry Granddad? Nineteen fifty-one?"

"Yeah, in the spring. They eloped."

"And you wonder where I got the idea."

"Sure, and look how they turned out."

"Divorce runs in our family. Should I just cut to the chase?"

"No, good grief, Taylor. Have some faith. I hate being divorced."

Taylor grimaced. "Sorry," she muttered, staring at the image, sinking into the scene, mystically searching for the third dimension below the flat, two-dimension image. Granny and Colette together? A sight she'd never seen in her twenty-nine years.

In this scene the sisters, with their beautiful forties hairstyles, neat, crisp dresses, and saddle oxfords, appeared to be friends.

Spice and Coach were young, good looking, kind

of brawny and masculine. "What do you suppose they were doing? Saying?"

Peg, Spice, Colette, and Jimmy.

"Picnic. Hanging out. Saying and doing what young adults do." Emma slowed, turning the car.

Taylor glanced up to see Walgreens instead of Del's Ice Cream. "What are we doing here?"

"I need a favor."

"What kind of favor?"

Emma slipped the picture from Taylor's hand. "Bring me a Diet Coke. A cold one. Get one from the back of the cooler and—"

"Excuse me? Why am I running your errand?"

"—a pregnancy test."

"What?" Taylor regarded Emma for a long moment. "Please don't tell me you're sleeping with your ex-husband. That's *reaallly* bad for the divorce."

"I am not. And the test is not for me."

Taylor made a face. "Then for who?"

"You."

Taylor laughed, slapping her hand over her heart, shaking her head. "It's happened. You've lost your mind."

"Yeah, well, you're in denial."

"How can I be in denial over something that isn't true? I'm not pregnant."

"Then get the test. Prove me wrong."

"I'm not falling for that trick," Taylor scoffed. But the conversation bugged her. Was she? Pregnant? "We've only been married six months."

"Oh, right—" *Snap-snap.* "The six-months rule," Emma said. "What is that, exactly?"

"It's too soon to be pregnant."

"Maybe? But have you two been, you know, *dancing*?" Emma raised her voice and wiggled her eyebrows.

Taylor snatched the photograph from her. "Yes, we've been dancing. That's one of the best parts about being married."

"And you've been using birth control?"

"Y-yes . . ." Taylor squirmed. Most of the time, but not always.

"Well, nothing is a guarantee. Seems the piper has come for his pay."

"Well, he's getting *nothing* from me." Taylor squeezed her hands together. "This can't be . . ."

"You've been queasy all weekend." Emma held up one finger.

"So was Alena. Did you buy her a pregnancy test?"

"She's four. Don't be daft." She popped up a second finger. "You've been skipping breakfast every day but eating like a horse at night. How many helpings of spaghetti did you have at Mama's?"

"One . . . two."

"Three. I counted." Emma held up a third finger. "Taylor, that's exactly how I was with both girls."

"Emma, this is typical when I'm on a deadline."

"Your deadline was finished this weekend."

"Or stressed."

"What stress? You're on vacation. When was your last period?"

"Emma, good grief—"

"Tell me. When?"

"I don't owe you an answer. Man, you're the bossiest sister ever."

But when was her last? Taylor couldn't remember. She and Jack were pretty careful. They'd married so quickly, they didn't have time for ironclad preventions, but they found a method that worked for them.

"When, Taylor?"

"I don't know, I'm not a freak list-maker like you. I don't keep a chart."

"Six, seven weeks ago?"

Taylor shoved open the door and stepped out. "If we're not getting ice cream, I'm going in for Milk Duds." Stress made her crave chocolate. And Emma was definitely stressing her out.

"Don't forget my Diet Coke and *your* pregnancy test!" Bigmouthed Emma.

"Shout it to the parking lot, will you?" Taylor moved through the automatic doors.

What did Emma know? Pregnancy? Impossible. Babies weren't even a germ of a dream. She and Jack were still figuring out marriage. Jack's obsession over Doug Voss created an awkward wedge between them.

Their communication skills earned an F minus.

At the candy aisle, Taylor stared at the rack of Milk Duds and slowly pressed her hand over her abdomen.

They'd talked about kids. Once. When they sat next to a noisy family at dinner one night.

Pretty noisy, huh?" Taylor said, smiling at the baby. He was a cutie with his round face and

dimpled cheeks. His mother called him Levi.
"What do you think about the name Levi?"
Taylor liked it.

"Fine." Jack was fixed on his phone. "For
another man's kid."

Taylor lowered her head to see his face. "No
kids?"

He peeked up at her. "No kids."

"Ever?"

"You know how I was raised, Taylor. Besides,
you said yourself this world is no place to bring
up a kid."

Yeah, she had said that once. But she didn't
mean it.

Taylor snatched up a box of Milk Duds. Then
another and another until her arms were laden. She
headed to the checkout with no intention of swinging
by the pregnancy tests. She had no room to carry one.

Jack's wedding day confession boomeranged
through her. *"If it doesn't work out we can walk away."*

Then what in the world were they doing?

Taylor passed the soda cooler. She arched her back,
balancing her Milk Duds, opening the cooler with
her fingertips. Grabbing a Diet Coke—first one in
the row—she got in line and scanned the magazine
headlines. Doug's *Gossip* was front and center with a
cover showing a baby-toting celebrity. Taylor glanced
away.

But all the magazines featured stars with their babies,

and the cast of a new sitcom, *Love 'Em or Leave 'Em,* in which the real-life actors were spitting out babies like springtime bunnies.

Love 'em or leave 'em. That was what it boiled down to, wasn't it? Love or leave. But what if she loved and he wanted to leave? He never said he wanted to go, but it was something Taylor felt in her gut. All the time. The time for guessing was coming to an end. She needed to talk to her husband.

Turning away from the headlines, Taylor came face-to-face with a display of pregnancy tests. On sale!

You've got to be kidding me.

"Next!"

Taylor stepped forward. Only one customer was in front of her. Her heart raced. Did she really need to buy a pregnancy test? She couldn't be pregnant. She *refused* to be pregnant.

From her shorts pocket, her phone rang. Probably Emma telling her to hurry up. But it was a New York number. One she didn't recognize.

Jack? Was he okay? "Hello?"

"Taylor, this is Justine Longoria, Colette Greer's cowriter for her autobiography."

She exhaled. "Hey, um, how can I help you?"

"I hope you don't mind, but she gave me your number. Said you were at her late sister's home and I thought, 'Perfect!' The publisher would love to have photos of Colette from when she was young. Any family pictures? Perhaps taken in England? It's weird, but Colette doesn't have any of her own."

"Wow, good question. I don't know. But I'll look around." Well, she did know of one. In the car.

"That would be fantastic. You have my number now so you can text me if you find any." Justine repeated her name and hung up.

Taylor hung up, tucking her phone in her pocket. She or Emma was going to have to go to the attic now. Granny's photo albums were up there. She knew only because Granny told her once.

Moving forward to check out, Taylor spied the bank of pregnancy tests again. There had to be fifty of them. Were they expecting a pregnancy epidemic in this town?

She couldn't remember her last cycle. Or when she had started waking up slow and tired, the fragrance of Jack's morning coffee making her nauseous.

Still, they were careful . . .

Until that dinner . . . two months ago . . .

Taylor moaned and stepped out of line. "Go ahead," she said to the woman behind her.

The evening in July was one for the memory bank. Jack had called around six. His client had been delayed and wouldn't make a scheduled dinner meeting at an upscale Manhattan restaurant. So, he said, did she want to join him? If so, he'd send the car for her.

She didn't hesitate. Absolutely. She slipped into a slinky black dress that accented a few features Jack liked best. She had her neighbor, a beauty school student, fix her hair in an updo. Jack's expression when she stepped out of the car filled her with flutters.

He, in turn, looked incredible, wearing his best blue

shirt, the top button open and his sleeves rolled up, his blue eyes snapping beneath a wave of his dark hair.

You look amazing, babe." He never called her anything but Taylor. Until that night.

"Back at you, babe."

He offered his arm, kissing her as they walked into the restaurant. But it was noisy, packed, exuding a different vibe than what moved between them. So Jack grabbed her hand and led her out to the street, hailing a cab.

They ate in the Village, at a small, homey restaurant he'd been dying to try. The food was amazing, the atmosphere romantic and intimate. When Michael Bublé's soothing voice came over the speakers and melted the atmosphere, Jack offered Taylor his hand.

"Dance with me." He led her to the garden, into the light of the moon, his arms, his heart.

Even more than their honeymoon night, she felt his love for her. A rare experience.

Between the melody and the movement, their walls came down. She became vulnerable, willing to let Jack see all of her. And in a husky, sweet, raw voice, Jack apologized for working too much, forgetting he had a wife at home.

"I want to be a good husband. I don't know how, but I want to try." He cradled her, touched her, overwhelmed her.

"I'm trying too."

"Let's go home." Jack hailed a cab and they

cuddled in the backseat, barely making it home before the fireworks began.

Later, she luxuriated in his arms, smoothing her hand over his chest. "Isn't the moon beautiful? I think it's shining just for us."

Jack raised his hand to its light. "The moon doesn't shine, babe. It just reflects the sun's light."

"Ha, you know what I mean."

He laughed and kissed her, settling between the sheets, his breathing even and content.

So this was love . . .

"Next!"

Taylor snatched up the pregnancy test and dropped it on the counter.

The night did not end as romantically as it began. Jack popped out of bed, panicked that their impromptu lovemaking would result in a baby.

Taylor, we didn't . . . I mean . . . I don't want kids, Taylor." He cut his hands through the air, pacing, raising his voice. "I do not want kids."

As the cashier rang up Taylor's order, she hoped, prayed, that as she was feeling particularly negative at the moment, the pregnancy test would be good enough to reflect the same.

CHAPTER TWENTY-ONE

COLETTE

Thursday morning Colette strode into the FRESH conference room flanked by Ford and Jack Forester feeling anxious yet determined, her spirit bolstered with the kind of strength that comes when one finally faces her fears.

While she appeared to be following Jack's plan for the visit, she had one of her own.

Jack leaned to say something to her, but for the life of her she could not focus on anything about this trip to FRESH. Only the matter beating in her own heart.

She thought it would be simple to sit through the FRESH presentation, then escape to her plan, but the enormity of what she was about to do settled on her aged shoulders heavier than expected.

But she'd set everything in motion before leaving New York and she refused to back out on it now.

Because if she did, she'd never find the courage again.

"Good morning, everyone." Evoking the bold and

self-focused Vivica Spenser, Colette walked into the boardroom, straight to the head of the table, like she'd done a million times on *Always Tomorrow*.

The team rose to their feet and chorused, "Good morning." A dozen well-dressed men and women lined the elongated glossy conference table and the perimeter of the room. A handsome gentleman approached, offering his hand.

"Lennon MacArthur. Welcome to our humble company. We are *thrilled* you've agreed to be our spokeswoman."

"I'm a fan of your product." That was Colette speaking, not Vivica. But since both women had lived in her soul for ages, Colette could hardly make the distinction. She scanned the room, taking in each face, making a mental note that they appeared to be honest, *fresh* folks.

She teetered on her plan. Could she really do it? Leave this safe place for one unknown?

"Please, Ms. Greer . . ." Lennon offered her a seat.

"Call me Colette, please."

"Colette, we have a lovely presentation for you."

But she remained standing. *Courage, Lettie.* If not today, never. "I appreciate that, Lennon, but I don't need a song and dance." She smiled for them all. "I've already heard the melody and I like it." She made a show of glancing around the room. "And I like you."

The room expanded with a collective exhale.

"Excellent. Then, what?" Lennon glanced at his team. "We can move on to the plant tour?" He motioned to the exit. "We do our own bottling right here, Ms. Greer, I mean, Colette."

"So I've heard. I read up on your practices. Very impressive." Colette noticed the large cake in the middle of the table. "I'll tell you what I'd like. A piece of that cake. It looks divine." She pressed her hand to her lean belly and angled toward one of the older women at the table. "One thing about getting older, you don't care about your figure quite as much."

The woman patted her own round middle. "Don't I know it."

Lennon barked that someone should cut Colette a piece of cake, which she accepted with gratitude. But really, she couldn't eat a thing. Her belly was full of anticipation, anxiety. Excitement.

She needed to get on with her plan, right or wrong. And she could feel her courage fading. Checking her watch, she realized the car she'd ordered would arrive any minute.

Yet she couldn't let *all* of FRESH's efforts go to waste.

So she forced down the cake and forced her attention on Lennon as he introduced staff members. Finally, when her cake was gone, she set her plate down and inquired about the ladies' room. "I'd like to freshen up."

"Of course, forgive us." He bustled about as if he expected neglecting to offer her a freshen-up minute might cost him. Fine, let him sweat a little. She'd need the credit in a few minutes. "Karli, can you show her to our executive lounge?"

"Please, Lennon, just point me in the right direction. A girl likes a bit of privacy in the loo." Colette lightly gripped his arm, offering the half wink she'd perfected that said, *"I like you."*

"Down the hall, on your right." He snapped his fingers and Karli passed over a key. "To the executive lounge. You'll find everything you need in there."

"Very nice." Colette clutched her wristlet by her side. Thank goodness she'd had the presence of mind to exchange her big handbag for a wristlet before she left her suite this morning. Lugging it just to the loo would've been ridiculous.

She almost made her exit alone, but Ford trailed out of the conference room behind her.

"What are you doing?"

"I'm going to the executive lounge." Colette dangled the key in front of him.

"We just got here. Why don't you sit and relax? Let them wine and dine you. Jack's put a lot on the line for this account." Ford's heavy stride thumped against the industrial carpet. "And we moved heaven and earth to get you here *this* week. This is not like you to be so disengaged."

"Ford, I'm grateful to Jack and FRESH. I'm sorry, I'm a bit distracted. But please assure everyone I will be their spokeswoman."

He made a face, then smiled. "Go freshen up. You can tell them when you return to the boardroom."

"Thank you. My eighty-two-year-old bladder is not what it used to be, and unless you want to call for 'cleanup on aisle four,' I'd better go."

Ford cleared his throat, stepping back. "See you in the room, then."

"Of course. Relax. Have another piece of cake." Colette pressed her back against the wall just inside the lounge door, breathing deep, feeling like a schoolgirl who had just escaped the headmaster. As she and Peg managed on one occasion or the other.

She waited another few seconds, then peeked out. But excitement took its toll on her heart, and she needed a moment to gather herself. She reclined in the nearest chair and breathed, not allowing herself to really ponder the next few minutes. Or the afternoon.

When she felt steady, she peeked out again. The hall was clear. Colette tossed the lounge key in the corner by the door and darted for the elevator.

The doors opened immediately and she stepped into the car, riding down to the main floor with her heart fluttering.

She'd not done anything so outlandish in years. And for a thrilling moment, it felt wonderful to *break* out. *Forgive me, Jack.*

On the main floor, Colette finally breathed. Tiptoeing past the receptionist, who was involved with something on her phone, Colette met her waiting car. A silver Mercedes parked by the door.

The things money could buy!

"Ms. Greer?" A man in a white shirt and dark slacks approached with the keys.

"That's me." She shoved past him and dropped in behind the wheel. She knew Ford. He'd be suspicious about now. "Show me how she works."

She'd owned a car back in the eighties but rarely drove it, so she'd sold it. Now her hands itched to grip the wheel and *drive*. Command her destiny.

"You hit this here." He touched a button by the

steering wheel and the car fired up. "And enter your destination into the GPS here."

"Push-button cars. What will they think of next?" She shooed the Hertz man aside and pulled out the map she'd carefully folded into her wristlet. "I don't need a GPS. I have a map. Just need to get out of Nashville."

Vivica Spenser, I learned so much from you.

"Where are you headed?"

"Heart's Bend."

"Turn right out of the parking lot." He pointed to the parking lot's edge. "Take a left and you'll see signs for I-40. Go west until you see route 70. Head—"

"North. Thank you. I can take it from there."

"You look familiar. Should I know you?"

Colette smiled. He couldn't be more than twenty-one, maybe twenty-two. "Did your granny or mamá watch soap operas?"

"My granny. Shoot, you couldn't move in her house when *Always Tomorrow* came on." He laughed, shaking his head. "See, it's ingrained in my psyche forever. Can't remember a chemistry formula for class, but I can remember a Vivica Spenser line, 'Never you mind, there's always tomorrow.' Then she'd toss water in someone's face and laugh."

Colette swallowed a moan. That line . . . one of the worst pieces of writing ever. The writers had come up with it early on, hoping to play off *Gone with the Wind* and get viewers quoting the show.

Sadly, it worked. The line was written into every script at least once. As much as Colette hated that line, it bought her parody commercials and funny sketches on late-night television, along with the water tossing. The line was the reason she even invented drink toss-ing. And why she was sitting here today.

"Well, I'm *that* woman. Vivica Spenser. And thank you so much for your help." Colette slammed the car door and shifted into gear while the Hertz man waved good-bye. She sped out of the parking lot, a death grip on the wheel.

It took her a few minutes to get the feel for this mod-ern motor, but once she hit I-40, she was feeling mighty proud of her driving prowess.

But that's when she realized her carefully executed plan had no second leg. She'd only planned to escape Nashville. What was she to do once she arrived in Heart's Bend?

· · ·

After the Winter Formal

February 1949

"What a sight you were tonight." Peg barged into the room the girls shared, her voice an icy wind. Her hair had slipped from its pins and curled against her flushed cheeks.

"Where have you been?" Colette, tucked down under her bedcovers, glanced at her sister through a short angle of light coming from the nightstand lamp. The round alarm clock tick-tocked 1:15 a.m. "I told Uncle Fred you were coming in straightaway."

"You made such a spectacle of yourself tonight." Peg teetered from side to side as she kicked off her heels and peeled away her gloves. "Showing off on the dance floor. The girls' restroom was all atwitter about you kissing Jimmy in the shadows."

"All atwitter? I never heard a single word." Colette reached for her minuscule dance-off trophy. She'd never won anything before, and this little trophy was her sign of good things to come.

"Everyone was talking . . ."

Everyone?

"That's not true. Peg, are you drunk?"

"No." Peg anchored her foot on the side of her bed and hitched up her skirt to roll down her stockings. "Well, are you *steady* with him now?"

"I smell beer on you." Old man Morley drank it often enough when they lived on the farm.

"Maybe."

"Peg!" Aunt Jean never should have let Peg go to the dance with a college chap.

"Don't lecture me, Miss Goodie-Goodie. Some-times—" Peg waved her stockings like nylon flags at Colette. "I really hate you."

"Peg, stop, you don't know what you're saying." Colette gripped the trophy, its sharp metal edges biting into her palm. "You don't mean it."

"I know *exactly* what I'm saying. You knew how I feel about him, yet you went to the dance with him anyway."

"He asked me. Was I to say no?"

"Yes, yes, a thousand times yes." Peg disappeared in the bathroom Uncle Fred built for them under the dormer eaves. From her place in bed, Colette watched her sister dunk her stockings in the sink and reach for the bar of soap. "He'd have asked me if you'd turned him down."

"You don't know that, Peg." This conversation went down like bitter dregs. "You're drunk. You don't know what you're saying."

"I know *full* well what I'm saying. I want, for once, *what* I want."

"For once? You always get what you want, Peg. We've lived in Heart's Bend six months and you're one of the most popular girls in school."

Colette shifted down under her covers. Drink made Peg even more cruel. Mr. Morley was a funny, sleepy drunk. But Peg seemed to be harsh and angry.

Since arriving in Tennessee, she and Peg fought constantly. Peg seemed to be fueled by some ridiculous jealousy. And mean. She was cold to Colette, demanding and arrogant.

"Why do you think Spice didn't have a date? He came for you. Then I could have Jimmy."

"That's ridiculous. Then why did you bring Drummond? He seems such a nice chap. Don't tell me you were going to leave him all alone."

"He's a college man. He'd have got on well enough." Peg emerged from the bathroom, slipping from her dress and stomping it on the floor beneath her feet.

"Peg, careful. Aunt Jean paid good money for that frock."

She stooped to pick it up, then swooned into the reading chair under the window. "I'm so tired."

Colette slid out of bed, reaching for her sister. "Here, let me help you. Where are your pajamas? Let's get you in bed."

"You're so selfish, Colette. You stole my papá from me."

Colette released Peg and sank down to the floor. "I don't want to fight with you. You're drunk."

"I didn't get to say good-bye." Peg waved her finger at Colette, her eyelids at half-mast, her speech slurred, and a single tear slipping from the corner of her eye.

"Neither did I."

"He loved you more." Peg shot forward, cupping her hand over Colette's mouth. "Everyone loved you more."

Colette tore her hand away. "Stop . . . This is ridiculous. No one loved me more." At times, Peg's jealousy knew no bounds. Truth didn't matter. Only the rage in her soul that she caged and fed like a personal pet. "I'm going to bed."

Peg could sleep in her bra and panties for all Colette cared.

"Just how did you get Jimmy to ask you to the dance? Hmm? Lure him out to the fir tree and promise him your virtue? Wouldn't Papá be proud?"

"You take that back." Colette swerved toward her sister, hand raised. "And yes, wouldn't he be proud. Look at you, with your mussed hair, your breath reeking of alcohol, and you traipsing in at this hour. What were you and Drummond doing, Peg?"

"Drummond Branson—" Peg sing-songed his name, drawing pins from her hair, her arms like jelly. "He's a *man*." Her forced laugh sent chills through Colette. "I'm tired of these *boys* at school."

"Except Jimmy?"

Peg regarded her. "He's not like the others. He's kind, sweet, wounded like you and me, Lettie." Peg's honest response was soft with sleep. "And now you take the one person that made me feel safe."

"Oh, Peg, I'm not taking him—"

"Yes, you are." Peg fired up from her chair, charging at Colette. "I told you I liked him."

"But you flirt with all the boys. I didn't know he made you feel safe." Colette stroked Peg's hair. "That's how he makes me feel."

Peg shrugged away from Colette's touch. "No one wants me." She curled her lip, then gagged, jumping from the chair and stumbling to the bathroom. "Not the Morleys, not Mamá or Papá."

Colette pressed against the wall as Peg wretched into the toilet. A moment later she appeared with her hair ratted, going every direction.

"Peg, please go to bed."

She fell forward on her twin mattress, mumbling in her pillow. Her muffled sob speared Colette's heart. "They sent me to the country when I begged them to let me stay at home."

"They sent both of us away, Peg. We were safer in the country."

"They were rid of us, that's what it was about."

"Peg, you can't mean that. You know it's not true."

"And then they died on us. How safe were we then?

And no one wanted us until Mrs. Morley made Aunt Jean take us."

"Honey, no. They wanted us. Remember, Mrs. Morley wrote to them right away, but she had the wrong address." Colette smoothed Peg's tangled hair, her cold fingers slipping against her hot face. "Now come on, go to bed. You'll see things more clearly in the light of day."

"Jimmy doesn't want me."

"It's cold tonight, isn't it?" Colette reached for the quilt draped over the footboard, covering Peg.

"Does he? He doesn't . . ."

"Peg, Jimmy and me, we fit together darling."

"You fit together? Well, don't you just fit with everyone." Peg rolled over on her side and gripped Colette's hand. And for a moment, they were sisters again. "But I-I *love* him. If you'd let him go, he'd choose me. I know he would."

Lord help her, but Colette was trying to understand. But Peg lived in her own world, with her own picture of things. Could she not see that Jimmy never picked her? Even when Colette stood aside?

"Peg, just let Jimmy choose. He's a big lad and knows his own mind."

"No!" Peg's nails cut into Colette's palm. "You always do this." She was on the verge of one of her rages. "Take, take, take. Just like when Papá came to visit you never made room for me. You just ran into his arms, his darling Lettie, and left me standing on the outside."

"Peg!" Colette jerked her hand free. "You chose to stay on the outside. Even when he called you to him, you ran the other way."

Peg flopped over on her side. "It haunts me, Colette. Their deaths haunt me."

"I know, Peg, me too. Say your prayers—"

She bolted upright with such force she nearly smacked Colette. "To a God who killed our parents? No, never."

Colette exhaled. "I can pray for us both."

"Do not pray for me."

If time healed all wounds, then it passed too slowly for them. As Colette hung up her robe and crawled into bed, the joy of her night with Jimmy long gone, she let her tears run as she whispered her prayers. The wind rushed against the house, rattling the windows, shaking Colette.

Help us, God. Please help us.

. . .

TAYLOR

Pink.

The dang test was pink. She had taken one yesterday and another again today, hoping for some sort of false positive. Or that one of these stupid sticks would tell her what she wanted—"You're not pregnant."

So craziness abounded as she took the test over and over, hoping for a different result. Sitting on the side of the tub, Taylor stared at the bright double-line result. Pink. Pink!

A soft knock sounded on the door. "Tay?" Emma. She'd stopped by on her way to work, her solicitude equal parts caring and nosiness. "Let me guess, you're still pregnant."

Taylor angled forward to open the door, holding up the test result. "Come in."

Emma peeked around. "Pink?"

"Does that mean it's a girl?"

"Absolutely." Emma slipped in and sat next to Taylor on the edge of the old clawfoot tub. "I think you can stop taking pregnancy tests now. You've clearly passed."

Taylor tossed the result stick in the trash. "But they were buy one get one free. I have six more under the sink."

Emma laughed, wrapping Taylor in a big sister's hug. "It's going to be fine."

"For who? You? I don't want to be pregnant. I can't be pregnant. He doesn't want kids." She peered at Emma. "Did I tell you when we got married he said, 'If it doesn't work out we can walk away, no fuss, no muss.'"

She balked. "Then why'd you marry him?"

"I thought he was kidding, you know. Or that I misunderstood. I'd put it out of my mind until the other day. Now I'm wondering if it's what he planned all along. Temporary marriage. And now I'm knocked up."

Emma brushed Taylor's hair away from her warm, sticky skin. "You're going to have a sweet, beautiful, cooing *baby*!"

"Who cries and poops and wants to be fed at all hours. Who won't cotton to being on a ten-hour photo shoot."

"Then it looks like you and Jack have some talking to do."

"I know." She sighed. "I keep thinking, 'I can't go back now.'"

"On your marriage?"

"No, on being pregnant. But yeah, I guess my marriage too. I can never be *un*-pregnant. Unless of course Superman *really* can fly around the earth counterclockwise and reverse time."

"Superman can reverse time?"

"Yeah, didn't you know that?"

"I just thought he could leap tall buildings in a single bound. And change clothes in a phone booth."

"He reversed time in one of the movies."

"Which one? Old or new?"

"Oh my word, really? The old one. With Christopher Reeve." Taylor stood and leaned on the sink, angling toward the mirror. "Do I look pregnant?"

"Do you mean are you glowing?" Emma's angular, pretty face appeared over Taylor's shoulder. "Maybe a little."

"What am I going to do?"

"Have a baby." Emma lightly turned Taylor by her shoulders. "Once you see your new baby's face, you are never going to regret bringing her—"

"Or him."

"Or him into the world."

Taylor dropped her head on Emma's shoulder, her tears tracing down the side of her nose. "I'm scared."

"So was I."

When Mama and Daddy divorced, Taylor was a sophomore in high school and alone in the battle of the parents, caught in between.

Emma was a freshman at Vanderbilt, and an hour away from the drama. But she called Taylor every night, nine o'clock sharp, just to check in and make sure she was all right.

"Thank you."

"For what?"

"Everything."

"You're welcome."

From below, they heard the front-door chimes. Taylor reached for a toilet paper tissue. "You expecting someone?"

Emma went down the hall to the foot of the stairs. "Yeah, the secondhand dealer said he'd come by this week to take the picnic table."

"No, not the picnic table," Taylor said, following her down.

"You cannot be sentimental over an old wooden table, chewed up by squirrels and covered in bird poop."

"Why not?"

The chimes sounded again. Emma bounded down the remaining stairs and across the living room to the front door. When she swung it open, Taylor peered over her shoulder.

Colette Greer stood on Granny's porch.

Taylor moved around Emma. "Colette, hey, what are you doing here?"

"May I come in?"

"Please do." Taylor stepped aside, letting her great-aunt, the great actress, into Granny's humble abode. It was a far cry from a Park Avenue penthouse.

Colette walked past her, shoulders back with an air

of confidence. But her pale complexion told another story. "Are you all right? What are you doing here?"

Taylor motioned for her to sit on the only piece of furniture left in the living room. The old Drexel sofa.

"Could I trouble you for a glass of water?"

"Water? Coming up." Taylor headed for the dining table for one of Granny's glasses. When she returned, she introduced Emma. "Colette, this is my sister, your niece, Emma."

"My aunt Colette." Emma took a seat next to her, not bothering to hide her wonder. "I think we met once, when I was real young."

Colette nodded. "I believe so."

Taylor reached for a three-legged stool and sat. "What're you doing here?"

Colette said nothing until she consumed her drink in one unladylike gulp. When she finished, she inhaled and handed her glass to Taylor.

"I drove over from Nashville. I was at a meeting with the FRESH Water people."

"So you agreed to be their spokeswoman?" *Good for Jack. Oh, good for Jack.*

"Yes, but I used a visit to the company as a ruse to visit Heart's Bend." Colette sat back, closing her eyes, drawing a long inhale. "I ducked out on them and drove over here myself. Mercy, I thought I wasn't going to make it. I left my manager and your husband at the FRESH offices."

"Jack's in Nashville?" They'd been texting through the week but nothing more than saying hello and good night. See, communication grade F minus.

Then, as if on some choreographed cue, Taylor's phone buzzed with Jack's ring.

"Hey," she said, low and intimate, walking to the bay of southern windows. A cut of the late-morning sun painted the edge of the porch in white gold.

"Please, by some wild chance, tell me Colette is with you."

"Yeah. Just now."

"Ford, she's in Heart's Bend. With Taylor. Yes, at Peg's. Taylor, keep her there. We're on our way."

"Keep her here? When you two and the whole of FRESH Water apparently couldn't keep her in Nashville?"

"Funny."

She thought so. "Jack, what happened?"

"She went to the executive lounge to freshen up and never came back. Intel is she had a car delivered and drove off."

Taylor went to the window. "Silver Mercedes."

"Just keep her there until we come. Ford is worried about her. It's not like her to just run off."

"I'll do my best." Hanging up, her back to Emma and Colette, Taylor whispered to the dark screen, "Jack, I'm pregnant."

She still didn't like the sound of it. But give her a few more dress rehearsals and she just might. Just might.

"Are they on their way?" Colette's trained voice brought Taylor around.

"Yes, they're worried about you. Colette, why'd you sneak out on them?"

"You snuck out? To come to Heart's Bend? That's a first." Emma's rolling laugh did not amuse Colette.

"Oh, I don't know. It seemed like a good idea . . . I wanted to come . . . needed to come. On my own. I suppose you don't understand." A bit of color had returned to Colette's cheeks, and by the steel in her blue eyes, she intended to complete her mission. "And if those two were so worried about me, how come it took them over an hour to call?"

"Men." All three. In unison.

Colette tapped Taylor's knee. "If you don't mind, I'd like you to take me to this wedding chapel. I heard it was for sale."

"The chapel? S-sure. And yes, it's for sale." Taylor glanced at Emma. *Interesting.* Then scrambled for her purse. "I can drive Granny's car." She motioned to the back door. "Looks like you've done enough driving for one day—"

"For a decade." Colette stood, so regal and elegant, her wristlet swinging from her hand.

"Just let me get my camera." She'd unloaded it from the Lincoln Monday evening. She had a feeling she was going to need it.

As she stooped for her camera bag by the dresser, tidbits of this and that shook together.

The chapel. Jimmy's unrequited love. Colette leaving HB and never returning. The photograph. Granny's strange letter.

Back downstairs, Taylor collected Colette, whispering to Emma, "Call Coach Westbrook. Tell him I'm on my way to the chapel to take pictures."

She pulled out her phone. "Just you? Alone?"

"Just me. Ask him to meet me." Taylor headed for the door. "Shall we, Colette?"

Emma followed, leaning into Taylor. "If you think you're leaving me out of this, you're crazy."

The women piled in the car, Colette riding shot gun, Emma in the back. Taylor headed northwest for the chapel, the sun rising high in the blue Southern sky, the fall breeze dancing with the ends of her hair.

Taylor glanced in the rearview window, her eyes meeting Emma's. Something was afoot. She started to speak, ask Colette if she knew Coach, but she just couldn't get the words out.

She would just wait and see.

At the Niven Realty For Sale sign—an ugly thing— Taylor slowed the car and turned down the gravel lane.

When they broke into the clearing, Taylor parked in the shade and cut the engine. Turning to Colette, she could no longer hold her curiosity.

"You're the one, aren't you, Colette? The one Jimmy built the chapel for."

Colette stepped out of the car, clapping the door gently behind her, her gaze fixed on the chapel wrapped in the afternoon light.

"He finished." She took a step, clutching her wristlet close.

Taylor glanced at Emma, getting out of the car. "You've not seen it, then?"

Colette angled around, her somber expression softened by tears. "No."

Joining Colette in the yard, Taylor said nothing, just

let Colette be in the moment. She could hear Emma rustling behind her, then bumping her elbow, passing over her camera bag.

Taylor slipped the strap on her shoulder, peeking sideways at Colette. Her cheeks were dewy, her blue eyes bright, her countenance free of that stiff reserve.

"You're the one."

One nod. "Yes," Colette said. "I'm the one."

CHAPTER TWENTY-TWO

JIMMY

For some reason, he paused by the bureau mirror on his way out of his room and smoothed his hand over the silver waves of his hair. He frowned. What did he care about his hair?

He didn't, but he did like his shirt tucked in nice and neat, so he double-checked that with a passing glance in the mirror.

Hmm . . . Jimmy leaned into his reflection. How had he gotten to be eighty-three when he was twenty-three just a day or two ago?

All this business of the chapel, and telling Doc his secrets, put him in mind of things he'd rather not recall.

But Keith Niven had just called, said to meet him at the chapel. He had a *big* fish on the hook. *Big fish.*

So Jimmy was heading out. This might be it. The end of an era, of his days with the old chapel.

He paused in his bedroom door, pressing his hand to his heart, breathing deep against a slight twinge.

After a moment he moved on down the stairs. Heartburn, was all.

In the kitchen, Jimmy cut off the coffeepot and

checked the roast he had going in the Crock-Pot. But when he looked out the window, he saw her, a ghost image in the shimmering waves of sunlight.

Colette . . .

How could he truly say good-bye? Maybe he should call Keith and stop this whole business.

Or maybe see if Taylor wanted the chapel. It was a long shot, but she was the closest thing he'd come to Colette in a good while. She didn't have to know he gave it to her as a way of "keeping it in the family."

But sure as shooting she'd ask questions.

On the other hand, sometimes a man just had to admit his failures. No matter how long it took.

He could put the money to good use. Finally take the trip to Normandy, to see the American gravesite he'd been thinking about since the 1970s.

The chapel was the past that didn't fit in his future. It was too late to fulfill the dreams that came with the chapel. Too late for children and grandchildren. Too late to leave his name, his father's name, on the earth.

Well, darn if his eyes weren't stinging. This maudlin thinking was getting him nowhere. Jimmy grabbed his keys just as the house phone rang.

"Coach here."

"Coach? This is Emma, Taylor Branson's sister. The photographer?"

"What can I do you for?"

"Taylor asked if you could meet her at the wedding chapel."

"What for?"

"She didn't say."

Jimmy frowned. *That's odd.* "I'm on my way there now. So I guess I'll see her when I see her."

Locking up, Jimmy headed to his truck thinking it'd be nice to see Taylor while he said good-bye to the chapel. She made him feel at rest, like they were old friends.

Braking at the bend in the drive, the popping gravel under his tires going silent, he reached for the radio knob and paused before turning onto River Road.

Vic Damone crooned a ballad. ". . . *knowing I'm on the street where you live.*"

Jimmy cut the wheel right, and instead of heading northwest toward the chapel, he took a southern detour. Toward the Clemsons' old place.

Toward the street where she'd lived.

If he could do it all over, would he? Maybe he would've gone back to New York, not given up on Colette so easily. But she'd said no in a way that crushed him. First in her letter. Then refusing to see him that cold day he stood outside her studio.

Nevertheless, he stayed true. What price could he put on following his heart, keeping his vow, even if she didn't?

He'd promised Colette Greer he'd love her to his dying day and darn it if he wasn't abiding by it.

But that didn't mean he had to hang on to the chapel. He'd spent more time away from Colette than with her, but that first day he laid eyes on her remained vivid and real. Like a technicolor motion picture. If he breathed deep and tried hard, he could even recall the fragrance of her hair.

Flowers.

The Clemson house sat dark now, save for a For Sale sign in the front. Ole Fred Clemson died before Dad. About twenty years ago. Jean had died in her sleep five years before that. But she'd never really recovered from Ted's death. Then Clem getting killed in Korea. And Colette running off.

On occasion, Jimmy would see Jean at the market and once, maybe twice, she asked, "Do you hear from Colette? We never do. I miss her. Do you think she knows about Clem? Peg says she writes but Colette never responds. Did you see she was on television now?"

Jimmy gunned the gas and U-turned back to the main road, resentment growing at what Colette had done. How could he love a woman so cruel as to abandon her family? He might have dodged a bullet there. Might have married a woman just like his mama. At least they didn't have no kid for her to run out on.

When he arrived at the chapel, he spied Peg's Lincoln. *Taylor must be here already.* Parking behind her, Jimmy made his way to the chapel, kicking acorns out of his way, glancing around for her.

He unlocked the front door, grateful for the solitude, for the moment to say good-bye.

Walking the center aisle, he heard it. The soft, echoing *whoosh-thump.* He froze, his heart leaping and beating to the same rhythm.

His skin tensed with gooseflesh, then eased with a warm peace.

"I know . . . ," he said, sliding into his pew. Third from the back, second from the front. "I'm sad too. But

it's over, ole girl. Your new owners will treat you kind,
I'll make sure."

Since he'd first heard the heartbeat that day Peg
stopped by, he knew the chapel was talking to him.
He couldn't make hide nor hair of it so he pretended
otherwise. But he knew. God was breaking in. The
supernatural world tapping into the natural.

"Lord, I reckon You're looking down and knowing
what's going on." Jimmy ran his hand along the top of
the pew in front of him. "I give her to You. Probably
should've done that a long time ago, but I reckon
Colette and I didn't exactly do things right. But I meant
what I said to her that night. Before I shipped to Korea.
I surely did."

His prayer, his confession weighted his heart. He'd
had plans for this place besides his own wedding.

He'd wanted to see friends marry here. His children
and grandchildren.

Whoosh-thump. Whoosh-thump.

I'll miss you too. Jimmy pressed the back of his wrist
to his watering eyes, memories surfacing with every
breath.

· · ·

JANUARY 28, 1951

THE GREAT NASHVILLE BLIZZARD

The *Tennessean* predicted clear skies, but on Sunday
afternoon, as Jimmy turned down the narrow lane

leading to his hideaway, the old Ford engine winding down, snow fell from blanketing gray clouds.

The wipers stuttered back and forth across the cold windshield, keeping the quarter-sized flakes from collecting.

The truck hit a hole and Colette laughed, bouncing in the seat next to him. "Where are we going, anyway?"

"You'll see." Jimmy turned on the defrost. Rats, it wasn't supposed to snow.

He'd set up the chapel for his scheme on his way home after church—when the skies were blue and the temperature a balmy fifty.

But by the time he headed to the Clemsons' to collect Colette, the temperatures had plummeted and snow thickened the air.

In the back of the truck, he had his secret picnic basket of fried chicken and hot chocolate. At the chapel, he'd set up a wrought-iron bench Dad had salvaged, along with a stack of blankets. He'd built a fire pit and stacked plenty of wood.

But snow? The chapel didn't have a roof. Jimmy was counting on the canopy of trees to catch the precipitation and keep the chapel clear.

"Do you have a surprise for me, Jimmy Westbrook?" Colette snuggled close to him, making his pulse thick and heavy.

"Just hold your horses."

She kissed his cheek and rested her head on his shoulder. Yep, his heart could burst this very minute and he'd die a happy man.

He was more confident than ever his idea to bring

her here was right. Even if her *surprise* was not complete.

He'd planned to show her the chapel when he was finished. He'd been sneaking off to work on it every spare hour, sometimes fibbing to Colette about his whereabouts on Saturday and Sunday afternoons, saying Dad needed him to work.

But Uncle Sam called him up two weeks ago and he couldn't wait any longer to tell her. He realized last night when they went to the pictures with Clem and his new wife, Marie, he'd made a mistake not telling her right away.

Clem shipped out tomorrow, and Marie cried all through the show.

So he made up his mind to tell Colette today. And to *show* her why he'd not already proposed. He prayed the stone walls of the chapel would demonstrate his love for her and hold her heart until he returned.

The truck hit an icy patch and skidded forward, the back end fishtailing. Jimmy gripped the wheel and eased off the gas, straightening out the truck's trajectory. Colette laughed, a free, sweet refrain.

"Lovely driving, Mr. Westbrook."

He soared. There was nothing like being a hero to the woman he loved. Made his blood pump and his heart ping.

Then the walls of the chapel came into view. He felt shy and nervous. What would she say?

"Here we are." He pulled up and cut the engine.

Through the gray light and flurrying snow, the chapel walls reached for the clouds, confident, ready to become what they were meant to be. Jimmy turned to Colette, slipping his arm around her shoulders. "If it's too cold, we can go."

"Go? After all you've done? Darling, I'm an English-woman. I lived through a war and plenty a cold night on a Carmarthenshire farm. Whatever this adventure you've planned, I'll not miss it." She scooted forward, peering through the windshield. "What is this?"

Jimmy nestled her close, the small light from the dash contouring the curves and planes of her face. Colette warmed his coldest corridors. She brought light where shadows had always lingered.

Her eyes searched his. "What's up with you? You're worrying me."

"You're beautiful. You know that, Colette?"

Her eyes glistened. "I believe it when you tell me, Jimmy."

He brought his lips to hers, the first tender touch igniting a fire that would heat him all night. She arched up, slipping her hand around his neck, returning his kiss with one of her own.

When they broke apart, he tapped the end of her nose. "Ready?" He had to keep moving or he'd whisper the words he'd been holding on to for over two years. *"Marry me."* He refused to utter them in the heat of the moment.

"Ready. Do you have your gloves and hat?" Colette raised her hand as she tugged on her thick, woolly gloves. "Aren't these divine? Aunt Jean found them at Loveman's."

"Let's hope they keep you warm. Here we go." Jimmy

tugged on his hat and jumped out, hurrying around to Colette's door.

Slipping his arm around her, he felt her lean into him, and everything was quiet and calm. Beautiful.

"Listen," she said, tipping back her head, catching a massive flake on her tongue. "You can hear the snow falling. Isn't it brilliant?"

"Yes, brilliant." Jimmy held her close and kissed her cheek. "If you get too cold, tell me."

"Love, you worry too much. But I adore that you worry about me." She faced the chapel. "Now, tell me, what is this place? Where are we?"

"Come on, you'll see." Jimmy plowed forward, kicking through the shallow accumulation of snow.

"Jimmy—" Her voice buoyed with wonder. "Is this a chapel?"

He stopped on the steps. Or what would be the steps. For now, it was only a couple of crooked limestones.

"It's your chapel, Colette. Your wedding chapel."

"My *wedding* chapel?" She stepped around him, walked to the walls, smoothing her gloved hand over the snow-kissed stone. "I don't understand." She turned to him. "Am I getting married?"

"Someday." Jimmy sidestepped the question, not ready to give a direct answer yet. "I tried to build it like the chapel in the picture, of you and Peg at that wedding. The one in the country."

"You remembered?" Her voice quivered. "I was babbling, running on with my stories of home."

"You said it was such a happy time in the midst of war."

"And you wanted to re-create it for me?" She let out a moan and ran to him, wrapping her arms around him. He dropped the basket and thermos and grabbed hold as she cradled her head against his coat and wept softly. "I love you, Jimmy. So very much. I'll spend my life showing you."

"I'll never let you go, Lettie." He buried his face against her hair. "I'll be your man. Your rock."

After a few moments, Colette released him and stepped back, drying her face with the cold, snowy sleeve of her coat. "You're too wonderful for me."

"Come on, I've set us up over here." He gestured about halfway up in what he intended to be the center aisle. If his plans worked out, this spot would be the third pew from the back and second from the front.

"I can't believe you did this. Who does such a thing? For a poor English girl? Jimmy, love, it must have cost you a fortune."

"Don't you know, Colette?" His confession burst to life. No more waiting for the planned moment by the fire. "I love you." A low laugh rumbled in his chest. "Since Clem showed me your picture, as crazy as it sounds. I just—"

She leapt at him, grabbing his shoulders and drawing him in for a kiss, holding on to him so tightly.

Jimmy responded, wrapping his arms about her, raising her off the ground, letting this moment be the rest of his answer.

How the chapel cost him practically nothing since Dad collected most of the stone. How the only expense was his time, which he freely gave.

"I love you too, Jimmy Westbrook. Since that night on the football field. With all my heart."

"I love you, Colette. I love you. I don't know much about marriage and all that, only one I ever took note of was your aunt and uncle's, but I'll give you everything I got."

"Me too, darling, me too."

He kissed her again, slowly this time, letting love defeat every one of their doubts. He didn't have to fear with Lettie. Ever.

When the kiss ended he tapped his forehead to hers. "Say it again, Lettie. That you love me."

She raised her gaze to his. "Jimmy Westbrook, I love you."

He laughed, swirling her around. "Hear that, world? My Lettie loves me. And I love her."

"Jimmy, put me down. Now, what is this place? *My* chapel." Colette moved to the middle of the square, dirt sanctuary, arms wide, embracing the snow and cold.

"Yessiree, she's all yours." The chill hit him and he stooped to start a fire.

"Whoo! I'm the richest girl in the world."

"I don't know about that, but you certainly got your own wedding chapel." He brushed the snow from the bench and the small woodpile, tugged a matchbox from his pocket, and set the delicate flame to the kindling.

She fell against him, throwing her arm around his neck. "My true love built a wedding chapel for me. What other girl can say such things? Not even Princess Elizabeth can say Prince Philip built a chapel just for her."

"What do you know about that? I bested Prince

Philip." Jimmy left the crackling fire and turned to her, cupping her cheek and kissing her.

"But, Jim?" Colette's voice sobered. "Why do I have a wedding chapel when I'm not getting married? Or even engaged?"

He slid onto the bench, pulling her down next to him. "That's the thing, Lettie. I want you to marry me. In your chapel."

"Jimmy . . ." The blue of her eyes radiated. "You're . . . p-proposing?"

He dropped to one knee. "Colette Greer, will you marry me?"

Her eyes glistened, reflecting the firelight. "Yes, James Westbrook. I'll marry you. Yes."

He tugged Colette down to the pallet of blankets, falling back, her fragrance and beauty igniting his passion for her.

"I'm going to be your wife," she said, her face hovering above his.

"I'm going to be your husband."

She smiled. "Mercy, it sounds so grown up."

"We *are* grown up, Colette. Twenty and nineteen. My dad was married at my age." She captured him more with every moment, with her dark hair curling from under the edges of her hat, her plump lips red and beckoning.

"We are, love. I'm ready."

The wind gushed through the open chapel, filling the air with snow and the scent of burning hickory.

What were cold temperatures compared to their love?

"I feel like I'm in a snow globe." Colette slipped off her gloves and twirled her hand through the falling crystals. "Jimmy, when did you decide to build me a chapel?"

"Two summers ago."

Her eyes widened. "Two summers." She pressed her warm palm to his cold cheek. "You *do* love me."

"With all my heart." He reached for the picnic basket. "I'm famished."

"What is that glorious aroma?" Colette leaned to see inside.

"Fried chicken, corn bread." Jimmy held up the thermos. "Hot cocoa."

"Does my true love cook?" Colette's wide-eyed expression made him laugh. "You *are* my hero."

Jimmy presented her with a tin of fried chicken. "Your true love's father cooks." He laughed, carefully filling two cups with hot cocoa.

"To us." He raised his cup.

"To us."

The fire found a bit of strength and the snow let up as the light began to fade from the gray clouds.

"See, darling, I told you the snow would let off."

"Never doubted you."

Snuggling under the blankets, resting against the iron bench, they talked, ate, and licked chicken grease from their fingers and dusted corn bread crumbs from their laps.

When Colette finished, she wiped her fingers on a cotton napkin and crawled out from the blankets, tucking her coat collar around her coat.

Jimmy shook the snow from the blankets, then warmed them by the fire while he watched Colette walk the chapel perimeter.

"To think, some girls get a diamond engagement ring, but I get a *chapel*. A lovely wedding chapel."

"I love that you see what it will be instead of this roofless structure I got going."

She turned to him, smiling, so beautiful standing between the brilliant firelight and the ghostly shadows of the snow. "When will it be finished? I want to be married as soon as possible. Before you change your mind."

Jimmy met her on the other side of the fire, encircled her in his arms, and kissed her. "I will never change my mind, but, honey, I need to tell you something."

"I'll need time to plan and save," she said. "I can't expect Uncle Fred to bear the expense of my wedding."

"Come sit by the fire."

"What?" Her expression darkened. "Why so serious when you've just proposed?"

Curling up with her by the fire, tucking the blankets all around them, he drew a long, deep inhale.

"I got my notice, Colette." He paused, searching her eyes, waiting for her response. Since Clem was leaving Monday bright and early, the war was fresh on his mind, her mind.

"Your notice?" Her lower lip quivered and her eyes pooled with sorrow.

"Two weeks ago."

"And you're just now telling me?" She gripped his hands, digging in her gloved fingers.

"I'm sorry, so sorry." He drew her toward him and kissed her. "We were having such a good time. And I didn't want to bring us down. Clem's leaving was doing enough of that—"

She flung her arms about him. "You can't go . . . you can't. How can I lose someone else I love to war? Bloody, stupid war. I won't let you go."

"I have to, Lettie." His response came off sharper than he'd intended. "Do you want me to write the War Department, tell them my fiancée won't let me?"

"Yes, please, yes. Tell them you can't go." Her tears glistened on her cheeks. "Y-you mean everything to me, Jimmy. I can't lose you. In England, I'd forgotten what true happiness felt like . . . You showed me different. You're so sweet and kind, and you make me laugh. Jimmy, who will make me laugh?"

He brushed a strand of hair from her face, then gently removed her wool hat, entwining his fingers with her soft hair. "I'll send you jokes from Korea."

"You make fun of me . . ."

"No . . ." Cupping her face, he kissed her, gently falling into her, wanting to forget he had no right to her body yet, to forget he'd be in a barracks with loads of other boys this time next week.

She stretched alongside him on the pallet, her pressing kiss an invitation. "Marry me, Jimmy."

He traced his finger along the planes of her beautiful face. "I'll come back to you, I promise. I will marry you."

"No, marry me now. In my chapel."

He buried his face against her breast, drawing strength from the *whoosh-thump* of her beating heart.

"We've no license. And by the time I run for the preacher—"

"I don't want any of that, just you."

"But, Colette, we won't be legal—"

"Yes, we will." She pressed his hand to her heart. "Here. In our hearts. I, Colette Elizabeth Greer, take you, James Allen Westbrook, to be my husband, for better or worse, in sickness and health, for richer or poorer, to love and cherish, 'til death us do part. Before God I pledge this vow."

He swallowed, the sovereignty of the moment pumping through his heart. He could hear the rhythm in his ears. "I, James Allen Westbrook, take you, Colette Elizabeth Greer, to be my wife, for better or worse, for richer or poorer, to love and cherish, in war and peace, in good and bad, no matter what, and before God I pledge this vow."

The sound of his voice lingered between them. Then he kissed her, feeling the finality of it all.

A slow grin pressed his lips. "We're married."

"So promise me, Jims, you will not die and leave me a war widow. I couldn't bear it. Not one bit."

His heart burst with the precious vulnerability of the woman in his arms. "I won't die, Mrs. Westbrook. Not in Korea, and not for a very long time. I'll be your old man husband."

"I'll be your old woman wife."

Snow began to fall once more, swirling down around them. Jimmy couldn't be sure, but in the distance he believed he heard a faint melody whistling through the trees.

"When I come home, I'm going to finish this chapel and marry you proper like, with all of our family and friends. Then we're going to have a bunch of kids and be 'those Westbrooks.'"

She laughed, snuggling against him, clinging to him. "I'll snub the women's league and club teas."

"I'll never hit the golf course or become an Elk. I'm going to be a . . . football coach. The best ever."

"A football coach? Really? Did you just decide?"

"I think I did."

"You'll be marvelous, darling. I know it."

She brushed her thumb over his lips, her eyes locked with his. "Just come home, Mr. Football Coach. Just come home."

The snow became a force of large flakes sizzling in the fire. Gathering her in his arms, he burrowed with her under the covers, his heart beating as he let go into the now, the beginning-middle-end of them, and followed his heart to where everything was warm, passionate, and beautiful.

CHAPTER TWENTY-THREE

COLETTE

She stood atop the rolling green knoll behind the chapel, looking out over a new development, memories rising, flooding the recesses of her mind.

The trickle started on the drive down River Road—it'd been so long since she'd traveled this way—and now that she'd arrived at the chapel, she couldn't seem to control her thoughts, her emotions, or the tremor running through her.

Taylor and Emma flanked her, submitting to the view and the silence.

"This used to be farmland," Colette said after a moment. "But now it's nothing but houses as far as the eye can see."

"There's a lot of development in Heart's Bend," Emma said.

"I heard a car door," Taylor said, gently touching Colette's shoulder. "I think Coach is here."

Colette nodded. "Go on, I'll be along."

"You all right?"

"Fine. Just need a moment." Colette was used to getting into character, preparing for a scene. But this was not pretend, reciting some writer's lines. This was real life and the character she needed to reckon with was her nineteen-year-old self.

The chapel was beautiful, displaying Jimmy's amazing craftsmanship. She could handle the outside of the place, but once she stepped inside . . .

The wind whispered past and she felt the thin ribbons knew her secret. That the night a blizzard threatened central Tennessee, she lay in her lover's arms.

For the first and the last time.

• • •

January 28, 1951

At the chapel

Snow swirled and danced, drifting down slowly through the open rafters, forming soft mounds on the chapel floor.

Her magical, wintry wedding chapel. Her living snow globe. A world in which no one existed but her and Jimmy.

She'd never been this close, this intimate with a man, but now that she let her heart and soul go to Jimmy, Colette knew it was the most *glorious* feeling. Her heart resounded beneath the layers of sweater and coat. "Is it real? All these happy feelings?"

Never mind the bother of him being called up. She'd not think of it.

"This is only the beginning, Colette." He loosened her scarf and brushed his warm hand along the base of her neck, causing her to tremble with passion.

"Aren't we the lucky ones, then."

"Very." He lowered his gaze, following the V line of her blouse. "Are you scared?"

"Not with you." She raised herself up, kissing him softly, slipping from her coat.

"I won't hurt you, Colette. Not now, not ever."

She knew then she'd follow him to wherever their passions led. And she would be safe inside their consummated love.

Peg would just have to understand.

"I trust you, Jimmy." She smiled, rolling her coat into a pillow. "My husband."

He pressed his lips to her forehead. "My wife."

Barely nineteen, Colette felt sage and mature, queen of the world. And Jimmy was her king.

He placed her hand over his heart, his chest firm and muscled beneath her palm. "It's racing."

Tentatively, she placed his hand over her heart. "As is mine."

His warm lips touched her as he drew her scarf from around her neck, and his touches spoke what words could not. Colette roped her arms around his shoulders, releasing into the movement of their bodies, moving to the *whoosh-thump* of her heart.

His eyes searched hers. "Tell me if you want to stop. We can be husband and wife in vow only."

"But I want to be your wife . . . in every way." She was

never more sure of anything in her life. Because he *was* her shield from the past, her hope in the present, and her promise for the future.

As the snow continued to fall and the fire flamed, their passion took them where lovers go. Colette surrendered everything to Jimmy, knowing that in this place of love she became who she wanted to be.

. . .

JIMMY

Jimmy collected his memories of Colette as the sanctuary door opened. Taylor and another woman entered with Drummond Branson, followed by Keith Niven and three fancy-looking suits.

Apparently they was all riled up over something. Drummond was going toe-to-toe with Keith.

"Drummond, you don't know what you're talking about."

"Keith, it's on record. I saw the city plans," Drummond said. "You're buying this property to build on it, not create a wedding venue."

"You know as well as I do they are just plans on record *just in case*. But there are no plans to put a development here." Keith laughed as if Drum walked the edge of crazy, making a face for Jimmy. "Coach, good to see you. Let me introduce your buyers. André Willet, Brant Jackson, and Dan Snyder."

"Pleased to meet you." Jimmy offered his hand, but Drummond stepped in between.

"Don't shake, Coach." What had Drummond so riled? "Keith, who are these men? And what's the offer?"

"Drum, I don't see how any of this is your business."

"Two hundred thousand." From the one named Brant. He seemed right confident, and two hundred grand didn't seem like a bad offer.

Drummond clapped him on the shoulder. "Coach, don't accept. This property is worth twice that."

"Are you accusing me of something, Drummond?" Keith said. "Then say it."

"What? Have I been unclear so far?"

Enough. Jimmy didn't want folks throwing stones in his chapel, in a place meant for love and joy.

But perhaps this argument was his just due—his sins coming home to roost. Fine, then let them be on him.

In fact, the buyers were standing right where he'd once lain with Colette.

He raised his hands. "Let's not argue—"

The Brant fella interrupted, his feathers all fluffed. "Two hundred is right at market value for this area. We've no intention of robbing Mr. Westbrook of a fair deal."

"The land alone is worth three hundred, maybe more. And this chapel? Throw in another hundred and fifty grand. Coach." Drummond took hold of Jimmy's shoulder. "The plan for this area is for big, ritzy row houses. These boys will sell each quarter acre for fifty thousand-plus. The six acres will gross well over a million dollars."

"It's called good business," André said. "We take the risk by buying the property, insuring it, making sure there are no environmental hurdles, and yes, eventually selling for a profit."

"No deal," Drummond said with all boldness but without any authority.

"This is not your business, Drummond." All red faced, Keith was fixing to blow.

Jimmy peered past Drummond at Taylor. He'd simmer down this argument by seeing what she wanted. "Did you need to see me?"

She glanced toward the door. "Yes, but—" She flashed her palm. "I'll be right back. Don't make any deals until I get back. Coach, this is my sister, Emma."

"Nice to meet you."

"You too, Coach."

"No deals . . . That's right, Taylor. Tell him." Drummond was like a dog with a bone on this one.

"Can we negotiate without this man?" Dan, the tall one, simmered beneath his fancy duds.

"Nothing less than five hundred thousand," Drummond pressed on. "For five acres. Leave the chapel on one. Plus an easement and parking."

"You must be out of your mind." The other suit looked like a shaken bottle of soda pop. "We want *all* six acres."

"Why? Take five. You'll still have plenty of land, along with the property you own, to build your suburb."

"Because—" Brant hesitated, glancing around at Keith and his partners. "The road goes right through here."

"Brant!" Keith's voice bounced among the rafters.

"Road? What road?" Jimmy said, his senses fully engaged, burning away any lingering emotion. "What road?"

"Yeah, Keith, what road?" Drummond angled back, arms crossed, clearly enjoying this.

"Coach, there's no road. Just, on the plans filed with the county"—he peered at Drummond—"plans we're not going to use, there might be a road." He motioned up and down the chapel aisle. "About here."

"But you can't have a road *about* here. You'd have to tear down the chapel."

"Exactly," Drum said. "The road to their community begins right there." He pointed to the back of the sanctuary. "At your little gravel entrance off River Road."

"But that can't be." Jimmy's heart jumped. No, no, no. "Keith? You said you were finding wedding venue buyers."

"Jimmy, listen . . ." Keith shoved Drummond out of the way and cupped his arm around Jimmy. "Yes, that *was* the original plan. But really, what do you care? As long as you make a good profit? And if it's good for Heart's Bend? Brant, André, and Dan here want to bring business and commerce, families, to Heart's Bend." Keith smiled down at him. "Which means more revenue, more money for schools, for football. Brant here is willing to donate a sizable sum to a new football field house."

Behind Jimmy, Drummond growled and grumbled. "A bunch of hoo-ha."

"Coach, you will be solely responsible for bringing

innovation and enterprise to Heart's Bend. Brant and the boys here have a vision of prosperity for our little town. What's good for one is good for all. What's good for all is good for one."

"Gobbledygook." Drummond again.

Jimmy took a breath. He meant to see this thing clearly. Like an opposing defense. "So, let me understand. You boys mean to bring more of Nashville over this way. We already got big communities on the east side of town. Shopping malls and movie theaters."

"Look around, Coach," Keith said. "The world's changing. You can talk to someone in Asia face-to-face on a device no bigger than a transistor radio. When you built this chapel we barely had television in these parts. Look, I know you had a plan when you built this place, but it didn't work out." The real estate agent shrugged. "Welcome to life. Plans change all the time. For you, what's most important is lining your nest egg. Who cares if your property is sold to a wedding venue or a developer?" Keith walked down the aisle, his arms wide. "Either way, you're making folks happy. Changing lives. Besides, Coach, you can't cling to the past."

"No, I can't cling to the past," Jimmy said slowly, thinking. "I've held on to this place too long. But I don't intend this chapel for destruction. She can't be torn down. My dreams might not have come true within these walls, but I'd like to help other couples make their dreams come true."

"So what are you saying?" Keith said.

"Coach," Brant said. "If you sell to someone else, we'll just buy from them. Just want to be up front about that, and might I add, I'm a big fan. My dad played against you in your last title game."

Jimmy regarded him through a narrow gaze. "We won that one as I recall."

Brant grinned, nodding. "Much to my father's regret."

"Enough memory lane," Drummond said. "Coach, don't sell."

"This development does have me reconsidering." Jimmy motioned to the high beam ceiling. "I hauled the lumber from downtown Nashville for this place during the rebuilding years, after the war. About broke my back hauling limestone out of the ground all over Tennessee. Stained the ground with my own sweat and tears. Boys, I can't let you tear her down."

"Interesting." Drummond walked around Keith, inspecting the ceiling beams. "I've got a buddy at the historical register. We might be able to claim this chapel as a historic site."

"Drummond, that's ridiculous," Keith said.

"Niven, you brought us into a circus." Brant started for the door, then whirled around to Jimmy. "This is not the end. We'll take legal action."

"Legal action? Brant, wait. Coach—" Keith stood between the two groups, a weak excuse for a peace bridge. "We can work this out. Let's go back to Drummond's idea of more money. How's five acres for five hundred thousand hit everyone?"

Like a match tossed on gasoline, Drummond, the suits, and Keith exploded one by one, protesting, their voices flying, their arms flailing, their reasons jabbing the air.

Jimmy jumped up on the nearest pew. "Take a knee!" His inner football coach roared from deep within. His baritone echoed about the beams, and every man, even the suits, took a knee. "Listen up, this is my place and I call the shots. There ain't going to be a lawsuit and—"

Ten feet away, the sanctuary doors opened and a stream of fall light rushed in. Jimmy squinted through the brilliance as a vision emerged from the hue of white and gold.

Colette.

His knees gave way and he buckled, slipping off the pew, his heart beating with the force of hummingbird wings. Drummond lurched forward, catching him by the arm, helping him to firm footing.

"Coach, I brought someone to see you." Taylor stepped around Colette, leading her down the aisle.

He couldn't speak. He couldn't move. Colette. His Colette. She was a statuesque beauty who seemed not to have aged one jot. Time had been kind to her. To his Lettie.

Keith stepped forward. "If you don't mind, we're in a meeting here."

"Everyone," Taylor said, ignoring that blowhard Keith. "This is Colette Greer, the soap opera star and the inspiration for the chapel."

"Colette Greer?" Brant said. "I thought she was dead."

"No, I'm very much alive." Colette spoke, so poised and gracious. "And this is *my* wedding chapel."

Keith laughed. "Is this some sort of joke?" He pointed

to the camera around Taylor's neck. "Are we on a reality show?" He danced about, waving his hands, looking the fool.

"No, no, she's right. This is Colette's chapel." Jimmy found a smattering of composure. He was breathing the same air as his true love. After sixty-four years. He felt suddenly aware of himself and smoothed his hand over his hair, tucked in the back of his shirt.

"Legally?" Brant said. "Does she have the deed? Because if she does, then why were you trying to sell it, Mr. Westbrook?"

The room seemed to expand, moving the other players out of the way. Jimmy only saw and heard Colette. "I knew you'd come." He kept the distance of one pew between them. "One day you'd come."

"Then why," she said in a whisper, "are you selling my chapel?"

From the corner of his eye, Jimmy spied Taylor behind her camera, capturing the moment. And he was grateful.

"What does she mean, this is her chapel?" Keith's whine broke the magic and interrupted Jimmy's sweet reunion. "Is she serious? Does she hold the deed? That's what we need to know, Coach."

"Everyone out!" Jimmy channeled his inner coach again and motioned to the exit. "Out. Out. Out. Stop yer yammering."

"We're not done here," Brant declared as he made his way down the aisle, his partners following.

"We're more than done here," Jimmy said. "Keith, take down your sign."

"We've got a contract, Jimmy."

"Not anymore. I'm not selling. And if I were, I'd not be in business with a man who lied to me."

"Way to go, Coach," Drummond said, clapping him on the back. "Way to go, Aunt Colette." He offered his hand. "I'm Peg's son, Drummond."

"Yes, I know." Then she did the oddest thing. She slipped her hand into Jimmy's and leaned into him. *Hold on, darling Lettie. I gotcha.* "My dear nephew."

"Daddy, Emma, why don't we give these two a moment?"

"Right, right. See you later?" Drummond walked toward the door with his daughters.

"Drummond," Jimmy said, "I owe you a Tennessee hill of gratitude."

"You don't owe me nothing, Coach. After all you did for me in high school, this is the least I can do."

The door opened, then closed, and silence filled the sanctuary. He was alone with *her.* He tried to speak but faltered, the thousands of words in his chest unable to find breath.

She squeezed his hand, her smile as bright as he remembered. "I'm sorry to come unannounced, but when I heard you were selling, I couldn't stay away."

"I'm glad." Jimmy cleared his throat, trying to sound like a man in this exchange. "I'm glad." He glanced down at his old boots. "You look good, Lettie."

Her soft laugh raised his chin. "My, no one has called me that in years. You look good too, Jims. And I'm not sure I have the right to demand anything of you, but please don't sell my chapel." She raised her gaze to the beams, surveyed the windows, the walls, the altar, soft sighs escaping. "It's more lovely than I imagined it would be."

"She's been waiting for you."

Colette glanced at him. "Jimmy, please, I—"

"Marry me." The words fired through the reservoir of the unspoken and into the room with the power of his heart. "I ain't waiting no more. You're here and I need to know if you'll marry me." He sank slowly to one knee, hanging on to the pew beside him.

"Marry you? Are you—"

"Proper this time. Not some vows only we knew about, vows we too easily walked away from."

She peered down at him, then turned, walking away. "I've not seen you in sixty-four years and this is what you ask of me?"

"What do you want me to ask? How's life? Or how was your trip down here? How long you staying? No, Colette." He shoved up from the floor. "You're here and I aim not to let you get away this time."

She whirled around to him. "And what about me? What I want?"

"Then is your answer no?"

"Jimmy . . . you . . . you have no idea what you're asking." She clasped her hands, pacing.

"But I do know what I'm asking. In fact, I asked you sixty-four years ago in this very spot and you said yes. What's changed?"

"What's changed?" She held out her arms and turned a slow circle. "Everything has changed, you old fool. How can you possibly want to marry me?"

"Because I ain't never stopped loving you. Isn't that enough?"

She shook, the wallet around her wrist visibly trembling. "You don't know me . . . what you're asking."

"Then tell me. What am I missing? Lettie, I never thought I'd see you again. But here you stand. Saving me. Saving the chapel. In that sense, nothing has changed at all."

She pressed her finger to her lips as tears slipped down her cheeks. "You silly old fool. You think we can just pick up where we left off? That we can be nineteen and twenty again?" She spun around and pushed through the door, leaving Jimmy to stand alone in the shadows, the echo of his proposal raining down over him.

CHAPTER TWENTY-FOUR

TAYLOR

She'd pretended she didn't, but she'd heard the *whoosh-thump* of the chapel's heart. She didn't know what else to call it. But it resounded loud and clear.

She'd peeked at Jimmy, but he didn't seem to hear it. He was so focused on Colette.

Just remembering gave Taylor chills, and now that she drove east toward Granny's with Emma oddly silent in the backseat and a stony Colette in the passenger seat, her heart spilled over.

So she released her questions to God. Who else could she ask about the supernatural but the One who created it? Existed above and beyond it? Why was He taking time to invade her world? Jimmy's world?

A low mutter came from Colette. "It was a mistake to come, a mistake."

"I saw Coach's face. He was . . . *really* glad to see you."

"You can never go back. You can't. Shouldn't have tried."

Colette's posture and tone invited no more questions, so Taylor settled in with her own thoughts with a peek in the rearview at Emma, who stared pensively at the passing trees.

They pulled into Granny's driveway, parking behind another dark rental car. Colette slipped out of the car, beelining for her rental. "Thank you, Taylor and Emma, for taking a foolish woman on a foolish journey."

"Won't you come inside? Maybe we can talk about it."

"No, I've seen and talked enough."

"Jack and Ford are inside."

"I need to be alone." She fumbled with a key, trying to unlock the car. When she couldn't manage it, she stomped her foot, swearing softly, her thin shoulders crumpling.

Emma walked over, gently taking the keys from her. "Colette, please come inside."

"Please unlock the door."

Emma passed the keys to Taylor. "I think you should drive her."

"No, I can drive myself." But Colette did not move.

Taylor unlocked the door and popped it open. "You don't have to block us out, you know. Just because Granny is dead or because trouble existed between you. It doesn't have to be that way with the rest of us."

At the sound of her own confession, Taylor felt the power of family. Good, bad, weak, or strong, family mattered. If not blood kin, then those who fit in one's heart.

"Yes, it must be this way." Colette stared down the shaded, tree-lined lane. "Because if you knew—"

"A secret?" Taylor tossed the word out on a hunch. "That there's a secret?"

Colette's countenance darkened. "You know?"

"That there's a secret? Yes, but I have no idea what. Colette, please come in. What could be so bad you can't tell us? Granny is gone and time has a way of healing things, you know?"

"Tell Ford I'll see him at the hotel." Colette's whole body trembled as she slipped behind the wheel.

"Colette, you're not in any shape to drive," Emma said. "When did you last eat?"

"I had cake not long ago."

"Cake? You need more than cake."

But the great Colette Greer was done talking. She slammed the door and fired up the engine.

From the curb, the sisters watched her drive off, the Mercedes' taillights disappearing around the corner. *Be safe, Colette.*

Making her way up to the house, Taylor regretted letting her go. But Colette wasn't a child. Or addled. She was hurting. And Taylor knew what it felt like to just want to escape.

When she and Emma entered the house, Jack and Ford leapt to their feet.

"Well?" Ford said, rushing to the door and peering out. "Where's Colette?"

"She left." Taylor set her camera on the remaining end table. "Said she wanted to be alone."

"You do realize she doesn't have a valid driver's license? And that she's a horrible driver?"

"We'll find her, Ford," Jack said, then moved to Taylor, wrapping her in a hug. She exhaled. He felt good. *I've something to tell you, Jack.* "What's going on, Tay?"

"Colette's the one. The one Coach built the chapel for."

"What? The wedding chapel Coach built, that you photographed, was for Colette Greer? When? Why?"

"Long time ago and I guess because he loved her. The details are sketchy."

Ford left the door but not his fretting. "What's this about a chapel?"

"Coach was in love with Colette?" Jack said.

Taylor gave a summary to Ford, who *hmm*'d. "That answers a few questions I've had over the years."

"So that's why she wanted to meet with FRESH." Jack glanced at Ford. "She wanted, needed, an excuse to see Coach."

"Jack, get your things," Ford said. "We need to find her and you're my ride. If it weren't for you and your wild ideas, we'd not be in this mess."

Jack went stony. "We'll find her." He checked with Taylor. "Did Colette say where she was going?"

"Her hotel. Said she'd meet Ford there."

"Then let's go." Ford popped open the door.

Jack hesitated with a glance at Taylor. "I need to go."

"I know, go." She shooed him off, flicking her hands. "We'll talk later."

"Okay." He started out, but returned and kissed her softly. "You okay? You look tired."

"She's been sick." Emma, the bullhorn. Just couldn't leave well enough alone.

Taylor made a face. "Was he talking to you?"

"Sick? What kind of sick?" Jack's furrowed expression of concern warmed her.

"Nothing. Just tired."

"Jack," Ford bellowed from the porch. "Daylight's burning."

Jack hesitated, like he wanted to say something. "I'd better go."

"Let us know if you find her." And, *I'm pregnant, Jack.*

Trying on the confession helped Taylor come to grips with her new reality. As mom.

"Burning daylight, Jack." Ford, loud and demanding.

Jack left without another word.

"New Yorkers," Emma said, shaking her head.

"Hey, I'm a New Yorker." Taylor gathered her camera and started for the stairs, bracing for Emma's commentary.

"No, you're not." Emma trailed after her. "It's why you're waffling on selling this house. You are a Heart's Bend girl through and through. You're stuck more to this place than Lorelai Gilmore is to Stars Hollow."

"You're crazy."

"So, you and Jack? What was that cordial exchange? Are you sure you're married?"

"You should really see a doctor, Emma," said Taylor, heading for the bum room.

"How you figure?"

"Get meds for the 'I-say-everything-that-comes-into-my-head' disease."

"As opposed to 'I-never-say-anything-that's-on-my-heart' disease." Emma plopped down to the bum room sofa as Taylor set her camera on the makeshift computer table. "You two act like friends-with-benefits, but I see some love and tenderness lurking beneath the surface."

Taylor plunked down, exhausted, into her favorite chair. "We can't seem to get on the same page at the same time. Eloping was a stupid idea. Maybe I should invoke the no muss, no fuss clause."

"Well, you can't until you tell him about—"

"Ahem. Excuse me." Jack's bass broke up the conversation.

Seeing him in the doorway, Taylor jumped to her feet. How long had he been standing there? What did he hear?

"Hey, Jack." Oh, too sweet and forced.

"Taylor, you need to move the Lincoln. You parked behind us." His parting glance was cold and quick.

"Jack—" She ran around Emma and the sofa, patting her pockets. Yep, that's where she'd tucked the car keys. "Wait."

But he didn't wait. He kept striding. "Just move the car, Taylor."

She pushed through the front door after him. "We were just talking, you know, sister talk."

He stopped in the middle of the yard. "No, I *don't* know."

"You know, random, just woo"—she whirled her hands in the air—"whatever comes to mind."

"Good to know." He turned to the rental. "Move the car."

Taylor fumed after him. "Jack, wait, please . . . Hey, you never wanted us to work anyway. I don't know why you're so upset."

He whipped around, his eyes dark. "I never wanted us to work? Wh-where did you get that malarkey? Is that what you tell yourself so you don't feel bad for slowly drifting out of our relationship?"

"Me? You're the one who said, 'If it doesn't work out we can walk away, no fuss, no muss.' Sound familiar?"

The rental car horn blasted, startling Taylor, pushing her back.

"Jack," Ford said from the open passenger door. "Colette could be in a ditch somewhere."

"Taylor, I've got to go." Jack backed away. "And I'm not the one who said that—you did."

"Me? No way. Don't blame me for your lack of commitment. You said it, I remember, Jack."

"Just move the car, Tay. I don't have time for this." Jack slipped behind the rental wheel.

Taylor flashed with anger, hot tears pooling as she climbed into Granny's car and reversed out of the driveway. She whipped the Lincoln alongside the curb.

She did not say, "No fuss, no muss." She only repeated him.

Jack drove off, the beam of his red brake lights burning into her heart.

Stop!

She dropped her head against the Lincoln's headrest. If this he-said, she-said miscommunication foreshadowed their relationship, how was the news going to go down when she told him she was pregnant?

They had to either bail out of this boatload of misunderstandings or get determined about maneuvering and steering this tiny canoe that was their relationship.

. . .

COLETTE

She remembered the way to his house like she'd driven over yesterday. Still, she circled for a half hour before she gathered the courage to turn down Dunbar Street.

The house looked the same, but the neighborhood had changed, houses springing up and down the lane. Back in 1951, the Westbrooks were the only ones here. Spying the redbrick foursquare-style home with white porch columns, Colette turned in, tapping the brake as she eased the car alongside Jimmy's truck.

Cutting the engine, she checked her mascara and lipstick in the rearview mirror. Her youthful eyes were the result of a surgeon's blade. Nevertheless, she peered at a woman who was tired, sad, and approaching the last years of her life.

She'd intended on driving to Nashville, stopping only when she landed at the hotel. But when she turned off Chelsea, she knew she had to see Jimmy again. The notion pulsed through every part of her.

With a breath of courage, she stepped out of the car and into the laughter of the neighborhood children as they tussled and played. Colette watched them for a moment, listening to a sound that should've been from their children, hers and Jimmy's. Their grandchildren.

She started for the house, then stopped, her adrenaline surging so forcefully that she felt positively weak.

Deep breath. All she had to do was channel a little Vivica Spenser.

At the side kitchen door, gripping her wristlet and car keys, she knocked. But, mercy, was she prepared to face him?

She had no lines. No script. What would she say to him? He'd proposed marriage, for heaven's sake! And she'd walked out on him. After a second, she knocked again.

But from one breath to the next, she lost her nerve. *Just go.* Then the door swung open and Jimmy stood there as tall, square-shouldered, and handsome as ever.

"I don't know what came over me back there. I just—"

"What do you want, Colette?" He remained on the other side of the door.

"I don't know. I was heading back to Nashville, then I realized I had to see you."

"Well, you've seen me." He started to shut the door. Stubborn ole coot.

"You took me by surprise, Jimmy. What did you expect me to do? Throw my arms around you like a schoolgirl, giggle and say yes?" Her legs betrayed her and slowly she sank down to the concrete stoop. "When I heard you were selling the chapel, something snapped inside of me. I had to come. I had to come."

One heartbeat, two . . .

The creak of the screen door opening caused her to raise her head and look at him. "You don't have to let me in. I can go. I just want to say I'm sorry."

"For what?"

She glanced up at him. "Well, if that isn't the million-dollar question. Everything, I suppose."

"Colette," he said with a sigh. "Just come in."

She hesitated, but when he tipped his head toward the kitchen with a "Please," she stepped up.

Taking her hand, Jimmy led her inside and back in time. The place was lovely, remodeled and up-to-date, but so much the same.

"The fragrance . . . Jimmy—" She squeezed his hand. "It still smells of pine."

"Pine?" He laughed, lightly holding her elbow and escorting her to the kitchen table. "Been here so long I don't even notice."

"The place is lovely. You've kept it up."

"Kept me busy." He held out a chair for her at the table. "W-would you like some coffee?"

"That would be nice."

She watched him move efficiently about his bright kitchen, moving through the golden light falling through the window as he retrieved fine china cups from a top shelf.

She would've exchanged her Park Avenue penthouse for this place. In a moment.

"Are you well, Jimmy?"

He set a cup and spoon in front of her. "My doc says I'll live to be a hundred."

But he had closed the door he'd opened so wide to her at the chapel. Colette felt it. Saw it in his movements.

"I had a meeting in Nashville with FRESH Water." She shifted into actress and spokeswoman mode.

Confident, settled, and centered. "I'm their new spokes-woman."

Jimmy settled a china sugar bowl with a matching pitcher of cream on the table, then pulled out a chair for himself while the coffee brewed. "That what brought you back to these parts?"

"Yes . . . No." She held his gaze, framed with the lines and wisdom of time. "I used them as an excuse, really. I owe Jack an apology I suppose, but I wanted to see you. And the chapel."

"You didn't need an excuse to see me. Or that chapel."

"Sure I did. After all, you left me for no reason." There. She'd said it. Jimmy wasn't the only one with boldness in his old bones. And so she'd left him—

Jimmy reared back. "Come again, woman?"

"Last I knew you were going to boot camp and coming back to me. But—"

"And you were going to wait for me."

"I waited."

"You left. If anyone left anyone, it was you leaving me, Lettie."

"Well, that part is true, but only after you left me." Plus, she didn't have much choice. She couldn't . . . stay.

"Where you get that?"

"Listen to us. Can't even figure what went wrong between us and you've made a marriage proposal."

He shoved back from the table, returning with the carafe, filling their cups. In silence, they each sweetened and creamed their coffee, their spoons clattering against the sides of the cups.

"Well . . . acting. That had to be an exciting life." Jimmy sat forward, his big hands cupped around the tiny, delicate cup.

"What about you? Football hall of fame I hear." For decades she received copies of the Heart's Bend *Hometown News*.

He might have rejected her, but she felt she must watch over him, even from the concrete and glass of New York.

"Yeah, it was an honor to be named." He nodded, sipped his coffee, and stared across the room, then at her. Without wavering, he reached for her hand. "Guess I was a fool proposing back there today."

"No, no, it's fine. I shouldn't have walked out. I've been doing that a lot today."

He shifted in his chair, long lines fanning from the corners of his eyes, deepening. "I never thought I'd see you again, Colette. Then Keith came around wanting to sell the chapel for me and I figured, 'Why not?' It was nothing but a symbol of something that weren't never going to happen. But then you walked in, right through the morning light like an angel sent from heaven. I lost my head there for a moment. And you're right"—he hoisted his coffee cup to her—"it is your chapel. I built it for you."

"I did leave you, Jimmy." Colette stared into her cream-colored coffee, grateful to have found her courage. "But only after I got your letter."

"Letter? I wrote you hundreds. Especially that first year."

She furrowed her brow. "I only got one." But what did

it matter? She had a grand secret that would be worthy of him leaving her. "No. If you knew the whole story—"

"Colette, whatever you came to say, say it. I'm eighty-three years old, and if the good Lord allows, I'll live a long life. I don't care what you done, past or present, or why you left me. I want to be with you. I want the truth. The time for confusion is over."

"We're not kids anymore. I've a home, a life, in New York."

Jimmy waved her off. "No matter. I feel like a kid, and you look like one."

Now he was being silly. But she laughed anyway.

"I'll move," he said. "Put this place, the chapel, all the land on the market and move. I've nothing without you. No kin, no one to inherit. I've rattled around this old place all my life, moved in when I was two and never left. I still put up the Christmas tree in the same spot Dad did. I take the same road I took to work for forty-five years. I've got some money put by. Never had a mother and now I don't have a wife, and forgive me, Lettie, but this old dog wants to learn a new trick. I want to try living with a woman. You." He released her hand and sat back. "That night in the chapel? When we said our own vows and we—"

Mercy, he was making her blush. "Yes, I remember."

"I ain't been with another woman since."

Heavy tears washed her eyes. "No one?"

"Why? I was married to you . . . in my heart. But you ran off with Spice Keating."

"Because of your letter." The nail in the coffin. "That you'd changed your mind."

Jimmy laughed. "You're joking. Why would I write such a letter? Why would you even believe it?"

"It was in an envelope addressed to me. On the table by the door. The day you left for boot camp. I thought you left me a final love letter."

"I was going to, but after our last night together, I couldn't bring myself to say good-bye again."

They had not made love again but sat for hours in the Clemsons' living room promising to wait for each other, to write daily.

"What did I say in this letter again?"

"That you'd reconsidered. You didn't feel it was fair to make me wait. That I should move on. In fact, I still have it," Colette said.

Jimmy pushed away from the table. "Why would I write such a thing? And you received no other letters?"

"None."

"Did you write me? Telling me we were a mistake, that 'our night' should've never happened. That you were too young to settle for one man. The world was changing and the new decade offered women all kinds of possibilities."

"I never wrote such a letter, Jimmy." Colette felt punched. Mocked. And jerked about.

"Then we have a conundrum." He tugged open a kitchen drawer and retrieved a yellowish envelope. He slid the letter across the table. "If you didn't write this, who did?"

With a trembling hand, Colette slipped the single sheet with her smooth, angled handwriting, faded with time, across the page.

. . . was all a mistake. I realize that now, Jimmy. Please forgive me. Move on . . . I'm too young . . . Going away . . .

Colette stopped on the last line. The lettering changed, the pen slipping off the edge of the paper. When she was younger, she hated writing to the end of the page. It messed up her neat penmanship.

Colette whirled up out of her chair with a ping of understanding. "No, she wouldn't . . . she couldn't."

"She? Who, Colette? Do what?"

Thinking, pacing, Colette tried to unwind the last sixty-four years. "She couldn't have been that evil, that cruel." But she was so bitter and so skilled at . . . Colette regarded the letter, turning it over to see her signature. Peg! Oh, that Peg!

"Jimmy, I did not write this." She shoved the letter at him. "Look at the signature. I always signed with a curly *C*. This is a straight *C*. And I never wrote to the edge of the page."

Colette sank back into her chair, hand to her middle, regret and sadness brewing there. How could she have been so blind? So ruled by fear? "Peg did this."

"Peg?" Jimmy said.

"Yes, Peg. Now she's dead and I can't confront her." A thin, sharp pang started around the back of Colette's head. The one she had since she was a girl on the Morleys' farm. "Remember? She was very proud of her copying skills. Used them to entertain the kids when we first moved here. Even tricked the girls into thinking she'd had tea with Princesses Elizabeth and Margaret."

Jimmy made a face. "Seems I remember her copying

homework for someone or another, but why would she do this?" He waved the fake letter, then dropped it to the table. "I can't think of anything more cruel."

Colette met his gaze. "Exactly. Peg was that cruel. She wanted what she wanted and didn't care who she hurt. She wanted you, Jimmy."

"But she was seeing Drummond Branson when I left for boot."

"And married him a few months later, but if you'd have whistled, she'd have come running."

Jimmy ran his hand over his silver hair. "Well, now, that makes sense. She wrote me a few times, after I heard you'd took off with Spice, saying she'd wait for me, but I told her to find her a nice man in Heart's Bend. It was too painful to hear from her, so I stopped writing back. Might have told her I met a Korean gal, just to get her to stand down."

"Peg was a liar and manipulator." Colette shook her head. But was she really any better? She'd been lying to folks for over sixty years.

"Then she came to the chapel once after I got back from the war, saying she'd run off with me if I wanted. And with Drummond's child on her hip, no less. I steered clear for a long time. Though she was the closest thing in town to you, Lettie."

"I never knew she was so twisted inside." But secrets had a way of deforming a girl's heart. Darkening and shadowing her view of the world.

"So you went to New York with Spice because she forged letters to the both of us. Surely we'd have figured it out over time. But you ran off so quickly."

"I had to, Jimmy."

"Had to?"

Colette sighed. Six decades and the news was no easier than the day she found out. "When Peg came to see you? That wasn't Drummond's boy on her hip, Jimmy." Colette moved to the kitchen door, drawing in a fresh, cool breath. "That was your boy. Our boy." She glanced back at Jimmy. "I left because of the letter and because I was pregnant. Drummond Branson is your son."

. . .

JACK

Friday afternoon unfurled before Jack with long limbs of light as he drove Ford around Heart's Bend looking for Colette.

They'd driven to Nashville, but Colette wasn't at the hotel so Ford made him turn around.

Ford called Colette's phone every other minute and bordered on panic.

"Pick up your phone, Colette." To Jack he said, "Let's stop by her sister's grave. Or her aunt and uncle's old place. Or by *that man's* house, Jimmy. The coach."

Jack navigated Ford's request while navigating the white water of emotions roaring through him. He held on to the steering wheel, his jaw tense, his arms taut.

Rotten. Rotten timing. Returning to the house and

bounding up the stairs just as Taylor voiced her honest, uninhibited feelings to Emma.

I agree, eloping was a stupid idea.

Or hey, maybe he'd finally happened across some serendipity. Because now he knew. Taylor believed their marriage to be stupid. If Ford hadn't been in the car laying on the horn, he'd have duked it out with her.

But hey, this made his London decision easier. He'd make Hops happy. Perhaps this was all a blessing in disguise. He could put some space between himself and Taylor. And if she wanted out of their marriage, she could walk away. No fuss, no muss.

What a waste to have worried over the London decision. Or Doug Voss.

"Jack, slow down, there's her car." Ford rapped on the passenger window.

Jack slowed. Sure enough, the car formerly parked outside Granny's was in Coach's driveway. But he didn't turn in. Instead, he cruised on by.

"Jack, stop. Turn in. Please."

"You're not going in there."

"I most certainly am. And in the vernacular of kindergarteners, 'You're not the boss of me.'"

"And you're not the boss of me. Or Colette. And you're certainly not the driver of this car."

"I need to check on her. See if she's all right. Now I demand you pull over."

"If she's with Coach, she's fine. Leave her be. She must have something powerful on her mind to bug out of the FRESH meeting the way she did. If Coach built that chapel for her, then I bet they have a lot to say to one another."

Jack turned around at the cul-de-sac and headed back to the main road, Ford sulking in the passenger seat. In the rearview mirror, Jack caught the pastoral scene of Coach's lawn and for a second he yearned.

He'd always wanted a place out this way, to raise a family. To create something he never had as a kid.

But it was all vanity. From now on, marriage and family would be something he admired from a distance, like a fine painting.

"I demand you pull over and let me out," Ford said.

"Leave her be." He'd fight for Coach and Colette, if not for himself.

"Jack—"

Rolling through the stop sign, Jack turned right and gunned the gas toward Heart's Bend proper.

His last thought boomeranged in his head. Why not fight for *his* marriage? Fight for himself?

He was letting his father, and every sour foster family experience he'd ever endured, control his life. Wasn't it time he became the man he wanted to be? Put his past behind him?

"Jack, I can't just leave her," Ford said.

"Tell you what, there's a charming inn you'd love. A restored plantation home that has the best cooking this side of the Mississippi. I'll drop you off—"

"Nothing doing. I won't be stranded without a car."

"Fine, then you drop me off."

"Where? What are you going to do?"

"I'm going to fight for something."

"The FRESH account? Don't worry about them. I can smooth that over."

"*I'll* smooth it over with them. This campaign will be a big hit. But for now, I've got something else to do."

The more he contemplated it, the more his spirit unlocked. He was going to go all-out for love like he did for advertising. For his job at 105. For the FRESH account.

Jack pulled up to the Fry Hut, shifted into park, and stepped out. "The inn is just down First Avenue," he instructed Ford. "All the way to the end. You can't miss it."

"What are you doing?" Ford scrambled out of the passenger seat, quick-stepping around to the driver's side. "Where will you be?"

"Fixing stuff." As he passed by, Jack gripped Ford's arm. "Don't go to Coach's. Give them time. Text Colette to tell her where you are, then go to the inn dining room and have a nice dinner. The back veranda overlooks the Cumberland River. It's storybook material."

"I suppose she can call if she needs me." Getting behind the wheel, Ford powered down his window and hung out his elbow. "Why do you care so much, Jack?"

He gazed at the Fry Hut, then over his shoulder toward Chelsea Avenue. "Because I might be starting to believe in second chances."

. . .

JIMMY

"Drummond Branson is my son?"

"Yes, conceived that night in the chapel."

"So you ran off without telling me?"

"You were in the army, and as far as I knew, done with me. I was scared, Jimmy. Embarrassed. How could I display my shame all over Heart's Bend? It's not the man who wears the scarlet letter but the woman. I couldn't do it to Aunt Jean and Uncle Fred."

"Why didn't you write to me? Dad would've taken you in, Lettie. I know he would've."

"I wanted to write to you, but Peg convinced me you'd only be with me for the baby. She said I couldn't tell you I was pregnant when you couldn't do anything about it. I told her we'd said our vows that night and she reminded me they were not binding. She reminded me of your letter and—" Colette shook her head. "I was ashamed, scared, and confused. By the time I knew I was pregnant, three months later, I'd not heard another word from you. Spice was heading to New York, so I went with him. His cousin had a job in television and he thought we could find work there. I imagined being an assistant or a secretary. Never in my wildest dreams did I imagine she'd send me on auditions. Jimmy, I had to go. A town scandal would've killed Aunt Jean right where she stood."

"I know, but . . ." He wrestled to understand, hearing her pain but not feeling it. But she was right. An unwed woman, in the eyes of 1950s society, brought shame on the family. He also knew that while their vows had been sincere, they'd not bound them publicly.

"Did Spice know? About my child?"

"I had to tell him. I was so sick on the drive to New York. He helped me hide it for a few months. I even hid it while I had a six-week job on *Love of Life,* but when I was seven months, I just popped. Couldn't hide any longer."

Her voice faded. She looked tired, beat up. Sixty years felt like a moment ago, her shame was so rich and real.

"Why didn't you marry him?"

"Because he also had a secret." Colette lifted her gaze to his.

"What secret?"

"I think you know."

Jimmy coughed. "So all that skirt chasing was a ruse?"

"Yes, so you see, we had equal shame to conceal. Of course today, those issues aren't so scandalous."

"It still weren't right for me not to know, Colette. I can't believe you'd not demand I step up and do my duty as a father, no matter what I said in a letter. Didn't you know me at all?"

"All reason was out the window. If I'd considered a way to let you know, those notions left when I went to New York."

"Well, do tell. How in the world did your sister end up with my boy?" The sharpness in his voice could not be helped.

Tears glistened in Colette's eyes.

"I tried to keep him, but there were no single moms

in New York or day care or help of any kind. I wondered, deep down, if when you came home you might accept us. If not me, then him."

"You know I would, Lettie."

She gazed toward the door. "He was born in the Salvation Army Booth House. I told them I was going home, so they let me leave with him. I didn't investigate adoption. I'd fooled myself into believing I could raise him on my own. But one week after bringing him back to my flat, I couldn't manage anything but crying. Even if you knew, even if you sent your entire army salary, I could not have managed on my own." The tone of her memory filled Jimmy with loneliness. "I wore a cheap wedding band, told people my husband was at war, but I was sinking so fast."

"Colette . . ."

"I couldn't get a job because I had no one to watch him. My flatmates were done with me and my little crying chap. My hands were red from washing nappies in the toilet."

He ran his hand over his face, along his jaw, the sheen in his eyes thick and spilling over. "Dad would've helped you."

"And how was I to know? Even if he agreed to help, was I to go around Heart's Bend with your bastard child? Ruin his reputation before he even had a chance?"

As she spoke, his understanding grew. He didn't like it, but he understood. "So you gave him to Peg?"

"Yes. Because I had nowhere else to go."

. . .

COLETTE

NOVEMBER 1951

HEART'S BEND

For more than an hour, she sat in Spice's truck, the engine rattling, heat blasting in spurts from the chrome vents. She held one hand on the door handle, the other on baby James's belly, sensing his heartbeat through the tips of her fingers. He'd cried these last two hours of the trip from New York. Wanting his dinner, not understanding why his mother made him wait. He was hungry, as was she.

But Colette had no choice. With only two cans of Similac remaining, she had to be wise. She would save one for tonight and one for the morning. Until the market opened.

But that would not be her concern, now, would it?

She'd stopped at a petrol station just north of Heart's Bend to prepare her little man for his adventure. In the loo, she'd changed his nappy, put on his best outfit, and wetted her fingers and smoothed his fine baby hair.

"You're going on an adventure, my darling. Mamá knows it will be marvelous for you. You'll be safe and dry, warm and fed." He watched her with wide eyes, kicking his feet. "I know that makes you happy. Dinner."

The nurse at the Booth House had showed her how

to bind her breasts to keep her milk from coming in, but how she ached every time James cried. Oh, what she would give now to nurse him until his belly popped round and full!

Perched on the toilet, she cradled him against her, rocked him from side to side, singing him her last song.

"Mamá will miss you, sweet boy / but don't you cry, it'll be all right / you'll have a warm bed tonight."

Colette's tears spilled down her dry cheeks. She was tired and weary, at her wit's end. She had never felt more alone.

James fussed, squirming against his tight blanket, his small cry like a kitten's mew. She loosened the wrap and kissed his tiny cheek.

"I've failed you, baby James. I've failed you." Colette's tears anointed her son's face.

Someone rattled at the door. "Anyone in there?"

"Yes, I'll be just a moment." Colette stood, legs trembling, shivering to her backbone. The room's block walls and bare white bulb brought no warmth at all.

But it wasn't the cold that bit through her and sank into her bones; it was the knowledge of what she was about to do.

She caught her reflection in the bathroom mirror. She looked tired and gaunt, a gray hue to her pale skin. She must work to eat, but there was no work for a single girl with a baby.

Exiting the small space, she smiled at the woman who waited with her little girl. "Sorry . . ."

"No worry, I see you've got a little'un. They're so

sweet, ain't they?" She bent for a peek at James. "He's a runt, now, ain't he. Well, never you mind, he'll fatten up when you feed him more."

Back in the cab of the truck, Colette exhaled, panic trapping her against the seat. She was starving her child. Wouldn't Peg have something to say about his gaunt wee cheeks? He was so thin and small, even for being only three weeks old.

Colette fired up the engine and moved the heat sliders to high. In the light of the dash, she peeled back James's blanket and looked at him, really looked. He was so frail.

Hands shaking, she fixed up the last can of Similac and took James in her arms. On his last night with her, he would feast like a little prince.

James winced at the cold formula, then suckled on the bottle with loud, slurping, hungry noises. The formula was gone in no time. Settling him back in the linen basket on the passenger side, Colette shifted into first, the gears grinding.

The road's rhythms and a full stomach rocked him to sleep for the final leg of the journey.

When Colette pulled the truck up outside Peg's house, the one she shared with Drummond, she wasn't sure how to execute her plan.

The small house glowed with lamplight and seemed to beckon Colette inside. Say what she would about Peg, she was not the one who had a baby out of wedlock.

Lord, please, for James, let Drummond and Peg be agreeable.

Hand on the door release, Colette faltered, sobbing. She couldn't . . . couldn't.

In the basket, James awoke and fussed, and her reality came into focus. She had no money. No job. No food for her child. Keeping him was only for herself, to ease her pain.

Looking through the streetlights, she peered toward Peg's home. "Come," she whispered to James. "It's warm and cozy at Aunt Peg's."

Then she caught sight of her sister passing by the window, taking up a magazine and sitting on the sofa. Drummond followed, a cigarette in one hand, the newspaper in the other.

"'Tis our cue, darling." Colette drew in a long, shaky breath. "Peg, if you love me at all . . . For Mamá and Papá."

Scooping James from the basket, Colette cradled him against her one last time, unable to stop the tears and her lips from pressing against his soft cheeks. She wanted to remember how sweet he tasted, how innocent he smelled.

"I'll never stop loving you."

Stepping out of the truck, Colette crossed the quiet, tree-lined street, the November chill about her legs as she marched toward the light, an eerie calm gripping her.

Ringing the doorbell, she stepped back, her maternal heart exploding, sending shards of love into every part of her being. She couldn't. She *just* couldn't.

Wheeling about, she aimed for the steps as Peg called her name.

"Colette?"

She turned round. "Hello, Peg."

"What are you doing here?" Peg stepped through the doorway wearing a smart housedress and a string of pearls about her neck. "Is that—"

"Baby James. He's three weeks old."

"Peg?" Drummond Branson appeared in the door, his imposing physique filling the frame and dimming the warm light. "What are you doing out here in the cold?"

"It's my sister, love."

"Colette? Well, haven't you been a stranger. Come in, it's cold out." He shoved open the screen.

"Drum, give us a moment, please?" Peg said.

"All right, but—" He paused. "Is that a *baby*?"

"Love," Peg sighed. "A moment? Please."

Drummond hesitated, then withdrew, leaving the door slightly ajar so a sliver of light fell across Colette's boots.

"I can't manage, Peg." Tears soaked Colette's confession. "I've no money because I can't work. My flatmates are weary of me. I've not slept—"

"So, what do you want? Money? I'll not just give you money."

"I don't want money." With one large draw on her shallow courage, Colette jutted forward, shoving James in her sister's arms.

"Take him. Raise him as your own."

"What?" Peg reached for the baby, clutching him close, fumbling with his loose blankets. "You can't be serious." The tenderness in her voice melted Colette.

"I can't take care of him," Colette cried. "I can't . . . Please, take him. Be good to him."

James squirmed, his small cry touching Colette so she nearly collapsed to the porch boards, her heart breaking, breaking, breaking . . .

"Well, I should have known it would come to this—"

Colette rose up. "I've no choice. Peg, do you hear me? He needs a family." She ran her hand over her tears, wiping her nose with the edge of her sleeve. "H-he likes to sleep on his back. But don't wrap him up tight—he likes to kick." Her voice faltered and she pressed her fingers to her eyes. *Please stop weeping.* "Feed him Similac, warm. He doesn't like it cold. One can every four hours, maybe more if he won't settle down. He's a good eater, this chap. He won't cry about a dirty nappy unless he's really in a mess. He likes singing . . . I-I sing to him every night."

"Colette, do you know what you're doing?"

"No, Peg, but I'm doing it." She turned to go.

"Colette, wait. I-I must tell you something."

Colette glanced back at Peg. "What could you possibly have to say?"

The front door opened again. "I know it's been awhile, but you two girls ought to come inside—Peg? Colette? What's going on?"

"Meet our son, Drummond." Peg eased the baby into her husband's arms. He fumbled, trying to hold him with care, his expression a mix of surprise and wonder. He looked toward Colette. "Yours?"

She nodded.

"Who's the father?"

"A chap you don't know, Drummond." Colette shot Peg a glance, silencing her. This was Colette's decision, and for once, Peg *would* do things her way. "I thought we were in love, but it turns out I was mistaken."

"And you're bringing him to Peg and me?"

"If you'll have him."

"Drum, we will, won't we? Please? You know how much I want a baby and we've not—"

"Colette." Six years older than Peg, Drummond was a seasoned businessman, and he sounded like one now. "If you do this, it's done. You hear me? This will be our boy and not another word will be said. Ever." Drummond's big bass commanded Colette.

"I understand." The inflation of it rocked Colette's façade. "And you must be a good father and mother to him."

"I'll need his birth certificate," Drummond said. "I've a college classmate who's a lawyer. He can do this up proper and legal like." The smoke from Drummond's cigarette curled through the cold air.

"Drum." Colette reached for the burning tobacco. "Cigarette smoke makes him cough." One of her flat-mates smoked like a chimney, always setting off James.

"No more smoking in the house, Drum," Peg said. "That's final."

Colette retrieved a folded document from her coat pocket. "Here's his birth certificate."

Drummond reached for it, handing the baby back to Peg. He glanced at Colette, his expression inquiring. "The baby's name is James?"

"I think it's best you stay away," Peg said as Drummond continued to read the certificate in the porch light. "We'll tell folks we adopted him from friends out of town."

"But I might want to see him."

"Then what? Break down? Want to take him back?" Peg stepped into Colette, her voice low, driving like a spear. "If we take him, you will not come back, you hear me? He will be our son. You will never, ever tell Jimmy."

Colette jerked with each word, hot tears creeping down her cheeks. "But, Peg, I can't just—"

"You can and you will. You go on back to New York and make whatever life you can for yourself. Leave us and the boy be. Swear it or so help me, I'll hand him right back to you."

"Can't I come for Christmas?"

"No."

Colette imploded, the sobs forcing her against the porch post, cracking her very being apart.

"Peg, take it easy. She's a kid," Drum said.

"Drum, pardon us a moment." Peg hooked her arm about Colette, leading her to side porch. "Just consider this the first unselfish thing you've ever done. James will have a good life with us."

"I'm so sorry, Peg, so sorry. I've ruined everything."

"Just promise me, Colette. You will stay away."

"What about Aunt Jean and Uncle Fred?"

"Write a letter, just tell them how busy you are . . ."

"Peg, you're asking too much."

James squirmed in Peg's arms, his tiny arm shoving out from under the blanket.

"Then are you prepared to leave with him? Go back the way you came?"

Colette wept, brushing her hand over James's head. This was her last moment with him as his mamá. Her last with Peg.

In stony silence, she retrieved James's basket from the truck and set it at Peg's feet. "There's a fuzzy bunny in here. I put it next to him at night. He has a few clothes and diapers, but you'll need more, much more. And this is the last bottle of formula. I don't know how you'll get through the night. He'll cry at two and—"

"Drummond's sister has a two-month-old. I'll run round to her place and get a few cans until the market opens."

"Good, he'll have a cousin to play with." Really, she must get on or she'd never leave at all.

"You're doing the right thing, Colette."

"Then why do I feel so empty?"

Drum appeared at the door, something in his hand. He passed it to Peg with a nod toward Colette.

Peg opened her hand to reveal a wad of bills.

Colette shoved them back. "I can't. No."

"For your trip home," Peg coaxed her. "Stay in a hotel. Have a nice meal. Do something with your hair. What a sight."

"I won't take your money, Peg. Not now, when I'm handing over my son. I want no implication now or ever that I *sold* him to you."

"All right, then." Peg leaned toward Colette's ear. "I'll take good care of Jimmy's boy. Because you know I love him."

"You're married to Drum, Peg. Don't be a fool."

Colette jammed her hands in her pockets and walked back to the truck, a blend of fury and sorrow brewing. She slipped behind the wheel and fired up the engine, exhaling one sob after another, her cries raging against the cold windshield.

But when she drove away, she dried her eyes and never looked back. Not once.

CHAPTER TWENTY-FIVE

TAYLOR

When she opened the front door Friday evening, she found Jack on the other side with Fry Hut bags in hand and a carrier of what appeared to be chocolate shakes.

She shoved the screen door open and stepped out. "Jack, I'm sorry—"

"No, Taylor, forget it."

"How can I forget it? You heard me say our elopement was stupid."

"Can we go for a ride in your granny's car?" He tipped his head toward the Lincoln. "Ford has the rental."

"Did you find Colette?"

"Sort of. She's at Coach's. Ford wanted to go in, but—"

"Oh no, those two needed to talk."

"That's what I said. So, what happened at the chapel?"

"I'm not sure. The real estate guy, Keith, was there with some buyers, but Dad showed up all hot about some development plans. Looks like Keith was lying to Coach. Then I brought Colette in, this big brouhaha started, and then Coach ordered everyone out. About five minutes later, Colette came steaming out of the chapel. She didn't say a word on the way home."

"There's more to this story, then." Jack offered up the Fry Hut bags. "What do you say? A ride in the Lincoln and a picnic?"

"Yeah, okay." Taylor went for the car keys. Whatever Jack was doing with his French fry peace offering, she liked it. And now that she knew her queasiness was from pregnancy, not Fry Hut fries, she was ready to go another round.

Fry Hut fries must remain associated with . . . with love. With Jack.

They walked to the car in silence, then Jack handed over the food. "Mind if I drive?"

"Suit yourself." She tossed him the keys.

"You can choose the radio station." Jack held the passenger door for her.

"Is that your sense of compromise?"

"For now." He winked, sending a warm flutter through her.

Okay, Jack Forester, she thought, *what are you up to?* With one eye on her man, still rocking his dress shirt and slacks, his tie riding at half-mast, she slid into the passenger seat.

Had he forgiven her? One aspect of their lousy communication was that they didn't fight much, so she didn't know the drill for arguments and their aftermath. Was this his way of saying sorry?

As he backed down the drive, she tuned the radio to country. After setting the volume on low, she settled back, cradling the food in her lap.

"Jack, I'm sorry you had to hear—"

He flashed his palm. "It can wait. We got to get where we're going or the fries will be cold. They're already cooling off since I walked here from the Hut."

"But I need to tell you something—"

"Taylor." He peered over at her. "I'm asking. Can it wait?"

"All right." She nestled against the smooth leather seat, raising her face to the early-evening breeze, the scent of fall and firewood in the current. "Can you at least tell me where we're going?"

"You'll see." Jack drummed his thumbs against the big round steering wheel. His broad smile and sincere, *real* twinkle in his eye stirred Taylor. She wanted to scoot over next to him and ride through town with his arm around her, kissing at the stop signs and red lights. Heart's Bend only had five, but that had still made for some good kissing.

She wanted to be his oasis. Where he came to rest, to be satisfied.

But she carried within her news that could change everything. For better or worse, she didn't know.

"I-I'm glad you're here." She wanted to start speaking her heart. To quit hiding behind fear.

When he looked at her, she caught the twinkle in his eye and sparked, feeling rewarded for her truth.

At the end of First Avenue, Jack turned left toward the football bleachers, the old car rocking in the ruts of a dusty road. He parked under a citadel of trees and upped the volume of the radio.

"Come on." He ushered her into the backseat, then

settled in next to her, stretching out his legs. "Got to love these big old cars." He held out his hand, palm up. "Fry me."

"Fry you?" Taylor handed him a bag of fries and a corresponding milk shake, grateful it was evening and her appetite was strong.

"Thank you, and oh, here . . . salt." Jack dug the packets from his shirt pocket.

For a long time, they just ate, enjoying the hot fries, sweet shakes, and the shift of the afternoon light toward evening.

Then Jack sat forward. "I have a job offer. In London."

"Excuse me?"

"One of our clients, WhiteWater Media, started a foundation there and Hops wants me to head it up."

"As in move to London?"

"As in yes. Look, Tay, I know this is out of the blue. I turned it down initially—"

"Without talking to me first?"

"I didn't think you'd want to go. So I told Hops no. You were just getting your business off the ground in New York. A move to London would kill your momentum. Starting over in a new city is one thing, but starting over in a new country . . ." He removed the lid from his shake and took a man-sized gulp. "Was I wrong?"

"No, but you don't get to be the only one who sacrifices. What if I was willing to give up my career for you?"

He grinned. "I'm not giving up my career by saying 'No.' Don't make me sound like a hero."

"But you are, kind of, by refusing your boss." Taylor

tore open a ketchup packet. "Did I tell you we found dozens of these in the glove box?"

"No . . ." Jack scooted toward her. "Are you saying you want to go to London?"

She dipped a salty fry in the ketchup. "Not if our commitment is only as thick as 'no fuss, no muss.'" Taylor shoved the fry in her mouth. "Jack, why did you tell me, 'If it doesn't work out we can walk away,' right before our wedding?"

"I never said that—you did."

"Jack, forgive me, but those were your *exact* words. I remember because you took my hand just as we started walking down to the beach."

"Funny, because I remember the *exact* moment you said it. Just as we started down to the beach."

"Exactly when *you* said it."

He swore, laughing to himself. "Why would I say that when I was the one who proposed?"

"Why would *I* say it since I'm the one who said yes?"

"To have a back door. A way out if things didn't go well."

"How you figure that?" Taylor folded the top of her French fry bag. This conversation had killed her appetite.

"Doug Voss."

She slapped her hand over her eyes. "Please, Jack, not Doug Voss again."

"Taylor, he texted you a dozen times inviting you to sneak off to LA with him. You were just out of a relationship with him when we met. We happened so fast maybe you do have lingering feelings for him. You never really told me what happened between you two."

Well, he was dealing the cards. She might as well pick up and start playing. "I lived with him for two months when I first moved to New York."

"I see."

"I'm not proud of it, but there you go. The whole truth."

"Why'd you move out?"

She picked at the hem of her shorts. The weather was almost too cool in the evening anymore for shorts. "Because . . ."

"Well, it couldn't have been me because we hadn't run into each other yet."

"No, I moved out long before I met you."

"What happened?"

"I don't want to say."

"Taylor, did he abuse you? Hurt you?"

"No, he's an egomaniac, but he's not a monster." She peeked at her husband. "If I tell you you'll think I'm crazy."

"What if I already think you're crazy?"

She popped his shoulder with the back of her hand. "Fine." Taylor adjusted in the seat, turning to Jack, pressing her back against the side of the car. "When I was with Doug I couldn't hear God's heartbeat anymore. There. You happy?"

"What?"

"I couldn't hear God's heart anymore. I know, weird, right? But ever since I was a kid, when I prayed or just sat and thought about God, I'd hear this faint, distant, maybe-I'm-all-wet-here heartbeat. And I'd feel this whoosh of love." She stared toward the empty football field. Friday night . . . the team must be playing an away game. "I never wanted to leave those moments. When I moved to LA and got caught up with life there, stopped praying, meditating on God, the heartbeats faded. I didn't really notice. I met Doug, moved to New York, and one day I realized something was missing from my life. I felt cold and empty, all shriveled and small on the inside. Spiritually anorexic. And I missed my heartbeats."

"Why didn't you ever tell me you were spiritual?"

"Why didn't you ask? Weren't you the Christian boy in high school?"

"Sometimes."

"Jack." Taylor tapped the cold side of her milk shake against her leg. "We can debate if we think marriage is a worthwhile endeavor—Lord knows my family track record is an argument against it—but I'd never cheat on you. I'd leave you first."

"Going to LA with Voss looked a lot like leaving."

"You really think so little of me? You think I'd just sneak off? Look, if I wanted to be with Doug, I'd be with him. I don't have time to play games. I've seen that side of marriage, and no thank you."

"Seen that side from who?"

"My father for one. Emma's husband for two."

"Your dad?" Jack's surprise softened her defenses. "I always thought he was a stand-up guy."

"He's not. When I was fifteen I caught him with another woman."

"Taylor, babe, really? I'm sorry. At least I knew my dad was a jerk from the get-go."

After that slight opening, she took a chance and recounted her photography class assignment and how she planned to surprise her dad for her candid shot. Instead, he had shocked her and rocked her world.

"I jumped from behind the door to snap a candid shot of him and he was kissing Ardell."

"Did he see you?"

"No, thank goodness. Dad's office was long and dark in the corners. I snuck around the door while he was locked with Ardell. He and Mom got divorced the next year. He married Ardell a year later."

"Don't take this wrong, but at least you had a dad. He didn't leave you. Deny you."

"Jack, I know your growing up was rough, but let's not play worst-dad Olympics. There're no winners."

"Did your dad look you in the eye when you were nine years old, just after your mom died, and say, with the coldest voice you'd ever heard, that you were not his child?"

"No . . . Jack, he actually said that, out loud?"

"To my freckled face."

"Okay, I was wrong, you win the gold medal. Babe, I'm so sorry . . ."

"Can I give the prize back? I'd have rather had a dad." Jack ducked his head forward, running his hand along the back of his neck. "When your dad outright rejects you, it's like scaling Mount Everest to come back. Your dad might have rejected the marriage, but he didn't reject *you*. He loved you."

Taylor sat up straight, Jack's truth twisting in her gut. Daddy didn't reject her, but she had rejected him. She grappled with the guilt of the realization.

She peeked at Jack. For all his flaws, he was a truth talker. "I guess I've let that day impact my view of life more than I imagined."

"We all do it, Taylor."

"Have you tried talking to your dad?"

He shook his head. "Not since Sam Gillingham mediated a meeting between us when I was seventeen. Should've known it would go bad when he showed up an hour late. Bad men produce bad fruit." He sat back, running his hands down his pressed slacks. His rolled-up shirtsleeves revealed the strength in his arms. "It's why I never want kids. I don't want to be like him. I don't know what baggage I carry around from being raised in ten foster homes. So I'm not passing it along to another generation."

Taylor felt all of her light fade. "Never? B-but you turned out, Jack. And it wouldn't be the same with you . . . you're not your father."

"No, true, but I'm a whole heap of what I experience in life because of him. Like it or not, I share his DNA. You know, I get this knot in my gut when I come to Heart's Bend because I'm nervous I'll run into him. It's like you said, I live with a ghost. One that haunts me. I so don't want to be like him I'm afraid to even think about kids." He winced. "I guess I never confessed that before."

"No, no, you haven't." She had no words as she glanced into the wind to dry her tears. Poor wee babe inside.

But the moment did something for Taylor. She wanted this baby, and the reality of its growing life inside her spread to the furthest ends of her being.

"Can't say my mom did a bang-up job before she died either, but she tried," Jack muttered more to himself than to Taylor. "And she loved me. But I will say the Gillinghams were good to me. They were the closest thing I ever had to a family. But I was fifteen when I moved in with them. I went to college three years later."

"Can I ask you something, Jack?"

He came back from his musings and fixed on her, the twinkle gone from his eyes.

"Are we going to make it? Did we think our marriage was forever? I've never seen one work, Jack. Not my grandparents', my parents', my sister's. Emma and Javier were supposed to be soul mates. Didn't last ten years. So if London is your dream—"

"Hops gave me some marriage advice."

"Can't wait to hear this."

"He said if working late was sexier than going home to my new wife, then maybe our relationship had run its course." He was watching her carefully as he talked. She was suddenly aware of her hands and legs, remembering the light dusting of freckles on her cheeks and nose that Jack said he loved on their wedding night. "Said I should cut you loose."

"Like a horse from the herd? Nice, Hops. So do you agree? Have we run our course?" When they eloped they'd started something. Taylor just wasn't sure they'd ever committed to finishing the race. "You'd rather work than come home to your wife?"

"No . . . I just thought we were building our careers. Wh-what do you think? Did we rush things when we eloped?" Jack smoothed his hand along his jaw. "And, Taylor, one last time and I'll never mention it again. You have no feelings for Voss?"

She raised up on one knee and grabbed his face in her hands. "I. Have. No. Feelings. For. Voss."

"Okay," he said, low, tentative. "End of Voss."

"But did we rush things when we eloped?" Taylor said. "Probably."

"What about that heartbeat thing? I mean, have you heard it since, you know, you left *him*? Since you married me?"

"I hadn't. Until a week ago. When I took the pictures at the chapel. That's why I had to get involved. I felt the heart of that place, like something was alive. I couldn't let Coach sell it. So I went to Daddy for help." She laughed at the sound of her description. "I'm cray-cray, right?"

"Not at all. What'd you hear at the chapel?"

"This *whoosh-thump*. Like a heartbeat under a stethoscope and magnified."

"Then what's God saying to you?"

She regarded him for a moment. "Now, that's a good question. I've not really thought to ask Him."

Jack set aside his fry bag and shake and pulled himself up, jumping from the car. He offered Taylor his hand. "Come on."

Taylor stopped for her shake and his, passed them to him, then hopped out of the car. "Where are we going?"

"To think."

Taylor jogged alongside him. It felt good to stretch, move, be in rhythm with him.

At the bleachers, Jack climbed to the top and faced the empty field. "Wonder where we're playing away tonight."

Taylor sat down next to him and shook the dew from her melting shake. "Lipscomb, I think."

"Were you there when my band played at that big bonfire my senior year? Our stage was right over there." Jack raised his shake toward a spot near the end zone.

"The Sonics! You guys were good."

"Good?" Jack sat back, putting his arms on the bench behind him. "We were horrible. Just horrible."

She laughed, taking another sip of chocolate goodness. "True, but the drummer was really *hot.*"

He grinned and kicked at her with his foot. "That's about all I brought to the table. My extreme hotness."

"You all were like this weird blend of rock-country-Christian."

"I'd be in jail if I hadn't become a drummer."

"Really?" Taylor sat back, loving this moment where he talked, like in the beginning, when they met in Manhattan. They talked of work, politics, news, where they wanted to be in ten years. Always the future and never the past.

So she enjoyed this reminiscing river.

"I was a really angry kid. Ticked off at the world, at the universe. Why did my mom die, the only parent who cared about me? What did I do to deserve a crappy life, going from foster family to foster family? One of the last families I lived with before moving in with the

Gillinghams had six kids. They all played an instrument. So when I moved in at fourteen, the dad handed me a set of drumsticks."

"He just threw you in? Sink or swim?"

"Pretty much." Jack sipped from his shake, dew running down the sides and dripping onto the bleachers. "I was horrible. The oldest boy, Simon, was a savant with instruments. He could play anything after hearing it once. Simon said, 'You look angry. You'll make a great drummer.' So he taught me and for the first time since Mom died, I felt like I belonged. I came home from school every day and practiced, sometimes until my hands bled."

Taylor loved the gentle flow of this moment. "So, ha, you lived with the Partridge Family?"

"Yeah, something like that." He glanced at her. "'I think I love you, so what am I so afraid of?' That's how their song went, right?"

The lyrics settled quietly on her heart. Sounded like *their* song. *I think I love you.*

"Just when I was getting good, falling into a rhythm, no pun intended, the dad transferred to a different job. They moved to Oregon or Washington, someplace far west. The state wouldn't let me go with them, so guess who got a new family. But deep down I don't think they wanted me to go."

"So you moved in then with the Gillinghams?"

"*Nooooooo*, I went from living with the Partridge Family–slash–Brady Bunch to living with the Monsters-slash–House of Horrors. Sex, drugs, and rock 'n roll, the works. Don't ask me how they got approved in the foster system. Remember Bobby Eastman?"

Her eyes widened. "Oh, wow, you lived with the Eastmans?"

"Yep. Bobby started offering me pot, coke, this pill, that pill, and bullying me into stealing from his parents. But I hated that place so much I joined the high school band just to stay away as long as possible. I never left school before six o'clock, even later if I could. Sometimes Stuart Greaves would invite me over for dinner and his mom always insisted I just spend the night. The first new pair of shoes I ever had came from them."

"First new? Ever?"

"I guess that explains my shoe obsession. And why I like new things."

"Jack, babe." Taylor scooted closer to him, brushing her hand over his shoulder.

"I was fifteen before I had a brand-new anything. Mrs. Greaves . . . she was a good lady. Bought me shoes, a couple pairs of jeans, and some shirts." His voice faded. "Fed me so I didn't have to eat from Dumpsters."

"No, you didn't."

He peered at her. "I don't like to talk about it because it makes me seem pitiful."

She linked her arm through his. "It makes you seem heroic. You survived. You overcame. Look at you, an ad exec in New York City for one of the best firms in the country. With a job offer in London to boot."

"Sometimes all I see is that unwanted kid who ate from a Dumpster."

"There's your ghost, then. It's not your dad at all. It's how you see yourself, Jack. You're not a failure, you're a survivor. And look what you've done with your life."

The shadows lengthened and the conversation fell silent as Taylor tried to picture sweet, handsome, fifteen-year-old Jack Dumpster diving.

"I'm glad you became a drummer," she said after a moment.

"Me too. Or we'd be having this dinner at the state penitentiary."

Or worse . . . She peered up at him. Not having it at all.

"Taylor?" Jack slipped an arm around her, drawing her close. "Have we taken this relationship as far as it can go?"

"You tell me. You're the one with the *sexy* office."

He laughed, lightly touching her chin, raising her face to his. "The only thing that's sexy in my life is you." His kiss encompassed her and disarmed her fears, stirring all of the stars and, if possible, bringing the Milky Way down to earth.

She clung to him, wanting him, yearning to feel beneath his chest, to *feel* his heart. When he pulled her onto his lap, she wrapped herself around him.

When the kiss faded, she pressed her forehead to his. "I never said if we don't work out we could walk away."

"Neither did I."

"Then how come we both heard it?"

"Maybe fear had a voice that day?" Jack slipped his hands around her waist and pulled her close. "Maybe

I said it and don't remember. But the truth is"—he paused for a long inhale—"I want us to work."

"We have some hurdles." Taylor smoothed her hands over his broad shoulders. But they were strong enough to carry her burdens. And she was willing to bear his.

"Taylor." His breathing deepened and his lips found hers. "I'm not good at telling you how I feel. I never grew up with a good exchange of emotions. Ask Sam and Sarah Gillingham."

"Okay, then just tell me one thing about how you feel, Jack. It doesn't have to be perfect or pretty, just true." She hungered, thirsted, for intimacy from his heart. He'd said so little in the six months they'd been man and wife.

"I want to, but the words get stuck and—"

"Do I matter to you? Do you care?"

"So much it hurts, Taylor." He brushed his hand over her hair, his warm breath scented with chocolate and Fry Hut fries. "When I think of how much I love you, it hurts. Corny, right? An eighties love song. Sometimes, if I imagine you and me ending, I can't think straight and my heart gets all fluttery."

"There, Jack, you're telling me how you feel."

In the distance, a dove cooed and the crickets sang their evening song. Taylor floated away on the wind of Jack's confession, her heart humming a melody of its own.

She wanted to trust love. Trust that the heartbeat of God was for them, not against them. All they had to do was surrender every one of their fears.

Turning to Jack, Taylor slipped her hands into his. "Babe, I have some news."

"Good or bad?"

"Good, I think. Shocking."

"Yeah? What?"

Taylor peered straight into his twinkling eyes. "I'm pregnant, Jack. I'm pregnant."

CHAPTER TWENTY-SIX

JACK

Stripped down to his slacks, he threw punches at the heavy bag swinging from the top of Sam Gillingham's detached garage.

Jab, cross, hook, upper cut. Followed by a round-house kick, sending the bag against the workbench.

Jab, cross, hook, upper cut . . .

Taylor's confession echoed through him. *"I'm pregnant."*

Jab-jab. Cross, hook, upper cut . . .

Okay, pregnant. Parenthood. Being a father. He could do this, right?

A memory flashed of when he was nine, right after his mama died and Rise dropped him off at the Martins', friends of his mama's.

"This is where you live now."

"But I want to live with you."

"Jack, you can't, you just can't."

Right cross, jab . . .

Bouncing from side to side, Jack worked the bag, punching and kicking each painful memory.

Jab, cross . . .

Freedom. He so craved freedom. But in the moment, Jack wondered if he'd ever be free.

With a yell, he hammered the bag over and over, finally falling back, exhausted.

Dropping to the old stool at the workbench, he snatched up his T-shirt to wipe the sweat from his eyes.

Poor Taylor. She didn't know what to think. She announced she was pregnant and Jack closed up. He drove her back to Granny's, then borrowed the car to drop in on the Gillinghams' punching bag.

Why? Why did finding out he was going to be a father bring up the ghosts of his past, of Rise Forester?

"I thought I heard someone out here."

Jack swung around to see Sam standing in the door, his reading glasses hooked through the top button of his shirt, slippers on his feet.

"I was going to come in when I was done."

"Didn't know you were in town."

"Wasn't planning on being, but my celebrity endorser got away from me."

Sam made a face. "Sounds challenging."

"Colette Greer. She came down to meet with FRESH Water but had business in town she needed to tend to."

"Ah, I see. Well, the Vanderbilt game is on tonight. I'd love some company. Sarah is baking. And she'd *love* someone to eat." Sam patted his belly. "My youthful physique is barely hanging on."

Jack laughed in spite of himself. In his late fifties, Sam was in good shape. Reaching for a folded lawn chair, Sam snapped it open and sat down, his manner and way so peaceful and confident. When he sat, he watched and waited.

"You do this to me, you know," Jack said, waving his gloved hand at Sam. "Get me off guard, talking about football and baking, then sit and wait." He leveled a punch at the bag and the ghosts swirling in his head.

"Blame it on doctor training."

Jack hooked his hands over the top of the bag, breathing, resting, trying to overcome the rattling of fears in his ears. "Taylor's pregnant."

"And that's what this is all about?"

Jack gave the bag a light punch. "Do you not know me? H-how can I be a good father when I was never fathered?" He shook his head. "Sorry, Sam. You were there for me."

"What'd I teach you about punching, Jack?"

"Pray. Punch and pray."

"Because you can punch that bag all day long and maybe do your physical heart some good, but exercise won't change you, cure you, or heal your hurts."

"But praying will?"

"You got anger? You talk to the Holy Spirit. 'Help me. Give me Your peace, Your joy.'"

"It's not as simple as you make it, Sam."

"That's right. It's not simple. You have to stick with it. Lean into the Spirit like you're leaning into those jabs and upper cuts."

"I'm not in the mood for a sermon."

"What sermon? You break into my garage—"

"I used the key." The one he kept on his ring, though he'd not been in Sam's garage for a long time. The sad

part about leaving Heart's Bend and not looking back
was leaving the Gillinghams. They'd visited him in
New York twice but he'd only been home, here, once in
about five years.

"—and beat up my punching bag. Looks like you've
been keeping in shape in New York."

"There's a gym in our office building."

"I see you're doing the physical work, but how about
emotional? Spiritual? You were never good at dealing
with your emotions."

"Gee, I wonder why . . ." Jab, jab, cross, cross.

"You know that excuse worked when you were fifteen. Even eighteen. I even gave you a pass when you
were twenty and figuring out who you wanted to be.
But now, Jack, you just look silly. You're thirty years old
and you've not reckoned that your earthly father has let
you down."

"Gee, Sam, I didn't realize I was ever supposed to be
okay with that."

"Is that what I said? Son, you're hearing what you
want to hear. Reckoning with it doesn't mean you
approve it. Your heavenly Father hasn't let you down.
Do you seek His approval? His advice? When was the
last time you prayed? Worshipped?"

"I've gone to church recently."

"I didn't ask you when you went to church."

"Then I don't know. A few months." Six? Seven?
A year?

"No wonder this baby news got to you."

"This should be a happy time, Sam, but I don't want
to be a father. I'm not ready to be a father."

"Too late. You already got a little one on the way. Jack, the good Lord has freely given you everything you need to heal from such a deep hurt, but you choose to keep walking around wounded. Eventually you'll walk further and further off the straight and narrow. One day, you'll be old and wonder where it all went wrong. Or worse, you'll be too far gone to even notice you've strayed, thinking God gave you a bum rap."

"I thought I *was* over it. Life was fine in New York. Then I ran into Taylor and *bam*! Everything turned upside down."

"Sarah and I were delighted when you called to say you'd eloped. Very romantic."

"Or very foolish." Jack reached for a folding chair and popped it open, sitting with a hard sigh, sweat trickling down his back and sides. These slacks were going straight to the cleaners. Sam was right—exercise alone couldn't heal him.

"How's it going with Taylor otherwise?"

"It's hard because I'm not good at telling her how I feel. What she means to me."

"What does she mean to you?"

"You sound like Taylor."

"Well?"

Jack knew Sam's game. He was good at getting him to talk by just waiting, being patient, listening.

For a moment the only sound in the garage was Jack catching his breath. He shifted his gaze from Sam to the garage floor, then to Sam.

"I think of her during the day." Once the first words spilled out, the rest came easy. "I love the idea that when I go home, she'll be there. Or *evidence* of her is there. But the moment I see her, I pull back. Clam up. And I walk past her like she's a bother instead of a joy."

"All right, you've identified the problem. How are you going to fix it?"

Jack glanced over at Sam, tapping his gloved hands together. "I don't know." Ah, there, he'd voiced it.

"So you keep one foot out the door. That way you can run first if it all goes south. But because you have one foot out the door, you're all but guaranteeing it *will* go south."

Jack jumped to his feet. "Don't you know, Sam, it *always* goes south! Even living here with you and Sarah . . . I turned eighteen and had to leave."

"Who said you had to leave?"

"The system. My case worker. Pack up, go to college, because I was one of the lucky ones—*ha!*—who earned a scholarship. Time to be on my own. I was done, out of the system. Besides, I didn't really belong here with you."

"But you had a place here. We told you."

"Yeah, but you and Sarah . . . had your own lives. You didn't need me—"

"Is that what you thought?"

Jack exhaled. "Yeah, I guess. Your friends and family didn't want me to be a permanent part of the clan."

"But Sarah and I did. We told you as much. Maybe it was you who didn't want to be a part of a family."

"That's not true and you know it."

"Then what's the problem?"

Jack laughed. "Me. There. Simple enough?"

"You know Sarah and I always wanted children, but it just never happened. Well, until we met you."

"A fifteen-year-old baby? What a bundle of joy."

Sam laughed. "Well, labor and delivery proved challenging at first, but then yes, you were a joy to us. Still are. When you walked into my office, face all busted up from that horrid situation you were in, I knew you were my son. I called Sarah and said, 'How would you like a beat-up, wounded, fifteen-year-old boy?'"

"You never told me that."

"She said, 'Bring him home.'" Sam leaned forward. "Jack, I'm going to tell you something and I want you to hear me. You were an answer to prayer."

"An angry teen with a broken face? That's what you and Sarah prayed for?" Sam was the plastic surgeon who'd fixed his broken cheekbone, jaw, and split eye.

"Not exactly, but we had such a desire for children. When we realized Sarah just couldn't keep a baby full term, we began to pray, 'Lord, we'll take children any way You want to give them to us.' We both felt kind of partial to a son. When you walked in, I *knew* you were the answer to our prayer."

An answer to prayer. Such a claim caused Jack to torque inside, messed with his right to be angry, to play the victim. Because if the God of all looked after him, even used him to *bless* someone else, then Jack had no excuse. God had a way of escape for him.

"Did I ever tell you I knew your mother?" Sam asked suddenly.

Jack perked up. "You did?"

"She volunteered at the hospital when she was in high

school. She was smart, kind, pretty. I always thought she'd do well in life."

"Yeah, well, she met the same force of evil I did. Rise Forester."

"And he destroyed her life, I admit. She made bad choices too, Jack. Some of the men she chose weren't the best. But she didn't mean to get killed the night she took off on a motorcycle."

"No, I guess she didn't."

"She was just trying to heal her broken heart, find a man who could appreciate her. But she was raised in church. She knew the truth."

"What's your point, Sam?"

"You have to decide, Jack. Choose. What kind of man do you want to be? You have the Holy Spirit. I saw you after your first summer camp, saw the change. I recognized His presence in your life. You were filled!" Sam rolled his voice like an old-time evangelist. "You have a Father."

"Then I got empty." Jack unlaced the gloves, tugging them off. "Never filled back up."

"It's not easy being a believer in a world with so many distractions, where there are so many other ways to solve problems. But, Jack, if you want to get over your anger at your father and be the father you want to be—"

"I don't even know what that looks like." Jack tossed the gloves onto the worktable.

"—you've got to go to the Lord. Really give it. You'll fail otherwise. Trust me. Because every little thing that happens will feed your fears, doubts, anger, and hurt. And it'll grow until you are consumed by it. I had a friend once who felt jilted by his father, thought he favored his siblings. Got married and had sons of his own. But he was so focused on the wrong done him by his father, he couldn't see he was doing the same to his own kids."

"Okay, I get it, Sam, I get it."

Sam's sigh was muted by his great big grin. "Well then." Sam opened a drawer under his workbench, pulled out a Bible, and tossed it to Jack. "Here's your passbook to your million-dollar account. Take a withdrawal and stop trying to make a good life on the devil's pennies."

Jack thumbed the pages. "I wouldn't know where to begin."

"How about, 'In the beginning was the Word, and the Word was God.' John 1. Be yourself, Jack. He's already seen the worst you have to offer and He still loves you." Sam made his way to the garage's sliding doors. "I'll leave you to it, but when you've found some peace, come on inside and help me cheer for the Commodores. Sarah would love to see you."

"I will. Thanks, Sam." Jack sat back in his chair, Bible resting on his leg.

"Can I say one more thing to you?"

"You have to ask?" Jack grinned. "Come on. Bring it."

"Sarah and I love you like a son. I'm sixty-six, thinking of retiring in a few years. A surgeon's hands get kind of shaky after a while."

"Not you, Sam. You're steady as a rock."

"So far . . . But we'll have some time on our hands. We've got some mission plans on the table, but to be honest, we'd like to spend time with family, be around our *son*, his wife. And their kids."

Jack shook his head. "Sam, think about what you're saying."

"I've thought about it for almost fifteen years. You're our son. Angry, sad, mad, or happy, that's how we see you, feel about you."

"Then you got cheated. I'm a horrible son."

"It's not too late to change, Jack. Thing is, you have to ask yourself if you want grandparents for your kids. And do *you* want parents? That's the crux of it right there. Are you ready to give up being angry? Because anytime you want to become a Gillingham, Jack, we'll go down to the courthouse and make it all legal."

"I'm thirty years old, Sam."

"I don't care if you're a hundred. I'm telling you, I want you as my son. Wouldn't it be nice to *know* you are a son right before you become a father?"

Jack glanced at Sam, who nodded, then turned for the house. "Take your time."

He might have been gone, but his confession hung around the garage, drilling through Jack and tapping his tears. *"I want you as my son."*

Pressing his head to the smooth leather Bible, Jack exhaled and let go of the first cord roping down his heart—the right to be angry—slipping from the chair to his knees as one freeing sob after another rolled over him.

CHAPTER TWENTY-SEVEN

TAYLOR

When the doorbell rang, Taylor hammered down the stairs from the bum room.

"Jack?"

He went silent when she dropped the baby news, asking her a half dozen times if she was sure, and everything sweet and romantic about him turned sour and cold.

When he dropped her off at home, he asked to borrow the car with a curt, "I got to do something."

She'd spent the last two hours putzing about the house, trying to sort through boxes, getting nowhere. She called Colette with no answer but left a voice message. Hopefully she was safe with Ford. Or better yet, Coach.

Jogging across the big, boxy, empty living room, she swung open the front door. "Where've you been?"

"At home." Daddy stood on the other side.

"Hey, wow." She pressed her hand to her thudding heart. "What are you doing here?" She didn't move but remained planted, leaning against the door.

"Can I come in?" he said.

"Um, yeah, sure?" Taylor glanced over her shoulder . . .

at nothing . . . There was no excuse to deny him. "Is this about the chapel?"

"No, nothing new on that front, but I've made some calls." The heels of Daddy's loafers skipped over the hardwood. "I take it you were expecting someone? Just not me."

"Jack. He . . . he went out on an errand."

Daddy nodded with a "Hmm" and left things there, making his way over to the one chair in the room. "Emma did a good job of clearing things out."

"Granny has an odd sense of humor, giving me the house and Emma the contents."

"Knowing her, she had some reason behind it. She always did." Daddy hesitated, then adjusted the pull of his slacks around his knees before perching on the edge of the chair. "Seeing Coach made me think of how she badgered him into mentoring me after she and Dad divorced. She got it stuck in her head I needed a male mentor and Coach was the man for the job." He laughed, shaking his head. "Poor Coach. Mama called him every night until he said yes. I was twelve or so, embarrassed, eavesdropping from my bedroom, muttering to myself, 'Leave him be, Mama.' I had Dad. He was just across town. She had some mysterious ways. Well, you know that, being as she left you that letter. And what was it, a key? Find anything yet?"

"No." Taylor took a seat on the sofa. "I have a feeling the search will take me to the attic."

Daddy chuckled, nodding. "Her secret cave. Chances are, you're right."

"Was it weird meeting Colette?" Taylor repositioned,

trying to relax. This common ground was a good place to reassess her feelings for her father.

Daddy shrugged. "A little. Mostly like meeting a long-lost relative, no context, no connection. Interesting about her and Coach, though."

Yeah, it was, and somehow that story was pinging in Taylor with the one Daddy just told.

"Do you think Peg loved Coach? Before she married Grandpa?"

"If so, she never said."

"But she was a woman of secrets."

Daddy leaned back, relaxing a bit. "Got me there, kiddo."

If she let herself not be mad, she liked Daddy. He was smart, funny, caring, handsome. A good citizen. And as far as she could tell, from her distant life perch, he was a good husband to Ardell.

More than that, he was her child's grandfather. A sweep of sentiment dusted the crusty edges of her fourteen-year-old offense.

"Can I talk to you?" His tone drew a serious shade in the room.

"S-sure." The tremor in her gut told her this was going to be personal.

"I don't mean to put you on the spot, Taylor, but I guess this chapel business and seeing Coach with Colette sparked something in me. I just have to know . . . What's wrong between us? I know it has something to do with the divorce, but, darling, I can't figure why you're so angry with me but not your mother."

Her vision glistened with tears. "Daddy, I can't—"

"I know this is hard, but I don't want this wall between us. I've asked Emma, your mama, and they don't know. Your mom blames the divorce and I get that. I was from a divorce too, Taylor. But I didn't hate one parent over the other. Did I do something—"

"Yes, and *you* know you did." She fired off the sofa, her emotions raw from the events of the day. "You and Mama wouldn't have gotten divorced if it wasn't for you and Ardell." Anger gas-pedaled her truth to the surface.

"What? Taylor, I didn't start up with Ardell until six months after the divorce."

"Really? That's the story you're sticking to?"

"It's the truth." The red tinge of frustration splashed his cheeks.

"I saw you. In your study. Kissing her."

"What? When?" He was on his feet now, hands propped on his belt.

"You were my hero, Daddy. How do you think it made me feel to see you in another woman's arms? Kissing her. And in your own home too." She walked around the couch, the conversation feeling so foreign. She'd imagined this moment but she'd never played it out.

"When was this?"

"You know when, Daddy. It's okay, you don't have to pretend. I know."

"Then tell me. I have no idea what you're talking about."

"Are you serious? In your study, about seven o'clock at night, fourteen years ago. Come on, you . . . Ardell . . . hugging . . . kissing."

Daddy frowned. "And you saw that?"

"I was hiding behind the door, waiting for you. Mr. Ellison gave my print photography class an assignment to photograph someone we admire. Our hero. I decided to do a candid shot, you at your desk working . . ." Taylor eased back down to the couch. "Because that's what you did, work to take care of us. Make us feel loved and safe."

"Oh, Taylor—"

"Instead, I learn you're a cheater."

"Why didn't you talk to me?"

"I was fifteen, Daddy. What was I supposed to say?"

"'What were you doing with Ardell?'"

"Right, and you'd have done what? Told me the truth? Apologized? Made it all better?"

He jutted out his chin. "No, no, I'd have told you it wasn't your business."

"Exactly. I got an F on that project because I couldn't think of another hero in time and I refused to turn in the one of you in the den."

"As I recall, that room didn't have a lot of light."

"I know what I saw."

"Did you see that she was crying? That I was comforting her? And yes, I did hug her and kiss her cheek."

"Well, it looked like lips from where I was standing."

Daddy sighed, sitting forward, pressing his forehead to his hands. Taylor's heartbeat counted the seconds as she waited. "Ardell came to me for advice. She'd found out her husband was having an affair."

"What? But I saw you—"

"Comforting an old friend. Taylor, this is why you've been angry at me all these years?"

"Yes, you cheated. So I thought. So I *saw*. I lost my family. My dad."

Daddy exhaled, rubbing his hand over his face. "Taylor, you're going to make me say things I don't want to say."

"I'd like the truth."

"Why don't you go talk to your mama?"

"Mama?"

"She had a hand in our marriage failing too."

"Like what? Wanting a faithful husband?"

"Taylor—"

She was pushing and knew it. "Say it, Daddy. Like what? You came over here to clear the air between us, so . . ."

"She was the one having an affair. With Ardell's husband, Trevor."

The truth punched her, plopping her against the sofa. "Mama?"

"That's right, Vicki had the affair. Not me. I wanted to work it out, as did Ardell with Trevor, but they both wanted out. Don't you remember him coming around after I moved out?"

"Yes, but I thought he was taking sides with her against the two of you." Daddy's truth brought light to the shades and shadows of Taylor's understanding.

"We never said anything to you girls 'cause we figured it wasn't something to put on your shoulders. Of course, I didn't know you saw me with Ardell."

"I-I don't know what to say."

"What's to say? You didn't know."

"But I've been mad at you for fourteen years. I watched

you and Mama fall apart and thought, 'Wow, marriage is rotten. Men stink.'"

"I never intended to divorce your mom, but if it's any encouragement, Ardell and I have been happily married for twelve years. Still going strong. And other than after a good workout or a day in the yard, we men-folk don't stink too bad."

A joke. He was easing the tension with a joke.

Taylor surrendered her rising, soft laugh. "Oh, Daddy . . . I don't know what to say."

"How about we can be friends again."

"Yes, yes, Daddy, I'm really sorry for the way I've been." She slipped from the couch as he stood, his arms open. Leaning into him, her head to his chest, Taylor sensed a shift in her soul and for the first time in a very long time, her world seemed to turn on the right axis.

"Kiddo, I wish you would've talked to me sooner."

They stayed there for a long while, hugging, rocking back and forth, wounds exposed and healing in the fresh light of truth.

. . .

JIMMY

Restless. Irritated. Frustrated. Overwhelmed. Mad. Astounded. Awed. Confused. Hurt. Remorseful.

Jimmy paced around his living room through each rising emotion into the kitchen and back again, doing his best to make peace with the news Colette had just dropped on him.

Drummond Branson was his son.

He sat in his recliner, positioned exactly where Dad's old chair used to sit, then popped to his feet again.

James. Colette had named the boy James.

Pacing, his adrenaline too hot for sitting, Jimmy let his gaze cruise past the curio cabinet, then back, stopping on the football tucked back on the top shelf behind the glass.

Walking over, he retrieved the old ball from its resting place. Dad's shadow box to encase Jimmy's game ball from '48 turned into a much bigger project. Clearly.

But for over six decades, the cabinet had been the ball's home. Coach took it out once a year, at the beginning of the football season, to inspire the boys.

Reaching in, he palmed the ball and tossed it between his hands. Walking over to the window, he shoved aside the curtain with the nose of the ball.

She was out there. Hurting. He couldn't console her once she confessed. She'd shrugged off his touch, assuring him she was the most despicable woman on the earth.

Finally she left. He waited until she pulled out of the driveway, then he followed her. So he knew Colette was in Heart's Bend. At the inn.

He came home thinking he'd leave her be, but the more he paced, the more he thought—the more time ticked by, the more he changed his mind.

Tucking the ball under his arm, he marched for

the kitchen, snatched up his keys, and fired out the back door.

If ever in his life he needed to score the winning touchdown, it was today. Right now. He'd heard Colette's story and now she was going to hear his.

At the inn, he asked for Colette's room and the clerk rang her from the desk.

"She'll be right out," she said.

So, more pacing. Back and forth through the lobby, tossing the ball in his hands, Jimmy prepared to have his say.

"I love you and it's high time we got married. In our chapel."

But when he turned to see a silver-haired, New York–looking man heading his way, he lost a bit of his nerve.

"Jimmy?"

"And you are?"

"Ford, Colette's manager." He offered his hand, which Jimmy took. No reason to be rude.

"Where's Colette? I need to talk to her."

"She's resting. We're flying home early in the morning. She sends her regrets."

Jimmy stepped back, needing space to think. Not this again . . .

If Colette needed rest, he did not want to disturb her. She was very upset this afternoon. But the way Jimmy saw things, he didn't have much time left.

He intended to speak his mind. Resting would have to wait.

He tucked the ball against his ribs and shoved around the manager. "What room is she in?"

"Hold on now . . ." Ford heeled after him. "She doesn't want to speak to you."

"I thought you said she was resting."

"And she doesn't want to speak to you. She's said all she intends to say."

"Then she can tell me to my face." Jimmy knocked on the first door on the right. "Colette? You in here?"

"You can't knock on every door, disrupting people."

"Don't blame me. You're the one with Colette's room number." Jimmy rapped softly on the door across the hall. "Lettie, it's Jimmy. I just need a word."

A bass growl came from the other side. "Wrong room, buddy."

"Sorry to disturb you." Jimmy moved down the hall. About to knock on the third door, Ford blurted, "Five. She's in room five. Stop pestering the rest of the guests."

With a backward glance at Ford, Jimmy moved down the hall. "Colette, darling, it's me, Jimmy. Can I speak with you?"

"Colette, you don't have to if you don't want to," Ford said over Jimmy's shoulder.

"Pardon me, but this don't concern you." Jimmy frowned. "Don't you have another client to tend to?"

"There's where you're wrong—it does concern me."

The door eased open and a weary but beautiful Colette greeted him. "Jimmy, please come in." She stood aside. "Ford, I'm famished for dinner. Can you order us something?"

"I'll see what I can do." He growled as he turned away.

"He's a peach," Jimmy said, gazing at Colette, gripping the ball between his hands.

"He's protective."

"I don't aim to harm you, Lettie."

"I know that and you know that, but—is that what I think it is?" She pointed to the ball.

"Game ball. Nineteen forty-eight. Had it with me the first night I talked to you."

"So, are we back to that? The beginning?" Colette reached for the ball, turned it in her hands, and flipped it back to Jimmy.

"If we could, I'd change a few things. I'd not be here now, with you on one side of a hotel room and me on the other, yes, almost like strangers." Jimmy stepped closer. "But we're not strangers, Colette. When you walked into the wedding chapel yesterday, I knew you. I felt like my heart had finally returned home. If that don't sound like a bunch of sentimental yuk from an ole bachelor football coach."

Colette retreated to the sitting area, reclining in a fancy upholstered chair, the evening light bright against the window. Yes, she was as lovely today as she'd been that night at the Clemsons. He even loved the time-earned lines of her face. Because each one had a story.

And in his chest beat a heart full of stories he longed to tell her, his one true love.

"I don't think we can go back, Jimmy." She shook her head, then rested her chin in her hand. "It's too late."

"More than too late, it's impossible." Jimmy took the

seat next to hers, tucking the ball beside him. "I'm talking going forward, Lettie. Having a life together."

She chortled. "Based on what, love? We're strangers."

"Then let's get to know each other. I'm game. Colette, I'm tired of waiting. Tired of living alone, of being in that old house, of saying I'll do things but never getting around to them."

"Then do them, Jimmy. You don't need me."

"Ah, but that's where you're wrong. I do need you, Lettie. You're the one I've been waiting for. Please marry me."

Her pretty, made-up eyes glistened. "We've lost so much time."

"Then let's not lose any more. If you don't love me, I'll understand, but I want you to give me a chance. I can win your heart all over—"

"It's not that, Jimmy."

"Do you love me?" He hung on, determined. The fear and misunderstanding, confusion and anger wedged between them by time and manipulation ended today.

"Do you love me?" She shivered, wrapping her arms about herself. "Though after what I did, you should show me the back of your head as you walk away."

"Lettie, yes, I love you. I never stopped loving you." He dropped to one knee in front of her. "I don't care what you did. I understand. I forgive. I want to marry you. I *must* marry you. What happened in the past is over. We can't change it. I reckon you did what you had to do." He cupped her hands with his. "So I'm asking you to do what you have to do now. Marry me. We'll deal with Drummond in time. And what Peg did."

Tears started down her cheeks. "I could've called your father. Talked to Aunt Jean and Uncle Fred—"

"You talked to the person you trusted most and she let you down, darling."

"Running seems so silly now. So far away. But I was so ashamed, felt so alone. So I made a whole new life for myself, a whole new Colette."

"But aren't you forgetting something? You married me that day in the chapel. Said vows to me. As I did to you."

"But it wasn't legal or proper, Jimmy. We both knew it."

"Maybe not in the eyes of the law. But in the eyes of my heart, I meant every word. The way I see it, it's time to honor our private vows with a public wedding."

"Surely after all these years apart, we're not still *married*. We can't possibly hold each other to youthful pledges."

"Why not? Did we mean what we said? We've not recanted, nor divorced each other?"

She shook her head, her chin quivering.

"Did you marry someone else?"

Again no.

"Me neither."

"Do we tell Drummond?" She angled for the square tissue box on the end table. "I wanted to tell you, Jimmy, so many times. But Drummond Sr. and Peg made it clear I was to be silent and stay away. So I did. And I didn't want to hurt James."

He caught the tear sneaking down her chin with the edge of his finger. "Why don't you stop throwing blocks and just say yes? We'll figure all of this out together. I love you, Colette Greer, heaven help me." He squeezed her fingers. "Marry me?"

She regarded him for a long, nearly heart-stopping moment. Then she nodded. Once. "Yes," she whispered. "I'll marry you, James Westbrook. I'll marry you."

CHAPTER TWENTY-EIGHT

JACK

He burst through Granny's front door. Man, Taylor had this place lit up like a Christmas tree. And she left the front door unlocked.

"Taylor? Babe?" He ran up the stairs two at a time. "Taylor?"

"Jack?" She stood in a narrow doorway, a lean set of stairs rising up behind her. "Where have you been?" She jumped into his arms, a white envelope crumpled in her hand.

He gripped her close, holding on to the one he loved. Cupping her face in his hands, he bent to kiss her. He'd never tire of her taste.

Taylor stumbled back when he released her. "J-Jack . . . what happened?" She laughed, touching his damp shirt. "Why are you all sweaty?"

"I went to Sam's. He's got a punching bag in his old garage."

A dark flicker shot from her eyes. "Wow, me being pregnant made you want to hit something?"

"No, I just needed to move, think. Get some space

between my head and heart. Taylor, you took me by surprise."

"Jack, I wasn't ready for this either. I didn't do it on purpose."

"I know, I know, I'm not saying you did."

"So what are you saying?"

"Look, I'm not perfect—"

She gasped. "Really?" She swirled her hand in the space between them. "Then this is off—"

Grinning, he pressed her against the wall and kissed her again. "Hush and listen. Sam came out and, well, we talked, and I had some God time, gained some perspective. Taylor, I'm in. I want to build a life with you. I want to get out from under the ghost of my father. I'm scared, unsure, and have a way to go to be the man you need me to be, but I'm . . ." He stepped back, sweeping his arms wide. "I'm in. I want this baby. Lord help the poor thing."

He braced himself, searching her face, ready for the pushback. For her to remind him he had yet to overcome his father's rejection, that he knew nothing about being a father, but either he could do all things through Christ who strengthened him or not. For the moment, he was banking on that verse being true.

"Are you sure? I mean, have you thought about this?"

"What's to think about? You're pregnant. The wheels are in motion. What are our options? Walking away? No, I don't want to walk away. I won't do that to my kid."

"So you boxed a bag and *snap*, just like that, you're all good?"

"Let's just say I've had a come-to-Jesus meeting, and while it's not adjourned yet, I have a clear sight of what I want, where I'm going, and how to get there. Sam and I are talking again tomorrow. I texted Hops to say I'd not be back until Wednesday."

She arched her brow. "Wow, I've never heard you talk like this."

"Weird?"

"Sort of, but I like it."

"So are you all in?"

"You said you know what you want. What is that, Jack?"

"Life with you."

The sheen in her eyes reflected her heart. "O-okay. And what about London?"

He pulled her to him. "It's a no unless *you* want to go." He kissed her, feeling her, sensing her, breathing in her response, her love filling his empty emotional bank.

She caught her breath as he released her. "This is not going to be easy. We've been living like we're not all in. Like if it doesn't work out we can walk away, 'no fuss, no muss.'"

"No more. We're not walking away. Our vows on the beach count."

She leaned against his chest and pressed her lips to his. "I love you, Jack."

The most beautiful words. Jack inhaled, peering into her eyes. "Taylor Branson, I love you. Very, very much. And God help me, I'm going to tell you every day."

He scooped her up, swaying from side to side until their bodies truly felt as one. When he set her down,

Taylor slipped her hand into his, leading him down the hall to her room.

"Taylor, I'm all sweaty," he said.

"You're about to be even more so."

With a sly grin, she set the envelope in her hand on the nightstand, eased the door closed.

This girl was his life adventure and he'd never tire of her. God help him.

. . .

TAYLOR

Evening settled over Heart's Bend as she lay in Jack's arms, more in love with him than the night they married.

He rolled on his side, brushing his hand over her hair. "I love you."

"So you've said. About a dozen times in the last hour."

"Now that I've said it, I like it." He nuzzled her neck, shoving the sheet away, and Taylor thought he might go for another round. Instead, he sat up. "Hey, listen, I want to run something by you. Sam told me I'm like a son to him. He wants to adopt me. Give me his name. Wh-what do you think about that?"

Taylor sat up. "Wow, that's . . . amazing. He knows you're thirty, right?"

Jack laughed. "That's what I said." He peered at her.

"He's been the only father I've ever really known. He wants to make me his son."

"I like the name Gillingham." She linked her fingers with his. "Do you think if you're not a Forester you wouldn't mind coming home to HB now and then?"

He searched her face. "I don't know. I'm a work in progress, Tay. But yeah, it might not be so bad."

"The baby would have two sets of grandparents."

"Yeah, that's true. But he'll have that either way."

"Guess it boils down to what you want, Jack. Do you want a new name with a new father, one who loves you? Or do you want to stay with the old name, being reminded of the man who out and out rejected you?"

He raised her chin, kissing her. "I married a smart girl."

"Was there ever any doubt?"

"Okay, what say we get some dinner." Jack bounded out of bed, reaching for his clothes. "You were doing something when I came in. What was it?"

She pointed toward the door. "Getting up the nerve to go into the attic."

"I thought Emma was in charge of cleaning out the house."

"She is, but Granny left me this weird letter." Taylor slipped out of bed, retrieving the letter, handing it to Jack. "Something about a box and a secret."

"A locked box apparently." Jack held up the key. "Why do you have to get up the nerve to go into the attic?" He skimmed the letter, laughing in the right places. "I like your granny."

"Only 'cause she said she liked you." Taylor slipped into her shorts and top.

"Naturally . . ." Jack finished reading and folded up the letter. "What is she talking about? A secret?"

"I have no idea, but since you're here . . . want to investigate the attic with me?"

"Why are you afraid of the attic? Can we order pizza? I'm starved."

"Yeah, I'll call Angelo's." She retrieved her phone. "And I'm terrified of the attic due to Emma and the great haunted house of 1995. By the way, our kid is never going to a haunted house."

"Shall I lead the way, then?" Jack stepped around her, easing open the attic door. He winked and her heart fluttered. Letting go meant she could fall all the way in love.

"Have at it. Light switch is on the right. By the way, Jack, Daddy came by tonight."

He glanced back at her. "And?"

"We talked. He didn't have an affair, Mama did."

Jack stopped midclimb and let out a low whistle. "You're kidding. You've been angry at him all this time for nothing? "

"Yes, and thank you for pointing that out."

He started for the attic landing. "How'd you leave things?"

"Like we have to start over, capture our lost years. I told him he was going to be a grandpa. That made him very happy."

Jack hit the landing and slipped his arm around Taylor. "I'm proud of you."

She pressed her hand to her forehead and stepped over to a pile of boxes under the eave. "Well, it's a start. We've a ways to go—"

"I'm proud you made it to the attic."

"Ha, very funny. And here." Taylor passed Jack what appeared to be an original Star Wars light saber. "For keeping the ghosts away."

Jack tapped the boxes with the tip of the plastic saber. "So what are we doing here?"

"Look for a box in a box." Taylor glanced around. "But once, when I was a teenager, I came over after school and found Granny up here putting something beneath the floorboards."

Jack knocked on the boards with the saber. When one echo responded hollow, he knelt down and tested the floorboards. And found a loose one.

When he raised it and peered in, he smiled at Taylor. "Could this be it?" He held up a deep, rectangular-shaped box. "Looks like something for jewelry."

Taylor took the box and glanced around for a place to sit. Nothing. So she reached for an old afghan and made a nest on the floor.

Jack propped open the sailor window, letting the heat out and the cool evening air in. Then he joined Taylor on the afghan.

"All right, box, show us what you got."

Taylor inserted the key. "I'm nervous." She peeked at Jack. "I'm glad you're here."

"No place I'd rather be."

Inside was another note and a bundle of letters bound by twine. "They're addressed to Colette." She flipped through the return addresses. "They're all from Jimmy. Looks like he was on a base."

"What's your granny doing with them?" Jack took the pack from her and thumbed through.

"I don't know." She spied the edge of a photograph. Pulling it free, she studied the black-and-white image. "That's Daddy as a baby." She passed it to Jack. "Does that look like a young Coach?"

"Yep." His gaze locked with hers. "I'm starting to figure out Granny's secret."

"She had an affair with Coach?"

"That's what I'm thinking. Read her letter, let's find out."

Taylor opened the note. "It's dated last year. Titled 'Confession.'" She made a face. "Sounds like a Danielle Steele novel."

> Confession:
>
> I've done some wrong. Lived with the guilt my whole life. And I'm weary. I've secrets bottled up inside and I don't feel I can bear them any longer.
>
> Though I must, for the sake of my sister. We've carried a burden together and I intended for it to die with me.
>
> Yet there is one secret I must confess.
>
> I broke them up. I forged letters from Colette to Jimmy and Jimmy to Colette because I loved him. I was so jealous of Lettie I couldn't see or think straight. If Jimmy wanted her, then I wanted Jimmy.
>
> So when Colette told me she was pregnant—

Taylor glanced at Jack. "Not Granny, Jack. Colette."

"The plot thickens. Go on." He tapped the letter.

> I devised a plan to get her away from him. I wrote
> letters, using my ability to copy handwriting. I'm full
> of regret, but what can I do now but say I'm sorry?

"Wait, wait, wait . . . what?" Taylor reread the line. "Granny forged letters?" She peeked at the stack bundled with twine. "Who does that?"

"I don't know, but I bet Granny had a reason." Jack flipped through the box's contents, coming up with a thin document. "Looks like a birth certificate."

Taylor read the first line over his shoulder. "'James Allen Westbrook Jr. Mother, Colette Greer. Father . . .'" Taylor raised her gaze to him. "Oh my gosh, oh my gosh, Jack, Colette and Coach had a *baby*." She slapped at his leg. "James Allen Westbrook *Jr*. This is huge."

"So why did she leave him? Why sixty years of silence?" Jack reached for Granny's note. "There has to be more."

"Jack, being an unwed mother back in the day was scandalous. She probably got sent away or chose to leave."

"He was born October 27, 1951."

"What?" Taylor slipped the birth certificate and Granny's note from his grasp. "Oh wow, oh wow, oh wow . . . Jack, come on."

She darted down the stairs, swinging by her room to grab her handbag, and ran out of the house, Jack trailing.

"Where we headed?"

"Daddy's." She jumped into the Lincoln like Batman. Jack jumped in like Robin.

"Ah, light dawns. He was born October 27, 1951?"

"Yep. Daddy is Jimmy and Colette's son. He has to be." She gunned the accelerator, beating the yellow light, the big car floating down the road.

When they pulled along the curb in front of Daddy and Ardell's, Taylor cut the engine and the lights. "Let's go."

"Hold up, Batman." He lightly gripped her arm. "What's the plan?"

"Um, ask Daddy how long he's known he was adopted."

"You assume he knows? Didn't Granny say she was tired of secrets? He's sixty-four years old, Colette. You can't just barge in waving that birth certificate. You don't even know the whole story."

"Yes, we do." She waved Granny's note. "She forged letters to break them up."

"But that doesn't explain how Colette's baby became Peg's." He held up his phone. "Why not give Colette a call? See if she'll confirm anything before you go to your dad."

"But I—" Taylor exhaled, her enthusiasm deflating. "How does it feel to be so smart?"

Jack grinned and ran his hand over her shoulder. "I'm not smart, just less emotionally invested."

She turned to him. "So Colette gets pregnant and leaves town? And Jimmy is away in Korea and he never knows?"

"According to your granny, she wanted to break them up."

"But she saved his letters to her?"

"This is life-changing for him, Tay. For Jimmy and Colette. Do you want to do this? Didn't your granny mention something about using caution?"

"Yeah, but, Jack, I can't keep this to myself. Look at what lies have done to the family. How lives have been altered. What if this is what led to Granny and Grandpa divorcing? What if *this* led to Jimmy and Colette never getting married in their chapel?"

"But those lives are in motion, babe. Have been for years. Colette's in New York, Jimmy's here. Your dad is Peg Branson's son, and she's not around to defend herself."

"Exactly." Taylor tapped the birth certificate against her hand. "That's why she wrote the letter. She's attempting to make amends."

"Babe, I'm not saying you can't bring this to light. I'm saying be sure."

Taylor glanced at her dad's place, the windows golden with the light. "I guess if you're going to change a man's life, it's best to do it after a good night's sleep. He and I have already had a come-to-the-truth day."

Jack drew her across the bench seat for a kiss. "Hey, I have an idea. Let's get married. In the chapel."

She regarded him. "Jack, really?"

His eyes glistened and sparked. It was the same look he got when he was onto a good ad campaign.

"I want to marry you. Properly. With friends, family, the church, the white dress and tuxedo, flowers, reception, the works. And neither one of us hearing, 'If it doesn't work out we can walk away . . .'" His proposal launched a soberness in the air and a weight settled over her. And she heard a faint but very real *whoosh-thump*. God's presence. *It's good to be home, Lord*.

"Okay, yes, I'll marry you. With the flowers and white dress."

"In the wedding chapel?"

"If Coach says yes." She held his face for a kiss. "But can we wait a little? I want to sort things out with Daddy. I have some mending to do and I want him to walk me down the aisle."

Jack cradled her cheek in his hand. "Absolutely, agreed."

"And I'd like not to be pregnant."

"You know I'm not going anywhere. Just tell me when."

"I love you, Jack Gillingham." She winked, touching her lips to his. "I like the sound of that."

"How about, 'I love you too, Taylor Gillingham'?"

"Nice."

"Guess I've made my decision. I'll talk to Sam tomorrow." He glanced back at Daddy's. "Come on, let's go home. We'll figure the rest of this out in the morning."

"Home? Heart's Bend?"

"Let's not get carried away. But yeah, home."

"So, no London?"

"No London. I want our kid to grow up knowing our wacky families."

Driving through the coming evening, twilight

already slipping through the horizon, Taylor listed *home* as her favorite word.

She'd come home to her heavenly Father, her earthly father, her husband, and to a truth that just might set everyone free.

. . .

COLETTE

She insisted on keeping their plans to themselves, taking the night to sleep on it, but Colette barely slept a wink, the dead parts of her heart coming alive and filling her with such joy.

She'd come home to her true love.

As she dressed, she hummed to herself, listening for Jimmy's rap on the door. She'd sent a disappointed Ford back to New York. Give him a few days and he'd come around. Poor fella wasn't used to Colette telling him what to do.

Crossing the warm, light room for a jacket, Colette peered out at the river easing along the edge of the grounds, the light of a late-September Saturday morning swimming along with the current.

If she wasn't sure last night, she was now. She loved Jimmy Westbrook and she'd not wait longer than necessary to marry him.

True love could not be defined by time or space.

Her heart raced when she heard his knock. Didn't he look handsome in his pressed shirt and creased jeans? His silver fox hair trimmed and neatly combed.

But it was the light in his blue eyes that spoke to her heart. Love. Pure, simple love.

"Ready?"

"I'm ready." She reached for her wristlet. "What do you think they'll say?"

"'What do we need to do to help?'"

Colette stopped, holding Jimmy back from another step. "And we're agreed? We will not tell Drummond? We'll be aunt and uncle, right?"

He nodded. "I think it's best all around."

So, to the grave. Just like she and Peg pledged from the start.

Jimmy drove slowly across town to Peg's old place. Colette rode next to him, like she used to, her arm tucked in by his side.

"Ready?" he said, helping her out his side, nodding toward the house.

A nervous prick raced through Colette. Like opening-night jitters. Or before she walked out on a talk show.

Jimmy rang the doorbell, gave her hand a squeeze.

Taylor opened the door, surprised, then welcoming them with a grand grin. "Jack, Jimmy and Colette are here."

He jogged down the stairs in a pair of golf shorts. "Hey, you two, what's going on? Where's Ford?"

"On his way to New York." Colette sat next to Jimmy on the sofa, still holding his hand.

"We've got some news," Jimmy said with a quick glance at Colette. "We're getting married."

"Married? Really?" They exchanged a look.

"Next Saturday," Colette pressed on. "At my wedding chapel."

"That's fantastic. It's about time." Taylor wrapped her in a hug. "This is amazing."

"What brought this on?" Jack said, still standing.

"We discovered we're still in love at eighty-two and eighty-three," Jimmy said. "Taylor, we'd like your help if you're willing."

"Absolutely. And I'll be your photographer."

"I was wondering if you'd be my matron of honor, Taylor." Colette thought the world looked lovely behind the wavy glass of tears. "I'll hire another photographer."

"Of course, yes, I'd be honored."

"I have a dress designer in New York and I have my assistant ringing her for a dress. Zoë will be here Monday to help, and my coauthor, Justine, is coming too. We're adding to the Colette Greer story."

"Have you told Daddy?" Taylor asked.

"We'll get over there later today," Jimmy said, standing, pulling Colette up with him. "Right now we're on our way to ask Doc to be my best man."

"Wait, wait—" Taylor bounced up the stairs, returning with an old jewel box.

"Where did you get this?" Colette reached for it as Taylor passed it over. "This belonged to my mother."

"I found it among Granny's things."

"I knew she had it. She kept telling me she didn't."

"Open it."

Colette checked with Jimmy, who nodded. She sat back down and lifted the lid. "Letters."

"They're from you, Jimmy."

He sank down next to her. "From the army."

Colette peered at him. "She took your letters."

"There's a note in there from her, a confession, if you will." Taylor angled up, tapping the white, folded note. "And Daddy's birth certificate."

Colette's hand trembled as she pulled it from the box. "Then you know."

"You're Daddy's parents. And my grandparents."

"I reckon the cat's out now, Lettie."

Oh, she was so glad to have Jimmy sitting next to her.

"Granny wrote me a note saying she didn't want to keep the secret any longer and gave me the key to this box, which Jack found under an attic floorboard. Seems to me she wasn't sure she wanted the truth to come out or not, but if you ask me, it always does."

"We weren't going to tell your father," Colette said, the shame of it all having weakened with time. But she still echoed some of 1951's sorrows.

"But don't you want to? After all this time. The secrets are out."

"We didn't want to disrupt his life," Jimmy said.

"But now I know," Taylor said.

"And she almost told him last night," Jack said.

Colette bumped Jimmy's shoulder. "What do you think, love?"

"I guess if Taylor here knows . . ."

"I don't understand." Taylor sat in the chair across

from the sofa. "If you loved each other, if you built the chapel for her, why didn't you get married?"

"The chapel wasn't complete when I went to Korea."

"But we said our own vows, didn't we, Jims?"

So they wove the story for Jack and Taylor, confirming what they'd guessed the night before.

When they finished, the reverb of their voices echoed through the nearly empty room.

Then Taylor's low question, "Why would Granny be so mean?"

"The war, the death of our parents, took its toll on her. She was always jealous of my relationship with our father. Her bitterness seeped deeper and deeper in time. But when I had the baby, I couldn't manage so I turned to her. She gladly took him but made me promise never to come back. To not tell Jimmy. To leave them alone. So I did. I think she felt she'd finally won something over me."

"But now it's like she's giving it all back to you."

"I suppose she is." Colette smoothed her hand over the box. "My mamá's box. She didn't have any jewels to put in it, but my father always promised her he'd fill it someday."

"Peg filled them with Coach's letters. Those are jewels," Jack said.

"Indeed they are." Colette clutched the packet over her heart. "I'm going to read them all slowly, savoring every word."

Jimmy laughed. "You'll get a bunch of details about how bad the mess food was and how much I missed you." He took up the birth certificate, clearing his throat.

"I guess Peg kept the original," Colette whispered.

"This means the world to me." The document shook in Jimmy's trembling hand.

"There's a picture of you too." Taylor reached past Colette and into the box. "I think this is you. With Daddy as a baby."

Jimmy's eyes brimmed as he pressed his fist to his lips. "Yes, that's me with DJ. Peg came by with him just as I was about to burn down the chapel."

"You were going to burn it down?" Jack said. "Really?"

Jimmy slipped his arm around Colette and she never wanted him to remove it. "I thought I'd lost her forever. The chapel was nothing more than a reminder."

"But this week we've found our way home. We're getting married. In our chapel." Colette took the image from him. "No more about the past for now. Full steam ahead into today, tomorrow, and our wedding next Saturday. Will you help us?"

Taylor got out her phone. "I can get Emma to help. She's a whiz at planning. We need cake, flowers, and music. Too bad the old wedding shop is closed down. If you want anything specific, tell me and we'll do our best to get it. Emma, get over here, we're planning a wedding. No, not mine. Just get over here. It's a surprise."

"It does my heart proud to see sisters getting along," Colette said. "As if Peg and I didn't make a royal mess of your lives."

"Lettie, we need to tell Drummond."

"But we agreed, Jims."

"That was before Taylor and Jack knew, before this box."

"I agree," Taylor whispered.

"Me too." Jack was on board as well.

She didn't like confrontation or delivering bad news, but wasn't that how she got into this mess in the first place? Brushing her hands over her skirt, as if to shoo away her jitters, Colette stood.

"I guess we'll be heading to see Drum, then." Colette glanced at Taylor. "Please call him, let him know we're coming."

So for the second time in her life, Colette drove through Heart's Bend, praying, hoping she was doing the right thing for her son.

CHAPTER TWENTY-NINE

JIMMY

White-gold evening light infused the chapel sanctuary as Jimmy took his place at the chapel altar, smoothing his hand down his new blue tie—the one Colette had bought for him and sent over to the house.

Darned if he wasn't nervous. Like a kid. But he'd take it. Today and every day 'cause it were a good kind of nervous. The sort that meant God still moved in a man's life. Even at eighty-three.

Beside him, Nick cleared his throat and sniffled. Jimmy glanced back at him. The gruff old doctor had more sentiment in his blood than the women's junior league.

Their eyes met and Doc gave him a nod, clapping his hand on Jimmy's shoulder. "I still expect to see you Friday mornings for coffee."

"Wouldn't miss it. I might need me some marital advice."

The whirlwind week had settled down to this one moment—Jimmy waiting for his bride to *finally* come down the aisle.

How his world had changed since the day he'd agreed

to let a photographer come take pictures of his chapel. His secret granddaughter, no less!

The guests, mostly family and friends, sat in the pews with tangible expectation. All of them were smiling to beat the band.

Emma and Taylor had worked tirelessly to pull off this wedding, but Colette was the force to be reckoned with. She had the energy of a forty-year-old.

Besides that, she had resources at her fingertips most folks only dreamed about.

After a honeymoon to New York, Hawaii, and Normandy, they were going to sit down with *Good Morning America* and appear on the *Tonight Show*. Apparently the folks there were big fans of Colette's.

Then she was going to finish her book and do more shows, and Jimmy didn't know what all. He only cared that he was going to be with her, watching from backstage. Suited him just fine.

Behind the altar, the string quartet began to play, the sentimental notes of "Because" causing Jimmy's eyes to crest with tears.

"Because you come to me . . ."

His Colette was coming to him.

Taylor entered first, pretty as a picture, and Jimmy felt such love for her. She wore a pretty blue dress that swept across the top of the floor. She nodded at Jimmy, but her eyes were all for Jack.

". . . a wider world of hope and joy I see . . ."

Then came his Colette, and Jimmy just knew his heart was going to explode.

She was a vision in a simple white gown befitting

her stature, leaning on the arm of Ford, her eyes glistening.

Jimmy swallowed the lump forming in his throat that threatened to undo him. He tugged at his shirt collar and tight bow tie.

In the midst of the wedding brouhaha, they had dealt with Drummond, who didn't take the news well.

But Monday evening Jimmy got a call. "Ardell and I want you and Colette to come to the house. We'd like to talk."

For the next three nights, they sat together talking, hashing out every emotion from anger to confusion to hurt to joy.

Drummond wrestled with the new knowledge that he was adopted. Jimmy grappled with missing the chance to raise his own son. Colette concluded it was time to finally forgive herself for "ruining everyone's life."

But in the end, it boiled down to the words Jack so wisely offered. "The way I see it, the family just got bigger, better, and more interesting."

Colette arrived at the altar as the strings bowed the final notes of the song.

Jimmy offered her his hand and Reverend Stebbins opened with a prayer.

Then he heard it, right above his head, the *whoosh-thump* of the chapel's heart. It started off distant and faint, then became louder, drawing near with each word of prayer.

It rushed through Jimmy with such a force he couldn't breathe. He raised his eyes to the light beyond the stained glass.

Lord?

Colette squeezed his hand and the *whoosh-thump* sank deeper and deeper, and little by little began beating in time to his own heart.

"Dearly beloved, it's a joy to be gathered here today . . ."

Jimmy peered at Colette. Now he knew. At last their two hearts had become one.

. . .

COLETTE

The strange look on Jimmy's face concerned her. He jerked, clutching his chest, his lips moving in silent recitation.

"Darling?"

He turned his gaze to her, smiling.

"Dearly beloved, it's a joy to be gathered here today . . ."

Reverend Stebbins's words drew them together, facing forward.

But she pressed her shoulder to Jimmy's, clinging to his broad, strong hand. "Are you quite all right?" she whispered.

"Never better, Lettie. Never better."

"Colette and Jimmy, will you face one another?" the reverend said.

Turning, Colette fell into Jimmy's eyes, the love

she had for him so many years ago maturing in this moment.

They repeated their vows, properly this time. "I, Colette Elizabeth Greer, take you, James Allen Westbrook . . ."

"I, James Allen Westbrook, take you, Colette Elizabeth Greer . . ."

They exchanged rings and bowed their heads for another prayer.

"Well, it gives me great pleasure to introduce to you Mr. and Mrs. James Westbrook. By the power vested in me—"

"Might I have a word?" Drummond was on his feet, hand in the air.

The reverend checked with Jimmy, who nodded.

"Go on."

Drummond smoothed his hands over his suit pockets, visibly nervous. "I learned this week that these two are my parents."

The collective gasp was small. Colette surveyed the sanctuary. Most everyone knew already, save for those few members of the *Always Tomorrow* family who were able to fly in.

"I've spent this week working through the news. Wearied these two with conversation after conversation. I've concluded the commercial had it right: life comes at you fast. Jack, I guess that phrase was a bit of brilliant advertising."

The small ripple of laughter broke the tension.

"Colette asked me to walk her down the aisle, but I

declined. In fact, I wasn't sure I wanted to come today."
He pressed his fist to his lips, clearing his throat. "The
more I thought about it, the angrier I got. Mom's dead,
Dad's dead, and I had no one to rail at but God." His
emotional monologue had the room captive. He'd have
been a good actor. "The more I ranted, the more He
showed me my own life, my own mistakes." He pointed
to Taylor. "I got some mending to do with this girl.
And, like finding out I was adopted, I didn't know
she'd been hurt by something I'd done."

Colette reached for Taylor's hand. They were going
to be good friends, she just knew it.

"I guess I just want to say it's easy to feel wronged.
To hold a grudge. Until we take a look at our own life.
Colette here made the best decision in the moment to
give me up to her sister to raise. She was a good mother
who gave everything for me, so I can't fault her. And
Coach here practically raised me on the football field,
so I feel kind of blessed to know I got my athletic genes
from him."

Colette could not imagine a more fitting, more
beautiful wedding. It was honest and real, without pre-
tense or the trappings of tradition.

Drummond stepped toward the altar. "I just want to
say, I'll be there for you both. Any hatchets that might
be remaining, I want to bury."

"I met a lovely young heiress once," Colette said.
"Corina Del Rey. She'd recently married a prince.
And she told me that what God taught her through a
very tremendous ordeal was to love well." She peered

at Jimmy. Then back to Drummond. "Shall we do the same? Love well. That doesn't mean it will be perfect, but we'll be like the Lord. Love anyway."

"I reckon that's the best we can all do." Drummond kissed Colette on the cheek and shook Jimmy's hand.

When he returned to his seat, a serenity passed through the chapel. It was finished. The pain, the heartache, the lies, righted toward love, peace, and healing.

"Jimmy, Coach, you may kiss your bride."

To cheers and a standing ovation, Colette received the kiss of her beloved, felt the sweetness of her tears blending with his.

"I love you, Jimmy." She wiped the water from his cheeks.

"And, Colette Westbrook, I love you!"

As they turned, the photographer stepped into the aisle, hitting the shutter, and the first day of the rest of their life began with a kiss and a photograph.

EPILOGUE

CHRISTMAS, ONE YEAR LATER

HEART'S BEND, TENNESSEE

"Taylor, you ready?" Daddy called up from Granny's living room. "Your carriage awaits. Emma and the girls have already gone to the chapel."

Ready? Yes. She was ready. Wait, diaper bag. Where was the diaper bag? With Ardell. Check. Who also had baby JJ. Check.

Because today Taylor was not a mama.

She was a bride. Check.

Emma had her bag of supplies—makeup, hair spray, water, bobby pins, toothbrush and toothpaste, second pair of shoes—and was waiting for her at the wedding chapel.

Her gown—a gift from Colette and her designer friend—was silk and tulle, trimmed in fur, and the wide, simple, creamy white skirt reminded Taylor of a first snow.

While she would always treasure her beach elopement, she was glad for this day to affirm her love and commitment to Jack in front of their friends and family.

"Tay?" Daddy's voice moved up the stairwell. "About time. You ready?"

With a final glance around the upstairs master suite in the house she and Jack spent the last year renovating, Taylor exited the room. She was ready.

From the bottom of the stairs, Daddy smiled up at her, looking dapper in his tuxedo, the lights from the Christmas tree bouncing over the gleaming hardwood.

"You look beautiful."

"I'm nervous!" She used the sleek polished banister to hold her steady, one hand gripping her skirt as the enormous folds glided over the stairs. "And I feel so empty without JJ in my arms."

"Enjoy it while you can. Besides, by the time Ardell, Sarah Gillingham, and your mother get done with him, he'll be so spoiled you might not want him back."

She laughed. "You have a point."

Daddy walked Taylor to the door, pausing before stepping onto the porch. "Thank you. For this past year, for giving me a chance to be your daddy again." His eyes glistened as he cleared his throat, glancing down at his new shoes. "Means everything to me."

"I'm the one who needs to be thanking you for this year. For helping Jack and me return to Heart's Bend, renovating Granny's house, and for forgiving me for being—" It still hurt to remember how wrong and bitter she'd been.

He wiped the dew from the corners of his eyes and

reached for the door. "Come on, it's your wedding day. Besides, we've been through all this. You're my girl and I never stopped loving you. I'm glad we finally got to the truth. Now, don't make your old man cry."

"Okay, but you started it." Taylor shot him a sly grin as she moved across the threshold, holding her skirt high while Daddy gathered her train.

Colette and Jimmy's journey had righted a lot of relationships this past year and set a course for new ones. But not without the tears that came with confession, repentance, and forgiveness.

Mama admitted to the affair and repented, seeking forgiveness from everyone. She and Daddy got along like old friends now, and Ardell finally took her place as a member of the family, playing the doting step-mother and grandmother.

Forgiveness went a long way in healing body and soul, and splashing the world with joy.

Like they agreed, Jack turned down London, and as they started collecting baby gear, they realized a cramped New York apartment was not where they wanted to raise little Jack James Samuel Drummond Gillingham either.

Back in January, Sam and Sarah Gillingham legally adopted Jack. What a beautiful day at the courthouse, watching God weave His tapestry of their family together, in spite of weakness and failings.

After that day, Jack changed. He'd been adopted, given a new name, and those old pains from his natural father began to shrivel and die.

FRESH offered Jack a job as vice president of advertising, but he didn't want the corporate grind so he launched out on his own. It was hard to do top-level advertising outside New York, but he found clients he adored who never would've fit under the 105 umbrella.

As for Taylor, she did work for Jack as he needed, but weddings and birthday parties became her primary photography venue, and—shocker—she loved it. It was the most fulfilling work she'd ever done.

She and Jack had come a long way in twelve months. It wasn't an easy trail, but one that was well worth it.

For the first six months, they decided to counsel with Jesus every morning, waking up to pray and read Scripture.

It was the least romantic endeavor Taylor ever tried. But the most glorious and rewarding.

Sometimes she and Jack sat across from each other in stony silence. Sometimes they prayed together or shared a verse. Sometimes they continued the argument from the night before. But they determined to stay faithful.

One morning, along about the six-month mark, the atmosphere changed. Their prayers came easy. Love blossomed between them.

There were a few times Taylor had heard the *whoosh-thump* heartbeat of God, but mostly she walked in faith. As she drew closer to Him and Jack, the need for a tangible reassurance began to fade. Like the removal of training wheels or a crutch.

But the day she heard baby JJ's heartbeat at their first ultrasound, she knew . . . The heartbeat she'd heard as a kid musing on God, those few times in the wedding chapel, was the sound of life. Of love.

After the ultrasound, she knew she'd not hear it again. It was God's last word to her on *that* particular matter.

He loved her, and He loved life.

"Let me help you now." Daddy offered Taylor his hand as she started down the porch steps, on her way to the—

"A horse and carriage?" There was supposed to be a limo parked by the curb.

"A gift from the Gillinghams."

At the edge of the walkway, Daddy and the driver assisted Taylor and her grand gown into the carriage, tucking her in with a thick blanket. Daddy climbed in next to her as the driver chirruped to the horses, the rhythm of their hooves trotting them into the crisp pink layers of twilight.

She'd see Jimmy and Colette for the first time all fall. They had arrived back in Heart's Bend just in time for the wedding. They'd been on a worldwide book tour to promote Colette's new memoir. Her story hit the *New York Times* number one slot the week it debuted. She and Justine changed the story to focus on the rekindled love of her life, and how being married at eighty-two proved God was in charge of the impossible.

With Him, love is never too late.

News spread about a little wedding chapel in the Tennessee woods and Jimmy handed the management over to Emma, who selectively booked weddings.

The carriage driver turned down the chapel lane,

the bare winter tree limbs leaving the stone structure exposed and in view. The shining mocha geldings tossed their heads so their harness bells rang out.

At the steps, Taylor descended the carriage, her hand in Daddy's, the fur-lined hem of her skirt swishing against the sidewalk.

Emma met her at the door, beautiful in a red fur-trimmed gown with the same full skirt and fitted bodice as Taylor's. She handed Taylor her Christmas bouquet of red roses and baby's breath. "Go time."

"Is *it* in there?" Taylor motioned to the flowers.

Emma made a face. "Yes, but I don't know why—"

"Shush, and walk down the aisle."

The music of "Because" wafted toward them on stringed notes. Emma clutched her bouquet and glided down the white runner.

Taylor leaned on Daddy, taking it all in. The chapel seemed to embrace her, welcome her, dancing over her with flickering candlelight. Fresh wreaths hung from each of the twelve pews, releasing the fragrance of Christmas pine.

The atmosphere was beautiful and serene.

"Happily ever after does exist, doesn't it, Daddy?"

"As long as you know it is sometimes disguised with trouble."

She laughed for him only. "You can say that again."

When they arrived at the altar, Taylor slipped her phone from her rose bouquet and snapped a picture of Jack's handsome, smiling face. "To remember."

He shook his head, grinning, and pulled his phone from his pocket. "To remember."

She slipped her hand into his and faced the preacher, ready for whatever came her way because she walked life with this man.

Jack, marriage, family were all pictures of God's love and she was going to frame them in her heart forever.

Not the End
  Just life continuing . . .

DISCUSSION QUESTIONS

1. Communication is one of the threads of this book. Jack and Taylor struggle to share their true hearts, and Jimmy and Colette lost sixty years of their relationship because they didn't press for the truth. Same with Taylor and her dad. What are ways you're weak in communication? Have you given up in some ways?

2. Taylor believes she saw her father cheating on her mother. But it wasn't what she imagined. The room was dark, draped in shadow. Talk about how we misunderstand each other and situations because we don't "see things properly." What are ways to combat these misunderstanding? What would you have done if you were Taylor?

3. Young Colette and Jimmy loved each other so much they said vows to each other before Jimmy shipped off to war. Were their words valid? Or does a recognized official have to pronounce a couple married? Talk about the power of words.

4. While I'd never advise young people to casually make a pledge of marriage without witnesses (that's the power of a contract or covenant), I would remind them the things they say to each other in

their youthful zeal *do* matter. How can we teach our kids, or ourselves, to be mindful of our words?

5. Jack didn't have a great childhood. But Sam Gillingham reached out, wanted to be his father. But Jack refused to see his effort, so ingrained in the pattern of the foster care system. How can we access the Father's love even when we've had a bad, or a great, earthly dad?

6. What did you think about Jack being adopted at age thirty? What's the significance of that event?

7. Taylor and Jack jumped into marriage before considering the cost. Often people "do," then "think." We condemn ourselves for making a mistake. But can God be in those moments too? Talk about a time in your life, or in the life of someone you know, when a supposed mistake worked for good.

8. Peg was a villain throughout the book but tried to make up for it in the end. Did her motivation make sense? The war and her parents' deaths seeded bitterness in her heart. And jealousy. What are those places in your life where envy, bitterness or jealousy have come in? Can you use the picture of Peg to realize how dangerous those attitudes can be?

9. Do you think love can last sixty-plus years without two people ever seeing each other? I wondered about that as I wrote this book, but then I'd hear a story or read something online where love endured the decades. Is there a Christlike picture here? We are waiting for the One we love to return too.

10. The Branson family seemed to have a track record of divorce. Sometimes families seem to perpetuate certain traits or situations, such as bad relationships, alcoholism, or financial woes. But God is a God of new life. How can we defeat those negative patterns in our families when we are in God?

11. The book has a happy ending. Was it what you expected? Wanted?

12. Who was your favorite character and why?

ACKNOWLEDGMENTS

I grew up with a great example of marriage, with kind parents who loved each other and us kids. There was warm light, laughter, and sweet aromas in our home as I grew up. Home was always a safe place to be.

My dad is with the Lord, but to my mama, I acknowledge and honor you for your life, your heart for the Lord, your worship, your devotion to family, and your visible and invisible demonstration of love for others. All with a gorgeous smile.

Love you, Mom.

This book started on a Tennessee vacation with my husband. I needed a "next book" idea and while driving down a hill to get enough bars on my phone for a phone call with my publisher, Daisy Hutton, I drove past a wedding chapel perched high above the road, surrounded by lush green trees.

I tossed out the idea to Daisy, "How about *The Wedding Chapel*?" And a story idea was born.

I appreciate everyone who walks with me on the publishing road. For those who help me live my dream, and above all, do what I sincerely believe God created me to do. I feel His presence when I write. I could not do this without Him or those who walk this walk with me.

Here's my humble appreciation to those people.

My husband, who listens, tosses out plot and character ideas, gives me time and space to meet deadlines, prays for me, and loves me. He is such a gift and blessing. Love you, babe!

My writing partner and all-around best girlfriend, Susan May Warren, who plotted this book with me one afternoon over the phone and I pretty much stuck to it. I know, shocker. Thank you for always being on the other end of the phone, Suz, to help me out of the ruts and get moving again. You make me laugh, inspire me, speak the truth to me when I need to hear it, and call me to be the best writer I can be. I thank the Lord for you.

My other writing buddy, Beth K. Vogt, who is a FaceTime call away whenever I need to talk. I'm so grateful for you and the blessing you are in my life. Thank you for being there to help with the story and writing process, even on a Saturday night. And I love seeing the wonderful author you are becoming.

My agent, the renowned Chip MacGregor. It took a dream and a glockenspiel to put us together, but here we are six years later. I'm grateful for you. Thanks for everything!

My editor, Becky Philpott, who also picks up the phone when I call. Who encourages me. Who listens. Who gives me wise counsel on how to take a story to the next level. Who loves the same books as me! Thank you for everything, Becky. You are such a blessing. I really appreciate you.

My other editor on this project, Karli Jackson. Thank you for your input and insight. Thank you for handling things like production and galleys. You are a delight.

The entire publishing team at HarperCollins Christian Publishing: Daisy Hutton, Katie Bond, Amanda Bostic, Becky Monds, Elizabeth Hudson, Kerri Potts, Jodi Hughes, Kristen Ingebretson, Kristen Golden, Jason Short and his team, the hardworking sales force. I really, really appreciate you. Thank you for all you do.

The kind and gracious Wes Yoder for sharing his chapel with me. Your ideas and advice helped me shape my own chapel. Thank you so much for the pictures and all the technical help. I hope to visit your chapel sometime.

The talented James Exley for insight into the life of a professional photographer and how that world works. For the fun, fame, or fortune truth. Praying God's abundant blessing on you!

All the readers who give their time and effort to read my stories. Thank you so very much. I can't tell you how much you mean to me.

To my Lord Jesus. How I love You, and all You are and have done and will do. Thank You for stories. Thank You for Your love and righteousness that surround me. For Your glory!

ABOUT THE AUTHOR

Rachel Hauck is the *New York Times, Wall Street Journal,* and *USA Today* bestselling author of *The Wedding Dress,* which was also named Inspirational Novel of the Year by *Romantic Times* and was a RITA finalist. Rachel lives in central Florida with her husband and two pets and writes from her ivory tower.

Visit her online at rachelhauck.com
Facebook: rachelhauck
Twitter: @RachelHauck